Paintings by the Master

Understanding the Gospels through Christ's Word Pictures

Donald P. Orthner

AMBASSADOR-EMERALD INTERNATIONAL
GREENVILLE, SOUTH CAROLINA • BELFAST, NORTHERN IRELAND

Paintings by the Master
Understanding the Gospels through Christ's Word Pictures
Copyright © 2001 Donald P. Orthner

ISBN: 1-889893-61-7

Published by:
Ambassador-Emerald International
427 Wade Hampton Blvd.
Greenville, SC 29609 USA
and
Ambassador Productions
Ardenlee Street
Belfast, BT6 8QJ
Northern Ireland

www.emeraldhouse.com

Cover design by Brad Sherman
Cover illustration by Mark Mulfinger
Cover design © 2001 Grand Design

Paintings by the Master

"A picture is worth a thousand words" — whether drawn with a brush, a pen, a parable, or an object lesson. The more important a picture's subject and the greater the artist's skill, the more powerful the message that picture can convey. How much more so when the picture portrays eternal life and the artist is the Son of God!

This book presents Christ's word paintings — pictures that equal thousands of words of detailed explanation. By using common objects and experiences drawn from everyday life, Christ conveyed volumes of truth in brief verbal vignettes. Thus He bridged the gap from the physical to the spiritual and from the temporal to the eternal. His paintings were as timely as they are timeless, and as practical as profound.

The Master used many forms of oral media to portray spiritual truth. These range from stories and parables (some longer than others and some with more than one lesson) to simple metaphors and similes (with more meaning than their brevity implies). He also crafted object lessons, historical parallels, and all manner of comparisons. All these made His remarkable teaching both clearer and more clearly applicable. Together, these paintings form a gallery of masterpieces — drawn by the greatest Master of all.

About the Author

Donald P. Orthner

The author's love for God and His Word was nurtured from childhood by godly parents and grandparents who faithfully served their Lord in the pastorate, foreign missions, and local churches. The Lord had a different avenue of service, however, for Don. A native of Michigan, he earned Bachelor's and Master's degrees in business administration at the University of Michigan, majoring in finance and economics. For the next 25 years, he worked in international finance and corporate financial management. He took time, however, to serve on the boards of directors of several Christian ministries and in his local church, with Christian education and outreach as priorities.

With a background of life-long Bible study and extensive experience in business analysis and management presentations, Don utilized both in authoring this work. It employs and expands the topical-outline and application-oriented approach he developed in his first book, *Wellsprings of Life—Understanding Proverbs*.

Don now resides in Greenville, South Carolina. His prayer is that God will use this book to exalt Jesus Christ in the heart and life of each person who reads it.

Dedicated with thankful memories
to my parents
Rudy and Edna Orthner
who loved their Savior and lived God's Word
through long and fruitful lives.

Preface

God's Word and daily life present a host of complementary messages. The more I grasp the lessons of each, the more I appreciate that a great many physical objects, events, and relationships are purposeful pictures of spiritual truth. These include tangible things such as bread, water, plants, and animals, as well as intangible things such as light and darkness and life itself. The same is true of major events such as birth, marriage, sickness, and death, and of human relationships as those of servants, friends, brothers, and children. God designed and created all of these at least in part to teach us about our spiritual needs and about His abundant and exclusive provision for meeting those needs.

On reflection, it is not surprising that the elements of creation so remarkably illustrate the messages of God's Word. God conceived both together as one integral package before time began. Thus we read that Christ is "the Lamb slain from the foundation of the world" (Rev. 13:8), and that God's grace "was given us in Christ Jesus before the world began" (II Tim. 1:9). Of the two, however, God's Word is the eternal reality of which creation is the passing picture. He declares, "Heaven and earth shall pass away, but my words shall not pass away" (Mt. 24:35); "for the things which are seen are temporal; but the things which are not seen are eternal" (II Cor. 4:18). How crucial that we see the eternal as we contemplate the temporal.

Christ was the Master at painting word pictures that relate everyday experiences to spiritual principles and precepts. Indeed, most of His teaching was in the form of pictures and comparisons or was illustrated by them. As the visible incarnate Word of God, He was uniquely qualified to depict the verbal inspired Word of God. Who better understood the purpose of every created thing, and who could better present these things as illustrations of spiritual truth? Observe and consider these "Paintings by the Master."

Donald P. Orthner

Contents

Helpful Notes

The chapters in this book are ordered in only one of many possible arrangements. There is benefit from reading the book straight through, but most chapters, and most sections of each chapter, can be used independently. Most of the text of the four Gospels is presented, as are the initial verses of Acts (an extension of Luke's account of Christ's life) and several of Christ's self-portraits in John's book of The Revelation (which are similar in style and content to the pictures of Christ in John's Gospel).

References to the individual Gospels are abbreviated throughout as follows: Matthew = MT, Mark = MK, Luke = LK, and John = JN. All words in parentheses in the Gospel text are as they appear in the King James translation. At times, portions of parallel passages from other Gospels are inserted in the passage being used, to form a conflation of these accounts. In such cases, the inserted words are in braces: { . . . }.

Whenever an explanatory word or phrase is added by this author within the Gospel text (e.g., to identify the speaker or audience, or to explain a term that may not be familiar to some readers), these words are placed in brackets [. . .] to show that they have been added. Some of the author's comments on the Gospel text include a paraphrase of part of that text. These paraphrases are not given as alternative translations but only to aid the reader's understanding of the original text.

It is the author's prayer that this book will exalt the Lord Jesus Christ, honor God's Word, and encourage God's children. May it especially be a help and guide to those who seek to learn about Christ or who yearn to know Him better.

1

Pressing Needs and Perfect Answers

Of all who ever lived, only Jesus Christ could evaluate with perfect accuracy and in complete detail every person He met. He alone could read each thought, motive, and feeling in every heart and mind. He knew who was lonely and hurting when outwardly all seemed well. He knew who was acting religious, but not worshipping God in spirit and truth. He saw the path and outcome of everyone's life — where a person was headed, the dangers he faced, and what would turn him toward God.

Christ could see inside people because of who He was and is. As God the Son, He is mankind's Creator who designed and constructed our physical, emotional, and spiritual natures and needs. As the sovereign Lord, He directs the circumstances in which we recognize and respond to our needs. Further, as omniscient God, He knows every detail of our deepest thoughts and motives — both currently and in advance. In every way, Christ "knew all men, and needed not that any should testify [to Him] of man; for *He knew what was in man*" (JN 2:24-25).

The same attributes that enable Christ to evaluate every person precisely and accurately also enable Him to satisfy fully every need and weakness He identifies. The needs He pictures in the following pages are common to all mankind. Likewise, the solutions He offers are available to one and all.

Pictures of Needy People

When seeing the crowds around him, Christ saw needy people far from God and going their own selfish ways. Many were floundering and suffering, vaguely sensing their needs but not able to satisfy them effectively. Christ's pictures of the multitudes depict these vital unmet needs. They picture too His deep love for all people and His great concern for their eternal welfare. In portraying the hearts of people, Christ also portrays the heart of God *for* people. Their needs were great, but His love and compassion were greater still.

I. His compassionate picture — Lost, scattered, helpless sheep.

A. The people were as sheep with no shepherd.

MT 9:35 And Jesus went about all the cities and villages, teaching in their synagogues, and preaching the gospel of the kingdom, and healing every sickness and every disease among the people.

36But when he saw the multitudes, he was moved with compassion on them, because they fainted, and were scattered abroad, as sheep having no shepherd.

Of all common animals, sheep are as dependent, helpless, and defenseless as any. Throughout scripture, therefore, God often pictures spiritually needy people as lost and helpless sheep. Isaiah 53:6 states, "All we like sheep have gone astray; we have turned every one to his own way; and the Lord hath laid on him [Jesus Christ] the iniquity of us all." Jesus was filled with compassion for these helpless sheep, knowing full well the meager, pitiful existence and the great dangers they faced without a divine shepherd.

B. The "lost sheep" of Israel were His first concern.

MT 10:5 These twelve [disciples] Jesus sent forth, and commanded them, saying, Go not into the way of the Gentiles, and into any city of the Samaritans enter ye not:

6But go rather to the lost sheep of the house of Israel.

7And as ye go, preach, saying, The kingdom of heaven is at hand.

C. There were other "lost sheep" He also loved.

JN 10:16 And other sheep I have, which are not of this fold: them also I must bring, and they shall hear my voice; and there shall be one fold, and one shepherd.

As Israel's promised Messiah, Christ initially focused His attention on "the lost sheep of the house of Israel." Early in His ministry, therefore, He commissioned His disciples to carry His message only to the Jewish people (MT 10). Later, as the nation's leaders hardened in their opposition to Him, Christ announced that He would bring "other sheep" into His "fold," including Gentiles who were not a part of the Jewish fold (JN 10).

II. His caring picture — Sick people in need of a physician.

MK 2:15 And it came to pass, that, as Jesus sat at meat in his [Matthew's] house, many publicans [tax collectors] and sinners sat also together with Jesus and his disciples: for there were many, and they followed him.

¹⁶And when the scribes and Pharisees saw him eat with publicans and sinners, they said unto his disciples, How is it that he eateth and drinketh with publicans and sinners?

¹⁷When Jesus heard it, he saith unto them, They that are whole have no need of the physician, but they that are sick: I came not to call the righteous, but sinners to repentance.

Verse 17 may be understood: "Those who think they are well see no need for a physician. Those who realize they are sick, however, are aware of their need. I came, therefore, not to call self-righteous people, but admitted sinners to repentance and salvation." Sin is not an involuntary "sickness," as some would claim in order to avoid their moral responsibility. God likens sin, however, to sickness and infirmity to illustrate its harmful effects. For example: "Ah sinful nation, a people laden with iniquity, . . . the whole head is sick, and the whole heart faint. From the sole of the foot even unto the head there is no soundness in it; but wounds, and bruises, and putrefying sores" (Isa. 1:4-6). The religious leaders, in contrast to known sinners, failed to recognize their terminal condition.

III. His concerned picture — People dwelling in darkness.

MT 4:13 And leaving Nazareth, he [Jesus] came and dwelt in Capernaum, which is upon the sea coast, in the borders of Zabulon and Nephthalim:

¹⁴That it might be fulfilled which was spoken by Esaias the prophet, saying,

¹⁵The land of Zabulon, and the land of Nephthalim, by the way of the sea, beyond Jordan, Galilee of the Gentiles;

¹⁶The people which sat in darkness saw great light; and to them which sat in the region and shadow of death light is sprung up.

JN 3:19 And this is the condemnation, that light is come into the world, and men loved darkness rather than light, because their deeds were evil.

Darkness pictures a lack of knowledge and understanding of God's truth and the resulting life of frustration and emptiness. Such darkness typified the people of Israel before their long-awaited Messiah finally came (MT 4:16). The nature of their darkness, however, became much more serious and ominous when Christ brought them God's *light* and they consciously chose, even *loved*, the darkness of their evil behavior rather than God's light (JN 3:19). Christ warned them of the permanent darkness that would come upon them if they persisted in refusing to respond to the light while the light was with them (see Sec. II on p. 99).

IV. His cautioning picture — A fruitless fig tree.

LK 13:6 He spoke also this parable; A certain man had a fig tree planted in his vineyard; and he came and sought fruit thereon, and found none.

⁷Then said he unto the dresser [gardener] of his vineyard, Behold, these three years I come seeking fruit on this fig tree, and find none: cut it down; why cumbereth it the ground?

⁸And he answering said unto him, Lord, let it alone this year also, till I shall dig about it, and dung [fertilize] it:

⁹And if it bear fruit, well: and if not, then after that thou shalt cut it down.

The parable may be interpreted as follows: God is the vineyard owner and Israel is His fig tee. (Similar imagery is employed in Hosea 9:10 and LK 21:29-32.) For three years, Christ as the gardener worked with the tree without visible fruit. By God's grace and mercy, Christ would give the Jewish people His fullest effort one more year. Then, if the tree did not bear fruit, God (in His time) would cut it down. The parable ends without revealing the outcome. Jesus was still offering Himself to the people as their Messiah, and they still had an opportunity to accept Him. Their opportunity, however, to repent of their sin and receive salvation would soon be closed. Then judgment.

V. His critical picture — Complaining and pouting children.

MT 11:16 But whereunto shall I liken this generation? It is like unto children sitting in the markets, and calling unto their fellows [playmates],

¹⁷And saying, We have piped unto you, and ye have not danced; we have mourned unto you, and ye have not lamented.

¹⁸For John [the Baptist] came neither eating nor drinking, and they say, He hath a devil [demon].

¹⁹The Son of man came eating and drinking, and they say, Behold a man gluttonous, and a winebibber, a friend of publicans and sinners. But wisdom is justified of her children.

The people, and particularly the religious leaders, had their own ideas regarding how prophets should conduct themselves and even what they should teach. Jesus here chides the Jews for acting like pouting children who complain that He would not "dance to their tune." It was as though they wanted to "play wedding" and dance, or "play funeral" and mourn. When He would not play along with them, they quickly turned against Him and caustically slandered His character and associations.

John the Baptist lived an ascetic life and did not eat or drink their normal fare (MK 1:6), and the Jewish leaders rejected him. Christ did eat the normal fare, but they criticized Him for eating with *sinners*. He asked, in effect, "What must John and I do to convince you that we speak for God ?" Two interpretations of verse 19b are possible: (1) The wisdom we proclaim to you is validated by *her children*, that is, by our deeds and lives, or (2) Wisdom is recognized and honored by *her children*, that is, by those who truly receive it. Either way, Christ claimed to speak God's wisdom and implied that the people rejected it.

      VI. His chastening picture — Blind people with blind leaders.
MT 15:12 Then came his disciples, and said unto him, Knowest thou that the Pharisees were offended, after they heard this saying [that they were hypocrites]?
¹³But he answered and said, Every plant, which my heavenly Father hath not planted, shall be rooted up.
¹⁴Let them alone: they be blind leaders of the blind. And if the blind lead the blind, both shall fall into the ditch.

Spiritual blindness was the greatest obstacle to the Jewish people's recognizing and accepting their Messiah. Their blindness stemmed from their sinful nature, which also prevented them from seeing how blind they were. As a result, they were unable to comprehend Christ's message, and would *fall into the ditch* of unbelief and its resulting condemnation. He also likened their leaders to worthless plants that God in time would uproot. In the end, only God's plants will remain.

      VII. His condemning picture — Rebellious, scattering little chicks.
LK 13:34 O Jerusalem, Jerusalem, which killest the prophets, and stonest them that are sent unto thee; how often would I have gathered thy children together, as a hen doth gather her brood under her wings, and ye would not!
³⁵Behold, your house is left unto you desolate: and verily I say unto you, Ye shall not see me, until the time come when ye shall say, Blessed is he that cometh in the name of the Lord.

In contrast to little chicks, which instinctively run to their mother's protective wings when danger threatens, the Jewish people repeatedly refused the spiritual refuge offered by their Messiah. He longed to gather them lovingly under His wings — but they would not come! Throughout their nation's history, their forefathers often rejected the love, protection, and blessing that God offered through His prophets. Now they had rejected God's own Son. With grief and heartache, Christ mourned their continued rebellion and forfeiture of God's blessing.

Christ also, however, is God the Righteous Judge. To be holy and just, He had to declare them guilty of their sin and sentence them to their deserved punishment (v. 35). Even then, He foretold the coming day of their nation's repentance and reconciliation to Himself, and the joy and blessing that will bring. (See the parallel passage in MT 23 on p. 423.)

> VIII. His compelling picture — Grain fields ready for harvest.
> **MT 9:37 Then saith he unto his disciples, The harvest truly is plenteous, but the laborers are few;**
> **38Pray ye therefore the Lord of the harvest, that he will send forth laborers into his harvest.**
>
> **JN 4:35 Say not ye, There are yet four months, and then cometh harvest? behold, I say unto you, Lift up your eyes, and look on the fields; for they are white [ripe] already to harvest.**
> **36And he that reapeth receiveth wages, and gathereth fruit unto life eternal: that both he that soweth and he that reapeth may rejoice together.**
> **37And herein is that saying true, One soweth, and another reapeth.**
> **38I sent you to reap that whereon ye bestowed no labor: other men labored, and ye are entered into their labors.**

Christ saw the multitudes as great fields of ripened grain ready for harvesting, but with few workers available to do the job. He challenged His followers to open their eyes and behold the great, unsatisfied spiritual needs of people all around them. Their first response should be to pray earnestly that God will enlist and empower laborers to work in His harvest (9:38). (Those who so pray, of course, must themselves be willing to labor in whatever way God directs them.)

In God's plan, one believer sows the seed of the Gospel in someone's life (4:37) and others nurture that seed with further testimony and encouragement (I Cor. 3:6). God alone produces the harvest of that person's salvation, but He assigns its reaping to His faithful servants (4:38). In eternity, those who have sown and those who have reaped will rejoice together with the eternal fruit of their faithful labor (v. 36).

Portraits of Christ as The Answer

God never identifies a need for which He does not prescribe a solution. Christ, therefore, sketched the following self-portraits to illustrate how He meets and satisfies the needs He identified in people. Most of these portraits begin with the words, "I am the . . . [e.g., Good Shepherd]." In each case, the full meaning is this: "I, and I alone, in distinction from and in contrast to all others, am the . . . [Good Shepherd, etc.]." Christ is not just "an answer" or "part of the answer" to peoples' problems. He is The Answer. He offers the only perfect, complete, and eternal solution to everyone's spiritual needs.

Christ's audiences typically included a mixture of curious observers, skeptical critics, and (relatively few) true believers. Regrettably, most of these people did not evidence much interest in or capacity for absorbing His spiritual instruction. To many, Christ's illustrations seemed as little more than pointless pictures of mundane things. Earnest seekers, however, could peer beneath His pictures' surface and perceive their life-giving message.

I. He is the Good Shepherd.

> **JN 10:11 I am the good shepherd: the good shepherd giveth his life for the sheep.**
>
> **¹²But he that is an hireling, and not the shepherd, whose own the sheep are not, seeth the wolf coming, and leaveth the sheep, and fleeth: and the wolf catcheth them, and scattereth the sheep.**
>
> **¹³The hireling fleeth, because he is an hireling, and careth not for the sheep.**
>
> **¹⁴I am the good shepherd, and know my sheep, and am known of mine.**
>
> **¹⁵As the Father knoweth me, even so know I the Father: and I lay down my life for the sheep.**

Christ previously described the multitudes as sheep having no shepherd (see Sec. I on p. 2). He came to be their shepherd. The religious leaders of the day had proved to be no more than hirelings that did not really care for the sheep. Christ as the Good Shepherd protects His sheep from the predators that would destroy them. In the ultimate demonstration of His love for the sheep and of His commitment to His role as their Shepherd, He gave His very life to save the sheep. (See pp. 114-118 for the full passage.)

II. He is the Door.

> **JN 10:7 Then said Jesus unto them again, Verily, verily, I say unto you, I am the door of the sheep.**
>
> **⁸All that ever came before me are thieves and robbers: but the sheep did not hear them.**
>
> **⁹I am the door: by me if any man enter in, he shall be saved, and shall go in and out, and find pasture.**
>
> **¹⁰The thief cometh not, but for to steal, and to kill, and to destroy: I am come that they might have life, and that they might have it more abundantly.**

In the Mideast, a shepherd at times would spend the night sleeping in the doorway of the sheepfold — keeping the sheep safely in and intruders out. He effectively became "the door of the sheep" (v. 7). Whoever enters God's fold through Christ the Door (by receiving Him as personal Savior) becomes His sheep and feasts in His pasture. Christ is the Door both to salvation and to the meaningful, abundant life that follows salvation.

III. He is the Great Physician.

LK 4:18 The Spirit of the Lord is upon me, because he hath anointed me to preach the gospel to the poor; he hath sent me to heal the broken-hearted, to preach deliverance to the captives, and recovering of sight to the blind, to set at liberty them that are bruised,
¹⁹To preach the acceptable year of the Lord.

Christ read this passage from Isaiah 61:1-2 in the synagogue in Nazareth. It prophesied that when the Messiah came, He would heal and deliver God's people from the bondage of their infirmities. Christ announced that this Great Physician was in their midst, and He performed many miracles of physical healing to prove His claim. His principal mission, however, was spiritual healing. Thus, He preached the good news of salvation, healed broken hearts, rescued the captives of sin, gave sight to the spiritually blind, and freed bruised spirits from Satan's oppression. (See Sec. II on p. 306 for the full passage.)

IV. He is the Light of the world.

A. He enlightens every person regarding his spiritual need.

JN 1:4 In him was life; and the life was the light of men. . . .
⁹That was the true Light, which lighteth every man that cometh into the world.

B. He shines into the lives of those who believe in Him.

JN 12:46 I am come a light into the world, that whosoever believeth on me should not abide in darkness.

C. He brightens each believer's path through life.

JN 8:12 Then spake Jesus again unto them, saying, I am the light of the world: he that followeth me shall not walk in darkness, but shall have the light of life.

These verses depict Christ as the Light of the world in several major respects:
1) He manifests in Himself the "true light" of God's purity and holiness, in contrast to the darkness of man's sinfulness (1:9).
2) He enlightens every man, through the evidence of creation and man's own moral nature, about God's perfection, power, and sovereignty and about man's accountability to Him (1:4, 9).
3) He proclaims the light of God's eternal truth, and illumines people's understanding of that truth, freeing them from the darkness of spiritual ignorance, bondage, and death (12:46).

4) He gives "the light of life" to every believer for his daily walk with Him by revealing God's will for each step along the way (8:12). (See also "Rays of Light in Darkness" on p. 98).

V. He is the Bread of Life.
> **JN 6:47 Verily, verily, I say unto you, He that believeth on me hath everlasting life.**
> **⁴⁸I am that bread of life.**
> **⁴⁹Your fathers did eat manna in the wilderness, and are dead.**
> **⁵⁰This is the bread which cometh down from heaven, that a man may eat thereof, and not die.**
> **⁵¹I am the living bread which came down from heaven: if any man eat of this bread, he shall live for ever: and the bread that I will give is my flesh, which I will give for the life of the world.**

God provided bread from heaven (manna) to sustain the Jewish people for 40 years in the wilderness. Manna was a picture of Jesus Christ, "the bread of life," that would come down from heaven almost 1,500 years later. After Christ fed a multitude with five loaves of bread and two fish (JN 6:1-14), He told them to seek the food "which endureth unto everlasting life" (v. 27). Neither the manna in the Old Testament nor the bread Christ multiplied from five small loaves could give such life. Christ Himself is the "living bread" (v. 51) that gives everlasting life. (See pp. 76-80 for the full passage.)

VI. He is the Burden Bearer.
> **MT 11:28 Come unto me, all ye that labor and are heavy laden, and I will give you rest.**
> **²⁹Take my yoke upon you, and learn of me; for I am meek and lowly in heart: and ye shall find rest unto your souls.**
> **³⁰For my yoke is easy, and my burden is light.**

A yoke is a wooden harness that joins draft animals together so they can work effectively as a team. If the animals, however, are unfit for the task, the yoke will be an unbearable burden. In this connection, the laws God gave Israel through Moses required absolute perfection and holiness. Because it was impossible to keep the law fully, it became "a yoke upon the neck . . . which neither our fathers nor we were able to bear" (Acts 15:10).

Christ invites all who are struggling under the heavy yoke of sin and guilt to come to Him for relief and rest. He will exchange our unbearable yoke for His *easy* yoke, in which He bears the full weight of our confessed sin and failure. Similarly, the *burden* of service He expects from us "is light." He gives us to carry only as much as He enables us to bear in our lives and in our service for Him.

VII. He is the Way, the Truth, and the Life.

    A. He is the answer to our troubles.

        JN 14:1 Let not your heart be troubled: ye believe in God, believe also in me.

        ²In my Father's house are many mansions: if it were not so, I would have told you. I go to prepare a place for you.

    B. He is the hope of our future.

        ³And if I go and prepare a place for you, I will come again, and receive you unto myself; that where I am, there ye may be also.

        ⁴And whither I go ye know, and the way ye know.

    C. He is the means of our salvation.

        ⁵Thomas saith unto him, Lord, we know not whither thou goest; and how can we know the way?

        ⁶Jesus saith unto him, I am the way, the truth, and the life: no man cometh unto the Father, but by me.

Christ's disciples were disheartened and troubled when He told them he would soon die and leave them. To comfort and encourage them, He promised to return and take them to be with Him in heaven. Then He said, "I am the way, the truth, and the life: no man cometh unto the Father, but by me." This declaration summarizes the principal purpose of His entire ministry. It pictures Christ as three basic and essential elements in anyone's salvation. Thus:

- He is "the Way" to God in every sense of that claim — for any person, at any time, and for any purpose. Because He paid the penalty for everyone's sin, He alone is qualified to intercede with the Father on our behalf. Christ, therefore, is the only Way by which we can enter God's presence and have a personal relationship with Him. Christ also will be our *physical* Way to heaven, by personally returning and taking every believer to be with Him there forever.

- He is "the Truth" in that He presented and exemplified God's message of essential truth to mankind. He revealed the truth about God's holy requirements, man's sin and guilt, God's means of salvation, and His own central role in God's plan. "Grace and truth came by Jesus Christ," who Himself is "full of grace and truth" (JN 1:14-17).

- He is "the Life" in the manifold sense of (1) having independent, self-sustaining life in Himself as God the Son (JN 5:26); (2) being the creator and sustainer of all life on earth (JN 1:3-4); and (3) giving abundant spiritual life to all who receive Him as their Savior and Lord (JN 5:24; 10:10). Later that evening He prayed, "And this is life eternal, that they may know thee, the only true God, and Jesus Christ whom thou hast sent" (JN 17:3).

2

Pictures In The Master's Name

A person's name in Bible times conveyed greater meaning than most names do today. Then, a name was more than merely a means of distinguishing one person from another. One's name often pictured the hopes and aspirations the parents had for their child, or a special event or circumstance associated with his birth. A name could also portray one's features or personality, or his heritage, vocation, or position. A name, therefore, often reflected the essence of its bearer's being and his principal characteristics and roles. With no one is this more true than in the names and titles given to Jesus Christ.

A Hebrew child typically received a single name at birth. Mary and Joseph knew the importance of appropriately naming her unique son, and they followed God's instructions precisely as He directed. Later, Jesus ascribed to Himself additional "names" (in the form of titles and descriptive designations) that further pictured His person and purpose. Taken together, these names form a gallery of portraits designed to provide a clear revelation of who He is and why He came.

Jesus — "Jehovah is Salvation"

The Teacher from Nazareth was known by many names and titles during His lifetime, but He had only one proper name, the name *Jesus*. (*Christ* originally was not a name but a title, as discussed in the following section.) *Jesus* was the name He received at birth and by which He was commonly known to friend and foe alike. It is the Greek equivalent of the Hebrew name *Jeshua* (or *Joshua*), meaning "Jehovah is salvation." Jesus, therefore, is both His human name and the principal appellation that identifies Him as mankind's Savior.

I. Jesus was The Savior from His birth.

A. He came to "save His people from their sins."

MT 1:18 Now the birth of Jesus Christ was on this wise: When as his mother Mary was espoused to Joseph, before they came together, she was found with child of the Holy Ghost.

¹⁹Then Joseph her husband, being a just man, and not willing to make her a public example, was minded to put her away privily [to break their engagement privately].

²⁰But while he thought on these things, behold, the angel of the Lord appeared unto him in a dream, saying, Joseph, thou son of David, fear not to take unto thee Mary thy wife: for that which is conceived in her is of the Holy Ghost.

²¹And she shall bring forth a son, and thou shalt call his name JESUS: for he shall save his people from their sins.

The name God selected for Mary's son emphasized Jesus' unique character and mission on earth. The angel expanded its meaning beyond "Jehovah is salvation" by indicating that (1) Jesus Himself was Jehovah in human flesh ("for *He* shall save . . .") and (2) *their sins* was the principal plight from which He would save His people.

B. He was Emmanuel — "God with us."

²²Now all this was done, that it might be fulfilled which was spoken of the Lord by the prophet, saying,

²³Behold, a virgin shall be with child, and shall bring forth a son, and they shall call his name Emmanuel, which being interpreted is, God with us.

²⁴Then Joseph being raised from sleep did as the angel of the Lord had bidden him, and took unto him his wife:

²⁵And knew her not till she had brought forth her firstborn son: and he called his name JESUS.

Verse 23 refers to Isaiah 7:14, which foretold that God would be with His people in a new and greater way through the virgin's son. Although He was not named "Emmanuel" (in the way He was named "Jesus" or called "the Christ"), He fulfilled completely Isaiah's characterization of Him as "God with us." God physically and visibly associated Himself with mankind in the person of Jesus.

    II. Jesus is The Savior announced by angels.

        A. He is the Savior for all people.

> **LK 2:8 And there were in the same country shepherds abiding in the field, keeping watch over their flock by night.**
> **⁹And, lo, the angel of the Lord came upon them, and the glory of the Lord shone round about them: and they were sore [very] afraid.**
> **¹⁰And the angel said unto them, Fear not: for, behold, I bring you good tidings of great joy, which shall be to all people.**

        B. He is the Savior and also the Lord.

> **¹¹For unto you is born this day in the city of David a Savior, which is Christ the Lord.**
> **¹²And this shall be a sign unto you; Ye shall find the babe wrapped in swaddling clothes, lying in a manger.**

        C. He is the Savior for the glory of God.

> **¹³And suddenly there was with the angel a multitude of the heavenly host praising God, and saying,**
> **¹⁴Glory to God in the highest, and on earth peace, good will toward men.**

The angels' announcement of Jesus' birth emphasized that He came to be "a Savior." They did not call Him "Jesus," probably because He had not yet been formally named (see Part III below). Rather, they stressed His purpose in coming and the "great joy" that would result from fulfillment of that purpose. The angels gave the good tidings to obscure shepherds, but their announcement is "*to all people*." Jesus was born "*unto you . . . a Savior*."

        D. He is the Savior to be sought and found.

> **¹⁵And it came to pass, as the angels were gone away from them into heaven, the shepherds said one to another, Let us now go even unto Bethlehem, and see this thing which is come to pass, which the Lord hath made known unto us.**
> **¹⁶And they came with haste, and found Mary, and Joseph, and the babe lying in a manger.**

        E. He is the Savior to be known and proclaimed.

> **¹⁷And when they had seen it, they made known abroad the saying which was told them concerning this child.**

¹⁸And all they that heard it wondered at those things which were told them by the shepherds.

F. He is the Savior to be worshipped and praised.

¹⁹But Mary kept all these things, and pondered them in her heart.
²⁰And the shepherds returned, glorifying and praising God for all the things that they had heard and seen, as it was told unto them.

The shepherds immediately responded to what God revealed to them, and they went to find the Savior. They found Him just as they had been told. Overwhelmed with wonder and joy, they widely proclaimed what they had seen and heard, glorifying and praising God. Mary treasured these experiences and pondered their meaning, in awe of her new-born son and Savior.

III. Jesus is The Savior revealed by the Holy Spirit.

A. He was presented as the Savior by godly parents.

LK 2:21 And when eight days were accomplished for the circumcising of the child, his name was called JESUS, which was so named of the angel before he was conceived in the womb.
²²And when the days of her purification according to the law of Moses were accomplished, they brought him to Jerusalem, to present him to the Lord; . . .

Hebrew sons were circumcised on their eighth day as a sign of God's covenant with His chosen people (Gen. 17:12), and Jesus was formally named at that time. After Mary's prescribed waiting period (33 days later, according to Lev. 12:4), she and Joseph brought Jesus to the temple to dedicate Him to God, as commanded in the Mosaic law.

B. He was promised as the Savior by God's Spirit.

²⁵And, behold, there was a man in Jerusalem, whose name was Simeon; and the same man was just and devout, waiting for the consolation of Israel: and the Holy Ghost was upon him.
²⁶And it was revealed unto him by the Holy Ghost, that he should not see death, before he had seen the Lord's Christ [Messiah].
²⁷And he came by the Spirit into the temple: and when the parents brought in the child Jesus, to do for him after the custom of the law,

C. He was proclaimed as the Savior by God's prophet.

²⁸Then took he him up in his arms, and blessed God, and said,
²⁹Lord, now lettest thou thy servant depart in peace, according to thy word:
³⁰For mine eyes have seen thy salvation,
³¹Which thou hast prepared before the face of all people;
³²A light to lighten the Gentiles, and the glory of thy people Israel.

³³And Joseph and his mother marvelled at those things which were spoken of him.

The Holy Spirit previously assured Simeon that he would live to see the Messiah, God's means of providing "the consolation [comfort and encouragement] of Israel" (vv. 25-26). At the right moment, the Spirit led Simeon to the temple to meet Jesus and His parents. While holding the baby, Simeon praised God that he had "seen thy salvation" (v. 30), the Savior God prepared for both Jews and Gentiles.

D. He would be persecuted as the Savior by God's people.

³⁴And Simeon blessed them, and said unto Mary his mother, Behold, this child is set for the fall and rising again of many in Israel; and for a sign which shall be spoken against;
³⁵(Yea, a sword shall pierce through thy own soul also,) that the thoughts of many hearts may be revealed.

The Holy Spirit also revealed through Simeon that many Jews would "fall" and speak out against this Savior (v. 34), thereby revealing the depravity of the human heart (v. 35). Mary herself would be "pierced through her soul" (as she saw her Son pierced on the cross). Many, however, would "rise again" from their fallen state by receiving salvation from this wonderful Savior.

IV. Jesus is The Savior preached by John.

JN 1:29 The next day John [the Baptist] seeth Jesus coming unto him, and saith, Behold the Lamb of God, which taketh away the sin of the world.
³⁰This is he of whom I said, After me cometh a man which is preferred before me: for he was before me.

John's initial public introduction of Jesus as "the Lamb of God" emphasized the same role cited by the angel before Jesus' birth — to save people from their sin. Both announced that Jesus would not just *tell* people how to have their sin forgiven, but that He personally would *take away* their sin and save them from it. Such a task could only be accomplished by God Himself. John affirmed Jesus' deity in stating "He was before me," even though John was born and began ministering before Jesus. (See "The Lamb of God" on p. 50.)

V. Jesus is the Savior received by sinners.

A. He seeks admitted sinners.

LK 19:1 And Jesus entered and passed through Jericho.
²And, behold, there was a man named Zacchaeus, which was the chief among the publicans [tax collectors], and he was rich.
³And he sought to see Jesus who he was; and could not for the press [the crowd], because he was little of stature.

⁴And he ran before, and climbed up into a sycamore tree to see him: for he was to pass that way.
⁵And when Jesus came to the place, he looked up, and saw him, and said unto him, Zacchaeus, make haste, and come down; for to day I must abide at thy house.

B. He accepts repentant sinners.

⁶And he made haste, and came down, and received him joyfully.
⁷And when they [the crowd] saw it, they all murmured, saying, That he was gone to be guest with a man that is a sinner.
⁸And Zacchaeus stood, and said unto the Lord; Behold, Lord, the half of my goods I give to the poor; and if I have taken any thing from any man by false accusation, I restore him fourfold.

C. He saves believing sinners.

⁹And Jesus said unto him, This day is salvation come to this house, forsomuch as he also is a son of Abraham.
¹⁰For the Son of man is come to seek and to save that which was lost.

Everyone, including Zacchaeus himself, knew that Zacchaeus was a "sinner." As the chief tax collector in his district, he was widely identified with extortion and dishonesty. He repented, however, of his sin and demonstrated his repentance by giving to the needy and restoring those he had cheated. Jesus responded to his repentance and faith by granting him full and immediate salvation. "Son of Abraham" (v. 9) in this context is not through physical descent but through faith in God. Abraham is "the father of all them that *believe*" (Rom. 4:11). Jesus seeks and saves all who will admit they are *lost* and will believe in Him as their Savior.

VI. Jesus was The Savior on the cross.

A. He sought salvation for those who killed Him.

LK 23:33 And when they were come to the place, which is called Calvary, there they crucified him, and the malefactors, one on the right hand, and the other on the left.
³⁴ᵃThen said Jesus, Father, forgive them; for they know not they do.

B. He refused to save Himself, to save others.

MK 15:29 And they that passed by railed on him, wagging their heads, and saying, Ah, thou that destroyest the temple, and buildest it in three days,
³⁰Save thyself, and come down from the cross.
³¹Likewise also the chief priests mocking said among themselves with the scribes, He saved others; himself he cannot save.

Jesus was fully man and also fully God. Only as a human being living on earth could He meet all the righteous and holy standards God requires of all people. And only as God in the form of a sinless man could He voluntarily die on the cross to pay the infinite penalty for everyone's sin. The perfect union of His humanity and His deity qualified Him fully and uniquely to be mankind's Savior. He could have saved Himself — if He had not resolutely determined to save us instead.

Jesus' prayer (in LK 23:34) for those who killed Him expressed His willingness, indeed His yearning, to forgive them their horrible sin. To receive God's forgiveness, however, they would first have to recognize and repent of their sin and trust in Jesus as their Savior, as did the thief in the following verses.

> C. He saved the thief who believed in Him.
> **LK 23:39 And one of the malefactors which were hanged railed on him, saying, If thou be Christ, save thyself and us.**
> **⁴⁰But the other answering rebuked him, saying, Dost not thou fear God, seeing thou art in the same condemnation?**
> **⁴¹And we indeed justly; for we receive the due reward of our deeds: but this man hath done nothing amiss.**
> **⁴²And he said unto Jesus, Lord, remember me when thou comest into thy kingdom.**
> **⁴³And Jesus said unto him, Verily I say unto thee, To day shalt thou be with me in paradise.**

The two thieves were condemned for breaking Roman law. Much more, they faced eternal condemnation for breaking God's law. One, however, genuinely repented of his sin and in simple faith called on Jesus to save him. Jesus immediately granted him full forgiveness and eternal salvation. That a guilty, dying thief could thus be saved demonstrates that anyone who repents and calls on Christ also can thus be saved.

> VII. Jesus is the Savior risen from the dead.
> **MK 16:2 And very early in the morning the first day of the week, they [three women] came unto the sepulchre at the rising of the sun.**
> **³And they said among themselves, Who shall roll us away the stone from the door of the sepulchre?**
> **⁴And when they looked, they saw that the stone was rolled away: for it was very great.**
> **⁵ And entering into the sepulchre, they saw a young man sitting on the right side, clothed in a long white garment; and they were affrighted.**
> **⁶And he saith unto them, Be not affrighted: Ye seek Jesus of Nazareth, which was crucified: he is risen; he is not here: behold the place where they laid him.**

Jesus' resurrection certified that His work of redemption was complete and that God had accepted His payment in full for mankind's sin. The fact of Jesus' resurrection, therefore, is as necessary for our salvation as the fact of His sacrificial death. Through these, He fulfilled the meaning of His name: "Jehovah is salvation."

VIII. Jesus is the Savior who will come again.

ACTS 1:9 And when he had spoken these things [to His disciples], while they beheld, he was taken up; and a cloud received him out of their sight.

¹⁰And while they looked steadfastly toward heaven as he went up, behold, two men stood by them in white apparel;

¹¹Which also said, Ye men of Galilee, why stand ye gazing up into heaven? this same Jesus, which is taken up from you into heaven, shall so come in like manner as ye have seen him go into heaven.

"This same Jesus" who ascended bodily into heaven will return to earth "in like manner" — that is, bodily from heaven. Jesus presently has a physical body, in glorified form (Rev. 1:17-18), and He will always have such a body. Thus, Jesus, the God-Man, identified Himself eternally with mankind when He came to be born in Bethlehem as our Savior.

Christ — "The Anointed One"

Old Testament writers foretold, in scores of instances and in wide-ranging detail, a coming Messiah. He would be God's unique man with miraculous power; He would deliver Israel from its enemies and its sins; and He would establish a world-wide kingdom with unprecedented peace, prosperity, and spiritual blessing. Jesus Christ was and is that Messiah. He fulfilled many of these prophecies during His life on earth; and He will fulfill the remainder when He comes again.

Christ is the Greek equivalent of the Hebrew *Messiah*, meaning "Anointed One." Hence, "the Christ" is a title rather than a name. The Gospel writers maintain the distinction between the name *Jesus* and the title *Christ*, and they cite His name many times more often than His title. In the epistles, however, *Christ* is often used interchangeably with His name, and much more often than *Jesus*. The change reflects the greater understanding believers had after Pentecost of the infinite nature and work of God's Son. Thus, the exalted meanings and implications of "the Christ" have been incorporated into our Lord's very name.

Elsewhere in this book, *Christ* generally is used as one of the Master's names. This section, however, deals with Him specifically as "the Anointed One" prophesied in the Old Testament. Each heading uses the title "The Christ" to emphasize a particular aspect of His Messianic mission and message. (Inserts from parallel passages are in braces: { . . . }.)

I. The coming Christ was prophesied in Scripture.

    A. His prophesied birth in Bethlehem.

MT 2:1 Now when Jesus was born in Bethlehem of Judaea in the days of Herod the king, behold, there came wise men from the east to Jerusalem,

²Saying, Where is he that is born King of the Jews? for we have seen his star in the east, and are come to worship him.

³When Herod the king had heard these things, he was troubled, and all Jerusalem with him.

⁴And when he had gathered all the chief priests and scribes of the people together, he demanded of them where Christ should be born.

⁵And they said unto him, In Bethlehem of Judaea: for thus it is written by the prophet,

⁶And thou Bethlehem, in the land of Judah, art not the least among the princes of Judah: for out of thee shall come a Governor, that shall rule my people Israel.

The prophecy in verse 6 is from Micah 5:2 (written about 700 B.C.). Through it, the Jews knew that the Christ would be born in Bethlehem. Micah 5:2 includes the additional significant statement, "whose goings forth have been from of old, from everlasting," asserting the Messiah's eternal pre-existence and deity. Note also that "King of the Jews" in verse 2 is used interchangeably with "Christ" in verse 4. Whether Jesus was indeed the Christ and King of the Jews became the central issue at His trials before the Jewish leaders and Pilate (in Secs. VII-VIII below).

    B. His prophesied life, death, and resurrection.

LK 24:25 Then he said unto them [two disciples], O fools [foolish ones], and slow of heart to believe all that the prophets have spoken:

²⁶Ought not Christ to have suffered these things, and to enter into his glory?

²⁷And beginning at Moses and all the prophets, he expounded unto them in all the scriptures the things concerning himself.

The principal theme of scripture from Genesis to Revelation is God's eternal plan for man's redemption through the sacrificial death of His Son, Jesus Christ. On the day of His resurrection, Christ walked, unrecognized, with two of His followers. To enlighten and encourage them, He began with *Moses* (the first five books of the Bible) and went through *all the scriptures*, explaining how they told of Him, including His death, resurrection, and future glory. These men undoubtedly heard the greatest exposition of the Old Testament ever given — presented by the Subject of those scriptures Himself.

II. The incarnate Christ was acknowledged by His disciples.

JN 1:40 One of the two which heard John [the Baptist] speak [about Jesus], and followed Him, was Andrew, Simon Peter's brother.

⁴¹He first findeth his own brother Simon, and saith unto him, We have found the Messias, which is, being interpreted, the Christ.

⁴⁵Philip findeth Nathanael, and saith unto him, We have found him, of whom Moses in the law, and the prophets, did write, Jesus of Nazareth, the son of Joseph. . . .

⁴⁹Nathanael answered and saith unto him [to Christ], Rabbi, thou art the Son of God; thou art the King of Israel.

MK 8:27 [LK 9:18] And Jesus went out, and his disciples, into the towns of Caesarea Philippi: and by the way he asked his disciples, saying unto them, Whom do men say that I am?

²⁸And they answered, John the Baptist: but some say, Elias; and others, One of the prophets.

²⁹And he saith unto them, But whom say ye that I am? And Peter answereth and saith unto him, Thou art the Christ {The Christ of God}.

The first five disciples to recognize and follow the Christ (in JN 1, above) did so before His public ministry had really begun. Although they were common men (fishermen for the most part), they had a desire for spiritual truth and righteousness. They had followed John the Baptist and had some knowledge of the scriptures pertaining to the Messiah (v. 45). Their openness to the Christ and willingness to follow Him contrasted sharply to the attitude of the crowds that came later mainly to see His miracles or obtain political or economic benefits.

    III. The omniscient Christ was identified through His words.

JN 4:25 The woman [at the well] saith unto him, I know that Messias cometh, which is called Christ: when he is come, he will tell us all things.

²⁶Jesus saith unto her, I that speak unto thee am he. . . .

³⁹And many of the Samaritans of that city believed on him for the saying of the woman, which testified, He told me all that ever I did.

⁴⁰So when the Samaritans were come unto him, they besought him that he would tarry with them: and he abode there two days.

⁴¹And many more believed because of his own word;

⁴²And said unto the woman, Now we believe, not because of thy saying: for we have heard him ourselves, and know that this is indeed the Christ, the Savior of the world.

The Samaritans (a mixed race, part Jewish) accepted only the five books of Moses as inspired by God. Yet they believed that the coming Christ "will tell us all things" (v. 25) and that He would be "the Savior of the world" (v. 42). After listening to the claims and teaching of Jesus, these Samaritans recognized the Christ more fully and accurately than did most in His Jewish audiences.

IV. The omnipotent Christ was certified by His miracles.

JN 10:24 Then came the Jews round about him, and said unto him, How long dost thou make us to doubt? If thou be the Christ, tell us plainly.
²⁵Jesus answered them, I told you, and ye believed not: the works that I do in my Father's name, they bear witness of me.

Jesus performed many miracles in many circumstances and for many apparent reasons. The principal purpose of His miracles, however, was to identify and certify Himself as the Messiah, the Christ. (For a review of Christ's miracles, please see chapters 14 and 15.)

VI. The human Christ was a puzzle to the people.

JN 7:25 Then said some of them of Jerusalem, Is not this he, whom they seek to kill?
²⁶But, lo, he speaketh boldly, and they say nothing unto him. Do the rulers know indeed that this is the very Christ?
²⁷Howbeit we know this man whence he is [from where he came]: but when Christ cometh, no man knoweth whence he is. . . .

³¹And many of the people believed on him, and said, When Christ cometh, will he do more miracles than these which this man hath done? . . .

⁴⁰Many of the people therefore, when they heard this saying [that He would give them living water], said, Of a truth this is the Prophet.
⁴¹Others said, This is the Christ. But some said, Shall Christ come out of Galilee?
⁴²Hath not the scripture said, That Christ cometh of the seed of David, and out of the town of Bethlehem, where David was?
⁴³So there was a division among the people because of him.

Most of the people did not have a proper understanding of the prophesied Messiah, especially the spiritual cleansing and restoration He had to bring (and they had to receive) before He could establish their desired political and economic kingdom. This failure led to their repeated misunderstanding of Christ's words, deeds, person, and purpose. Ultimately, it led to Christ's crucifixion. (See also "Puzzles of Going and Coming" on p. 418.)

VII. The rejected Christ was condemned by the religious leaders.

A. For alleged blasphemy — claiming to be the Christ and God.

MK 14:60 And the high priest stood up in the midst [of the ruling Sanhedrin], and asked Jesus, saying, Answerest thou nothing? what is it which these witness against thee?
⁶¹But he held his peace, and answered nothing. Again the high priest asked him, and said unto him, Art thou the Christ, the Son of the Blessed?

⁶²And Jesus said, I am: and ye shall see the Son of man sitting on the right hand of power, and coming in the clouds of heaven.
⁶³Then the high priest rent his clothes, and saith, What need we any further witnesses?
⁶⁴Ye have heard the blasphemy: what think ye? And they all condemned him to be guilty of death.

After failing to find any fault in Jesus (in spite of contrived testimony from false witnesses), the chief religious and civil leaders of the nation condensed their interrogation of Him into one pivotal question: "Art thou the Christ?" Based on His affirmative reply, they condemned Him to death for blasphemy, by making Himself equal with God.

B. For alleged heresy — perverting the nation with His teaching.
LK 23:1 And the whole multitude of them arose, and led him unto Pilate.
²And they began to accuse him, saying, We found this fellow perverting the nation, and forbidding to give tribute to Caesar, saying that he himself is Christ a King.
³And Pilate asked him, saying, Art thou the King of the Jews? And he answered him and said, Thou sayest it.
⁴Then said Pilate to the chief priests and to the people, I find no fault in this man.
⁵And they were the more fierce, saying, He stirreth up the people, teaching throughout all Jewry, beginning from Galilee to this place.

The Jews rejected Christ's teaching regarding God's requirements for their lives. The standards of godliness He both espoused and demonstrated were more than they could countenance. Rather than admit and address their own sinfulness, they tried to find fault with Christ's message. They falsely accused Him of stirring up the people and perverting the nation with His teaching.

C. For alleged treason — making himself a king against Caesar.
JN 19:12 And from thenceforth Pilate sought to release him: but the Jews cried out, saying, If thou let this man go, thou art not Caesar's friend: whosoever maketh himself a king speaketh against Caesar.
¹³When Pilate therefore heard that saying, he brought Jesus forth, and sat down in the judgment seat in a place that is called the Pavement, but in the Hebrew, Gabbatha.
¹⁴And it was the preparation of the passover, and about the sixth hour: and he saith unto the Jews, Behold your King!
¹⁵But they cried out, Away with him, away with him, crucify him. Pilate saith unto them, Shall I crucify your King? The chief priests answered, We have no king but Caesar.

The crowds previously tried to make Jesus their king by force after He fed the 5,000, but He refused and withdrew from them. Now, the Jews alleged that Jesus was trying to make Himself a king and that He opposed Caesar. The very people who claimed to be looking for a Messiah who would free them from Roman domination, now cried: "We have no king but Caesar."

VIII. The innocent Christ was sentenced by Pilate.

MT 27:17 Therefore when they [the chief priests and elders] were gathered together, Pilate said unto them, Whom will ye that I release unto you? Barabbas, or Jesus which is called Christ? . . .

²⁰But the chief priests and elders persuaded the multitude that they should ask Barabbas, and destroy Jesus.

²¹The governor answered and said unto them, Whether of the twain will ye that I release unto you? They said, Barabbas.

²²Pilate saith unto them, What shall I do then with Jesus which is called Christ? They all say unto him, Let him be crucified. . . .

²⁶Then released he Barabbas unto them: and when he had scourged Jesus, he delivered him to be crucified.

Pilate's belief in Jesus' innocence, his wife's pleas based on her dream (MT 27:19), and statements Christ made to him privately regarding His kingdom (JN 18:36-37) caused Pilate to try to release Jesus. When he succumbed to the pressure from the Jews, he focused their attention again on the central issue, "What shall I do then with Jesus which is called Christ?" This remains the all-important question that every person must answer for himself before God.

IX. The crucified Christ was reviled by His killers.

A. By religious leaders after His trial.

MT 26:67 Then did they spit in his face, and buffeted him; and others smote him with the palms of their hands,

⁶⁸Saying, Prophesy unto us, thou Christ, Who is he that smote thee?

B. By Roman soldiers after His scourging.

MT 27:27 Then the soldiers of the governor took Jesus into the common hall, and gathered unto him the whole band of soldiers.

²⁸And they stripped him, and put on him a scarlet robe.

²⁹And when they had platted a crown of thorns, they put it upon his head, and a reed in his right hand: and they bowed the knee before him, and mocked him, saying, Hail, King of the Jews!

³⁰And they spit upon him, and took the reed, and smote him on the head.

³¹And after that they had mocked him, they took the robe off from him, and put his own raiment on him, and led him away to crucify him.

C. By the people and their leaders at His cross.

> LK 23:35 And the people stood beholding [Christ on the cross]. And the rulers also with them derided him, saying, He saved others; let him save himself, if he be Christ, the chosen of God. {Let Christ the King of Israel descend now from the cross, that we may see and believe. And they that were crucified with him reviled him [MK 15:32].}

The Christ, who rightfully deserved to be crowned King of the Jews with reverence and honor, was crowned instead with thorns and contempt. Instead of a throne, He was put on a cross. The religious leaders sarcastically offered to believe in Him if He came down from the cross. But when He rose from the dead — a far greater feat — they still refused to believe that Jesus was the Christ.

X. The risen Christ was revealed to believers.

A. The testimony of fulfilled prophecy.

> LK 24:44 And [after Christ's resurrection] he said unto them, These are the words which I spake unto you, while I was yet with you, that all things must be fulfilled, which were written in the law of Moses, and in the prophets, and in the psalms, concerning me.
> ⁴⁵Then opened he their understanding, that they might understand the scriptures,

B. The testimony of His resurrection.

> ⁴⁶And said unto them, Thus it is written, and thus it behoved Christ to suffer, and to rise from the dead the third day:
> ⁴⁷And that repentance and remission of sins should be preached in his name among all nations, beginning at Jerusalem.
> ⁴⁸And ye are witnesses of these things.

C. The testimony of the Holy Spirit.

> ⁴⁹And, behold, I send the promise of my Father [the Holy Spirit] upon you: but tarry ye in the city of Jerusalem, until ye be endued with power from on high.

D. The testimony of His ascension.

> ⁵⁰And he led them out as far as to Bethany, and he lifted up his hands, and blessed them.
> ⁵¹And it came to pass, while he blessed them, he was parted from them, and carried up into heaven.

E. The testimony of changed lives.

> ⁵²And they worshipped him, and returned to Jerusalem with great joy:
> ⁵³And were continually in the temple, praising and blessing God. Amen.

Their is no record that the Christ who had been utterly rejected by His nation appeared publicly to unbelievers during the 40 days between His resurrection and ascension. To true believers, however, He revealed Himself more fully than He did before His death (v. 45). After His ascension, fully confident that Jesus is the Christ, they worshipped Him openly and boldly — continually "praising and blessing God." Amen!

The Lord — "Master and God"

The Lord is one of the simplest yet most exalted titles given to Jesus Christ. Its basic meaning is "master," and it pictures one's authority, competence, and/or ownership in a particular realm. Lord also suggests the master's function as protector and benefactor of his realm. Applied to Christ, *Lord* pictures all of these qualities as they pertain to His rule and supervision over all creation. It particularly applies to His relationship to mankind, and especially to those who acknowledge Him as *their* Lord and *their* Master.

The Lord (*Kyrios* in Greek) is also used in the New Testament to translate two of the principal Hebrew names for God — Jehovah and Adonai. (Adonai pictures essentially the same attributes and qualities as *Lord*.) At times, *the Lord* refers to Jesus' own divine lordship — and identifies Him as the incarnate Jehovah and Adonai.

Lord was commonly used in Jesus' time for addressing people whose positions deserved respect, such as civic and religious leaders and owners of slaves or employers of servants. Jesus was often called Lord by the general public and by His followers — typically implying this respect for His status as a teacher and prophet. For the most part, He did not object to these lesser uses of Lord — leaving the extent to which people recognized His lordship to each individual. From time to time, however, He clearly indicated that He was also the fully divine Lord. The following passages refer to Him with that exalted meaning.

I. Announcements from God that Jesus is Lord.

A. By the Holy Spirit through Elisabeth.

LK 1:41 And it came to pass, that, when Elisabeth heard the saluta-tion of Mary, the babe [John the Baptist] leaped in her womb; and Elisabeth was filled with the Holy Ghost:

⁴²And she spake out with a loud voice, and said, Blessed art thou among women, and blessed is the fruit of thy womb.

⁴³And whence is this to me, that the mother of my Lord should come to me?

B. By the angels at Jesus' birth.

LK 2:11 For unto you is born this day in the city of David a Savior, which is Christ the Lord.

C. By God's prophets regarding the Messiah.

MT 3:1 In those days came John the Baptist, preaching in the wilderness of Judaea,

²And saying, Repent ye: for the kingdom of heaven is at hand.

³For this is he that was spoken of by the prophet Esaias, saying, The voice of one crying in the wilderness, Prepare ye the way of the Lord, make his paths straight.

D. By the angel at Jesus' resurrection.

MT 28:5 And the angel answered and said unto the women, Fear not ye: for I know that ye seek Jesus, which was crucified.

⁶He is not here: for he is risen, as he said. Come, see the place where the Lord lay.

Each of these four passages pictures a different aspect of Jesus' divine lordship. Elisabeth referred to Mary's unborn son as "my Lord," foretelling His role as her personal Deliverer and Savior. The angel's announcement of Jesus' birth suggests His supreme and universal governing authority by linking His titles *Christ* and *Lord.* John the Baptist's citation of Isaiah's prophecy stressed the Messiah's deity when he referred to the coming "Lord," which in Isaiah 40:3 is "Jehovah." The angel's announcement at the empty tomb associates the risen Lord with those who follow Him as their Master and Leader. Jesus is fully Lord in all of these respects.

II. Announcements by Jesus that He is Lord.

A. He is the Lord and Rock of true believers.

LK 6:46 And why call ye me, Lord, Lord, and do not the things which I say?

⁴⁷Whosoever cometh to me, and heareth my sayings, and doeth them, I will show you to whom he is like:

⁴⁸He is like a man which built an house, and digged deep, and laid the foundation on a rock: and when the flood arose, the stream beat vehemently upon that house, and could not shake it: for it was founded upon a rock.

⁴⁹But he that heareth, and doeth not, is like a man that without a foundation built an house upon the earth; against which the stream did beat vehemently, and immediately it fell; and the ruin of that house was great.

B. He is the Lord and Master of His servants.

JN 13:12 So after he had washed their feet [at the Last Supper], and had taken his garments, and was set down again, he said unto them, Know ye what I have done to you?

¹³Ye call me Master ["Teacher"] and Lord: and ye say well; for so I am.

¹⁴If I then, your Lord and Master, have washed your feet; ye also ought to wash one another's feet.

¹⁵For I have given you an example, that ye should do as I have done to you.

¹⁶Verily, verily, I say unto you, The servant is not greater than his lord; neither he that is sent greater than he that sent him.

¹⁷If ye know these things, happy are ye if ye do them.

C. He is the Lord and Judge of everyone's destiny.

MT 7:21 Not every one that saith unto me, Lord, Lord, shall enter into the kingdom of heaven; but he that doeth the will of my Father which is in heaven.

²²Many will say to me in that day, Lord, Lord, have we not prophesied in thy name? and in thy name have cast out devils? and in thy name done many wonderful works?

²³And then will I profess unto them, I never knew you: depart from me, ye that work iniquity.

These passages present three additional aspects of Jesus' lordship. First, He is the Lord in the lives of those who not only hear His Word, but do it (LK 6). He was not saying that anyone is saved by how he lives, but that all those who are saved will obey His Word and thus give evidence of their salvation. The choice of whether to accept Jesus as Savior and Lord is up to each individual, but the consequences of that choice are as predetermined as the fate of a house built either on rock or on sand.

For those who willingly accept His lordship, Jesus also is their teacher, guide, and example, as He illustrated in washing His disciples' feet (JN 13). Note how He reversed the order His disciples used, and their implied ranking of importance, when they called Him "Teacher and Lord." In His sermon on the mount (MT 7), Jesus declared that He is the judge and final authority of who enters heaven. Those who profess Him as Lord with their mouths, but not in their hearts (in spite of abundant religious deeds), do not know Him as Lord at all.

III. Announcements by believers that Jesus is Lord.

A. By the former blind man after his healing.

JN 9:35 Jesus heard that they had cast him out [the Jews had excommunicated the blind man Jesus healed]; and when he had found him, he said unto him, Dost thou believe on the Son of God?

³⁶He answered and said, Who is he, Lord, that I might believe on him? ³⁷And Jesus said unto him, Thou hast both seen him, and it is he that talketh with thee.

³⁸And he said, Lord, I believe. And he worshipped him.

B. By Thomas after Jesus' resurrection.

JN 20:24 But Thomas, one of the twelve, called Didymus, was not with them when Jesus came [the day He arose].

²⁵The other disciples therefore said unto him, We have seen the Lord. But he said unto them, Except I shall see in his hands the print of the nails, and put my finger into the print of the nails, and thrust my hand into his side, I will not believe.

²⁶And after eight days again his disciples were within, and Thomas with them: then came Jesus, the doors being shut, and stood in the midst, and said, Peace be unto you.

²⁷Then saith he to Thomas, Reach hither thy finger, and behold my hands; and reach hither thy hand, and thrust it into my side: and be not faithless, but believing.

²⁸And Thomas answered and said unto him, My Lord and my God.

²⁹Jesus saith unto him, Thomas, because thou hast seen me, thou hast believed: blessed are they that have not seen, and yet have believed.

C. By the apostles after Jesus' ascension.

MK 16:19 So then after the Lord had spoken unto them, he was received up into heaven, and sat on the right hand of God.

²⁰And they went forth, and preached every where, the Lord working with them, and confirming the word with signs following. Amen.

Before the former blind man understood who Jesus was, he called Him "Lord," the common title of respect (v. 36). When he learned of Jesus' deity, however, he worshipped Him as *his* Lord (his Savior and Master). Thomas, although one of the twelve, also had to progress from recognizing Jesus as "*the* Lord" to "*my* Lord and *my* God." In both cases, Jesus acknowledged their new-found faith and accepted their worship. After His ascension, Jesus became "the Lord" more fully to His disciples than ever before as they increasingly comprehended the great implications of His divine lordship and proclaimed Him as Lord and God everywhere they went.

One day, Jesus' lordship will be universal and complete. "Wherefore, God also hath highly exalted him, and given him a name which is above every name: that at the name of Jesus every knee should bow . . . and that every tongue should confess *that Jesus Christ is Lord*, to the glory of God the Father" (Phil. 2:9-11).

3

Portraits Of Christ "The Son"

"Whose son is he?," Jesus asked the Pharisees regarding their expected Messiah (MT 22:42). Although they correctly answered from the Old Testament, "the son of David," they could not see (or admit) that Jesus was that Son. Similarly, when the people in Jesus' home town of Nazareth were astonished at His teaching and miracles, they asked, "Is not this the carpenter's son?" (implying, "How can this mere carpenter's son, whom we all know, say and do such great things?"). The people generally, and their leaders especially, repeatedly gave erroneous answers to the crucial question, "Whose son is Jesus?"

The more clearly Jesus demonstrated that He was the Son of David and the Son of God, the more strongly the religious leaders alleged the exact opposite. They implied that He was "born of fornication" (JN 8:41). They added more strongly, "Say we not well that thou art a Samaritan, and hast a devil?" (v. 48). Their blasphemy peaked when they claimed: "He hath Beelzebub [Satan], and by the prince of the devils casteth he out devils" (MK 3:22).

Jesus often referred to Himself as "the Son of Man." Yet near the end of His ministry, the people were still asking, "Who is this Son of Man?" When He asked His disciples, "Whom do men say that I the Son of man am?", they said, "one of the prophets." Then He asked, "But whom say *ye* that I am?" Peter answered, "Thou art the Christ, the Son of the living God" (MT 16:13-16). Jesus Christ is all three — the Son of David, the Son of Man, the Son of God.

These portrayals of Christ correspond closely to the three in the prior chapter. *Son of David* is inseparably tied to the titles *Christ* and *Messiah*. *Son of Man* often parallels His name Jesus as the man from God who came to be our Savior. *Son of God* portrays His deity as does *The Lord* in its divine and exalted sense. To comprehend Christ involves seeing Him in all of these marvelous roles and relationships.

Jesus is "The Son of David"

God's covenant with King David (about 1,000 B.C.) included the unconditional and immutable promise: "thine house and thy kingdom shall be established forever" (II Sam. 7:16). At the time, God did not divulge how He would fulfill that promise. Later, however, He revealed through David's Messianic Psalms many details of the coming eternal King's life and reign. A number of additional prophecies (particularly in Isaiah and Jeremiah) confirm that the Messiah would come through David's lineage and occupy his throne. Jesus Christ is that Son of David.

I. The Son of David came as God promised.

A. He came through a virgin in David's line.

MT 1:1 The book of the generation [genealogy] of Jesus Christ, the son of David, the son of Abraham.

²Abraham begat Isaac; and Isaac begat Jacob; and Jacob begat Judas ["Judah", the father of David's tribe] and his brethren; . . .

⁶And Jesse begat David the king; and David the king begat Solomon . . .

¹⁶And Jacob begat Joseph the husband of Mary, of whom was born Jesus, who is called Christ.

The first verse in the New Testament proclaims: "Jesus Christ, the son of David, the son of Abraham." The miraculous means by which He entered David's lineage is reflected in verse 16 in the change from the long series of male-begat-male to "of Mary, of whom was born Jesus." Isaiah had prophesied: "Hear ye now, O house of David . . . the Lord himself shall give you a sign; behold, a virgin shall conceive, and bear a son, and shall call his name Immanuel [i.e., God with us]" (7:13-14). God also had promised Abraham that the Messiah would descend from him, saying: "In thy seed shall all the nations of the earth be blessed" (Gen. 22:18). The Son of David and Son of Abraham would bring both righteous government and bountiful blessing to the whole world.

B. He came to reign as king forever.

LK 1:30 And the angel said unto her, Fear not, Mary: for thou hast found favor with God.

³¹And, behold, thou shalt conceive in thy womb, and bring forth a son, and shalt call his name JESUS.

³²He shall be great, and shall be called the Son of the Highest: and the Lord God shall give unto him the throne of his father David:

³³And he shall reign over the house of Jacob for ever; and of his kingdom there shall be no end.

The angel's announcement reflected Isaiah's prophecy: "For unto us a child is born, unto us a son is given: and the government shall be upon his shoulder:

and his name shall be called Wonderful, Counselor, The mighty God, The everlasting Father, The Prince of Peace. Of the increase of his government and peace there shall be no end, upon the throne of David, and upon his kingdom, to order it, and to establish it with judgment and with justice from henceforth even for ever. The zeal of the Lord of hosts will perform this" (9:6-7). Christ's genealogy in Luke 3 is generally viewed as Mary's, who was also of the house of David.

C. He came to redeem and save His people.

LK 1:67 And his [John the Baptist's] father Zacharias was filled with the Holy Ghost, and prophesied, saying,

⁶⁸Blessed be the Lord God of Israel; for he hath visited and redeemed his people,

⁶⁹And hath raised up an horn of salvation for us in the house of his servant David;

⁷⁰As he spake by the mouth of his holy prophets, which have been since the world began:

⁷¹That we should be saved from our enemies, and from the hand of all that hate us;

⁷²To perform the mercy promised to our fathers, and to remember his holy covenant;

⁷³The oath which he sware to our father Abraham, . . .

Three months before Christ's birth, the Holy Spirit proclaimed through Zacharias that God was "visiting" His people through a descendant of David. That One would be a "horn of salvation." A "horn" in scripture pictures sovereign authority and power. Here, the reference is to the Messiah's mighty power, especially over His foes and the foes of His people. God's "horn of salvation" would redeem and save His people by overcoming their greatest enemies of sin and death.

D. He was born as God planned in the city of David.

LK 2:1 And it came to pass in those days, that there went out a decree from Caesar Augustus, that all the world should be taxed [registered for tax purposes].

²(And this taxing was first made when Cyrenius was governor of Syria.)

³And all went to be taxed, every one into his own city.

⁴And Joseph also went up from Galilee, out of the city of Nazareth, into Judaea, unto the city of David, which is called Bethlehem; (because he was of the house and lineage of David:)

⁵To be taxed with Mary his espoused wife, being great with child.

⁶And so it was, that, while they were there, the days were accomplished that she should be delivered.

> ⁷And she brought forth her firstborn son, and wrapped him in swaddling clothes [strips of cloth], and laid him in a manger; because there was no room for them in the inn.

Through God's sovereign providence, Caesar required that everyone in the Roman empire be registered to facilitate the collecting of taxes. Jews, who meticulously maintained genealogical records, had to return to their ancestral towns for this registration. Hence, Joseph and Mary arrived in Bethlehem as she was about to give birth. With much of the population similarly traveling, "there was no room for them in the inn."

It is likely that Christ was born in a cave, of which there were many in the Judaean hills, rather than in a building. The manger probably was of solid stone, with a trough cut into it, in which the animals' feed was placed. In caves that were used as stables, mangers often were cut into the walls of the caves or into ledges of rock within the caves. Thus, the infinite, eternal Son of David, probably began His earthly life wrapped in strips of cloth and laid on a carved-rock bed inside a borrowed cave — much as the way He ended it.

II. The Son of David revealed Himself through miracles.

> MT 12:22 Then was brought unto him one possessed with a devil, blind, and dumb: and he healed him, insomuch that the blind and dumb both spake and saw.
> ²³And all the people were amazed, and said, Is not this the son of David?

> MT 15:21 Then Jesus went thence, and departed into the coasts of Tyre and Sidon.
> ²²And, behold, a woman of Canaan came out of the same coasts, and cried unto him, saying, Have mercy on me, O Lord, thou son of David; my daughter is grievously vexed with a devil. . . .
> ²⁸Then Jesus answered and said unto her, O woman, great is thy faith: be it unto thee even as thou wilt. And her daughter was made whole from that very hour. (See Sec. II on p. 176 for the full passage.)

> MT 20:30 And, behold, two blind men sitting by the way side, when they heard that Jesus passed by, cried out, saying, Have mercy on us, O Lord, thou son of David. . . .
> ³⁴So Jesus had compassion on them, and touched their eyes: and immediately their eyes received sight, and they followed him.

It was commonly expected that the Son of David, the Messiah, would perform miracles to certify His identity. Although a few needy individuals readily confessed their belief that Jesus was the Son of David (e.g., the Gentile woman and the blind men, above), the people as a whole seemingly could not progress beyond a tentative supposition that He was that One. Whenever they appeared ready to accept the undeniable evidence of His miracles, they soon would stumble over His teaching.

III. The Son of David is David's Lord.

> MT 22:41 [MK 12:35; LK 20:39] While the Pharisees were gathered together, Jesus asked them,
>
> ⁴²Saying, What think ye of Christ? whose son is he? They say unto him, The son of David.
>
> ⁴³He saith unto them, How then doth David in spirit call him Lord, {For David himself said by the Holy Ghost, in the book of Psalms,} saying,
>
> ⁴⁴The Lord [Jehovah] said unto my Lord [Adonai], Sit thou on my right hand, till I make thine enemies thy footstool?
>
> ⁴⁵If David then call him Lord, how is he his son?
>
> ⁴⁶And no man was able to answer him a word, neither durst any man from that day forth ask him any more questions.

The passage Christ cited is Psalm 110:1, in which David describes his Lord's ascension to Jehovah's right hand and His subsequent return to earth to claim David's throne. Verse 45 could be read: "How could David call the Christ his Lord [Adonai being one of the principal names of God in the Old Testament], when the Christ is also David's son?" Only the deity of the Son of David can account for this. The Pharisees could not (or would not) give the correct answer.

IV. The Son of David offered Himself as King.

A. The common people wanted Him king.

> MT 21:6 And the disciples went, and did as Jesus commanded them,
>
> ⁷And brought the ass, and the colt, and put on them their clothes, and they set him thereon.
>
> ⁸And a very great multitude spread their garments in the way; others cut down branches from the trees, and strawed them in the way.
>
> ⁹And the multitudes that went before, and that followed, cried, saying, Hosanna to the son of David: Blessed is he that cometh in the name of the Lord; Hosanna in the highest.
>
> ¹⁰And when he was come into Jerusalem, all the city was moved, saying, Who is this?
>
> ¹¹And the multitude said, This is Jesus the prophet of Nazareth of Galilee.

These verses describe Christ's triumphal entry into Jerusalem on Palm Sunday only five days before His crucifixion. His final offer of Himself as King, and the crowd's response, fulfilled Zechariah 9:9, "Rejoice greatly, O daughter of Zion; shout, O daughter of Jerusalem: behold, thy King cometh unto thee: he is just, and having salvation; lowly, and riding upon an ass, and upon a colt the foal of an ass."

Hosanna means "Save now, we pray" — a call for immediate establishment of the Messianic kingdom. The multitude's cries and praise fulfilled Psalm 118:25-26: "Save now, I beseech thee, O Lord: O Lord, I beseech thee, send now prosperity. Blessed be he that cometh in the name of the Lord". Most, however, viewed Christ only as a prophet (v. 11), not as the Son of God.

B. The Pharisees resisted His becoming King.

> LK 19:37 [MK 11:9] And when he was come nigh, even now at the descent of the mount of Olives, the whole multitude of the disciples began to rejoice and praise God with a loud voice for all the mighty works that they had seen;
>
> ³⁸Saying, Blessed be the King {Blessed be the kingdom of our father David} that cometh in the name of the Lord: peace in heaven, and glory in the highest.
>
> ³⁹And some of the Pharisees from among the multitude said unto him, Master, rebuke thy disciples.
>
> ⁴⁰And he answered and said unto them, I tell you that, if these should hold their peace, the stones would immediately cry out.

The Pharisees were most upset that the common people (whom they considered unlearned and ignorant) acknowledged Jesus as the Son of David — and that He accepted their praise. They demanded that He put a stop to such nonsense! His reply alludes to Habakkuk 2:11: "For the stone shall cry out of the wall, and the beam out of the timber shall answer it." That verse is from a passage that condemns those who are greedy of position and honor (which, here, belong to Christ alone).

C. The nation misunderstood Him as King.

> ⁴¹And when he was come near, he beheld the city, and wept over it,
>
> ⁴²Saying, If thou hadst known, even thou, at least in this thy day, the things which belong unto thy peace! but now they are hid from thine eyes.
>
> ⁴³For the days shall come upon thee, that thine enemies shall cast a trench about thee, and compass thee round, and keep thee in on every side,
>
> ⁴⁴And shall lay thee even with the ground, and thy children within thee; and they shall not leave in thee one stone upon another; because thou knewest not the time of thy visitation.

The people of Israel did not understand what (and who) would bring them peace, or what that peace would entail (v. 42). They failed to recognize, therefore, "the time of [their] visitation" when the Son of David offered them His kingdom and its perfect peace. As a result, they would have no peace, but only tribulation and desolation, until Christ returns and becomes their eternal Prince of Peace.

D. The chief priests rejected Him as King.

> MT 21:14 And the blind and the lame came to him in the temple; and he healed them.
>
> [15]And when the chief priests and scribes saw the wonderful things that he did, and the children crying in the temple, and saying, Hosanna to the son of David; they were sore displeased,
>
> [16]And said unto him, Hearest thou what these say? And Jesus saith unto them, Yea; have ye never read, Out of the mouth of babes and sucklings thou hast perfected praise?
>
> [17]And he left them, and went out of the city into Bethany; and he lodged there.

Christ replied to His critics from Psalm 8:2, which reads: "Out of the mouth of babes and sucklings hast thou ordained strength [praise] because of thine enemies, that thou mightest still the enemy and the avenger." The praise in this Psalm is for God alone. By applying this Psalm to the people's praise of Himself, Jesus indicated He was God. One of the saddest statements in the Bible follows: "He left them, and went out" — unrecognized, uncrowned, and unwanted.

V. The Son of David is building His church, while awaiting His kingdom.

> REV 22:16 I Jesus have sent mine angel to testify unto you these things [concerning His second coming] in the churches. I am the root and the offspring of David, and the bright and morning star.
>
> [17]And the Spirit and the bride [His church of all true believers] say, Come. And let him that heareth say, Come. And let him that is athirst come. And whosoever will, let him take the water of life freely.

Throughout scripture, the primary significance of "the Son of David" lies in Christ's relationship to Israel as its Messiah and King. Here, however, in His revelation to John about 65 years after His ascension, Christ cites His Davidic lineage as grounds for publicizing *in the churches* the prophecies of His second coming. The *root* of David depicts Christ as David's divine predecessor and creator, whereas the *offspring* of David portrays Him as David's human successor and heir (as discussed in III above). Both the church and redeemed Israel will reign with Christ in His millennial kingdom, and He will be the supreme Lord and King of both peoples.

Jesus is "The Son of Man"

Son of Man is the principal title Jesus used in referring to Himself. In the Gospels, only He used it, and He did so often (about eighty times). His audiences were puzzled by the term, and they asked on one occasion, "We have heard out of the law that Christ abideth for ever: and how sayest thou, The

Son of man must be lifted up [on the cross]? Who is this Son of man?" (JN 12:34). In essence, they were asking, "Where in scripture is there a prophecy about a "Son of Man" who would die?" They clearly misunderstood Isaiah 53 and other passages that foretold the Messiah's sacrificial death.

It is sometimes said that *Son of Man* refers to Jesus' human nature in the way *Son of God* refers to His divine nature. Jesus did use *Son of Man* to refer to His humanity, and did so with a broad range of applications, from His deprivation and humiliation on earth to His future coming as exalted and glorified Messiah. At times, however, He used *Son of Man* in the same way He would use *Son of God*. For example, He essentially equated the two terms at His trial before the Sanhedrin (see I.E, below). *Son of Man*, therefore, encompasses the full nature and character of Jesus Christ as the God-Man.

I. The Son of Man is God incarnate.

A. He "came down from heaven."

JN 3:11 Verily, verily, I say unto thee [Nicodemus], We speak that we do know, and testify that we have seen; and ye receive not our witness.

¹²If I have told you earthly things, and ye believe not, how shall ye believe, if I tell you of heavenly things?

¹³And no man hath ascended up to heaven, but he that came down from heaven, even the Son of man which is in heaven.

B. He has power to forgive sins.

MT 9:2 [LK 5:18] And, behold, they brought to him a man sick of the palsy, lying on a bed: and Jesus seeing their faith said unto the sick of the palsy; Son, be of good cheer; thy sins be forgiven thee.

³And, behold, certain of the scribes said within themselves, This man blasphemeth. {Who can forgive sins, but God alone?}

⁴And Jesus knowing their thoughts said, Wherefore think ye evil in your hearts?

⁵For whether is easier, to say, Thy sins be forgiven thee; or to say, Arise, and walk?

⁶But that ye may know that the Son of man hath power on earth to forgive sins, (then saith he to the sick of the palsy,) Arise, take up thy bed, and go unto thine house.

C. He is greater than the temple and the sabbath.

MT 12:1 At that time Jesus went on the sabbath day through the corn; and his disciples were an hungred [hungry], and began to pluck the ears of corn, and to eat.

²But when the Pharisees saw it, they said unto him, Behold, thy disciples do that which is not lawful to do upon the sabbath day.

³But he said unto them, Have ye not read what David did, when he was an hungred, and they that were with him;

⁴How he entered into the house of God, and did eat the shew-bread, which was not lawful for him to eat, neither for them which were with him, but only for the priests?

⁵Or have ye not read in the law, how that on the sabbath days the priests in the temple profane the sabbath, and are blameless?

⁶But I say unto you, That in this place is one greater than the temple.

⁷But if ye had known what this meaneth, I will have mercy, and not sacrifice, ye would not have condemned the guiltless.

⁸For the Son of man is Lord even of the sabbath day.

D. He is Lord over the angels and all mankind.

MT 13:40 As therefore the tares [weeds in the wheat field] are gathered and burned in the fire; so shall it be in the end of this world.

⁴¹The Son of man shall send forth his angels, and they shall gather out of his kingdom all things that offend, and them which do iniquity;

⁴²And shall cast them into a furnace of fire: there shall be wailing and gnashing of teeth.

In each of the above cases, the Son of Man ascribed to Himself particular attributes or prerogatives of God that no mere human could rightfully claim. In talking with Nicodemus, He claimed firsthand knowledge and experience obtained in heaven. He not only claimed but proved His power to forgive sins when He healed the paralytic. He claimed supremacy over both the temple and the sabbath — two of the most holy institutions in Judaism. He called the angels "His angels" and claimed that He was the one who would consign sinners to hell.

E. He is God the Son and the God-Man.

MK 14:60 [LK 22:66] And the high priest stood up in the midst [of the Sanhedrin], and asked Jesus, saying, Answerest thou nothing? what is it which these witness against thee?

⁶¹But he held his peace, and answered nothing. Again the high priest asked him, and said unto him, Art thou the Christ, the Son of the Blessed?

⁶²And Jesus said, I am: and ye shall see the Son of man sitting on the right hand of {the} power {of God}, and coming in the clouds of heaven.

At His trial before the Sanhedrin (a court of 71 Jewish leaders), Jesus quoted from Daniel's prophecy (7:13-14), which His accusers knew pertained to the Messiah, and which proclaimed the Son of Man's deity. It reads: "I saw in the night visions, and, behold, one like the Son of man came with the clouds of heaven, and came to the Ancient of days, and they brought him near before him. And there was given him dominion, and glory, and a kingdom, that all people, nations, and languages, should serve him: his dominion is an everlasting dominion, which shall not pass away, and his kingdom that which shall not be destroyed."

The religious leaders did not fully comprehend Daniel's prophecy, but they clearly understood that Jesus was applying it to Himself and thereby claiming to be God. Therefore, they accused Him of blasphemy and sentenced Him to death. (See also Sec. VII.A on p. 21.)

> II. The Son of Man's coming was foretold by the prophets.
>> LK 18:31 Then he took unto him the twelve, and said unto them, Behold, we go up to Jerusalem, and all things that are written by the prophets concerning the Son of man shall be accomplished.
>>
>> MK 9:11 And they asked him, saying, Why say the scribes that Elias [Elijah] must first come [before Messiah's kingdom is established]? ¹²And he answered and told them, Elias verily cometh first, and restoreth all things; and how it is written of the Son of man, that he must suffer many things, and be set at nought [treated with contempt].
>>
>> MT 26:24 The Son of man goeth [in death] as it is written of him: but woe unto that man by whom the Son of man is betrayed! it had been good for that man if he had not been born. ²⁵Then Judas, which betrayed him, answered and said, Master, is it I? He said unto him, Thou hast said.

Jesus indicated that the Old Testament contains many prophecies regarding the Son of Man's life and death on earth. Yet, other than the passage in Daniel cited in Section I.E above, the term rarely is used in a Messianic context. Jesus evidently was referring, therefore, to the many passages pertaining to His coming in human form, beginning with the "seed" of Eve (Gen. 3:15) and the "seed" of Abraham (Gen. 22:18). Isaiah 53 and Psalm 22, among others, surely were in His mind when He said, "It is written of the Son of man, that he must suffer many things" (MK 9:12).

> III. The Son of Man was a servant of men.
>> A. He relinquished comfort to serve others.
>>> MT 8:19 And a certain scribe came, and said unto him, Master, I will follow thee whithersoever thou goest. ²⁰And Jesus saith unto him, The foxes have holes, and the birds of the air have nests; but the Son of man hath not where to lay his head.
>>
>> B. He befriended outcasts and sinners.
>>> MT 11:18 For John [the Baptist] came neither eating nor drinking, and they [unbelievers] say, He hath a devil.

¹⁹The Son of man came eating and drinking [normal fare], and they say, Behold a man gluttonous, and a winebibber, a friend of publicans and sinners. But wisdom is justified of her children.

C. He ministered to others as a servant.

MT 20:26 . . . whosoever will be great among you, let him be your minister;
²⁷And whosoever will be chief among you, let him be your servant:
²⁸Even as the Son of man came not to be ministered unto, but to minister, and to give his life a ransom for many.

In these passages, Jesus cites two related purposes of the Son of Man. One is His personal calling to a life of self-sacrifice and service to both God and man. The second is to call His followers to a similar view and practice of life. That the Creator of the universe "hath not where to lay his head" puts the comforts and seeming necessities of this life in perspective, compared with the importance of preparing for our eternal abode.

The Son of Man also was derided for being "a friend of tax-collectors and sinners." Yet where would we be if He were not so? We should have the same concern that He has for those who clearly need His salvation. We must also think and act as "servants and ministers" in our relationships with one another, following His example.

IV. The Son of Man is the Savior of men.

A. He came to save lost and dying people.

LK 19:10 For the Son of man is come to seek and to save that which was lost. [See Sec. V on pp. 15-16 for the full passage].

LK 9:52 And [Jesus] sent messengers before his face: and they went, and entered into a village of the Samaritans, to make ready for him.
⁵³And they did not receive him, because his face was as though he would go to Jerusalem.
⁵⁴And when his disciples James and John saw this, they said, Lord, wilt thou that we command fire to come down from heaven, and consume them, even as Elias did?
⁵⁵But he turned, and rebuked them, and said, Ye know not what manner of spirit ye are of.
⁵⁶For the Son of man is not come to destroy men's lives, but to save them. And they went to another village.

B. His death and resurrection secured our salvation.

JN 3:14 And as Moses lifted up the serpent in the wilderness, even so must the Son of man be lifted up:

¹⁵That whosoever believeth in him should not perish, but have eternal life.

MT 20:18 Behold, we go up to Jerusalem: and the Son of man shall be betrayed unto the chief priests and unto the scribes, and they shall condemn him to death,
¹⁹And shall deliver him to the Gentiles to mock, and to scourge, and to crucify him: and the third day he shall rise again.

MT 12:40 For as Jonas [Jonah] was three days and three nights in the whale's belly; so shall the Son of man be three days and three nights in the heart of the earth.

C. He gives salvation to all who receive Him.

JN 6:27 Labor not for the meat [food] which perisheth, but for that meat which endureth unto everlasting life, which the Son of man shall give unto you: for him hath God the Father sealed.

The Son of Man came to save people's lives, not to destroy them (LK 9:56). To do so, he lived on earth for 33 years as a perfect man and as "the last Adam" (I Cor. 15:45). Then, as our sinless substitute, He died to redeem us from the spiritual death that the first Adam, as the first representative man, brought upon the whole human race when he sinned. Christ stated His purpose succinctly: "The Son of man is come to seek and to save that which was lost."

V. The Son of Man will reign over men.

A. He will come in glory, seen by all.

MT 24:27 For as the lightning cometh out of the east, and shineth even unto the west; so shall also the coming of the Son of man be. . . .

³⁰And then shall appear the sign of the Son of man in heaven: and then shall all the tribes of the earth mourn, and they shall see the Son of man coming in the clouds of heaven with power and great glory.

B. He will reign over all the earth.

MT 25:31 When the Son of man shall come in his glory, and all the holy angels with him, then shall he sit upon the throne of his glory:
³²And before him shall be gathered all nations: and he shall separate them one from another, as a shepherd divideth his sheep from the goats:

C. His disciples will reign with Him.

MT 19:28 And Jesus said unto them [His disciples], Verily I say unto you, That ye which have followed me, in the regeneration [the millennial kingdom] when the Son of man shall sit in the throne of his glory, ye also shall sit upon twelve thrones, judging the twelve tribes of Israel.

When the Son of Man returns to earth with power and glory, He will fulfill all the Messianic prophecies not fulfilled during His first advent. He will rule with complete authority over the world-wide kingdom God's people have long awaited. Not only will His first disciples reign with Him, but all those who trust Him as Savior after them will do so too.

VI. The Son of Man will judge all men.

JN 5:26 For as the Father hath life in himself; so hath he given to the Son to have life in himself;

²⁷And hath given him authority to execute judgment also, because he is the Son of man.

MT 16:27 For the Son of man shall come in the glory of his Father with his angels; and then he shall reward every man according to his works.

The Son of Man experienced "the feeling of our infirmities" and "was in all points tempted like as we are, yet without sin" (Heb. 4:15). He is uniquely qualified, therefore, to "execute judgment" over all mankind (JN 5:27). When He returns, the glorified Son of Man will preside with supreme authority, wisdom, and power over everyone's final judgment and eternal reward. (The several judgments involved here are reviewed on p. 440 ff.)

Jesus is "The Son of God"

Jesus is "The Son of God" primarily in that He is "God the Son" — coequal in the Trinity with God the Father and God the Holy Spirit.

Human minds cannot fully comprehend the infinity of God, the tri-unity of God, the ways of God, the incarnation of God, or many of the other glorious aspects of God. Jesus used, therefore, every means available to bridge these gaps in human understanding. Many of His parables and illustrations portrayed God's nature, purposes, and desires, as did His own life and ministry. To "see" Jesus with comprehension and appreciation is to see God Himself.

Although many prophecies regarding the Messiah indicate He would be a God-Man, the term *Son of God* is not used prophetically in the Old Testament. As with *Son of Man*, therefore, Jesus' audiences initially did not know what to make of the term. It became increasingly clear, however, to His followers and foes alike, that in claiming to be the Son of God, Jesus meant no less than that He was fully God in human flesh. This section presents the principal instances in which Jesus is so identified as the Son of God.

I. Jesus' affirmation that He is God.

A. He is God who came from Heaven.

JN 3:16 For God so loved the world, that he gave his only begotten Son, that whosoever believeth in him should not perish, but have everlasting life.

¹⁷For God sent not his Son into the world to condemn the world; but that the world through him might be saved.

¹⁸He that believeth on him is not condemned: but he that believeth not is condemned already, because he hath not believed in the name of the only begotten Son of God.

B. He is God who deserves honor and worship.

JN 5:21 For as the Father raiseth up the dead, and quickeneth them [gives them life]; even so the Son quickeneth whom he will.

²²For the Father judgeth no man, but hath committed all judgment unto the Son:

²³That all men should honor the Son, even as they honor the Father. He that honoreth not the Son honoreth not the Father which hath sent him.

C. He is God who gives salvation.

²⁴Verily, verily [most assuredly], I say unto you, He that heareth my word, and believeth on him that sent me, hath everlasting life, and shall not come into condemnation; but is passed from death unto life.

²⁵Verily, verily, I say unto you, The hour is coming, and now is, when the [spiritually] dead shall hear the voice of the Son of God: and they that hear shall live.

Jesus often referred to God as "my Father" and to Himself as "the Son." Interestingly, others called Him the Son of God more often than He used the full term Himself (five of the latter are recorded, all in John). Jesus focused more on *demonstrating* that He was the Son of God, through His sinless life, profound teaching, and miraculous works, than on frequently declaring His deity to largely skeptical audiences. Whenever appropriate, however, He clearly stated His heavenly origin, His equality with the Father, His ability to give spiritual life, and mankind's accountability to Him alone as its ultimate judge and rewarder.

II. Heaven's confirmation that Jesus is God.

A. By God's angel before Jesus' birth.

LK 1:30 And the angel said unto her, Fear not, Mary: for thou hast found favor with God.

³¹And, behold, thou shalt conceive in thy womb, and bring forth a son, and shalt call his name JESUS.

³²He shall be great, and shall be called the Son of the Highest: . . .

³⁵And the angel answered and said unto her, The Holy Ghost shall come upon thee, and the power of the Highest shall overshadow thee: therefore also that holy thing which shall be born of thee shall be called the Son of God.

B. By God the Father at Jesus' baptism.

MT 3:16 And Jesus, when he was baptized, went up straightway out of the water: and, lo, the heavens were opened unto him, and he saw the Spirit of God descending like a dove, and lighting upon him:

¹⁷And lo a voice from heaven, saying, This is my beloved Son, in whom I am well pleased.

C. By God the Father at Jesus' transfiguration.

MT 17:1 And after six days Jesus taketh Peter, James, and John his brother, and bringeth them up into an high mountain apart,

²And was transfigured before them: and his face did shine as the sun, and his raiment was white as the light.

³And, behold, there appeared unto them Moses and Elias talking with him.

⁴Then answered Peter, and said unto Jesus, Lord, it is good for us to be here: if thou wilt, let us make here three tabernacles; one for thee, and one for Moses, and one for Elias.

⁵While he yet spake, behold, a bright cloud overshadowed them: and behold a voice out of the cloud, which said, This is my beloved Son, in whom I am well pleased; hear ye him.

God the Son also became the human "Son of God" when the Holy Spirit came upon and "overshadowed" Mary at Jesus' conception (LK 1:35). Thus, He received through His birth a human nature that in its sinlessness parallels the original innocence of Adam, the first "son of God" (LK 3:38). In contrast to Adam, however, Jesus never sinned or failed to please His Father in any way (JN 8:29). Only as God the Son "was made flesh and dwelt among us" (JN 1:14) was it possible for a human being to live a perfect, sinless, God-pleasing life. The Father could declare, therefore, both at Jesus' baptism and at His transfiguration, "This is my beloved Son, in whom I am well pleased."

III. Believers' declarations that Jesus is God.

A. By John after Jesus' baptism.

JN 1:32 And John bare record, saying, I saw the Spirit descending from heaven like a dove, and it abode upon him.

³³And I knew him not: but he that sent me to baptize with water, the same said unto me, Upon whom thou shalt see the Spirit

descending, and remaining on him, the same is he which baptizeth with the Holy Ghost.

³⁴And I saw, and bare record that this is the Son of God.

B. By Jesus' disciples when seeing His miracles.

MT 14:33 Then they that were in the ship [when He calmed the storm] came and worshipped him, saying, Of a truth thou art the Son of God.

C. By Peter in affirming Jesus' deity.

MT 16:13 When Jesus came into the coasts of Caesarea Philippi, he asked his disciples, saying, Whom do men say that I the Son of man am?

¹⁴And they said, Some say that thou art John the Baptist: some, Elias; and others, Jeremias, or one of the prophets.

¹⁵He saith unto them, But whom say ye that I am?

¹⁶And Simon Peter answered and said, Thou art the Christ, the Son of the living God.

D. By Peter when many stopped following Jesus.

JN 6:66 From that time [when He claimed to be "the bread of life"] many of his disciples went back, and walked no more with him.

⁶⁷Then said Jesus unto the twelve, Will ye also go away?

⁶⁸Then Simon Peter answered him, Lord, to whom shall we go? thou hast the words of eternal life.

⁶⁹And we believe and are sure that thou art that Christ, the Son of the living God.

E. By Martha after Lazarus' death.

JN 11:25 Jesus said unto her, I am the resurrection, and the life: he that believeth in me, though he were dead, yet shall he live:

²⁶And whosoever liveth and believeth in me shall never die. Believest thou this?

²⁷She saith unto him, Yea, Lord: I believe that thou art the Christ, the Son of God, which should come into the world.

F. By Thomas after Jesus' resurrection.

JN 20:28 And Thomas answered and said unto him, My Lord and my God.

[See Sec. III.B on p. 28 for the full passage.]

During Jesus' public ministry, His disciples acknowledged Him as "the Son of God" on several occasions. They recognized that He clearly was more than a man and was in some way divine. Based, however, on their frequent lapses of faith, on scripture's statements of their limited understanding, and on their demoralized response to Jesus' arrest and crucifixion, it does not appear that they really grasped that He was fully God the Son. Jesus, however, accepted their acknowledgments as given. He gently and patiently nurtured their limited understanding and faith until they could say with full assurance after His resurrection, "My Lord and my God."

IV. The demons' consternation that Jesus is God.

A. They fear His authority and power.

MK 3:10 For he had healed many; insomuch that they pressed upon him for to touch him, as many as had plagues.

¹¹And unclean spirits, when they saw him, fell down before him, and cried, saying, Thou art the Son of God.

¹²And he straitly charged them that they should not make him known.

LK 4:41 And devils [demons] also came out of many, crying out, and saying, Thou art Christ the Son of God. And he rebuking them suffered them not to speak: for they knew that he was Christ.

B. They know He will banish them to hell.

MT 8:28 And when he was come to the other side [of the Sea of Galilee] into the country of the Gergesenes, there met him two possessed with devils, coming out of the tombs, exceeding fierce, so that no man might pass by that way.

²⁹And, behold, they cried out, saying, What have we to do with thee, Jesus, thou Son of God? art thou come hither to torment us before the time?

The demons know the Son of God firsthand. He created them in their initial perfect state, ejected them from heaven when they fell with Satan, and has been their avowed enemy ever since. They also know that God has set a future date for their final banishment to hell. They asked Jesus, therefore, why He was tormenting them "before the time" (MT 8:29). Although they acknowledged His superior being and omnipotent power, Jesus would not permit demons to influence the people regarding His identity as the Messiah and Son of God. He left that decision for each individual to make by his own volition.

V. The leaders' condemnation of Jesus as God.

A. For claiming equality with God.

JN 5:16 And therefore did the Jews persecute Jesus, and sought to slay him, because he had done these things [a miracle of healing] on the sabbath day.

¹⁷But Jesus answered them, My Father worketh hitherto, and I work.

¹⁸Therefore the Jews sought the more to kill him, because he not only had broken the sabbath, but said also that God was his Father, making himself equal with God.

Many Jews in Jesus' time apparently conceived of the promised Messiah as being less than fully God — perhaps because of assumed limitations imposed by His known humanity. This is reflected in their somewhat greater tolerance (at least initially) of Jesus' statements indicating that He was the Christ than of those that He was God. Whenever the religious leaders perceived He was claiming deity, they wanted to kill Him immediately. God restrained them, however, until His appointed time. "My Father" in verse 17 means "My very own unique Father." The Jews correctly discerned that Jesus was claiming deity, and they reacted accordingly.

> B. For "making Himself God."
> **JN 10:30 [Jesus said,] I and my Father are one.**
> **³¹Then the Jews took up stones again to stone him.**
> **³²Jesus answered them, Many good works have I showed you from my Father; for which of those works do ye stone me?**
> **³³The Jews answered him, saying, For a good work we stone thee not; but for blasphemy; and because that thou, being a man, makest thyself God.**

> C. For claiming His works were God's works.
> **³⁴Jesus answered them, Is it not written in your law, I said, Ye are gods?**
> **³⁵If he called them gods, unto whom the word of God came, and the scripture cannot be broken;**
> **³⁶Say ye of him, whom the Father hath sanctified, and sent into the world, Thou blasphemest; because I said, I am the Son of God?**
> **³⁷If I do not the works of my Father, believe me not.**
> **³⁸But if I do, though ye believe not me, believe the works: that ye may know, and believe, that the Father is in me, and I in him.**
> **³⁹Therefore they sought again to take him: but he escaped out of their hand,**

The Jews were ready to stone Jesus for blasphemy because "thou, being a man, makest thyself God" (v. 33). Jesus responded by citing Psalm 82, which rebuked Israel's unjust judges for their wicked practices. In spite of their wrong-doing, they were still addressed as "gods" (82:6) because their role was to picture God's equitable governing of His people. Jesus asked, in effect, "If human judges were called 'gods,' how much more should I, who was 'sanctified and sent into the world' by the Father, be called the Son of God?" (v. 36). He then cited His miracles as proof that He was God. The Jews again tried to seize Him, but could not because His time to die had not yet come.

> D. For claiming to be the Son of God.
> **LK 22:70 [MT 26:63] Then said they all [at His trial before the Sanhedrin], Art thou then the Son of God? And he said unto them, Ye say that I am.**

⁷¹And they said, What need we any further witness? for we ourselves have heard {his blasphemy} of his own mouth.

JN 19:4 Pilate therefore went forth again, and saith unto them, Behold, I bring him forth to you, that ye may know that I find no fault in him.
⁵Then came Jesus forth, wearing the crown of thorns, and the purple robe. And Pilate saith unto them, Behold the man!
⁶When the chief priests therefore and officers saw him, they cried out, saying, Crucify him, crucify him. Pilate saith unto them, Take ye him, and crucify him: for I find no fault in him.
⁷The Jews answered him, We have a law, and by our law he ought to die, because he made himself the Son of God.

When none of their false accusations against Jesus could be sustained, the religious leaders in desperation relied solely on His claim of deity to demand His death. His reply: "Ye say that I am" in LK 22:70 may be read: "You are correct in saying that I am" — a clear affirmation that He was God. Jesus was condemned and crucified "because He made Himself the Son of God" (JN 19:7).

    VI. The soldiers' observation that Jesus was God.
MT 27:50 Jesus, when he had cried again with a loud voice [on the cross], yielded up the ghost.
⁵¹And, behold, the veil of the temple was rent in twain from the top to the bottom; and the earth did quake, and the rocks rent; . . .
⁵⁴Now when the centurion, and they that were with him, watching Jesus, saw the earthquake, and those things that were done, they feared greatly, saying, Truly this was the Son of God.

The Roman soldiers knew that Jesus was crucified for claiming to be the Son of God. Throughout His scourging and crucifixion, they had taunted Jesus and made cruel sport of Him regarding these claims. They obviously were startled, however, when the skies suddenly became dark at high noon. Three hours later (and still in darkness), the extraordinary events listed above frightened them greatly. From the centurion to the lowest conscript, they could not help but acknowledge, "Truly this was the Son of God."

    VII. Scripture's proclamation that Jesus is God.
JN 20:30 And many other signs truly did Jesus in the presence of his disciples, which are not written in this book:
³¹But these are written, that ye might believe that Jesus is the Christ, the Son of God; and that believing ye might have life through his name.

John's Gospel declares from beginning to end that Jesus is the Christ, the Son of God and God the Son. In support of this great truth, John related a number of Jesus' miracles and fulfillments of prophesies that attest to His deity. Jesus gave the people generally, and His disciples particularly, many more such signs, including those recorded in the other Gospels. John closed the book with: "And there are also many other things which Jesus did, the which, if they should be written every one, I suppose that even the world itself could not contain the books that should be written" (21:25). More than enough is written, however, so that anyone and everyone can understand that Jesus Christ is the Son of God, and that whoever believes in Him as his personal Savior will receive God's gift of eternal life.

4

The Cross and the
Tomb in Bold Relief

Why begin viewing Christ's word paintings with those that depict His death and resurrection? These pertain to the *end* of His life and ministry; why not view them *last*?

Perspective is critical in art, and Christ always drew from the perspective of eternity. From that vantage point, His death and resurrection were the primary focal points of His time on earth. Whatever other subjects He portrayed, those are best understood in the broader context of His blood-stained cross and His empty tomb. His crucifixion revealed His life's greatest purpose, and His resurrection proved its spiritual power.

The principal requirement for fully appreciating the Master's art is personally knowing the Master Himself. That relationship begins with rightly understanding His sacrificial death and bodily resurrection.

Pictures of Christ's Sacrificial Death

Christ told the Jews, "I lay down my life, that I might take it again. No man taketh it from me, but I lay it down of myself. I have power to lay it down, and I have power to take it again" (JN 10:17-18). Jesus Christ was not a martyr. He died voluntarily, intentionally, and purposefully. His death was also substitutionary. He died on our behalf, in our place, and for our benefit. The following pictures illustrate the purposeful and sacrificial nature of Christ's death and the great price He willingly paid for our redemption. (Inserts from parallel passages are placed in braces: { . . . }.)

I. Christ is the Lamb of God.

A. He is God's sacrifice for sin.

JN 1:29 The next day John [the Baptist] seeth Jesus coming unto him, and saith, Behold the Lamb of God, which taketh away the sin of the world.

B. He was the Lamb before His birth.

³⁰This is he of whom I said, After me cometh a man which is preferred before me: for he was before me.

³¹And I knew him not [as to His full identity]: but that he should be made manifest to Israel, therefore am I come baptizing with water.

C. God certified His deity and ministry.

³²And John bare record, saying, I saw the Spirit descending from heaven like a dove, and it abode upon him.

³³And I knew him not: but he that sent me to baptize with water, the same said unto me, Upon whom thou shalt see the Spirit descending, and remaining on him, the same is he which baptizeth with the Holy Ghost.

³⁴And I saw, and bare record that this is the Son of God.

D. Believers acknowledge and follow God's Lamb.

³⁵Again the next day after John stood, and two of his disciples;

³⁶And looking upon Jesus as he walked, he saith, Behold the Lamb of God!

³⁷And the two disciples heard him speak, and they followed Jesus.

For his Jewish audience, John's declaration that Jesus was the Lamb of God carried immense meaning and shocking implications. From the beginning, the sacrificial offerings prescribed by God to cover people's sins required the death of innocent animals. When Adam and Eve first sinned, God covered them with coats of skins from animals He slew in their stead (Gen 3:21). From Abel to Moses, God taught His people the necessity of such sacrifices for their sins.

After the Exodus and for the next 1,400 years, the Jewish people meticulously performed numerous daily, weekly, monthly, and annual sacrifices as commanded by God, using the blood of innocent animals to cover their sins. These all pointed ahead to God's perfect sacrifice, who would be "brought as a lamb to the slaughter" when God "laid on Him the iniquity of us all" (Isa. 53). Christ came as "the Lamb slain from the foundation of the world" (Rev. 13:8), "a lamb without blemish and without spot" (1 Peter 1:19). He would take away not only Israel's sin, but "the sin of the [whole] world" (v. 29).

II. Christ is our Passover meal.

A. The meal pictured His sacrificial death.

LK 22:14 And when the hour was come [for the Passover meal], he sat down, and the twelve apostles with him.

¹⁵And he said unto them, With [great] desire I have desired to eat this passover with you before I suffer:

¹⁶For I say unto you, I will not any more eat thereof, until it be fulfilled in the kingdom of God.

No recurring celebration or memorial was more revered by the Jews than the feast of Passover. It commemorated God's "passing over" the Jews in Egypt, when He commanded each household to kill an unblemished male lamb and apply its blood to the doorposts, to spare their eldest son from death (Ex. 12:1-30). This particular Passover was unique because Christ was about to fulfill, once and for all by His own death and shed blood, the eternal redemption that the Passover prefigured. "For even Christ, our passover, is sacrificed for us" (1 Cor. 5:7).

B. The bread pictured His broken body.

MT 26:26 [LK 22:19] And as they were eating, Jesus took bread, {and gave thanks,} and blessed it, and brake it, and gave it to the disciples, and said, Take, eat; this is my body {which is given for you: this do in remembrance of me}.

As the pictures in the Passover meal neared fulfillment, Christ ordained a new "memorial supper" for His followers. The bread pictures His body, freely given in death for us. Much as He broke the unleavened bread used in Passover meals, He permitted His sinless body to be broken through the horrible scourging and crucifixion He endured on our behalf.

C. The cup pictured His shed blood.

²⁷And he took the cup, and gave thanks, and gave it to them, saying, Drink ye all of it [i.e., Drink of it, all of you];

> ^{28}For this is my blood of the new testament, which is shed for many for the remission of sins. {this do ye, as oft as ye drink it, in remembrance of me [I Cor. 11:25].}
> ^{29}But I say unto you, I will not drink henceforth of this fruit of the vine, until that day when I drink it new with you in my Father's kingdom.

Christ not only had to die to pay for our sins, He had to die by shedding His blood. God had said, "The life of the flesh is in the blood . . . for it is the blood that maketh an atonement for the soul" (Lev. 17:11). Christ commanded His followers to eat the bread and drink the cup "in remembrance of me." We should do so "until He comes" (I Cor. 11:26). Then He will feast with us forever in His kingdom (v. 29).

III. Christ gave His all to purchase treasures.

A. He gave all He had for a "treasure hid in a field."

> **MT 13:44 Again, the kingdom of heaven is like unto treasure hid in a field; the which when a man hath found, he hideth, and for joy thereof goeth and selleth all that he hath, and buyeth that field.**

B. He gave all He had for "one pearl of great price."

> ^{45}Again, the kingdom of heaven is like unto a merchant man, seeking goodly pearls:
> ^{46}Who, when he had found one pearl of great price, went and sold all that he had, and bought it.

The eight parables in MT 13 picture various aspects of Christ's kingdom. These two form a pair with similar messages. (See Chapter 19 for the others.) In a prior parable, "the field" is the world (v. 38), and the "man" is Christ Himself (v. 37). That seems to be the case here too. Because sinful people cannot purchase any part of God's kingdom with anything they can offer, the man in these parables could not be a mere human. The Son of man, however, could and did give "all that he had" to purchase these costly treasures.

With this view, the "treasure hid in a field" most likely depicts the people in every place and time whose salvation Christ would purchase through His sacrificial death. These include Old Testament believers (who trusted in their future redemption) as well as all who receive Christ as Savior either in this age or in times to come. Christ's principal goal was to purchase the treasure, but He also purchased the field (this world over which He ultimately will reign). His anticipated "joy" (v. 44) of possessing the treasure was sufficient motivation for Christ to give His all to obtain it.

Similarly, but more narrowly, the "one pearl of great price" seems to picture Christ's church, the single universal body of all who truly believe in Him during this present age. Again, He purchased it with all He had. "Christ also loved the church, and gave himself for it . . . that he might present it to himself a glorious church" (Eph. 5:25-27). The word pearl comes from a Sanskrit word meaning "pure." That Christ would foresee a body of sinful, rebellious people as a "pearl of great price" pictures both the immeasurable extent of God's grace and the transforming power of the gospel.

IV. Christ drank the cup of God's judgment for sin.

A. He "sorrowed unto death" in facing His cup.

MT 26:36 Then cometh Jesus with them unto a place called Gethsemane, and saith unto the disciples, Sit ye here, while I go and pray yonder.

³⁷And he took with him Peter and the two sons of Zebedee [James and John], and began to be sorrowful and very heavy.

³⁸Then saith he unto them, My soul is exceeding sorrowful, even unto death: tarry ye here, and watch with me.

³⁹And he went a little farther, and fell on his face, and prayed, saying, O my Father, if it be possible, let this cup pass from me: nevertheless not as I will, but as thou wilt.

"Cups" in scripture picture a person's intense involvement in an event or a series of experiences. There are cups of God's blessing, as in "my cup runneth over" (Psa. 23:5), and cups of God's wrath and judgment for sin, as in Isaiah 51:17. The latter declares: "O Jerusalem, which hast drunk at the hand of the Lord the cup of his fury; thou hast drunken the dregs of the cup of trembling, and wrung them out". The cup Jesus faced in Gethsemane was full to the brim with God's wrath and judgment for all the sins of all mankind of all time.

B. He agonized in prayer regarding His cup.

⁴⁰And he cometh unto the disciples, and findeth them asleep, and saith unto Peter, What, could ye not watch with me one hour?

⁴¹Watch and pray, that ye enter not into temptation: the spirit indeed is willing, but the flesh is weak.

⁴²He went away again the second time, and prayed, saying, O my Father, if this cup may not pass away from me, except I drink it, thy will be done. {And there appeared an angel unto him from heaven, strengthening him. And being in an agony he prayed more earnestly: and his sweat was as it were great drops of blood falling down to the ground [LK 22:43-44].}

In Gethsemane, Jesus confronted the supreme issue of submitting to the horrible death and separation from God that awaited Him on the cross. These verses provide an unusual glimpse into that struggle and reveal the interplay between Jesus' full deity and His full humanity. Consider the following:

1) Although the matter of His sacrificial death had been settled within the Godhead "from the foundation of the world," Jesus' human will had to make the same final and irrevocable commitment to go to the cross. Also, His human emotions had to bear the vicious ridicule and rejection of His own people, and His human body had to accept the extreme abuse and torture of scourging and crucifixion.

2) As God the Son praying to God the Father, Jesus agonized over His looming rejection by His Father while He bore mankind's sin. The Father and the Son had never experienced anything less than perfect harmony and unity from eternity past; but the Son would soon cry, "My God, my God, why hast thou forsaken me?" Jesus knew full well that bearing mankind's sin would include full separation from His Father.

3) The disciples' complete failure to provide any support or encouragement to Jesus, and their inability to comprehend the gravity of the situation only added to the crushing loneliness and isolation that Jesus faced as a human being. He truly was "a man of sorrows, and acquainted with grief: and we hid as it were our faces from Him" (Isa. 53:3).

    C. He accepted God's will by accepting His cup.

        ⁴³And he came and found them asleep again: for their eyes were heavy.

        ⁴⁴And he left them, and went away again, and prayed the third time, saying the same words.

        ⁴⁵Then cometh he to his disciples, and saith unto them, Sleep on now, and take your rest: behold, the hour is at hand, and the Son of man is betrayed into the hands of sinners.

        ⁴⁶Rise, let us be going: behold, he is at hand that doth betray me.

Although Jesus prayed initially for relief (v. 39), He submissively added, "Thy will be done." In His second prayer (v. 42), He submitted further to His Father's will in saying, "If this cup may not pass away from me, except I drink it, thy will be done". After His third prayer (the same as the second; v. 44), He returned to His sleeping disciples with the issue irrevocably settled. With full peace and assurance, He took the cup that awaited Him.

    D. He refused to escape drinking His cup.

        ⁴⁷And while he yet spake, lo, Judas, one of the twelve, came, and with him a great multitude with swords and staves, from the chief priests and elders of the people.

> **JN 18:10** Then Simon Peter having a sword drew it, and smote the high priest's servant, and cut off his right ear. The servant's name was Malchus.
>
> ¹¹Then said Jesus unto Peter, Put up thy sword into the sheath: the cup which my Father hath given me, shall I not drink it?

In refusing all opportunities to avoid His cup, Jesus sealed His commitment to fulfill God's plan for our salvation. Knowing both the horrible death and "the joy that was set before Him" (Heb. 12:2), He willingly drank the cup the Father had given Him. (See also Sec. IV.C under "Crucifixion" on p. 60.)

V. Christ paid our overwhelming debts.

> **JN 19:28** After this [six hours on the cross], Jesus knowing that all things were now accomplished, that the scripture might be fulfilled, saith, I thirst.
>
> ²⁹Now there was set a vessel full of vinegar: and they filled a sponge with vinegar, and put it upon hyssop, and put it to his mouth.
>
> ³⁰When Jesus therefore had received the vinegar, he said, It is finished: and he bowed his head, and gave up the ghost.

"It is finished" (v. 30) is a single Greek word, *tetelestai*. In business and financial records from the time of Christ, *tetelestai* often is written beside or over a record of indebtedness, meaning "paid in full." Christ's cry, "It is finished," signified His payment in full for the greatest transaction of all time — His purchased redemption of the fallen human race.

Under Roman law, many infractions carried specified monetary penalties. An offender was not released until he or someone else paid the stated amount. If the penalty was not paid promptly, the offender was imprisoned and a "certificate of debt" was posted nearby listing his crime(s) and the payment required for his release.

Under God's law, "There is not a just man upon earth, that doeth good, and sinneth not" (Eccl. 7:20). Further, "the soul that sinneth, it shall die" (Ezek. 18:20). Each person's sins create a staggering debt to God far beyond anyone's ability to pay. With all the sins of the billions of people who have ever lived and will yet live, the magnitude of mankind's sin debt is beyond measure. Hence, only an infinite payment by One with no sin debt of His own could satisfy the righteous demands of God's law.

Through Christ's sacrificial death, "He made you [all believers] alive together with Him, having forgiven us all our transgressions, having *cancelled out the certificate of debt* consisting of decrees against us and which was hostile to us; and He has *taken it out of the way, having nailed it to the cross*" (Col. 2:13-14, NASB).

When Christ went to Calvary, He took all of our "certificates of debt" and cancelled every one, paying them in full with His blood. Thus, He could proclaim in victory, "tetelestai!" Our purchased redemption was complete.

Portrayals of Christ's Crucifixion

Christ portrayed His coming death not only as a voluntary sacrifice for sin (as shown in the preceding section), but also as a violent execution at the hands of His enemies. Although God sovereignly governed every detail of the life and death of His Son, He permitted Christ's adversaries (both human and spiritual) to carry out their darkest designs within His divine plan. These culminated in their crucifying Jesus Christ.

Crucifixion was a Roman, not a Jewish, form of capital punishment. It was undoubtedly one of the most cruel and painful means of execution ever devised. Based on Deuteronomy 21:23, the Jews considered that anyone hanged on a tree (or a cross) was cursed by God. Galatians 3:13 applies this verse to Christ, who was "made a curse for us; for it is written, Cursed is everyone that hangeth on a tree." Thus, even the form of Christ's horrible death is a picture of His bearing our curse to atone for our sin.

I. The bronze serpent "lifted up" on a pole.

A. Christ was "lifted up" to save those who look to Him.
JN 3:14 And as Moses lifted up the serpent in the wilderness, even so must the Son of man be lifted up:
¹⁵That whosoever believeth in him should not perish, but have eternal life.

Although the Israelites experienced God's miraculous deliverance from Egypt, they complained bitterly against God in the wilderness. He sent "fiery serpents" among them, and many people died from their bite. When the people acknowledged their sin and repented, God told Moses to put a bronze serpent on a pole. If anyone bitten by a serpent looked to the bronze serpent, he lived (Num. 21:5-9). Christ told Nicodemus that He similarly would be "lifted up" (v. 14) and that those who look in faith to Him "should not perish, but have eternal life."

B. His crucifixion opened salvation to everyone.
JN 12:32 And I, if I be lifted up from the earth, will draw all men unto me.
³³This he said, signifying what death he should die.

³⁴**The people answered him, We have heard out of the law that Christ abideth for ever: and how sayest thou, The Son of man must be lifted up? who is this Son of man?**

Christ's statement that He would be "lifted up" perplexed the Jews. They knew the Messiah would "abide for ever" (v. 34), and apparently had concluded He could not (or would not) die. They could not reconcile that view with an intervening death, especially such a cruel and ignominious death as crucifixion.

C. His "lifting up" proved He is God.

JN 8:28 Then said Jesus unto them, When ye have lifted up the Son of man, then shall ye know that I am he [lit. I AM], and that I do nothing of myself; but as my Father hath taught me, I speak these things.

Christ declared that, when He was "lifted up," the Jews would finally realize that He was "I AM" — the God who revealed Himself to Moses at the burning bush. (The he after "I AM" was supplied by translators and is better omitted.) Thus, His crucifixion and resurrection (and many of their details) would prove His deity. (See Sec. II under "I AM" on pp. 341-343.)

II. The heir killed by wicked farmers.

A. God leased His vineyard to tenant farmers.

MT 21:33 [LK 20:9] Hear another parable: There was a certain householder, which planted a vineyard, and hedged it round about, and digged a winepress in it, and built a tower, and let it out [leased it] to husbandmen, and went into a far country {for a long time}:

This parable was directed primarily at the "chief priests and elders" (MT 21:23). These religious leaders and their predecessors are the husbandmen (tenant farmers or sharecroppers) to whom the householder (God Himself) leased His specially-prepared vineyard (His chosen people, Israel). Then he left "for a long time."

B. God sent His servants to receive His rightful fruit.

³⁴**And when the time of the fruit drew near, he sent his servants to the husbandmen, that they might receive the fruits of it.**

³⁵**And the husbandmen took his servants, and beat one, and killed another, and stoned another.**

³⁶**Again, he sent other servants more than the first: and they did unto them likewise.**

C. God finally sent His only Son.

³⁷**[MK 12:6] But last of all {having yet therefore one son, his well-beloved} he sent unto them his son, saying, They will reverence my son.**

The sharecroppers were accountable to the owner for maintaining the vineyard and giving him his share of its produce. Israel's religious leaders, however, wanted the nation's *fruit* for *their own* benefit, not God's. Hence, they mistreated and even killed the many prophets and other servants God sent to direct their service and worship toward Him. At long last, God sent His only and well-beloved Son in a final effort to bring them into a right relationship with Him.

    D. The tenants killed the Son.

> **³⁸[LK 20:14] But when the husbandmen saw the son, they said among themselves, This is the heir; come, let us kill him, and let us seize on his inheritance {that the inheritance may be ours}.**
> **³⁹And they caught him, and cast him out of the vineyard, and slew him.**

The tenants killed the owner's son because he was the heir and they wanted the vineyard for themselves (v. 38). This pictures the religious leaders' vendetta against Christ. God deserves the pre-eminent position of honor and authority among His people, and this position is Christ's *inheritance*. The leaders, however, coveted that honor and authority. So they killed the Son.

    E. The leaders pronounced their own judgment.

> **⁴⁰When the lord therefore of the vineyard cometh, what will he do unto those husbandmen?**
> **⁴¹They say unto him, He will miserably destroy those wicked men, and will let out his vineyard unto other husbandmen, which shall render him the fruits in their seasons.**

The judgment the religious leaders predicted for the tenants (v. 41) was precisely the judgment that befell them. The "other husbandmen" who received stewardship over God's vineyard are believers in Christ whom He appoints to labor in His church. (The new stewards must avoid the self-centered attitudes and behavior that caused the former stewards' downfall.)

Christ's audiences often missed the point of His parables. The religious leaders initially did not grasp the meaning of this parable either. Moments later, however, they got the picture (v. 45) and "perceived that He spake of them." In their anger, they sought to kill Christ, just as He foretold in the parable.

    III. The "stone the builders rejected."

      A. The "rejected stone" will become the "chief cornerstone."

> **MT 21:42 [continued from above] Jesus saith unto them, Did ye never read in the scriptures, The stone which the builders rejected, the same is become the head of the corner: this is the Lord's doing, and it is marvelous in our eyes?**

⁴³Therefore say I unto you, The kingdom of God shall be taken from you, and given to a nation bringing forth the fruits thereof.

Christ applied Psalm 118:22-23 to Himself in verse 42, referring both to His rejection by the religious leaders during His first coming and His ruling over Israel and all the earth as "the head of the corner" at His second coming. In the interim, He is building a new *nation* (v. 43), His Church, "Jesus Christ himself being the chief corner stone" (Eph. 2:20).

    B. The "stumbling stone" will become God's "grindstone."
        ⁴⁴And whosoever shall fall on this stone shall be broken: but on whomsoever it shall fall, it will grind him to powder.

In verse 44a, Christ applied to Himself Isaiah 8:14-15, which pictures the Lord as "a stone of stumbling and for a rock of offense to both the houses of Israel . . . and many among them shall stumble, and fall, and be broken, and be snared, and be taken." Verse 44b may refer to Daniel 2:34-35, which predicts that Christ as "a stone cut out without hands" will fall upon and crush to powder the Antichrist's final human government. Christ eventually will crush all opposition to His authority, including the religious and political opposition typified by the Jewish leaders — and that of our time as well.

    C. Hearts of stone rejected God's "living stone."
        ⁴⁵And when the chief priests and Pharisees had heard his parables, they perceived that he spake of them.
        ⁴⁶But when they sought to lay hands on him, they feared the multitude, because they took him for a prophet.

As their forebearers did in the Old Testament, the Jewish leaders "made their hearts as an adamant stone, lest they should hear the law, and the words which the Lord of hosts hath sent" (Zech. 7:12). Peter, probably recalling this incident years later, referred to Christ as "a living stone, disallowed indeed of men, but chosen of God, and precious" (I Pet. 2:4). The leaders sought to kill Christ, but His time had not yet come.

    IV. The fire and baptism of agonizing death.

    A. The fire of God's wrath would envelope Him.
        LK 12:49 I am come to send fire on the earth; and what will I, if it be already kindled?

Fire in scripture often pictures God's judgment of sin. Here, in context with verse 50 (below), Christ likely is referring to the fire of God's wrath He would incur at Calvary as He bore the penalty for the sin of all mankind. Verse 49b may be read: "And how I long that it were already burning!" Knowing that His fiery judgment would be intensely painful, He longed to get through it and beyond it and accomplish its purpose as soon as possible.

B. The baptism of excruciating death would engulf Him.

⁵⁰But I have a baptism to be baptized with; and how am I straitened [pressed beyond measure] till it be accomplished!

Baptize and *baptism* are forms of Greek words that mean "to immerse, dip, or submerge" (see "Baptism" on p. 169). In referring to His impending death as a baptism, Christ meant that He would plunge fully into it and submerge Himself completely within it. As with the "fire" He wished were already burning, He agonized over the flood of rejection, torture, and grief that soon would engulf Him, longing for its conclusion.

C. The cup and the baptism of God's judgment would overwhelm Him.

MK 10:37 They [James and John] said unto him, Grant unto us that we may sit, one on thy right hand, and the other on thy left hand, in thy glory.

³⁸But Jesus said unto them, Ye know not what ye ask: can ye drink of the cup that I drink of? and be baptized with the baptism that I am baptized with?

³⁹And they said unto him, We can. And Jesus said unto them, Ye shall indeed drink of the cup that I drink of; and with the baptism that I am baptized withal shall ye be baptized:

⁴⁰But to sit on my right hand and on my left hand is not mine to give; but it shall be given to them for whom it is prepared.

The disciples had no comprehension of "the cup" and "the baptism" Christ faced. Nor did they understand His prediction that they too would suffer persecution and even martyrdom for their faith later on. Christ's "cup" and "baptism" were primarily for our salvation, but they also picture the suffering that believers can expect in an antagonistic world (v. 39).

V. The Shepherd smitten by God.

MT 26:31 Then saith Jesus unto them [His disciples], All ye shall be offended because of me this night: for it is written, I will smite the shepherd, and the sheep of the flock shall be scattered abroad.

³²But after I am risen again, I will go before you into Galilee.

³³Peter answered and said unto him, Though all men shall be offended because of thee, yet will I never be offended.

³⁴Jesus said unto him, Verily I say unto thee, That this night, before the cock crow, thou shalt deny me thrice.

³⁵Peter said unto him, Though I should die with thee, yet will I not deny thee. Likewise also said all the disciples.

Zechariah 13:7, written over 500 years before, states: "Awake, O sword, against my shepherd, and against the man that is my fellow, saith the Lord of hosts: smite the shepherd, and the sheep shall be scattered." God Himself would "smite the Shepherd" and sacrifice the Shepherd for the sheep, that He might bless the sheep for all eternity. Romans 8:32 states: "He that spared not his own Son, but delivered him up for us all, how shall he not with him [Christ] also freely give us all things?"

Zechariah also prophesied that "the sheep shall be scattered" when the Shepherd was smitten. The disciples all vehemently denied that they would desert Christ, even if everyone else forsook Him. Their good intentions and brave promises, however, went for naught, and Zechariah's prophecy was fulfilled that same night.

These verses give rise to the question: "If God 'smote the Shepherd,' how could the Jews, Romans, or anyone else be held responsible for Christ's death?" The answer lies in God's foreknowledge that all mankind would choose to sin, and in His planning before creation for Christ's atoning death for that sin. God's foreknowledge and sovereignty, however, do not remove or diminish men's responsibility for their sin or for Christ's crucifixion. Both God's "smiting the Shepherd" and men's responsibility for it were proclaimed in Peter's message on Pentecost: "Jesus of Nazareth . . . being delivered by the determinate counsel and foreknowledge of God, ye have taken, and by wicked hands have crucified and slain" (Acts 2:22-23). God smote the Shepherd because He knew nothing else could accomplish our salvation from our sin.

VI. Crucifixion at Calvary
(A conflation based on MT 27:32-37, MK 15:21-26, LK 23:33-38, and JN 19:17-24)

A. The place of Golgotha.
JN 19:17 And he [Jesus] bearing his cross went forth {And as they came out [of the city], they found a man of Cyrene, Simon by name: him they compelled to bear his cross} into a place called the place of a skull, which is called in the Hebrew Golgotha {which is called Calvary}:
[18]Where they crucified him, and two other with him, on either side one, and Jesus in the midst.

Golgotha in Hebrew and Calvary in Latin mean "skull." One possible site of Golgotha is near a hill just outside the old city wall. The hill has a strong skull-like appearance and its location seems consistent with other scriptural criteria as well. Most important is what Christ did at Golgotha. None of the details of the extreme physical torture He endured there are related in the Gospels;

rather, all four writers simply report, "they crucified him." The salvation that He purchased there is their overriding focus.

B. The palliative of gall.
MT 27:34 They gave him vinegar [sour wine] to drink mingled with gall: and when he had tasted thereof, he would not drink.

Gall is a general term for something bitter. (Mark reports that it included myrrh.) The drink was intended to drug its recipient and alleviate his pain. Christ chose, however, to suffer the full force of His physical and spiritual ordeal with no means of relief.

C. The placard of guilt.
JN 19:19 And Pilate wrote a title, {the superscription of his accusation} and put it on the cross {over his head}. And the writing was, {THIS IS} JESUS OF NAZARETH THE KING OF THE JEWS.
²⁰This title then read many of the Jews: for the place where Jesus was crucified was nigh to the city: and it was written in Hebrew, and Greek, and Latin.
²¹Then said the chief priests of the Jews to Pilate, Write not, The King of the Jews; but that he said, I am King of the Jews.
²²Pilate answered, What I have written I have written.

The superscription listed Christ's indictment, the charged offense for which He was crucified. After all the false testimony and rigged trials, the only charge that remained was that He was "the king of the Jews." Pilate may have intended only to mock his Jewish adversaries with this title, but God intended to declare who truly was on the cross.

D. The parting of garments.
²³Then the soldiers, when they had crucified Jesus, took his garments, and made four parts, to every soldier a part; and also his coat [tunic]: now the coat was without seam, woven from the top throughout.
²⁴They said therefore among themselves, Let us not rend it, but cast lots for it, whose it shall be: that the scripture might be fulfilled, which saith, They parted my raiment among them, and for my vesture they did cast lots. {And sitting down they watched [kept watch over] him there;} These things therefore the soldiers did.

The garments of an executed person typically were taken by the executioner (four soldiers in Jesus' case). The soldiers gambled for His garments by casting lots (possibly using dice). Their action fulfilled the prophecy cited in verse 24 from Psalm 22:18. That Psalm foretells many details of Christ's crucifixion —

even though crucifixion was not devised as a means of capital punishment until hundreds of years after the Psalm was written.

>   VII. The veil torn in two.
>   **MT 27:50 [As He hung on the cross] Jesus, when he had cried again with a loud voice, yielded up the ghost.**
>   **⁵¹And, behold, the veil of the temple was rent in twain from the top to the bottom; and the earth did quake, and the rocks rent;**

The veil in the temple separated the Holy of Holies from the outer areas and signified God's unapproachable holiness except through the strictly limited means He prescribed. Only the high priest could enter within the veil once a year on the Day of Atonement, and only with blood from a sin offering. He would sprinkle the blood on the mercy seat above the ark of the covenant to atone for all of the people's sins in that year that had not been covered by other sacrifices. It was the most sacred and solemn event in Israel.

As Christ's torn body hung on the cross and His spirit departed His body in death, the veil in the temple also was torn — from the top down, by God Himself. The tearing of the veil pictures the opening of access to God's holy presence that Christ's death affords those who come to God through Him. Redeemed sinners, therefore, now may have "boldness to enter into the holiest [place] by the blood of Jesus, by a new and living way, which he hath consecrated for us, through the veil, that is to say, his flesh" (Heb. 10:19-20).

Scenes of Christ's Burial

Christ often pictured His coming death and resurrection, but He left it largely to others to present the scenes and lessons of His burial. Whether they were devoted believers or avowed adversaries, they were all guided by God's sovereign hand in each picture they presented and each prophecy they fulfilled. The following portrayals of Christ's burial demonstrate God's amazing superintending of every detail of Christ's death and our redemption.

>   I. Mary's anointing pictured Christ's burial.
>
>   A. She anointed Him before His death.
>   **MK 14:3 [JN 12:1; MT 26:6] And being in Bethany in the house of Simon the leper, as he sat at meat, there came a woman having an alabaster box of ointment of spikenard very precious; and she brake the box, and poured it on his head {and anointed the feet of Jesus, and wiped his feet with her hair: and the house was filled with the odor of the ointment}.**

John reveals that the woman was Mary of Bethany, sister of Martha and Lazarus. Mary seems to have listened to Jesus' teaching as intently and perceptively as anyone (LK 10:38-42), and she understood that He was about to die. Full of adoration for her Master, she quietly but unabashedly demonstrated her love in the most generous and tender fashion that she could devise. (Spikenard was a fragrant ointment obtained from the roots of a plant from India.)

B. The disciples saw her "waste," not her worship.

⁴And there were some {his disciples} that had indignation within themselves, and said, Why was this waste of the ointment made? {Then saith one of his disciples, Judas Iscariot, Simon's son, which should betray him, Why was not this ointment sold} ⁵For it might have been sold for more than three hundred pence [denarii], and have been given to the poor. {This he said, not that he cared for the poor; but because he was a thief, and had the bag, and bare what was put therein.} And they murmured against her.

Three hundred denarii was approximately a laborer's annual wage. Contrast the materialistic, short-sighted attitude of Jesus' disciples, led by Judas, to Mary's valuation and veneration of her Lord. They were so temporally-minded that they completely missed the point of Mary's sacrificial worship. Instead, they criticized both her and her wasteful extravagance.

C. Christ received her worship and honored her deed.

⁶And Jesus said, Let her alone; why trouble ye her? she hath wrought a good work on me. ⁷For ye have the poor with you always, and whensoever ye will ye may do them good: but me ye have not always. ⁸She hath done what she could: she is come aforehand to anoint my body to the burying {for in that she hath poured this ointment on my body, she did it for my burial}. ⁹Verily I say unto you, Wheresoever this gospel shall be preached throughout the whole world, this also that she hath done shall be spoken of for a memorial of her.

Jesus very recently had clearly told His disciples of His imminent betrayal, trial, and crucifixion (MT 20:18-19). Here He tells them with equal clarity that Mary has anointed His body for its burial. She was aware of the Jews' inflamed desire to kill Jesus and probably expected His death to be sudden and violent. In such circumstances, she might not have an opportunity to anoint His dead body later in accordance with Jewish custom. Therefore, "she has done what she could: she came beforehand to anoint my body for burial" (MT 26:12).

II. Christ would fall as a seed "into the ground."

JN 12:23 And Jesus answered them, saying, The hour is come, that the Son of man should be glorified.

²⁴Verily, verily, I say unto you, Except a corn of wheat [kernel of grain] fall into the ground and die, it abideth alone: but if it die, it bringeth forth much fruit. . . .

²⁷Now is my soul troubled; and what shall I say? Father, save me from this hour: but for this cause came I unto this hour.

A seed that remains above ground produces nothing. When properly planted, however, it multiplies itself many times over. Christ was deeply troubled about His rapidly approaching death, but He knew that if He did not "fall into the ground and die," He would be as unfruitful as an unplanted kernel of grain. "For this cause came I unto this hour" — to die as a seed in the ground, and bring forth "much fruit."

III. The soldiers treated Christ's body as prophesied.

A. "They broke not His legs" as the Passover Lamb.

JN 19:31 [When Christ died] The Jews therefore, because it was the preparation, that the bodies should not remain upon the cross on the sabbath day, (for that sabbath day was an high day,) besought Pilate that their legs might be broken, and that they might be taken away.

³²Then came the soldiers, and brake the legs of the first, and of the other which was crucified with him.

³³But when they came to Jesus, and saw that he was dead already, they brake not his legs: . . .

³⁶For these things were done, that the scripture should be fulfilled, A bone of him shall not be broken.

Christ died at about 3:00 in the afternoon, and a dead body could not remain unburied when a sabbath commenced at 6:00 in the evening. That *high sabbath* was the first day of the Feast of Unleavened Bread, which God said "shall be an holy convocation to you" (Ex. 12:16). The religious leaders, who had just murdered God's Son, now scrupulously sought to obey God's ceremonial law. They asked Pilate, therefore, to hasten the death of the crucified men by breaking their legs. This typically was done with an iron hammer or rod, causing the one hanging on a cross to suffocate by restricting his diaphragm through lack of support. Christ, however, had already "given up the spirit" and died (v. 30).

God did not permit the soldiers to break Christ's legs because that would have violated the Passover lamb's picture of Christ. God told Moses: "They shall leave none of it [the roasted lamb] unto the morning, *nor break any bone of it*" (Num. 9:12). Thus, "Christ, our passover, sacrificed for us" (I Cor. 5:7), could not have had any of His bones broken. David also had prophesied, "He keepeth all his bones: not one of them is broken" (Psa. 34:20).

B. They pierced His body as God foretold.
> ³⁴But one of the soldiers with a spear pierced his side, and forthwith came there out blood and water.
> ³⁵And he that saw it [John, the author] bare record, and his record is true: and he knoweth that he saith true, that ye might believe. . . .
> ³⁷And again another scripture saith, They shall look on him whom they pierced.

The soldier may simply have wanted to satisfy himself that Christ was dead. God intended, however, that he prove to all that Christ had truly died. God also intended that he mark Christ's body for unmistakable identification when He arose from the tomb and when He comes again. Christ later told Thomas, who doubted He had risen, "reach hither thy hand, and thrust it into my side: and be not faithless, but believing" (JN 20:27). Regarding Christ's second coming, Zechariah wrote: "The inhabitants of Jerusalem . . . shall look upon me whom they have pierced" (12:10). When He returns in glory, "every eye shall see him, and they also which pierced him" (Rev. 1:7).

IV. Believers buried Christ's body with honor.
   (A conflation of all four Gospel accounts)

A. A disciple boldly claimed Christ's body.
> MT 27:57 When the even [evening] was come, there came a rich man of Arimathaea, named Joseph, {an honorable counselor} who also himself was Jesus' disciple {but secretly for fear of the Jews}:
>
> LK 23:51 (The same had not consented to the counsel and deed of them;) {and he was a good man, and a just} . . . who also himself waited for the kingdom of God.
> ⁵²This man went {boldly} unto Pilate, and begged the body of Jesus.
>
> MK 15:44 And Pilate marvelled if he were already dead: and calling unto him the centurion, he asked him whether he had been any while dead.
> ⁴⁵And when he knew it of the centurion, he gave the body to Joseph {and he took it down}.

Joseph and Nicodemus (see Sec. B below) were members of the Sanhedrin which condemned Christ to death, but they "had not consented" at His trial. Although Joseph had been a "secret disciple," the Sanhedrin certainly would learn quickly of his claiming and burying Jesus' body. But that did not deter him. Their deed of allegiance to Christ undoubtedly cost these men their seats on the Sanhedrin and probably resulted in their excommunication from the synagogue and exclusion from Jewish society (cf. JN 9:22).

> B. Jesus was buried "with the rich in His death."
> **JN 19:39 And there came also Nicodemus, which at the first came to Jesus by night, and brought a mixture of myrrh and aloes, about an hundred pound weight [about 65 pounds avdp.].**
> **⁴⁰Then took they the body of Jesus, and wound it in linen clothes with the spices, as the manner of the Jews is to bury.**
> **⁴¹Now in the place where he was crucified there was a garden; and in the garden a new sepulchre, wherein was never man yet laid.**
>
> **MT 27:60 And [Joseph] laid it [Jesus' body] in his own new tomb, which he had hewn out in the rock: {There laid they Jesus therefore because of the Jews' preparation day; for the sepulcher was nigh at hand.} And he rolled a great stone to the door of the sepulchre, and departed.**

If the Romans had disposed of Jesus' body, they undoubtedly would have abused it greatly. (Under Roman law, a condemned criminal lost his right to a burial.) But God did not permit unbelievers to defile any further the body of His Son. Instead, Joseph and Nicodemus reverently gave Jesus a proper burial. This fulfilled Isaiah 53:9: "He made His grave with the wicked [when buried at the same time as the unrepentant thief] and with the rich in His death [when laid in a rich man's tomb]."

The "manner of the Jews" regarding burial (v. 40) included (1) interment on the day of death or within 24 hours; (2) wrapping the body fully and tightly with strips of cloth, spreading aromatic spices between layers, and covering the face with a separate cloth; (3) burial in a family tomb, if available, typically located outside the city and often in a cave cut from rock; and (4) placing the bones in a stone container (an "ossuary") in the tomb a year later. Mourning for the dead was a major part of the ceremony, beginning as soon as possible after death and continuing openly and intensely for seven days (as for Lazarus in JN 11).

Burial differed, however, for a criminal condemned by a Jewish court. His body could not be carried in a traditional funeral procession, nor could it be placed in a tomb with deceased relatives until the reburial of his bones a year later. Further, his death could not be mourned publicly. Thus, Christ's body was quietly placed in "a new sepulchre, wherein was never man yet laid" (v. 41). Also, scripture records no public mourning for Christ, even though His mother and many of His followers were in Jerusalem when He died. (They mourned, however, in private, as reported in JN 20:11 and MK 16:10.)

C. Faithful women prepared to anoint Christ's body.

LK 23:55 And the women also, which came with him from Galilee, followed after, and beheld the sepulchre, and how his body was laid. {And there was Mary Magdalene, and the other Mary {the mother of Joses}, sitting over against the sepulchre.}

⁵⁶And they returned, and prepared spices and ointments; and rested the sabbath day according to the commandment.

The women who traveled with Jesus and His disciples and "ministered unto Him of their substance" (LK 8:1-3) now planned their final deed of devoted service. Jesus was buried shortly before the sabbath began on Friday evening. The women, therefore, did not have sufficient time to obtain and prepare spices and also anoint His body until Sunday morning. God certainly was pleased with their devotion and desires, but He had greater plans for Sunday morning.

Previews of Christ's Resurrection

To both His detractors and His disciples, Christ presented a variety of pictorial previews of His promised resurrection. These gave clear notice to the people in general and His foes in particular that even though they would crucify Him, He was fully in control of the course and consummation of His life. Additionally, these previews indicated how He would prove conclusively that He was the Messiah and God the Son. In so doing, they also make everyone accountable to Him as the ultimate Lord and Judge of all mankind.

For His disciples, these pictures should have provided comfort and encouragement during the dark days accompanying Christ's crucifixion. Each one promises His ultimate and complete victory. When the previews became reality, they confirmed and strengthened the disciples' faith and emboldened them to proclaim the good news of salvation far and wide.

I. Christ's "temple" would be destroyed but raised in three days.

A. The Jews made God's temple "a house of merchandise."

JN 2:13 And the Jews' passover was at hand, and Jesus went up to Jerusalem,

¹⁴And found in the temple those that sold oxen and sheep and doves, and the changers of money sitting:

¹⁵And when he had made a scourge of small cords, he drove them all out of the temple, and the sheep, and the oxen; and poured out the changers' money, and overthrew the tables;

¹⁶And said unto them that sold doves, Take these things hence; make not my Father's house an house of merchandise. . .

Many Jews traveled long distances to the feast in Jerusalem, and it was difficult to take along animals to sacrifice in the temple. Also, the Roman and other coins they used for ordinary business had to be exchanged for Hebrew shekels to pay the required temple tax. The profit opportunities were too attractive for greedy merchants to resist, and the temple court became a bustling market place. Jesus was incensed that the traders (with the religious leaders' evident approval) had made "my Father's house a house of merchandise," and He drove them out.

B. Christ would "raise this temple" to prove His authority.

¹⁸Then answered the Jews and said unto him, What sign showest thou unto us, seeing that thou doest these things?

¹⁹Jesus answered and said unto them, Destroy this temple, and in three days I will raise it up.

²⁰Then said the Jews, Forty and six years was this temple in building, and wilt thou rear it up in three days?

²¹But he spake of the temple of his body.

The Jews challenged Christ to produce a sign (an attesting miracle) to prove His right to control the temple and drive out the merchants. He replied that although they would "destroy this temple" (speaking of His body), He would "raise it up" again in three days. Here at the outset of His ministry, Christ indicated that His resurrection (still three years away) would be the ultimate sign of His rightful authority over all of God's "house" and realm.

C. The Jews distorted Christ's claim at His trial.

MT 26:59 Now the chief priests, and elders, and all the council, sought false witness against Jesus, to put him to death;

⁶⁰But found none: yea, though many false witnesses came, yet found they none. At the last came two false witnesses,

⁶¹And said, This fellow said, I am able to destroy the temple of God, and to build it in three days. {We heard him say, I will destroy this temple that is made with hands, and within three days I will build another made without hands [MK 14:58].}

D. They mocked His claim at His crucifixion.

MT 27:39 And they that passed by [His cross] reviled him, wagging their heads,

⁴⁰And saying, Thou that destroyest the temple, and buildest it in three days, save thyself. If thou be the Son of God, come down from the cross.

E. They realized later that His temple was His body.

MT 27:62 Now the next day [after His death], that followed the day of the preparation, the chief priests and Pharisees came together unto Pilate,

⁶³Saying, Sir, we remember that that deceiver said, while he was yet alive, After three days I will rise again.

⁶⁴Command therefore that the sepulchre be made sure until the third day, lest his disciples come by night, and steal him away, and say unto the people, He is risen from the dead: so the last error shall be worse than the first.

⁶⁵Pilate said unto them, Ye have a watch: go your way, make it as sure as ye can.

⁶⁶So they went, and made the sepulchre sure, sealing the stone, and setting a watch.

The Jews recalled Christ's initial preview of His promised resurrection, and they viciously threw it back at Him at His trial and crucifixion. That they eventually understood what He meant is evident in their appeal to Pilate after Christ's death to take all possible measures to prevent its fulfillment.

F. Christ raised His temple, and strengthened His followers' faith.

JN 2:22 [continued from Sec. B above] When therefore he was risen from the dead, his disciples remembered that he had said this unto them; and they believed the scripture, and the word which Jesus had said.

The same picture that, upon its fulfillment, confounded and condemned Christ's enemies, gladdened and encouraged His disciples. "And they believed the scripture," i.e., Old Testament prophecies of Christ's resurrection. These include Psalm 16:10, "For thou wilt not leave my soul in hell [*sheol*, the grave]; neither wilt thou suffer thine Holy One to see corruption." Also, Isaiah 53:10 foretold, "When thou shalt make his soul an offering for sin, he shall see his seed, he shall prolong his days, and the pleasure of the Lord shall prosper in his hand."

II. Christ's resurrection is "the sign of the prophet Jonah."

A. It proves that He is the Messiah.

MT 12:38 Then certain of the scribes and of the Pharisees answered, saying, Master, we would see a sign from thee [that you are the Messiah].

³⁹But he answered and said unto them, An evil and adulterous generation seeketh after a sign; and there shall no sign be given to it, but the sign of the prophet Jonas [Jonah]:

> **⁴⁰For as Jonas was three days and three nights in the whale's belly; so shall the Son of man be three days and three nights in the heart of the earth.**

Christ had already provided a multitude of signs that He was the Messiah, and He refused to cater to the Pharisees' desire for more proof at that time. Like Jonah in the great fish (Jonah 1:7), however, Christ would remain "in the heart of the earth" for three days, and then rise again. This would be the ultimate sign that He is God's "Anointed One" — not only to the unbelieving Pharisees, but to all the world.

> B. It makes everyone accountable to Him.
>
> **⁴¹ The men of Nineveh shall rise in judgment with this generation, and shall condemn it: because they repented at the preaching of Jonas; and, behold, a greater than Jonas is here. {For as Jonas was a sign unto the Ninevites, so shall also the Son of man be to this generation [LK 11:30].}**

Christ was greater than Jonah in that He was a greater person (the sinless Son of God), presented greater credentials (including miracles, which Jonah did not perform), and offered a greater deliverance (eternal life vs. delayed death). The Ninevites' repentance following Jonah's warning will be held as condemning evidence against the unrepentant Pharisees, and against all who reject Christ's greater gospel.

> C. It shows His greatness and glory.
>
> **⁴²The queen of the south shall rise up in the judgment with this generation, and shall condemn it: for she came from the uttermost parts of the earth to hear the wisdom of Solomon; and, behold, a greater than Solomon is here.**

Christ was greater than Solomon in person, power, and preaching, as well as in Solomon's hallmark, wisdom. The Queen of Sheba will "condemn" those who reject Christ because she acknowledged and admired Solomon's (lesser) wisdom and glory. She recognized that God Himself had elevated Solomon, and said: "Blessed be the Lord thy God, which delighted in thee, to set thee on the throne of Israel: because the Lord loved Israel for ever, therefore made he thee king, to do judgment and justice "(I Kings 10:9). In contrast, the Jews failed to recognize Christ's greater and divine origin, wisdom, authority, and glory.

> D. It is the last sign He would give.
>
> **MT 16:1 The Pharisees also with the Sadducees came, and tempting desired him that he would show them a sign from heaven.**
>
> **²He answered and said unto them, When it is evening, ye say, It will be fair weather: for the sky is red.**

> ³And in the morning, It will be foul weather to day: for the sky is red and lowering. O ye hypocrites, ye can discern the face of the sky; but can ye not discern the signs of the times?
>
> ⁴A wicked and adulterous generation seeketh after a sign; and there shall no sign be given unto it, but the sign of the prophet Jonas. And he left them, and departed.

Again, the Jews sought a sign of Christ's identity and authority. Although they could predict the weather by observing changes in meteorological conditions, they completely misread "the signs of the times" — the epoch-marking conditions and events that heralded the Messiah's arrival and the imminent inauguration of His kingdom. Having missed and/or rejected all of these signs, the only further sign that Christ would give them would be that of the prophet Jonah — His resurrection from the dead.

III. Christ's resurrection was a "joyful birth" after "painful labor."

> JN 16:20 Verily, verily, I say unto you [His disciples], That ye shall weep and lament, but the world shall rejoice: and ye shall be sorrowful, but your sorrow shall be turned into joy.
>
> ²¹A woman when she is in travail hath sorrow, because her hour is come: but as soon as she is delivered of the child, she remembereth no more the anguish, for joy that a man is born into the world.
>
> ²²And ye now therefore have sorrow: but I will see you again, and your heart shall rejoice, and your joy no man taketh from you.

Christ forewarned His disciples that they would sorrow while the world rejoiced as He was crucified. Their sorrow, however, would only be temporary, like that of a woman in painful labor. His resurrection would erase their sorrow and replace it with joy, as when a baby "is born into the world." Best of all, that joy would abide permanently in their hearts, and no one would ever take it from them (v. 22).

IV. Christ Himself is "the resurrection and the life."

> JN 11:25 Jesus said unto her [Martha], I am the resurrection, and the life: he that believeth in me, though he were dead, yet shall he live:
>
> ²⁶And whosoever liveth and believeth in me shall never die. Believest thou this?
>
> ²⁷She saith unto him, Yea, Lord: I believe that thou art the Christ, the Son of God, which should come into the world.

Christ previously had shown His power to raise the dead, and He had just told Martha that her brother Lazarus (who died four days earlier) would rise again. Here, He declares that He Himself is "the resurrection and the life." Christ alone possesses resurrection power, resurrection glory, and resurrection life (i.e., perfect, complete, unending life). He would prove this claim with His own resurrection soon thereafter. His resurrection would also prove that He is fully able to raise in similar fashion all those who trust in Him for salvation and eternal life. (See Sec. VII on p. 17 and Sec. X on p. 24 for additional comments on Christ's resurrection.)

V. Christ is the "First Fruits" from the dead.

A. He arose on the first day of the week.

LK 24:1 Now upon the first day of the week, very early in the morning, they [three women] came unto the sepulchre, bringing the spices which they had prepared, and certain others with them.
²And they found the stone rolled away from the sepulchre.
³And they entered in, and found not the body of the Lord Jesus.

B. He arose "the third day" — the day of First Fruits.

⁴And it came to pass, as they were much perplexed thereabout, behold, two men stood by them in shining garments:
⁵And as they were afraid, and bowed down their faces to the earth, they said unto them, Why seek ye the living among the dead?
⁶He is not here, but is risen: remember how he spake unto you when he was yet in Galilee,
⁷Saying, The Son of man must be delivered into the hands of sinful men, and be crucified, and the third day rise again.

As God commanded at Sinai, the Jews celebrated the Feast of First Fruits to commemorate the beginning of the barley harvest. The feast signified that the first produce of the ground belonged to God and was sacred to Him. It also demonstrated the people's faith that God later would give them the full harvest. (See Lev. 23:4-11.)

First Fruits was celebrated on the first day of the week that followed the sabbath that fell during the seven-day Feast of Unleavened Bread. Christ was crucified on Passover, a Friday. The Feast of Unleavened Bread began the next day (Saturday, the sabbath), and First Fruits came the following day (Sunday). The Jews counted the days on both ends of a period; by that reckoning, Sunday was "the third day" after Christ's crucifixion (v. 7). The day Christ arose was the day of First Fruits.

Christ fulfilled the pictures in the Feast of First Fruits in several ways. First, He arose from the ground that day as the first sheaf of grain from the seed that was planted through His burial. Second, He presented Himself before believers that day as a "wave offering" (Lev. 23:11) dedicated to God's honor and glory. Third, He was the forerunner of the full harvest still to come, comprised of all believers who will be resurrected in the future.

Paul wrote: "But now is Christ risen from the dead, and become the firstfruits of them that slept" (I Cor.15:20). He added: "For as in Adam all die, even so in Christ shall all be made alive. But every man in his own order: Christ the first-fruits; afterward they that are Christ's at his coming" (vv. 22-23). As the "First Fruits," Christ's resurrection is both the pattern and the guarantee for every believer's future resurrection.

5

Mosaics of Salvation and Life

The Jews tended to view salvation more as a national than an individual matter. Most thought that when the Messiah came and brought national deliverance and prosperity, the benefits would "trickle down" to them as individuals. Also, in their mind, salvation was defined primarily in political, economic, social, and physical terms, rather than in spiritual terms. Their hope of personal salvation was based more on their loyalty to their nation and its religious practices than on a personal relationship with God based on faith in Him and His saving grace.

Christ sought throughout His ministry to correct these fundamental misunderstandings. He taught that individuals, saved by Him one by one, would make up God's kingdom — rather than the King automatically saving them en masse. He taught that salvation occurred in the *heart* of each believer, and that external benefits (e.g., popular approval, earthly possessions, and physical comfort) may be *lost*, not gained, by His true disciples. Inner conversion would produce right attitudes toward religious practices, not vice-versa.

Christ's pictures of salvation and spiritual life greatly puzzled or upset most of His hearers. Nicodemus, a national leader, asked, "How can these things be?" Although Christ drew many illustrations of these essential truths, much of the Master's art was not understood or appreciated until after His rejection and death.

The Bread of Life

Christ's most widely observed and acclaimed miracle was His feeding of 5,000 men (plus women and children) from five small loaves and two fish. It marked the pinnacle of His popularity and resulted in the people trying to make Him king. Christ's purpose in feeding the multitude, however, was to demonstrate that their dependence on Him for physical bread was a picture of their greater need for Him as their spiritual bread. He portrayed Himself, therefore, as "the bread of life" and "the true bread from heaven."

All four Gospels report the miracle, each with details not given by the others. (A conflation of those accounts is given in Section IV on pp. 296-298.) Only John records Christ's discourse on the Bread of Life, which followed the miracle and is presented here.

I. The people wanted physical bread more than spiritual bread.

A. They wanted Jesus to be their benefactor.

JN 6:14 Then those men, when they had seen the miracle that Jesus did, said, This is of a truth that prophet that should come into the world. ¹⁵When Jesus therefore perceived that they would come and take him by force, to make him a king, he departed again into a mountain himself alone. . . .

B. They primarily sought physical benefits.

²⁴When the people therefore saw that Jesus was not there, neither his disciples, they also took shipping, and came to Capernaum, seeking for Jesus. ²⁵And when they had found him on the other side of the sea, they said unto him, Rabbi, when camest thou hither? ²⁶Jesus answered them and said, Verily, verily, I say unto you, Ye seek me, not because ye saw [perceived] the miracles, but because ye did eat of the loaves, and were filled.

Christ's miracle so excited the crowd that they forcibly tried to make Him king on the spot. He desired, however, first and foremost to be their *spiritual* Messiah, and later to provide the political and economic benefits they sought. They did not see His miracles with spiritual understanding, or they would have recognized His true identity and purpose in coming. Rather, they followed Him primarily for their own temporal interests (v. 26).

II. Christ Himself is the Bread from heaven.

    A. He offers eternal food for man's eternal need.

        [27]Labor not for the meat [food] which perisheth, but for that meat which endureth unto everlasting life, which the Son of man shall give unto you: for him hath God the Father sealed.

        [28]Then said they unto him, What shall we do, that we might work the works of God?

        [29]Jesus answered and said unto them, This is the work of God, that ye believe on him whom he hath sent.

    B. He is the True Bread, given for the whole world.

        [30]They said therefore unto him, What sign showest thou then, that we may see, and believe thee? what dost thou work?

        [31]Our fathers did eat manna in the desert; as it is written, He gave them bread from heaven to eat.

        [32]Then Jesus said unto them, Verily, verily, I say unto you, Moses gave you not that bread from heaven [the manna]; but my Father giveth you the true bread from heaven.

        [33]For the bread of God is he which cometh down from heaven, and giveth life unto the world.

Christ admonished the people to pursue not the food that perishes but the eternal food that He would give them (v. 27). The "work of God" they must do for this food is simply to "believe on Him" (v. 29). They replied, "Show us a sign, as Moses gave manna as a sign that he was God's spokesman, and we will believe you." Had they not just witnessed His greatest sign to date, and many other signs before that (v. 2)? As the "True Bread from heaven" who "gives life to the world", Christ Himself and what He was doing was all the sign they needed.

III. Christ is the Bread of Life, offered to everyone.

    A. He satisfies every hungry heart that comes to Him.

        [34]Then said they unto him, Lord, evermore give us this bread.

        [35]And Jesus said unto them, I am the bread of life: he that cometh to me shall never hunger; and he that believeth on me shall never thirst.

        [36]But I said unto you, That ye also have seen me, and believe not.

        [37]All that the Father giveth me shall come to me; and him that cometh to me I will in no wise cast out.

    B. He gives eternal life to all who believe in Him.

        [38]For I came down from heaven, not to do mine own will, but the will of him that sent me.

> ³⁹And this is the Father's will which hath sent me, that of all which he hath given me I should lose nothing, but should raise it up again at the last day.
>
> ⁴⁰And this is the will of him that sent me, that every one which seeth the Son, and believeth on him, may have everlasting life: and I will raise him up at the last day.

Knowing that most in the crowd did not believe in Him, Christ invited individuals to accept Him as their personal Bread of Life. Whoever does so will "never hunger" again for salvation (v. 35) but will have everlasting life (v. 40). Christ also will "raise him up" (by resurrection from the dead or by the rapture of living believers) "at the last day" (at the end of this present age), to live eternally with God.

IV. God draws those who come to Christ.

A. Those drawn by the Father will receive His Bread.

> ⁴¹The Jews then murmured at him, because he said, I am the bread which came down from heaven.
>
> ⁴²And they said, Is not this Jesus, the son of Joseph, whose father and mother we know? how is it then that he saith, I came down from heaven?
>
> ⁴³Jesus therefore answered and said unto them, Murmur not among yourselves.
>
> ⁴⁴No man can come to me, except the Father which hath sent me draw him: and I will raise him up at the last day.

B. Those taught by God will come to Christ.

> ⁴⁵It is written in the prophets, And they shall be all taught of [by] God. Every man therefore that hath heard, and hath learned of [from] the Father, cometh unto me.
>
> ⁴⁶Not that any man hath seen the Father, save he which is of God, he hath seen the Father.
>
> ⁴⁷Verily, verily, I say unto you, He that believeth on me hath everlasting life.

The Jews took offense that one they had known from childhood, and whose family still lived among them, would claim to be "bread from heaven" (v. 41). Christ replied that God the Father must supernaturally *draw* people to His Son for them to be saved. One of the Father's principal drawing tools is His Word, and all who heed its message will come to Christ (v. 45).

This passage balances God's sovereignty in saving individual people and our personal responsibility to come to Christ and accept Him. God must draw, and everyone He draws will come (vv. 44-45). But we must come willingly to Christ as the Father draws us. Christ promised, "he that cometh to me I will in no wise cast out" (v. 37). Everyone that believes in Him *has* (immediately and fully) everlasting life (v. 47).

IV. We receive life by partaking of Christ.

A. He is the Living Bread and universal sacrifice.

⁴⁸**I am that bread of life.**

⁴⁹**Your fathers did eat manna in the wilderness, and are dead.**

⁵⁰**This is the bread which cometh down from heaven, that a man may eat thereof, and not die.**

⁵¹**I am the living bread which came down from heaven: if any man eat of this bread, he shall live for ever: and the bread that I will give is my flesh, which I will give for the life of the world.**

B. We must partake of His flesh and blood.

⁵²**The Jews therefore strove among themselves, saying, How can this man give us his flesh to eat?**

⁵³**Then Jesus said unto them, Verily, verily, I say unto you, Except ye eat the flesh of the Son of man, and drink his blood, ye have no life in you.**

⁵⁴**Whoso eateth my flesh, and drinketh my blood, hath eternal life; and I will raise him up at the last day.**

⁵⁵**For my flesh is meat [food] indeed, and my blood is drink indeed.**

C. He lives in those who partake of Him.

⁵⁶**He that eateth my flesh, and drinketh my blood, dwelleth in me, and I in him.**

⁵⁷**As the living Father hath sent me, and I live by the Father: so he that eateth me, even he shall live by me.**

⁵⁸**This is that bread which came down from heaven: not as your fathers did eat manna, and are dead: he that eateth of this bread shall live for ever.**

Because most in the crowd were not prepared to believe in Him, Christ spoke to them increasingly in metaphors. They had already rejected His clear statements that "the work of God" is to *believe* on Him (v. 29), that such *believing* would eternally satisfy the hunger and thirst of their souls (v. 35), and that through *believing* on Him they would have everlasting life (v. 47).

Eating Christ's flesh and *drinking His blood* are vivid illustrations of what it means to receive Christ as personal Savior. These include accepting His sacrificial death on our behalf (He gave His flesh for the life of the world, v. 51) and assimilating both Him and His Word into our souls and daily lives. Those who so eat and drink "shall live forever" (v. 58). (See also Sec. II under "Passover Meal" on p. 51.)

V. Salvation depends on faith, not works.

A. The Bread of Life is received spiritually, not physically.

⁶⁰Many therefore of his disciples [followers], when they had heard this, said, This is an hard saying; who can hear it [accept it]?

⁶¹When Jesus knew in himself that his disciples murmured at it, he said unto them, Doth this offend you?

⁶²What and if ye shall see the Son of man ascend up where he was before?

⁶³It is the spirit that quickeneth [gives life]; the flesh profiteth nothing: the words that I speak unto you, they are spirit, and they are life.

B. Those who do not receive Christ will eventually leave Him.

⁶⁴But there are some of you that believe not. For Jesus knew from the beginning who they were that believed not, and who should betray him.

⁶⁵And he said, Therefore said I unto you, that no man can come unto me, except it were given unto him of my Father.

⁶⁶From that time many of his disciples went back, and walked no more with him.

C. Those who believe in Christ will steadfastly follow Him.

⁶⁷Then said Jesus unto the twelve, Will ye also go away?

⁶⁸Then Simon Peter answered him, Lord, to whom shall we go? thou hast the words of eternal life.

⁶⁹And we believe and are sure that thou art that Christ, the Son of the living God.

Christ's disciples (v. 60) included a mixture of true believers, tentative followers, miracle seekers, and wishful thinkers desiring a utopian kingdom. Most of them could not accept His "hard saying" that they must *eat His flesh* to receive eternal life. To dissuade them from thinking they must literally eat His body and drink His blood, He stated clearly, "It is the [Holy] Spirit that gives life; flesh accomplishes nothing: my words are spirit and life" (v. 63). The people, however, had no real appetite for the Bread of Life. As a result, "many of His disciples went back, and walked no more with Him" (v. 66).

Turning to the twelve and testing their faith, Christ asked, "Will ye also go away?" Peter replied that there was no one else to whom they could turn; only He had "the words of eternal life." With unusual clarity and certainty, Peter affirmed their faith and confidence that Jesus is "the Christ, the Son of the living God." He was their Bread of Life.

The Nature of Salvation

The Gospels are full of messages and illustrations regarding God's plan for saving people from their sin. From the angelic announcements of Christ's birth to the accounts of His resurrection and ascension, the theme of salvation through Christ is paramount throughout. Many aspects of our salvation, however, are more clearly explained in the epistles than in the Gospels. There are major reasons for this difference. First, until Christ had died and risen, these essential foundations of saving faith were not fully revealed. (Although Christ previewed these foundations, He typically did so in veiled form, leaving their full revelation until after the Holy Spirit came on Pentecost.) Second, Christ was still offering Himself as the Messiah promised to Israel in the Old Testament. His message of salvation, therefore, often was designed and phrased as much for those living under Mosaic law as it is for us in this age of grace. Observe how the Master conveyed that message through pictures and illustrations perfectly suited to the people of both eras.

I. Salvation is a new birth.

A. We must be "born again" to see God's kingdom.
JN 3:1 There was a man of the Pharisees, named Nicodemus, a ruler of the Jews:
²The same came to Jesus by night, and said unto him, Rabbi, we know that thou art a teacher come from God: for no man can do these miracles that thou doest, except God be with him.
³Jesus answered and said unto him, Verily, verily, I say unto thee, Except a man be born again, he cannot see the kingdom of God.

B. As flesh gives physical birth, God's Spirit gives spiritual birth.
⁴Nicodemus saith unto him, How can a man be born when he is old? can he enter the second time into his mother's womb, and be born?
⁵Jesus answered, Verily, verily, I say unto thee, Except a man be born of water and of the Spirit, he cannot enter into the kingdom of God.
⁶That which is born of the flesh is flesh; and that which is born of the Spirit is spirit.
⁷Marvel not that I said unto thee, Ye must be born again.

C. This new birth is God's doing.
JN 1:11 He [Jesus] came unto his own [creation], and his own [people] received him not.
¹²But as many as received him, to them gave he power to become the sons of God, even to them that believe on his name:
¹³Which were born, not of blood, nor of the will of the flesh, nor of the will of man, but of God.

Nicodemus wondered how a man could be "born again" when he is old (v. 4). The new birth that Christ described is spiritual, not physical, and internal, not external (vv. 5-6). John added that it is "not of blood [through physical descent], nor of the will of the flesh [one's own desire or effort], nor of the will of man [one's desire for someone else], but of God [by His will and His doing alone]" (v. 13).

II. Salvation is like the wind.

A. Both are invisible, but effective and perceivable.

JN 3:8 The wind bloweth where it listeth [pleases], and thou hearest the sound thereof, but canst not tell whence it cometh, and whither it goeth: so is every one that is born of the Spirit.

B. Earthly illustrations teach spiritual truth.

⁹Nicodemus answered and said unto him, How can these things be? ¹⁰Jesus answered and said unto him, Art thou a master of Israel, and knowest not these things? ¹¹Verily, verily, I say unto thee, We speak that we do know, and testify that we have seen; and ye receive not our witness. ¹²If I have told you earthly things, and ye believe not, how shall ye believe, if I tell you of heavenly things?

Both the wind and the working of the Holy Spirit are beyond human control. By recognizing their presence and power, however, and by submitting to their influence and direction, we can benefit from their activity. The wind's effects on our environment are only temporary, but the Spirit's accomplishments in our hearts are eternal. For an unbeliever being drawn to God by His Spirit, the latter's working may, at first, go as unnoticed as a gentle breeze. After salvation, however, and with spiritual hindsight, we can appreciate where the Wind came from and what it was doing in our hearts and lives.

III. Salvation is everlasting life.

JN 3:16 For God so loved the world, that he gave his only begotten Son, that whosoever believeth in him should not perish, but have everlasting life.

¹⁷For God sent not his Son into the world to condemn the world; but that the world through him might be saved.

Physical life is so taken for granted that we seldom see it as a picture of spiritual life (as faint, imperfect, and incomplete as it is). Although physical life is temporal and fraught with difficulties, it is like spiritual life in several major respects. These include the supreme value both God and man assign to each (as man perceives his spiritual need), our unavoidable dependence on God for granting and sustaining each, and God's bountiful provision that more than meets the needs of each.

God simultaneously created both physical and spiritual life as complementary aspects of mankind's initially perfect nature. Adam's sin brought death on both fronts. Salvation gives each believer spiritual life through his new birth, and that life is everlasting life. Salvation also guarantees each believer that he will ultimately experience perfect physical life in a glorified body forever. In contrast, the fragility and brevity of our present physical life underscore the importance of receiving everlasting life while it still may be obtained. (See "Life and Death" on p. 107.)

IV. Salvation requires child-like faith.

A. Child-like faith is simple trust and belief in Christ.

MK 10:13 And they brought young children to him, that he should touch them: and his disciples rebuked those that brought them.

¹⁴But when Jesus saw it, he was much displeased, and said unto them, Suffer the little children to come unto me, and forbid them not: for of such is the kingdom of God.

¹⁵Verily I say unto you, Whosoever shall not receive the kingdom of God as a little child, he shall not enter therein.

¹⁶And he took them up in his arms, put his hands upon them, and blessed them.

B. Child-like faith includes humble repentance and submission.

MT 18:2 And Jesus called a little child unto him, and set him in the midst of them,

³And said, Verily I say unto you, Except ye be converted ["turned around"], and become as little children, ye shall not enter into the kingdom of heaven.

⁴Whosoever therefore shall humble himself as this little child, the same is greatest in the kingdom of heaven.

C. Child-like faith excludes intellectual pride and human effort.

MT 11:25 At that time Jesus answered and said, I thank thee, O Father, Lord of heaven and earth, because thou hast hid these things [the way of salvation] from the wise and prudent, and hast revealed them unto babes.

²⁶Even so, Father: for so it seemed good in thy sight.

Christ gladly received little children — and those adults who came to Him in child-like humility and faith. They trusted Him without reservation and followed Him without hesitation. In contrast, those who see themselves as "wise and prudent," and who disdain the "babes" who accept and follow Christ with child-like trust and obedience, cannot experience the blessings that God shares only with His "little children."

V. Salvation is portrayed by the repentant son.

MT 21:28 But what think ye? A certain man had two sons; and he came to the first, and said, Son, go work to day in my vineyard.

²⁹He answered and said, I will not: but afterward he repented, and went.

³⁰And he came to the second, and said likewise. And he answered and said, I go, sir: and went not.

³¹Whether of them twain did the will of his father? They say unto him, The first. Jesus saith unto them, Verily I say unto you [the religious leaders] That the publicans and the harlots go into the kingdom of God before you.

³²For John [the Baptist] came unto you in the way of righteousness, and ye believed him not; but the publicans and the harlots believed him: and ye, when ye had seen it, repented not afterward, that ye might believe him.

Christ cited the "publicans [tax-collectors] and harlots" as representative of sinners who clearly had violated God's moral laws. Under John the Baptist's preaching, many such sinners admitted their wrong-doing, repented of their disobedience, and began to do "the will of their Father" (v. 31). The religious leaders, in contrast, claimed at the outset that they were obeying God, but never did His will. As with the repentant son, salvation requires a turning from sin with a desire to please God and obey His will.

VI. Salvation is a narrow gate, open for a while.

A. The gate to life is narrow; the road to hell is wide.

MT 7:13 Enter ye in at the strait [narrow] gate: for wide is the gate, and broad is the way, that leadeth to destruction, and many there be which go in thereat:

¹⁴Because strait [narrow] is the gate, and narrow [hard] is the way, which leadeth unto life, and few there be that find it.

B. Many desire eternal life but miss the narrow gate.

LK 13:23 Then said one unto him, Lord, are there few that be saved? And he said unto them,

²⁴Strive to enter in at the strait gate: for many, I say unto you, will seek to enter in, and shall not be able.

God's arms are open wide to whoever will come to Him for salvation. The gate of salvation, however, is *narrow* because Christ alone is the Door (JN 10:9) and no one can come to God except through Him (JN 14:6). The way is *hard* in that salvation is on God's terms alone and requires full submission to Christ as both Savior and Lord. The striving that Christ called for in verse 24 is not one's working for his salvation but rather his making absolutely certain that he has entered the narrow gate through Christ in the manner God has prescribed.

C. The Lord will close the door some day, and suddenly.

²⁵When once the master [owner] of the house is risen up, and hath shut to the door, and ye begin to stand without, and to knock at the door, saying, Lord, Lord, open unto us; and he shall answer and say unto you, I know you not whence ye are [where you came from]:

²⁶Then shall ye begin to say, We have eaten and drunk in thy presence, and thou hast taught in our streets.

²⁷But he shall say, I tell you, I know you not whence ye are; depart from me, all ye workers of iniquity.

The door of salvation is wide open now, but one day the "Master of the house" will shut it — suddenly and without warning. All who fail to enter beforehand will be barred from His presence forever. The supposed friends of the Master in verse 25 made the same mistake, and experienced the same result, as the foolish wedding guests (see Sec. III on p. 436 ff). They presumed a relationship with the Master that never existed. When He shut the door, they cried "Lord, Lord" with double piety and double urgency. They had never come to Christ, however, while the door was open. Worse yet, the religious deeds they relied on as their ticket of entry were judged to be works of iniquity that deserve retribution, not reward.

VII. Salvation is like a needle's eye.

MT 19:23 Then said Jesus unto his disciples, Verily I say unto you, That a rich man shall hardly enter into the kingdom of heaven.

²⁴And again I say unto you, It is easier for a camel to go through the eye of a needle, than for a rich man to enter into the kingdom of God.

²⁵When his disciples heard it, they were exceedingly amazed, saying, Who then can be saved?

²⁶But Jesus beheld them, and said unto them, With men this is impossible; but with God all things are possible.

For some, and particularly for those who are materialistic, the narrow gate to salvation may seem as restrictive and demanding as a needle's eye. They are more inclined to rely on their own resources and abilities than to trust solely in God for their salvation. Some also fear that God will somehow deprive them of their possessions if they commit themselves to Him. In fact, He gives greater purpose and value to our resources when they are dedicated to Him. Christ declared that, with men, achieving salvation through earthly means "is impossible" (v. 26). With God, however, "all things are possible" — including anyone's salvation, whether rich or poor or in between. (See Sec. II on p. 244 ff for the full passage on the rich young ruler.)

The Benefits of Salvation

There are many facets on the gem of salvation. A number of these relate to what we are saved *from*; and others, what we are saved *to*. The benefits that flow from each are incomparable. The former include deliverance from our sin's eternal penalty and from its oppressive control over our lives. The latter include everlasting life, the ability and freedom to live as we should, and abundant daily life with true peace, satisfaction, and joy. (Other facets of salvation — what we are saved *for*, e.g., worship, service, and discipleship — are covered in chapters 9, 11, and 13.) The following pictures illustrate several of the major benefits that accompany our salvation.

I. Salvation cancels overwhelming debts.

A. The critical Pharisee and the sinful woman.

LK 7:36 And one of the Pharisees desired him that he [Jesus] would eat with him. And he went into the Pharisee's house, and sat down to meat.

³⁷And, behold, a woman in the city, which was a sinner, when she knew that Jesus sat at meat in the Pharisee's house, brought an alabaster box of ointment,

³⁸And stood at his feet behind him weeping, and began to wash his feet with tears, and did wipe them with the hairs of her head, and kissed his feet, and anointed them with the ointment.

³⁹Now when the Pharisee which had bidden him saw it, he spake within himself, saying, This man, if he were a prophet, would have known who and what manner of woman this is that toucheth him: for she is a sinner.

The Pharisee's motive for inviting Jesus to dinner is not given. He did not extend the basic courtesies given guests (vv. 44-46 below), and he may have invited Jesus only out of curiosity or to find fault with Him. Verse 39 indicates he saw Christ only as a man and not even as a prophet. In contrast, the woman apparently had heard Christ's teaching and repented of her sinful life before she came, as shown by her worship and the costly gift she brought. Her tears reflected both her sorrow for her sin and her great appreciation for the One who forgives sin.

B. The parable of two debtors.

⁴⁰And Jesus answering said unto him, Simon, I have somewhat to say unto thee. And he saith, Master, say on.

> ⁴¹There was a certain creditor which had two debtors: the one owed five hundred pence [denarii] and the other fifty.
>
> ⁴²And when they had nothing to pay, he frankly forgave them both. Tell me therefore, which of them will love him most?
>
> ⁴³Simon answered and said, I suppose that he, to whom he forgave most. And he said unto him, Thou hast rightly judged.

The larger debt was equivalent to 500 days' wages for a laborer; the smaller, to 50 days' wages. Although neither debtor could pay anything, the first debtor must have had a greater sense of helplessness and hopelessness, given the tenfold greater magnitude of his debt. Likewise, his gratitude toward the creditor must have been greater when his unpayable debt was completely forgiven.

Regarding our sin-debt to God, no one can atone for any of his sins and everyone must rely solely on God's mercy and grace for forgiveness. The woman's sins were so great, and her deserved condemnation so clear, that when she was fully and freely forgiven, she was overwhelmed with relief, gratitude, and love for her merciful Savior.

C. The woman's repentance, versus Simon's indifference.

> ⁴⁴And he turned to the woman, and said unto Simon, Seest thou this woman? I entered into thine house, thou gavest me no water for my feet: but she hath washed my feet with tears, and wiped them with the hairs of her head.
>
> ⁴⁵Thou gavest me no kiss [of greeting]: but this woman since the time I came in hath not ceased to kiss my feet.
>
> ⁴⁶My head with oil thou didst not anoint: but this woman hath anointed my feet with [expensive] ointment.

Simon failed to provide Jesus any of the three customary courtesies listed in these verses. In contrast, the woman demonstrated her genuine repentance and faith in Christ by devotedly performing each one. She served Him with all her heart and all her resources.

D. The result of salvation: forgiveness and peace.

> ⁴⁷Wherefore I say unto thee, Her sins, which are many, are forgiven; for she loved much: but to whom little is forgiven, the same loveth little.
>
> ⁴⁸And he said unto her, Thy sins are forgiven.
>
> ⁴⁹And they that sat at meat with him began to say within themselves, Who is this that forgiveth sins also?
>
> ⁵⁰And he said to the woman, Thy faith hath saved thee; go in peace.

The woman was forgiven when she first repented and placed her faith in Christ (even before she came to Simon's house). If she had any lingering doubt, that was dispelled when Christ confirmed her forgiveness (v. 48) and bestowed on her His divine peace (v. 50). The other guests (probably Pharisees) were amazed that Christ claimed to forgive sins, not recognizing that the only One through whom God provides forgiveness, salvation, and peace was in their very midst.

II. Salvation frees slaves of sin.

    A. The gospel frees sinners from bondage.

JN 8:31 Then said Jesus to those Jews which believed on him, If ye continue in my word, then are ye my disciples indeed;
³²And ye shall know the truth, and the truth shall make you free.

To "continue in [Christ's] word" is to believe it, to be committed wholly to it, and to obey it as a rule of life. Those who do so are true disciples. They will understand God's truth and will be freed by that truth from sins that would prevent them from living as God desires and directs.

    B. Many refuse to admit they are slaves of sin.

³³They answered him, We be Abraham's seed, and were never in bondage to any man: how sayest thou, Ye shall be made free?
³⁴Jesus answered them, Verily, verily, I say unto you, Whosoever committeth sin [habitually] is the servant [bond-slave] of sin.

Based on their negative response, which intensified in the following verses and through verse 59 when they tried to kill Jesus, it is clear that these people did not really "believe on Him" (v. 31) as their spiritual Savior. They apparently saw Him only as a potential earthly Messiah. They rejected His contention that they were in bondage by claiming to be Abraham's descendants. This, they assumed, guaranteed their personal freedom. Christ replied, "Whoever [whether Jew or Gentile] habitually sins is the bond-slave of sin" — whether he recognizes and admits it or not.

    C. Christ frees sinners fully and forever.

³⁵And the servant [bond-slave] abideth not in the house for ever: but the Son abideth ever.
³⁶If the Son therefore shall make you free, ye shall be free indeed.

Christ introduces another slave analogy in verse 35. Bond-slaves do not have any rights in their master's household. They may be sold, traded, or otherwise disposed of at any time. Christ, however, as the eternal Son of God has all the rights, privileges, and prerogatives of the owner of the estate. When He frees a slave of sin, that person is truly free. Further, He places that former slave in His family as a full son and causes him to abide in God's house forever. That is freedom indeed!

III. Salvation is a bountiful feast.

A. A Pharisee invited Christ to dinner.

LK 14:1 And it came to pass, as he went into the house of one of the chief Pharisees to eat bread on the sabbath day, that they watched him. . . .

¹⁵And when one of them that sat at meat with him heard these things [Christ's teachings], he said unto him, Blessed is he that shall eat bread in the kingdom of God.

B. God invites many to His feast.

¹⁶Then said he [Christ] unto him, A certain man made a great supper, and bade many:

¹⁷And sent his servant at supper time to say to them that were bidden, Come; for all things are now ready.

C. The invited guests make many excuses.

1. "I have to take care of my property."

¹⁸And they all with one consent began to make excuse. The first said unto him, I have bought a piece of ground, and I must needs go and see it: I pray thee have me excused.

2. "I have to take care of my business."

¹⁹And another said, I have bought five yoke of oxen, and I go to prove them: I pray thee have me excused.

3. "I have to take care of my wife."

²⁰And another said, I have married a wife, and therefore I cannot come.

The invited guests picture the Jewish people who had received many prior invitations to the coming feast through Old Testament prophets and John the Baptist. Their refusal to come when everything was ready was inexcusable. They gave the same kind of excuses that many people give today for not accepting God's invitation to salvation. They were preoccupied with physical things, business pressures, and family responsibilities. They let the seemingly urgent preempt the truly important.

D. The poor and needy are invited in their place.

²¹So that servant came, and showed his lord these things. Then the master of the house being angry said to his servant, Go out quickly into the streets and lanes of the city, and bring in hither the poor, and the maimed, and the halt, and the blind.

The poor, the maimed, and so on represent the "sinners and tax-collectors" who were disdained by the Pharisees. Christ was particularly sensitive to their needs and invited them to come to Him. As in the parable, many of these people were acutely aware of their helpless estate and readily accepted the invitation to the Lord's bountiful feast.

E. Outsiders are invited to "fill His house."
> ²²And the servant said, Lord, it is done as thou hast commanded, and yet there is room.
> ²³And the lord said unto the servant, Go out into the highways and hedges, and compel them to come in, that my house may be filled.
> ²⁴For I say unto you, That none of those men which were bidden [and refused to come] shall taste of my supper.

The outsiders include Gentiles to whom the gospel message was taken when the Jewish people as a nation rejected it. The parable ends without stating that the lord's house was filled. In that respect, it leaves off where we are today. The Lord's invitation is still being extended, and the opportunity remains for many more to come.

This parable resembles another in MT 22 in which a king prepares a wedding feast for his son and the invited guests do not come (see Sec. III on p. 130). The details differ, but the messages are similar.

IV. Salvation provides "living water."
A. Physical thirst pictures spiritual thirst.
> JN 4:5 Then cometh he [Jesus] to a city of Samaria, . . .
> ⁶Now Jacob's well was there. Jesus therefore, being wearied with his journey, sat thus on the well: and it was about the sixth hour.
> ⁷There cometh a woman of Samaria to draw water: Jesus saith unto her, Give me to drink. . . .
> ⁹Then saith the woman of Samaria unto him, How is it that thou, being a Jew, askest drink of me, which am a woman of Samaria? for the Jews have no dealings with the Samaritans.

B. Christ gives people "living water."
> ¹⁰Jesus answered and said unto her, If thou knewest the gift of God, and who it is that saith to thee, Give me to drink; thou wouldest have asked of him, and he would have given thee living water.

C. Many do not understand this water or its source.
> ¹¹The woman saith unto him, Sir, thou hast nothing to draw with, and the well is deep: from whence then hast thou that living water?
> ¹²Art thou greater than our father Jacob, which gave us the well, and drank thereof himself, and his children, and his cattle?

    D. Living water satisfies fully and eternally

> **¹³Jesus answered and said unto her, Whosoever drinketh of this water shall thirst again:**
>
> **¹⁴But whosoever drinketh of the water that I shall give him shall never thirst; but the water that I shall give him shall be in him a well of water springing up into everlasting life.**

Satisfaction of spiritual needs is likened in scripture to the satisfaction of thirst with cool, refreshing water from a deep well or gushing spring. In Isaiah, God calls, "Ho, every one that thirsteth, come to the waters" (55:1). Christ was preparing the woman for salvation by picturing it as a unending spring of fresh, pure, satisfying water. But she still thought He was referring to some kind of physical water for her physical thirst.

    E. Some want it, but do not know how to obtain it.

> **¹⁵The woman saith unto him, Sir, give me this water, that I thirst not, neither come hither to draw.**
>
> **¹⁶Jesus saith unto her, Go, call thy husband, and come hither. . . .**
>
> **²⁸The woman then left her waterpot, and went her way into the city, and saith to the men,**
>
> **²⁹Come, see a man, which told me all things that ever I did: is not this the Christ?**
>
> **³⁰Then they went out of the city, and came unto him.**

    F. It is received by believing in Christ.

> **³⁹And many of the Samaritans of that city believed on him for the saying of the woman, which testified, He told me all that ever I did.**
>
> **⁴⁰So when the Samaritans were come unto him, they besought him that he would tarry with them: and he abode there two days.**
>
> **⁴¹And many more believed because of his own word;**
>
> **⁴²And said unto the woman, Now we believe, not because of thy saying: for we have heard him ourselves, and know that this is indeed the Christ, the Savior of the world.**

Between verses 16 and 28, Christ revealed to the woman her sinful life and His identity as the Messiah (see Sec. II. on p. 159). Through her testimony and invitation (v. 29), but more importantly, through Christ's speaking to them in detail (for two days), many Samaritans believed in Him as the Messiah and "the Savior of the world."

    G. Christ gives living water to all who come to Him.

> **JN 7:37 In the last day, that great day of the feast, Jesus stood and cried, saying, If any man thirst, let him come unto me, and drink.**

>³⁸He that believeth on me, as the scripture hath said, out of his belly [inmost parts] shall flow rivers of living water.

>JN 6:35 And Jesus said unto them, . . . he that believeth on me shall never thirst.

The basic thirst of every heart can be satisfied only by the living water that Christ offered to the Samaritan woman and to the Jews at their national feast (JN 7:37). His last invitation in the Bible is to thirsty people to come to "the fountain of the water of life" and drink freely (Rev. 21:6). Whoever drinks Christ's living water "shall never thirst" again (JN 6:35).

Heaven's View of Our Salvation
(Luke Chapter 15)

What does our salvation look like from heaven's portal? How does God picture us before we receive it, and with what does He compare His work of grace? How does God "feel" when we repent of our sin and trust in Him? Christ told three parables in LK 15 that portray our salvation as viewed from God's vantage point. Seeing our salvation as God sees it should increase our appreciation of both it and Him. It should also increase our joy over others' salvation and our compassion for those still without it.

I. Christ and the Pharisees saw "sinners" differently.

>LK 15:1 Then drew near unto him all the publicans and sinners for to hear him.

>²And the Pharisees and scribes murmured, saying, This man receiveth sinners, and eateth with them.

The Pharisees used the term "publicans [tax-collectors] and sinners" to refer in general to those of ill repute. They had already written off such reprobates as spiritually unworthy and hopeless. They would never associate with such people, much less eat with them! Christ, however, saw the publicans and sinners as among the lost He came to save. Many of them sensed His concern for their spiritual welfare (especially in contrast to the Pharisees' disdain for them) and gladly came to hear Him.

II. Heaven rejoices when one lost sheep is saved.

A. The shepherd seeks the one sheep that is lost.

>³And he spake this parable unto them, saying,

>⁴What man of you, having an hundred sheep, if he lose one of them, doth not leave the ninety and nine in the wilderness, and go after that which is lost, until he find it?

>⁵And when he hath found it, he layeth it on his shoulders, rejoicing.

⁶**And when he cometh home, he calleth together his friends and neighbors, saying unto them, Rejoice with me; for I have found my sheep which was lost.**

B. Heaven delights in the one who repents.

⁷**I say unto you, that likewise joy shall be in heaven over one sinner that repenteth, more than over ninety and nine just persons, which need no repentance.**

In the context of verses 1-2, the lost sheep represents a sinner who knows that he is lost. The ninety-nine other sheep picture the Pharisees who think they are in the fold but in fact are "in the wilderness." Verse 7b may be understood: "rather than ninety-nine self-righteous people who do not see their need to repent." (Christ used similar language in LK 5:32 in contrasting the same two groups; see Sec. II on p. 3.) Heavenly observers know the immeasurable value of one repentant soul. They rejoice when it is "found" and brought home.

III. God rejoices when one lost coin is found.

A. The owner seeks the one coin that is missing.

⁸**Either what woman having ten pieces of silver, if she lose one piece, doth not light a candle, and sweep the house, and seek diligently till she find it?**

⁹**And when she hath found it, she calleth her friends and her neighbors together, saying, Rejoice with me; for I have found the piece which I had lost.**

B. Heaven rejoices in each sinner's salvation.

¹⁰**Likewise, I say unto you, there is joy in the presence of the angels of God over one sinner that repenteth.**

God Himself leads the rejoicing in the presence of His angels for each sinner who repents. The angels obviously join in that celestial celebration, knowing God's plan of redemption, having served God in the circumstances that led to the sinner's repentance, and having seen His rejoicing over each prior soul that turned to Him for salvation.

IV. The Father rejoices when one lost son comes home.

A. The son's request.

¹¹**And he said, A certain man had two sons:**

¹²**And the younger of them said to his father, Father, give me the portion of goods that falleth to me. And he divided unto them his living.**

¹³**And not many days after the younger son gathered all together, and took his journey into a far country, and there wasted his substance with riotous living.**

B. The son's remorse.

¹⁴And when he had spent all, there arose a mighty famine in that land; and he began to be in want.

¹⁵And he went and joined himself to a citizen of that country; and he sent him into his fields to feed swine.

¹⁶And he would fain have filled his belly with the husks that the swine did eat: and no man gave unto him.

¹⁷And when he came to himself [his senses], he said, How many hired servants of my father's have bread enough and to spare, and I perish with hunger!

C. The son's return.

¹⁸I will arise and go to my father, and will say unto him, Father, I have sinned against heaven, and before thee,

¹⁹And am no more worthy to be called thy son: make me as one of thy hired servants.

²⁰ªAnd he arose, and came to his father.

The younger son's share of the family estate was one third (Deut. 21:17). Although the father obviously was grieved by the son's self-centeredness, he permitted his son to have his own way — and to reap his own results. When the son "came to himself," he repented of his sin, not just his circumstances. Also, he recognized that his sin first and foremost was "against heaven" (i.e., the God of heaven), and also against his father. Repentance requires action, and he "came to his father."

D. The Father's response.

²⁰ᵇBut when he was yet a great way off, his father saw him, and had compassion, and ran, and fell on his neck, and kissed him.

E. The son's repentance.

²¹And the son said unto him, Father, I have sinned against heaven, and in thy sight, and am no more worthy to be called thy son.

F. The son's restoration.

²²But the father said to his servants, Bring forth the best robe, and put it on him; and put a ring on his hand, and shoes on his feet:

G. The Father's rejoicing.

²³And bring hither the fatted calf, and kill it; and let us eat, and be merry:

²⁴For this my son was dead, and is alive again; he was lost, and is found. And they began to be merry.

These verses parallel the celebrations for the rescued sheep and the found coin. The heavenly Father knows perfectly of each believer's true repentance and gladly welcomes him home even as he is approaching. He also adds to each son's salvation His gifts of love, blessing, and honor, as the earthly father did with his returning son. In every case, the Father's house is full of rejoicing when the *dead* is *alive again* and the *lost* is *found.*

> H. The brother's reaction.
>
> **25Now his elder son was in the field: and as he came and drew nigh to the house, he heard music and dancing.**
> **26And he called one of the servants, and asked what these things meant.**
> **27And he said unto him, Thy brother is come; and thy father hath killed the fatted calf, because he hath received him safe and sound.**
> **28And he was angry, and would not go in: therefore came his father out, and entreated him.**

> I. The brother's reply.
>
> **29And he answering said to his father, Lo, these many years do I serve thee, neither transgressed I at any time thy commandment: and yet thou never gavest me a kid, that I might make merry with my friends:**
> **30But as soon as this thy son was come, which hath devoured thy living with harlots, thou hast killed for him the fatted calf.**

> J. The Father's reassurance.
>
> **31And he said unto him, Son, thou art ever with me, and all that I have is thine.**
> **32It was meet that we should make merry, and be glad: for this thy brother was dead, and is alive again; and was lost, and is found.**

Whether the elder son represents legalistic Jews or selfish and critical Christian brothers (an oxymoron), Christ's point is the same as in the two prior parables. It is that God is willing to receive, forgive, and restore anyone who truly repents of his sin and comes to Him for salvation. He rejoices over each repentant sinner, and so should all believers. We should do whatever we can to welcome and encourage each brother who "was lost, and is found."

6

Physical Reflections
of Spiritual Reality

In using illustrations from human experience to teach spiritual truth, Christ generally taught from the well known to the less known, from the physical to the spiritual, and from the temporal to the eternal. He used common but important objects, such as bread and clothing, to picture spiritual needs, principles, and relationships that are of far greater import than the objects themselves.

This chapter demonstrates that even the most precious and irreplaceable earthly benefits and experiences, such as sunlight and eyesight, are but faint shadows of greater spiritual realities. Even life itself is a picture of a much greater gift that God desires to give us. Whether beginning, therefore, with images of shining light or priceless life, Christ still taught from the lesser to the greater. For what is greater than receiving spiritual light, spiritual sight, and spiritual life?

Rays of Light in Darkness

Light in the Gospels pictures the presentation, comprehension, and acceptance of God's revealed truth. Each of these stages in the illumination of a believer is called light at various times, but the full dawning of spiritual light involves all three. The source of God's light is His Word — both the written Word of scripture and the Living Word of Jesus Christ. Christ is portrayed as "the true light" and the "light of the world." As such, He proclaimed the "light of life" "to them that sit in darkness."

Darkness is the exact opposite of light in each of its forms and applications.It variously pictures spiritual ignorance, sinfulness, unbelief, the forces of evil, and eternal condemnation. Unbelievers are bound in such darkness as fully as the dead are bound in the darkness of their graves. If they are exposed to God's light, however, and receive it, they can escape the darkness in all of its forms and become God's "children of light."

I. The world was in darkness, in need of God's light.

    A. God had promised a coming "sunrise."

    LK 1:76 And thou, child [John the Baptist], shalt be called the prophet of the Highest: for thou shalt go before the face of the Lord to prepare his ways;
    [77]To give knowledge of salvation unto his people by the remission of their sins,
    [78]Through the tender mercy of our God; whereby the dayspring [sunrise] from on high [the Messiah] hath visited us,
    [79]To give light to them that sit in darkness and in the shadow of death, to guide our feet into the way of peace.

    B. God's Light "sprung up" through the darkness.

    MT 4:13 And leaving Nazareth, he [Jesus] came and dwelt in Capernaum, which is upon the sea coast, in the borders of Zabulon and Nephthalim:
    [14]That it might be fulfilled which was spoken by Esaias [Isaiah] the prophet, saying, . . .
    [16]The people which sat in darkness saw [a] great light; and to them which sat in the region and shadow of death light is sprung up [has dawned].

In the physical realm, complete darkness immobilizes and imprisons its captives. They are forced to wait helplessly until a ray of light shines their way. Similarly, scripture often refers to the absolute darkness of sin and the debilitating condition it imposes. For a world locked in such darkness, Christ came as the long-awaited "sunrise" (LK 1:78). He was the Light that dawned and became a "great light" to free people from darkness and the shadow of death.

II. Light portrays God's truth, which penetrates the darkness.

A. Christ brought the light of the Gospel to men.

JN 1:4 In him [Christ] was life; and the life was the light of men.

⁵And the light shineth in darkness; and the darkness comprehended it not [i.e., could not overpower or conquer it].

⁶There was a man sent from God, whose name was John.

⁷The same came for a witness, to bear witness of the Light, that all men through him might believe.

⁸He [John] was not that Light, but was sent to bear witness of that Light.

⁹That was the true Light, which lighteth every man that cometh into the world.

Perfect spiritual life resides eternally in Christ as God (v. 4). The revelation and manifestation of that life to mankind is called "the light of men," that is, the light to men and for men. This revelation culminated in the coming into the world of the true Light and His message of light and life. As the true, perfect, and complete Light, He gives light to every man that is born in the world (v. 9). Christ shines rays of spiritual truth into the heart of "every man" on earth through a divinely-orchestrated combination of his moral nature, the world about him, and the Word of God.

B. The "Light of the world" offers the light of salvation.

JN 12:46 I am come a light into the world, that whosoever believeth on me should not abide in darkness.

JN 8:12 Then spake Jesus again unto them, saying, I am the light of the world: he that followeth me shall not walk in darkness, but shall have the light of life.

Christ came as "a light into the world" (v. 46) so that people would not have to "abide" (remain continually) in the darkness of unbelief and condemnation. Those who follow Him (v. 12), by trusting Him as Savior and Lord, will no longer "walk" (as a normal practice) in the darkness of selfish pride and disregard of God. Christ's "light of life" dispels both the darkness of condemnation (through salvation) and the darkness of self-centered living (through sanctification, i.e., through being made more like Him).

C. Christ's light shines only for a while.

JN 9:4 I must work the works of him that sent me, while it is day: the night cometh, when no man can work.

⁵As long as I am in the world, I am the light of the world.

JN 12:35 Then Jesus said unto them [the Jews], Yet a little while is the light with you. Walk while ye have the light, lest darkness come upon you: for he that walketh in darkness knoweth not whither he goeth. ^{36a}While ye have light, believe in the light, that ye may be the children of light.

Christ's ministry on earth lasted only three and one-half years. Although the Jewish people had many opportunities to acknowledge Him as their Messiah during that time and during the apostles' ministry thereafter, most did not do so. When their nation's "light" eventually was withdrawn, their national opportunity to receive it came to an end. People today similarly have many opportunities to trust in Christ as the Light for salvation. Those who do so become children of light (v. 36) and acquire the characteristics of His light in their lives. For the others, their opportunities one day will come to an end. Then, "the night will come" (v. 4) and "darkness will come upon them" (v. 35).

D. The light cannot coexist with darkness.

JN 3:18 He that believeth on him [Christ] is not condemned: but he that believeth not is condemned already, because he hath not believed in the name of the only begotten Son of God.
¹⁹And this is the condemnation, that light is come into the world, and men loved darkness rather than light, because their deeds were evil.
²⁰For every one that doeth evil hateth the light, neither cometh to the light, lest his deeds should be reproved.
²¹But he that doeth truth cometh to the light, that his deeds may be made manifest, that they are wrought in God.

A person cannot embrace both light and darkness. He will love one and hate the other, with his choice based on his attitude toward sin (vv. 19-20). God's light is like a searchlight that finds and exposes our wrong thoughts and deeds. Because everyone's life before salvation is inherently evil (v. 19), people naturally resist and flee from God's light. Those who have received God's salvation, however, should place themselves willingly and regularly under His spotlight to make certain their lives are in conformity with His will (v. 21).

III. Light pictures a believer's spiritual understanding.

A. Perceiving God's will is like seeing the sunlight.

LK 11:34 The light of the body is the eye: therefore when thine eye is single [healthy], thy whole body also is full of light; but when thine eye is evil [defective], thy body also is full of darkness.
³⁵Take heed therefore that the light which is in thee be not darkness.
³⁶If thy whole body therefore be full of light, having no part dark, the whole shall be full of light, as when the bright shining of a candle doth give thee light.

As physical light enters the eye so that the body can function with purpose and effectiveness, so spiritual light illumines the believer's mind with spiritual understanding and godly wisdom so that he can function with purpose and effectiveness in every area of life. (See also Sec. I.B on p. 251.)

B. Doing God's will is like walking in sunlight.
JN 11:8 His disciples say unto him, Master, the Jews of late sought to stone thee; and goest thou thither [to Judaea] again?

⁹Jesus answered, Are there not twelve hours in the day? If any man walk in the day, he stumbleth not, because he seeth the light of this world.

¹⁰But if a man walk in the night, he stumbleth, because there is no light in him.

Jewish daytime was divided into twelve hours, from 6 a.m. to 6 p.m. Christ's reply, in essence, meant: "If I walk in the daylight of God's will and direction for my life [including His will for the time and manner of my death], I will not stumble [or die prematurely]." The same is true for all believers with respect to any aspect of God's will for our lives. As long as we walk in the light of His purposes and plans for our lives, His light will illumine our way regardless where He leads us. Conversely, if we walk "in the night" outside of God's will, we will stumble badly in the darkness.

IV. Light pictures a believer's testimony for Christ.

A. John the Baptist was a light to the Jews.
JN 5:33 Ye sent unto John, and he bare witness unto the truth. . . .

³⁵He was a burning and a shining light: and ye were willing for a season to rejoice in his light.

John was "a burning and a shining light" because he openly and boldly proclaimed the truth (v. 33) that God committed to his charge regarding the coming Messiah. The Jews initially "rejoiced in his light," i.e., in his announcements that "the kingdom of heaven is at hand." But they did so only "for a season" until he and then Christ more fully revealed the spiritual requirements for entering that kingdom.

B. Believers are a light to the world.
MT 5:14 [LK 11:33] Ye are the light of the world. A city that is set on an hill cannot be hid.

¹⁵Neither do men light a candle, and put it {in a secret place, neither} under a bushel, but on a candlestick; {that they which come in may see the light} and it giveth light unto all that are in the house.

¹⁶Let your light so shine before men, that they may see your good works, and glorify your Father which is in heaven.

Until Christ returns, believers are to be "the light of the world" as His representatives and emissaries. They do so by reflecting His light in their lives and by directing His light to those in darkness. If His light truly burns in His disciples' lives, (1) it "cannot be hidden," like a Mideastern city on a hill that reflects bright sunlight off its light-colored buildings (v. 14); (2) it will give light to all that are nearby, as a lamp in a dark house (v. 15); and (3) it will "shine before men" through good works that point to and glorify God (v. 16).

V. Light represents openness and public display.

A. The gospel should be proclaimed "in light."

MT 10:26 Fear them not [the scoffers] therefore: for there is nothing covered, that shall not be revealed; and hid, that shall not be known. 27What I tell you in darkness, that speak ye in light: and what ye hear in the ear, that preach ye upon the housetops.

These verses may be understood: "There is nothing covered [in God's plan of salvation and will for men's lives] that shall not be revealed. And nothing is hidden or veiled in secrecy that shall not be known and understood. What I tell you in the privacy of `darkness' and confidence, you must proclaim openly in the `light' of full public disclosure. What you hear quietly in your ear, you must preach resoundingly from the housetops." Christ was referring to the gospel message, which was "covered" (veiled) in the Old Testament and "hidden" from the Jews of His day. That message would be revealed fully to His disciples after His resurrection for them to proclaim boldly and openly for all to hear.

B. Sins in the darkness will be brought to light.

LK 12:1 In the mean time, when there were gathered together an innumerable multitude of people, insomuch that they trode one upon another, he began to say unto his disciples first of all, Beware ye of the leaven of the Pharisees, which is hypocrisy. 2For there is nothing covered that shall not be revealed; neither hid, that shall not be known. 3Therefore whatsoever ye have spoken in darkness [secrecy] shall be heard in the light [openly]; and that which ye have spoken in the ear in closets shall be proclaimed upon the housetops.

At first glance, Christ's statement in verse 2 seems identical to that in MT 10:26 in Part A above. One major difference, however, completely changes its meaning. Here, He addresses what "ye (not `I')" have spoken in darkness and in closets. In the context of verse 1, which warns against hypocrisy, verse 2 should be understood: "For there is nothing covered [by hypocrisy] that shall not be revealed [at the judgment, if not before]; neither is anything hidden [by deceit] that shall not be uncovered and disclosed openly." These verses warn both believers and unbelievers that all "hidden" and unconfessed sins will be brought to light for judgment.

> VI. Light is fought by "the power of darkness."
>> **LK 22:52 Then Jesus said unto the chief priests, and captains of the temple, and the elders, which were come to [arrest] him, Be ye come out, as against a thief, with swords and staves?**
>> **⁵³When I was daily with you in the temple, ye stretched forth no hands against me: but this is your hour, and the power of darkness.**

At its core, spiritual darkness is not a passive, neutral, or impersonal condition. It is willful rejection of God's truth and active opposition to His revealed will. Just as spiritual light emanates from and is energized by the Triune God, spiritual darkness stems from and is powered by the unholy alliance of Satan, the world system he dominates, and man's sinful nature.

Satan is the ultimate power in, of, and behind this darkness. When he was unable to defeat Christ with temptations, religious opposition, and attempts to take His life prematurely, he marshalled all of "the power of darkness" to make Christ's crucifixion as terrible, painful, and disgraceful as possible in a final effort to prevent our salvation. He and his religious and political allies combined, however, could not extinguish the Light or His light of life. JN 1:5 (in II.A above) can be understood: "The light of God's truth shines into a world full of spiritual darkness; and all the powers of darkness could not overwhelm or conquer it."

Views of Sight and Blindness

Christ used analogies of "sight" and "seeing" to picture the reception and understanding of God's revealed truth. When a person "sees" God's desire and will for him personally, he is able to respond knowledgeably and obediently. The more he applies and obeys what he sees, the more light God will give him, and the more of God and His will he will see. For a believer, full sight is embracing and following God's light as the guiding beacon for his life.

"Blindness" is the opposite condition. It pictures the ignorance of God's truth in general and especially the willful disregard or rejection of truth already presented. The religious leaders of Israel, who of all people should have been the most prepared for their Messiah and been the first to recognize Him when He came, were the most intractably blind of all. Even believers can be blind in certain respects if they close their eyes to some command or other revelation of God's will. They too will suffer the

consequences of their blindness until they open their eyes and their life to
God's light.

    I. Spiritual sight is accepting and heeding God's truth.

        A. Christ's message brought sight to some and blindness to others.

> **JN 9:39 And Jesus said, For judgment I am come into this world, that they
> which see not might see; and that they which see might be made blind.**
>
> **⁴⁰And some of the Pharisees which were with him heard these
> words, and said unto him, Are we blind also?**
>
> **⁴¹Jesus said unto them, If ye were blind, ye should have no sin: but
> now ye say, We see; therefore your sin remaineth.**

Verse 39 may be understood: "I came into this world to judge all people (and
reward them accordingly), so that those who do not have spiritual sight but
desire it, might see; and so that those who think they can see (but in fact are
blind) might be confirmed in their blindness." The latter group included the
Pharisees in verse 40. In context, verse 41 may be understood: "If you were
blind (because you had no knowledge of God's law), you would have no consciousness of sin. But because you now claim, `We can see' (when you have
rejected God's light), your sin remains (and you are blind indeed!)"

        B. Christ's parables either increased sight or confirmed blindness.

> **LK 8:10 And he said [to His disciples], Unto you it is given to know the
> mysteries of the kingdom of God: but to others [I speak] in parables;
> that seeing they might not see, and hearing they might not understand.**
>
> **MT 13:13 Therefore speak I to them in parables: because they see-
> ing see not; and hearing they hear not, neither do they understand.**
>
> **¹⁴And in them is fulfilled the prophecy of Esaias, which saith, By
> hearing ye shall hear, and shall not understand; and seeing ye shall
> see, and shall not perceive:**
>
> **¹⁵For this people's heart is waxed gross [become calloused], and
> their ears are dull of hearing, and their eyes they have closed; lest
> at any time they should see with their eyes, and hear with their ears,
> and should understand with their heart, and should be converted,
> and I should heal them.**
>
> **¹⁶But blessed are your eyes, for they [understand and accept what
> they] see: and your ears, for they [understand and accept what
> they] hear.**

Christ designed His parables to increase the understanding of those who had
some spiritual sight, even if it was minimal. Those who genuinely desired to
learn and obey God's truth could see at least dimly, and Christ's parables were
given to improve their vision. On the other hand, those who repeatedly

"closed their eyes" to God's Word (v. 15), thinking they already could see, only confirmed their own blindness to what Christ was teaching.

II. Spiritual blindness leads to false beliefs and hopeless conditions.

A. Blind leaders and blind followers will "fall into the ditch."

MT 15:12 Then came his disciples, and said unto him, Knowest thou that the Pharisees were offended, after they heard this saying?

¹³But he answered and said, Every plant, which my heavenly Father hath not planted, shall be rooted up.

¹⁴Let them alone: they be blind leaders of the blind. And if the blind lead the blind, both shall fall into the ditch.

Christ had just condemned the Pharisees for elevating their man-made traditions above God-given doctrine. Because they effectively negated God's commands and replaced them with their own, He calls them "blind leaders of the blind." Worse yet, the people of Israel, who desperately needed spiritual guidance, were instead being blinded by their leaders' false beliefs. Both the blind leaders and their blind followers were falling "into the ditch" of false religion.

B. Willfully blind people cannot be healed.

JN 12:37 But though he had done so many miracles before them, yet they believed not on him:

³⁸That the saying of Esaias the prophet might be fulfilled, which he spake, Lord, who hath believed our report? and to whom hath the arm of the Lord been revealed?

³⁹Therefore they could not believe, because that Esaias said again,

⁴⁰He hath blinded their eyes, and hardened their heart; that they should not see with their eyes, nor understand with their heart, and be converted, and I should heal them.

It is interesting to compare Isaiah's original prophecy with Christ's reference to it in MT 13 (in I.B) and John's reference to it above. In Isaiah 6:9-10, God commands Isaiah to "shut their eyes" by proclaiming His message to the people. Christ states, "their eyes *they* have closed" to God's truth. John writes, "He (God) hath blinded their eyes" because they refused to believe His message. Taken together, these passages make it clear that all three parties (God, His messenger, and the hearer) have indispensable and interrelated roles in the opening or closing of a hearer's eyes. Christ stressed, however, that every blind person is fully responsible for his own blindness and its consequences. (See His condemnation of the Pharisees' blindness in Sec. II .B on p. 393.)

III. Spiritual sight can be dimmed by spiritual failure.

A. By failing to learn from prior lessons.

MK 8:15 [MT 16:6] And he charged them [His disciples], saying, Take heed, beware of the leaven of the Pharisees, and of the leaven of Herod.

¹⁶And they reasoned among themselves, saying, It is because we have no bread.

¹⁷And when Jesus knew it, he saith unto them, Why reason ye, because ye have no bread? perceive ye not yet, neither understand? have ye your heart yet hardened?

¹⁸Having eyes, see ye not? and having ears, hear ye not? and do ye not remember?

¹⁹When I brake the five loaves among five thousand, how many baskets full of fragments took ye up? They say unto him, Twelve.

²⁰And when the seven among four thousand, how many baskets full of fragments took ye up? And they said, Seven.

²¹And he said unto them, How is it that ye do not understand? {Then understood they how that he bade them not beware of the leaven of bread, but of the doctrine of the Pharisees and of the Sadducees.}

Soon after Christ provided bread to over 4,000 people, His disciples lacked bread themselves. Instead of trusting Christ to meet their need (as they twice in recent days had witnessed His feeding of whole multitudes), they fretted over their plight. Christ rebuked them for "having eyes, and seeing not" (v. 18). They failed to see that Christ was desirous and fully capable of meeting their every need if they would only trust Him to do so. In short, they failed to live by faith — largely because they failed to learn from prior experiences in which He fully met even greater needs.

The text suggests that the disciples also failed to see the danger of the leaven of the Pharisees and the leaven of Herod. Leaven is yeast that ferments and raises dough; it pictures harmful influences that furtively pervade and control its host. The Pharisees' leaven was their self-righteousness and hypocrisy. Herod's leaven was his trusting in his own strength and living for this life alone. Christ warned His disciples to beware of the sinfulness and dangers of these insidious "doctrines" and of natural human tendencies in these directions.

B. By failing to be like Christ and thereby misleading others.

LK 6:39 And he spake a parable unto them, Can the blind lead the blind? shall they not both fall into the ditch?

⁴⁰The disciple is not above his master: but every one that is perfect shall be as his master.

Although verse 39 appears similar to MT 15:14 in II.A above, it has an entirely different meaning. The whole passage in LK 6:20-49 addresses how Christ's followers should live godly lives day by day. In this context, the "blind leaders" are professing Christians who misrepresent Christ to others by failing to "be as their Master" (v. 40). Those who observe them (especially new and weak believers) are in danger of following them into the same "ditch" of wrong behavior and spiritual failure.

> C. By failing to see and remove the "planks" in our own eyes.
> **⁴¹And why beholdest thou the mote that is in thy brother's eye, but perceivest not the beam that is in thine own eye?**
> **⁴²Either how canst thou say to thy brother, Brother, let me pull out the mote that is in thine eye, when thou thyself beholdest not the beam that is in thine own eye? Thou hypocrite, cast out first the beam out of thine own eye, and then shalt thou see clearly to pull out the mote that is in thy brother's eye.**

Luke follows verses 39-40 with Christ's admonition that we not be blind to our own faults. Before we can pull "tiny specks" of failure or wrong-doing out of another believer's eye, we must first pull the "large planks" of our sins and shortcomings out of our own eyes. Only then can we "see clearly" enough to help remove any specks from our brother's eyes.

Forms of Life and Death

To what possession does mankind ascribe a higher value, or cling more tenaciously, than life itself? People will go to any length and sacrifice anything else to protect and preserve it. Christ, therefore, often used the precious and irreplaceable nature of physical life to picture the infinitely more glorious and more enduring spiritual life that God gives to those who will receive it.

As though the benefits of spiritual life were not enough incentive to receive it, the only alternative to it is an existence Christ pictured as eternal death. Mortal man's greatest fear and greatest acknowledged enemy is physical death. As dreaded and frightening, however, as death can be, it is only a mild and momentary representation of spiritual death that continues through eternity in hell.

Because of everyone's sin — both his inborn sin nature and the multitude of individual sins that flow regularly from it — God's Word declares that everyone without Christ already is hopelessly dead. In a miracle of re-creation, however, Christ imparts His own perfect life to every sinner who acknowledges his helpless state and by faith receives that life from Him.

I. "Life" or "death" depends on our relationship to God.

    A. Life is inherent in God alone.

JN 5:26 For as the Father hath life in himself; so hath he given to the Son to have life in himself;

JN 5:21 For as the Father raiseth up the dead, and quickeneth them [gives them life]; even so the Son quickeneth whom he will.

God is self-existent and self-sufficient. The members of the Godhead (Father, Son, and Holy Spirit) not only have life, they are life. Further, they impart life, when and to whom they will to do so (v. 21). They can readily "raise the dead" — the physically dead to physical life and the spiritually dead to spiritual life. With God, we may have complete, satisfying, eternal life. Without God, there is no life at all.

    B. Spiritual life is a personal relationship with God through Christ.

JN 17:1 These words spake Jesus, and lifted up his eyes to heaven, and said, Father, the hour is come; glorify thy Son, that thy Son also may glorify thee:

²As thou hast given him power over all flesh, that he should give eternal life to as many as thou hast given him.

³And this is life eternal, that they might know thee the only true God, and Jesus Christ, whom thou hast sent.

Because God is life, anyone who truly knows Him through personal experience (as in v. 3) receives His life as his own. Believers thereby become "partakers of the divine nature" (II Peter 1:4). Among its characteristics, God's nature is complete and eternal. The life, therefore, that believers receive upon "knowing God and Jesus Christ" is "life eternal" with all of its qualitative and quantitative perfections.

    C. Spiritual death is the state of those apart from God.

MT 8:21 And another of his disciples said unto him, Lord, suffer me first to go and bury my father.

²²But Jesus said unto him, Follow me; and let the dead bury their dead.

JN 5:25 Verily, verily, I say unto you, The hour is coming, and now is [has already arrived], when the dead shall hear the voice of the Son of God: and they that hear shall live.

Christ termed living unbelievers "the dead," referring to their unregenerate spiritual condition. Dead people obviously are powerless to overcome their lifeless state. Unless they are raised by God to life in Christ, they will remain spiritually dead forever. To "hear" Christ's voice means to respond positively to it. The "hour" for responding to His voice "now is." The duration of this hour is known only to God, but the term implies that its length is both fixed and limited.

> D. Life or death is a personal choice.
>
> **MT 7:13 Enter ye in at the strait [narrow] gate: for wide is the gate, and broad is the way, that leadeth to destruction, and many there be which go in thereat:**
>
> **¹⁴Because strait is the gate, and narrow [constricted, or difficult] is the way, which leadeth unto life, and few there be that find it.**

Everyone is on one of two roads. Most are on the popular and easy "way to destruction." In contrast, relatively few find "the way to life." The latter, though available to all, is narrow and constricted. Its gate is narrow in that it is exclusive and exact; it can only be entered through Christ and on God's terms alone. Its path is constricted and difficult in that it requires self-denial and sacrifice; Christ must be the undisputed Lord of each entrant's life. Whichever road a person chooses determines both his current condition and his eternal destination.

> II. Christ is the means by which the dead become alive.
>
> A. He is the source of all life.
>
> **JN 1:1 In the beginning was the Word [Christ Himself], and the Word was with God, and the Word was God.**
>
> **²The same was in the beginning with God.**
>
> **³All things were made by him; and without him was not any thing made that was made.**
>
> **⁴In him was life; and the life was the light of men.**
>
> **JN 10:10b I am come that they might have life, and that they might have it more abundantly.**

Christ created "all things" (v. 3), including all forms and aspects of physical life. Also, life itself resides in Him (v. 4, and as shown in I.A), referring here primarily to His perfect, eternal, spiritual life. The latter is the life that He now offers to all people. He came from God to earth that we might have such life, and have it abundantly.

> B. He is the only means of spiritual life.
>
> **JN 14:6 Jesus saith unto him, I [and I alone] am the way, the truth, and the life: no man cometh unto the Father, but by me.**

JN 5:39 [to legalistic Jews] Search the scriptures; for in them ye think ye have eternal life: and they are they which testify of me.
⁴⁰And ye will not come to me, that ye might have life.

Christ claimed clearly that He is the one and only means of spiritual life for all mankind (v. 6). He rebuked those who sought to earn such life by observing religious rites and regulations. Their preoccupation with the rules of scripture obscured its basic message that spiritual life is available only through Him (v. 39). As a result, they missed the way to God and the eternal life they zealously sought.

C. He gives life through the words of life.

JN 6:63 It is the spirit that quickeneth [gives life]; the flesh profiteth nothing: the words that I speak unto you, they are spirit, and they are life.

JN 6:68 Then Simon Peter answered him, Lord, to whom shall we go? thou hast the words of eternal life.
⁶⁹And we believe and are sure that thou art that Christ, the Son of the living God.

The Living Word spoke "words of life," that the spiritually dead might hear Him and live. His words were "spirit" and "life" (v. 63) in that His message was a spiritual message, addressing spiritual needs, for the purpose of giving spiritual life. In acknowledging Christ's deity, Peter declared that He alone spoke "the words of eternal life." No one else had such a convicting and transforming message or was worthy of their allegiance and worship.

III. Faith in Christ is the only requirement for life.

A. Saving faith relies on His death in our place on the cross.

JN 3:14 And as Moses lifted up the serpent in the wilderness, even so must the Son of man be lifted up [on the cross]:
¹⁵That whosoever believeth in him should not perish, but have eternal life.
¹⁶For God so loved the world, that he gave his only begotten Son, that whosoever believeth in him should not perish, but have everlasting life.

The Israelites who were bitten by poisonous snakes in the wilderness, and who repented of their sin, had only to look to the bronze serpent Moses made — and they lived (see Sec. I.A on p. 56). Similarly, any repentant sinner who looks in faith to Christ and His sacrificial death on the cross for salvation from his sin "should not perish but have everlasting life."

B. It trusts solely in Him for salvation.

JN 6:35 And Jesus said unto them, I am the bread of life: he that cometh to me shall never hunger; and he that believeth on me shall never thirst. . . .

⁴⁷Verily, verily, I say unto you, He that believeth on me hath everlasting life.

JN 20:30 And many other signs truly did Jesus in the presence of his disciples, which are not written in this book:

³¹But these are written, that ye might believe that Jesus is the Christ, the Son of God; and that believing ye might have life through his name.

Believe, trust, receive, and accept are all synonymous in the context of our response to Christ's offer of eternal life. They go beyond mental assent and acknowledgment of certain facts to an active embracing of and commitment to Christ as the only possible means of our salvation. To believe in "His name" (v. 31) is to rely fully and solely upon who Christ is and what He did to purchase our redemption. There is nothing more (or less) that anyone can do to receive God's gift of salvation and life.

C. It frees us from death and condemnation.

JN 5:24 Verily, verily, I say unto you, He that heareth my word, and believeth on him that sent me, hath everlasting life, and shall not come into condemnation; but is passed from death unto life.

Those who believe in Christ with saving faith will never again face spiritual death or condemnation. They were eternally delivered from these when they trusted in Him, because He bore all of God's judgment and punishment for their sin. As a result, every believer has passed "from death to life," from sin to salvation, and from condemnation to glorification. "If the Son therefore shall make you free, ye shall be free indeed!" (JN 8:36).

IV. The life Christ gives is guaranteed forever.

A. It begins when received and never ends.

JN 3:36 He that believeth on the Son hath [presently has] everlasting life: and he that believeth not the Son shall not see life; but the wrath of God abideth on him.

JN 6:51 I am the living bread which came down from heaven: if any man eat of this bread, he shall live for ever: and the bread that I will give is my flesh, which I will give for the life of the world.

All who believe in Christ for salvation already have eternal life. Their eternal relationship with God, their position in Christ's body of believers, their heavenly inheritance, and much more, are irrevocably guaranteed at the moment they receive Christ as their Savior. Spiritual life, therefore, is both a present and an everlasting possession. Christ promised that those who partake of Him as the Living Bread "shall live forever" (6:51). To the same degree, unbelievers already are under God's condemnation, and His wrath continually "abides" on them. The same verse (3:36) declares both certainties regarding present and eternal life and present and eternal condemnation.

B. It includes future and eternal physical life.

JN 11:25 Jesus said unto her, I am the resurrection, and the life: he that believeth in me, though he were dead [even if he dies], yet shall he live:

²⁶And whosoever liveth [whoever is now alive] and believeth in me shall never die. Believest thou this?

Believers may die physically, but not permanently. Christ also won the victory over physical death when He vanquished its cause, namely, sin and spiritual death (I Cor. 15:54-57). When He returns for His believers, those who previously died will be resurrected and join those who are alive at that time. Together they will live in glorified bodies and share perfect, wonderful physical life with Christ for all eternity. (See Mankind's Resurrection on p. 440, and particularly Sec. IV on p. 442.)

C. It is kept and assured by God alone.

JN 10:27 My sheep hear my voice, and I know them, and they follow me:

²⁸And I give unto them eternal life; and they shall never perish, neither shall any man pluck them out of my hand.

²⁹My Father, which gave them me, is greater than all; and no man is able to pluck them out of my Father's hand.

³⁰I and my Father are one.

God assumes all the responsibility for guaranteeing that every believer's eternal life is in fact eternal. Christ confirmed this with several additional guarantees. First, its recipients will "never perish"; Christ obligated Himself to protect every one of His sheep forever. Second, no one will ever be able to remove them from His omnipotent grasp. And third, God the Father, who "gave them" to Christ (v. 29) as His eternal inheritance, has added His own guarantee that no one will ever be able to terminate either their eternal life or Christ's position as their eternal Lord. (See Sec. VI on p. 117.)

7

Family Portraits of Christ and His Own

Since the church began at Pentecost, some of the questions most widely debated in professing Christendom include "Who is a member of Christ's family?"; "How does one join it?"; and "How are its members identified?" The first three Gospels each record an illustration that summarizes Christ's answer. In it, He declares, "For whosoever shall {hear the word of God, and} do the will of my Father which is in heaven, the same is my brother, and sister, and mother" (MT 12:50; LK 8:21).

To remove all doubt on this vital issue, Christ presented a number of parables and parallels that illustrate who is, and who is not, in His family. He used simple pictures of the well-known relationships listed above to give the clearest possible answer. He wants everyone to know how to become His "brother, and sister, and mother."

The Shepherd and His Sheep
(John 10:1-30)

Shepherds and sheep were common fixtures on the hillsides of Israel. The people's familiarity with the nature of sheep and the task of shepherds provided a ready canvas for the Master's illustrations. He frequently used their knowledge of sheep to picture their own nature and needs — and His role as their shepherd. This section and the next highlight these comparisons.

I. Christ is the True Shepherd.

A. He alone is the rightful Shepherd.

JN 10:1 Verily, verily, I say unto you, He that entereth not by the door into the sheepfold, but climbeth up some other way, the same is a thief and a robber.

²But he that entereth in by the door is the shepherd of the sheep.

³ᵃTo him the porter openeth;

B. He knows His sheep and leads each one.

³ᵇand the sheep hear his voice: and he calleth his own sheep by name, and leadeth them out.

⁴And when he putteth forth his own sheep, he goeth before them, and the sheep follow him: for they know his voice.

⁵And a stranger will they not follow, but will flee from him: for they know not the voice of strangers.

C. Those who are not His sheep do not understand Him.

⁶This parable spake Jesus unto them: but they understood not what things they were which he spake unto them.

The Pharisees to whom Christ spoke this parable considered themselves the rightful shepherds of God's flock, Israel. They had not, however, entered the sheepfold "by the door" of divine appointment but tried to climb in by their own devices. The Spirit of God, as porter of the sheepfold, ordained Christ as the True Shepherd (see LK 4:18) and opened the door for Him to care for the sheep. The True Shepherd gently guides, aids, and encourages His sheep (not mercilessly driving them as did the Pharisees) and prepares the way before them. Similarly, the true sheep readily recognize and respond to the Shepherd's voice and willingly follow wherever He leads.

II. The Shepherd is also the Door to the fold.

A. He is the only means of entering the fold.

⁷Then said Jesus unto them again, Verily, verily, I say unto you, I [and I alone] am the door of [for] the sheep.

⁸**All that ever came before me are thieves and robbers: but the sheep did not hear them.**

⁹**I am the door: by me if any man enter in, he shall be saved, and shall go in and out, and find pasture.**

B. He gives His sheep true life, and abundantly.

¹⁰**The thief cometh not, but for to steal, and to kill, and to destroy: I am come that they might have life, and that they might have it more abundantly.**

The Shepherd also claimed to be the door through which the sheep enter the fold. How He could be both simultaneously is explained in Section II on page 7. This "double exposure" can be compared with Hebrews 9:11-10:22 which combines three pictures of Christ in one sweeping scene. There He is pictured as (1) the veil (the "door" to the Holy of Holies) in the tabernacle through which (2) He as our High Priest entered God's presence with (3) His own blood as the sacrifice for our sins. In both JN 10 and Hebrews 9 and 10, Christ is both the door and the One who enters the door. Because He thus entered God's presence on our behalf, we too may enter it through Him, our "Door" to God.

III. He is the Good Shepherd who loves the sheep.

A. He is willing to die to save the sheep.

¹¹**I am the good shepherd: the good shepherd giveth his life for the sheep.**

B. "Hirelings" do not really care for the sheep.

¹²**But he that is an hireling, and not the shepherd, whose own the sheep are not, seeth the wolf coming, and leaveth the sheep, and fleeth: and the wolf catcheth them, and scattereth the sheep.**

¹³**The hireling fleeth, because he is an hireling, and careth not for the sheep.**

Christ first pictured Himself as the True Shepherd (vv. 1-5) and the Pharisees as impostors and usurpers. Starting in verse 11, He portrays Himself as the Good Shepherd, emphasizing His care for His sheep to the point of willingly dying for them. In contrast, He depicts the religious leaders of the day as "hirelings." Their positions of leadership were originally ordained by God for the benefit of His sheep. However, they had perverted their assignment for their own prestige, power, and economic benefit. Because they did not really care for the sheep, they left the sheep to the wolves.

C. He knows His sheep intimately and loves them infinitely.

¹⁴**I am the good shepherd, and know my sheep, and am known of mine.**

¹⁵**As the Father knoweth me, even so know I the Father: and I lay down my life for the sheep.**

D. He unites all of His sheep in one fold.

¹⁶And other sheep I have, which are not of this fold: them also I must bring, and they shall hear my voice; and there shall be one fold, and one shepherd.

A key characteristic of the relationship of each sheep with its Shepherd is that they know each other fully and intimately. His knowledge of us is complete in every detail and is coupled with His unbounded love, devotion, and attention to our good. So are we to know Him. This intimate relationship was not restricted to His first disciples, or to believers who walked with Him in Israel, but is intended as well for the "other sheep I have" (including Gentile believers not of the Jewish fold). "Them also I must bring," through the centuries and from around the world, to complete His "one fold" of all true believers.

IV. The Shepherd died and arose for His sheep.

A. He voluntarily died and rose again.

¹⁷Therefore doth my Father love me, because I lay down my life, that I might take it again.

B. He alone controlled His destiny.

¹⁸No man taketh it from me, but I lay it down of myself. I have power to lay it down, and I have power to take it again. This commandment have I received of my Father.

Christ was not a defeated victim of bigoted murderers. He voluntarily, even purposefully, laid down His life for His sheep. He did so for their good and their benefit, as well as in their stead as their substitute. The sheep were on their way to slaughter, but He interposed His own life in their place. On several occasions, His enemies sought to put Him to death, but to no avail because His "hour" had not yet come. At precisely the time appointed by His Father, He laid down His life by Himself. Others may willingly die for a cause, but He alone could take up His life again after He died — all as planned by the Father.

V. The Jews were divided over Christ's identity.

A. They could not deny His miracles, but they would not believe.

¹⁹There was a division therefore again among the Jews for these sayings.

²⁰And many of them said, He hath a devil, and is mad; why hear ye him?

²¹Others said, These are not the words of him that hath a devil. Can a devil open the eyes of the blind?

B. They challenged Him to say He was the Messiah.

²²**And it was at Jerusalem the feast of the dedication, and it was winter.**
²³**And Jesus walked in the temple in Solomon's porch.**
²⁴**Then came the Jews round about him, and said unto him, How long dost thou make us to doubt? If thou be the Christ, tell us plainly.**

C. They had already decided in spite of the evidence.

²⁵**Jesus answered them, I told you, and ye believed not: the works that I do in my Father's name, they bear witness of me.**
²⁶**But ye believe not, because ye are not of my sheep, as I said unto you.**

Jesus' pictures of Himself caused "division among the people." When unbelieving Jews demanded He tell them plainly if He was the Christ, He replied He had already done so — by the sayings (v. 19) and miracles (v. 21) that they refused to acknowledge. The real reason some of them demanded an explicit affirmation that He was the Christ became clear later at His trials before the Sanhedrin and Pilate. They sought to condemn Him to death for blasphemy against God and treason against Rome.

VI. The Shepherd's sheep have eternal life.

A. He guarantees their eternal salvation.

²⁷**My sheep hear my voice, and I know them, and they follow me:**
²⁸**And I give unto them eternal life; and they shall never perish, neither shall any man pluck them out of my hand.**

Christ has sealed the eternal salvation of each of His sheep with an unqualified three-fold guarantee: (1) He has given them eternal life as a free gift that does not depend on any sustaining effort of their own; (2) they shall never perish, because He has assumed all the responsibility for maintaining their security; and (3) no force, human or otherwise, can ever dislodge them from His protecting hand.

B. The Father guarantees their salvation, as Christ's inheritance.

²⁹**My Father, which gave them me, is greater than all; and no man is able to pluck them out of my Father's hand.**
³⁰**I and my Father are one.**

Verse 29 is not merely a restatement of Christ's guarantee in verse 28. It is of a different order and is based on different grounds. God the Father guarantees each believer's eternal salvation based on the fact that He has given that one to Christ for Christ's own benefit. Christ prayed, "Holy Father, keep through thine own name those whom thou hast given me" (JN 17:11). The Father keeps securely and forever — in His own hand and based on His own immutable character — every believer that He has given to His Son. He will not take away, or let become lost in any way, anyone He has given to Christ.

The Father also has ordained Christ's inheritance, which includes His future kingdom and all believers who will inhabit it. Christ will receive His inheritance "when He shall come to be glorified in His saints, and to be admired in all them that believe" (II Thess. 1:10). Thus, the Father has guaranteed our inheritance of eternal salvation by guaranteeing Christ's inheritance of all believers, who will worship Him forever.

Christ and the Father "are one" (v. 30) in the essence of their nature, their character, and their attributes. They are also one in their eternal purposes and plans for all creation and in the perfect harmony of their respective functions and activities with mankind. They are also one in their loving personal relationship with every sheep in the Shepherd's flock.

Other Scenes of the Shepherd and Sheep

The following brief sketches supplement those in JN 10 in illustrating the many ways in which Christ is the Good Shepherd and we are His dependent sheep. These or parallel passages are included and discussed further in other chapters on the pages indicated.

I. The Shepherd's love for His sheep.

MT 9:36 But when he saw the multitudes, he was moved with compassion on them, because they fainted, and were scattered abroad, as sheep having no shepherd.

MT 18:12 How think ye? if a man have an hundred sheep, and one of them be gone astray, doth he not leave the ninety and nine, and goeth into the mountains, and seeketh that which is gone astray?

¹³And if so be that he find it, verily I say unto you, he rejoiceth more of that sheep, than of the ninety and nine which went not astray.

¹⁴Even so it is not the will of your Father which is in heaven, that one of these little ones should perish.

Christ's heart went out to these helpless sheep when He saw their desperate spiritual plight. He not only observed their great need, but resolutely and selflessly set out to rescue and restore them. Finding even one "little one" in the wilderness was sufficient motivation and reward for all His effort. (See Sec. I on p. 2 and Sec. II on p. 92.)

II. The Shepherd's care for His sheep.

MT 12:10 And, behold, there was a man which had his hand withered. And they [some Pharisees] asked him, saying, Is it lawful to heal on the sabbath days? that they might accuse him.

¹¹And he said unto them, What man shall there be among you, that shall have one sheep, and if it fall into a pit on the sabbath day, will he not lay hold on it, and lift it out?

¹²How much then is a man better than a sheep? Wherefore it is lawful to do well on the sabbath days.

¹³Then saith he to the man, Stretch forth thine hand. And he stretched it forth; and it was restored whole, like as the other.

The question in verse 11 obviously calls for a "yes" answer. Rescuing a helpless sheep is an act of mercy that is always right and proper. Christ called showing such mercy one of "the weightier [most fundamental] matters of God's law" (MT 23:23). He mercifully cared for the handicapped man and met his need — as He cares for every believer in His flock and meets the needs of each one. (See Sec. XI on p. 318.)

III. The Shepherd's death for His sheep.

MT 26:31 Then saith Jesus unto them [His disciples], All ye shall be offended because of me this night: for it is written, I [God the Father] will smite the shepherd, and the sheep of the flock shall be scattered abroad.

The Good Shepherd knew that even though His sheep would be scattered when He was smitten on the cross, it was for their salvation that He should so die. Accordingly, He accepted that horrible death so that His sheep could be saved and gathered into His eternal fold. (See Sec. V on p. 60.)

IV. The Shepherd's feeding of His sheep.

JN 21:15 So when they had dined, Jesus saith to Simon Peter, Simon, son of Jonas, lovest thou me more than these? He saith unto him, Yea, Lord; thou knowest that I love thee. He saith unto him, Feed my lambs.

¹⁶He saith to him again the second time, Simon, son of Jonas, lovest thou me? He saith unto him, Yea, Lord; thou knowest that I love thee. He saith unto him, Feed my sheep.

¹⁷He saith unto him the third time, Simon, son of Jonas, lovest thou me? Peter was grieved because he said unto him the third time, Lovest thou me? And he said unto him, Lord, thou knowest all things; thou knowest that I love thee. Jesus saith unto him, Feed my sheep.

The Chief Shepherd would soon return to heaven and leave the direct care and feeding of His sheep to His disciples. He made this critical task Peter's supreme responsibility and also the test of his love for Him. Similarly, Christ gave pastor/teachers (or, "shepherd/feeders") to His church so that all believers may be trained and strengthened to carry out His ministry on earth (Eph. 4:11-12; I Pet. 5:2-4). (See Sec. IV on p. 265.)

V. The Shepherd's commission for His sheep.

MT 10:6 But go rather to the lost sheep of the house of Israel.

> [7]And as ye go, preach, saying, The kingdom of heaven is at hand. . . .
> [16]Behold, I send you forth as sheep in the midst of wolves: be ye therefore wise as serpents, and harmless as doves.

LK 10:3 Go your ways: behold, I send you forth as lambs among wolves.

Christ commissioned His disciples (first the twelve in MT 10, then seventy in LK 10) to go and preach the gospel as "lambs among wolves." This indicated the gentleness, simplicity, and innocence with which they were to proclaim the Good News. These instructions are similar to those He gave later regarding the opposition they would face in fulfilling their Great Commission (JN 15:18-16:4). Although faithful believers may seem at times to be as vulnerable and defenseless as sheep among wolves, Christ promised, "Lo, I am with you always" (MT 28:20). (See "The Disciples' Commission" on p. 267 ff.)

VI. The Shepherd's warning for His sheep.

MT 7:15 Beware of false prophets, which come to you in sheep's clothing, but inwardly they are ravening wolves.

One of the sheep's greatest dangers is being misled and ravaged by religious wolves who masquerade as sheep. Such wolves not only lull unbelievers into a false sense of security short of salvation, they also can wreak great havoc among God's flock. Christ urgently warned, "Beware of them!" His sheep do so by carefully comparing the supposed sheeps' doctrine with scripture and by examining the fruit of their lives and ministries. (See Sec. I on p. 383 ff.)

VII. The Shepherd's reward for His sheep.

MT 25:31 When the Son of man shall come in his glory, and all the holy angels with him, then shall he sit upon the throne of his glory:
[32]And before him shall be gathered all nations: and he shall separate them one from another, as a shepherd divideth his sheep from the goats:
[33]And he shall set the sheep on his right hand, but the goats on the left.
[34]Then shall the King say unto them on his right hand, Come, ye blessed of my Father, inherit the kingdom prepared for you from the foundation of the world:

LK 12:32 Fear not, little flock; for it is your Father's good pleasure to give you the kingdom.

At His return, the Great Shepherd will gather His sheep from among all the nations and usher them into His and their glorious kingdom. With this incomparable blessing in store, Christ encourages His "little flock" not to fear the problems and trials of life, but to rest upon His promise of their great and eternal reward. (See Sec. VIII on p. 444 ff.)

The Vine and Its Branches
John 15:1-17

The Jews were well acquainted with grape vines and the husbandry vines required to produce a bountiful harvest. They also knew from the Old Testament that Israel was God's special vine, which He cultivated for bearing spiritual fruit. Israel failed, however, to produce the fruit God desired. He said, "What could have been done more to my vineyard, that I have not done in it? wherefore, when I looked that it should bring forth grapes, brought it forth wild grapes?" (see Isa. 5:1-7). "Yet I had planted thee a noble vine, wholly a right seed: how then art thou turned into the degenerate plant of a strange vine unto me?" (Jer. 2:21).

To receive the quality of fruit God desired, He planted a new and perfect Vine. Further, to produce the quantity of fruit He desired, He would tend the branches with new and more intensive means. On the eve of His crucifixion, Christ pictured for His disciples how God would accomplish these objectives through Him and through them.

  I. Christ is the Vine; believers are branches.

    A. The Vine and branches are to bear fruit for God.
    JN 15:1 I am the true vine, and my Father is the husbandman.

This verse may be read: "I myself am the vine, the true one [in contrast to Israel]; and my Father is the gardener." The gardener tills the soil and cares for the vine, working particularly with its branches. The Father provided Christ as the Vine, places believers as branches in the Vine, and assures that the branches receive the nourishment they need to bear fruit for Him.

    B. To bear fruit, each branch must
      1. Be pruned of unproductive elements;
      ²Every branch in me that beareth not fruit he taketh away: and every branch that beareth fruit, he purgeth it, that it may bring forth more fruit.

      2. Be cleansed by God's Word;
      ³Now ye are clean through the word which I have spoken unto you.

      3. Abide fully in the Vine.
      ⁴Abide in me, and I [will abide] in you. As the branch cannot bear fruit of itself, except it abide in the vine; no more can ye, except ye abide in me.

For maximum fruit-bearing, grape vines must be pruned so severely that uninitiated observers often wonder how the remaining stubby limbs could ever again produce grapes. Believers similarly must be pruned severely of self-centered goals, un-Christlike attitudes and traits, and possessions and activities that inhibit their spiritual growth. One of God's pruning hooks is His Word, which is "sharper than any two-edged sword, piercing even to the dividing asunder of soul and spirit . . . and is a discerner of the thoughts and intents of the heart" (Heb. 4:12).

That same Word is also God's cleansing agent (v. 3). He uses it both in "the washing of regeneration" (our new birth; Titus 3:5) and our ongoing sanctification and cleansing "with the washing of water by the Word" (Eph. 5:26). When a branch is so pruned and cleansed, it is fit to abide in the Vine and begin bearing fruit. There is more to abiding in Christ, however, than being pruned and cleansed, as the following verses explain.

II. Christ's life gives strength to His branches.

A. "Abiding branches" bear much fruit.
> ⁵I am the vine, ye are the branches: He that abideth in me, and I in him, the same bringeth forth much fruit: for without me ye can do nothing.

To abide in Christ is to maintain close, intimate communion with Him. He makes it possible for us to have such communion when we trust Him as our Savior, and He seeks to develop and perfect it within us throughout our lives. In spite of His provision, however, we abide in Him only to the degree that we genuinely desire to do so and act in accordance with that desire by faithfully obeying, serving, and communicating with Him.

Christ always desires to abide in close communion with us, and He acts perfectly in accord with His desire. He encourages and helps us to learn more fully of Him, to fellowship more intimately with Him, and to live more identically like Him. We abide in Him by embracing and furthering His abiding in us. To that same degree, we "bring forth fruit" — whether little or much. Without His abiding presence and power, "ye can do [absolutely] nothing."

B. "Barren branches" are discarded and burned.
> ⁶If a man abide not in me, he is cast forth as a branch, and is withered; and men gather them, and cast them into the fire, and they are burned.

A supposed "branch" that does not abide in the Vine and bear fruit to any degree whatsoever probably is not a true branch at all. The vinedresser recognizes all pretense and deception, and He separates the fruitless branches from the true. Under His supervision, every false and fruitless branch will be rejected, "cast into the fire, and burned."

C. "Faithful branches" thrive on God's Word and prayer.

⁷If ye abide in me, and my words abide in you, ye shall ask what ye will, and it shall be done unto you.

One of the principal ways we abide in Christ and He in us is through His words abiding in us. We learn of Him, appreciate Him, and receive instruction for following Him primarily through His words. By believing His Word, we show our faith in Him, and by obeying His Word, we show our love for Him. Our union and our communion with Him both depend upon His Word. By filling our mind and life with God's Word, we abide in Christ more fully, and we provide for His abiding more fully in us. Answered prayer, likewise, depends on this mutual abiding of us in Him and His Word in us (see Sec. I on p. 187).

D. "Fruitful branches" glorify God.

⁸Herein is my Father glorified, that ye bear much fruit; so shall ye be [become] my disciples.

Scripture identifies three major categories of fruit that all believers are to bear: (1) the "fruit [singular] of the Spirit" (Gal. 5:22-23), which is the full array of Christ-like graces and virtues He desires to reproduce in each of us, (2) the fruit of good works and good words (e.g., MT 12:33-34) that flow from Christ-like character, and (3) the fruit of evangelism (JN 4:35-36), which is the eternal life reproduced in others through the faithful witness of believers. The more such fruit we bear, the more God is glorified and the more we become Christ's disciples (v. 8). Our discipleship increases in scope, maturity, and fruitfulness as we abide more fully in Him. (See "Other Pictures of Spiritual Fruit" on p. 125 ff.)

III. Christ's love gives joy to His branches.

A. Be steadfast in love and obedience to Him.

⁹As the Father hath loved me, so have I loved you: continue [abide] ye in my love.

¹⁰If ye keep my commandments, ye shall abide in my love; even as I have kept my Father's commandments, and abide in his love.

Christ makes two staggering comparisons here. First, He loves us just as (in the same way and to the same degree) the Father loves Him — perfectly, wholeheartedly, unconditionally, and continuously. Given the quality and magnitude of His love for us, how great our desire and effort should be to continue in it (v. 9). Second, we are to continue in Christ's love by keeping His commandments even as (in the same way and to the same degree) Christ kept His Father's commandments — perfectly, wholeheartedly, unconditionally, and continuously.

B. Fill up your joy with His love and His Word.

> **¹¹These things have I spoken unto you, that my joy might remain [abide] in you, and that your joy might be full.**

Christ spoke "these things" (vv. 1-10) not to burden His disciples with unachievable standards and responsibilities, but that His own joy might abide in them and that their joy may be complete. His joy flowed from His eternal relationship with His Father (not from earthly circumstances), and that joy is perfect, complete, and unending. Similarly, our joy is full to the extent of our abiding relationship with Christ and our loving relationship (v. 12 below) with other believers.

C. Love others sacrificially, as Christ loved you.

> **¹²This is my commandment, That ye love one another, as I have loved you.**
> **¹³Greater love hath no man than this, that a man lay down his life for his friends.**

Using another "just as" comparison, Christ commands us to love other believers as perfectly, wholeheartedly, unconditionally, and continuously as He loves us. The hallmark of such love is willing self-sacrifice for one another. He set the standard and illustrated such love by dying for us — in our place and for our benefit. To the same degree, we should put the interests and benefits of other believers above our own.

IV. Christ's friendship gives purpose to His branches.

A. We show our friendship through obedience to Him.

> **¹⁴Ye are my friends, if ye do whatsoever I command you.**

B. He shows His friendship by revealing God to us.

> **¹⁵Henceforth I call you not servants; for the servant knoweth not what his lord doeth: but I have called you friends; for all things that I have heard of my Father I have made known unto you.**

Friendship with Christ goes far beyond a master-servant relationship. Although He remained the Master of His disciples and they remained His servants, He elevated their (and our) relationship with Him to that of intimate friendship. Such friendship is based on selfless love and includes mutual giving and receiving. We lovingly give to Christ primarily though ready and willing obedience to His commands (v. 14) and seeking to please Him. Among the gifts we receive from Him are His revelations of God's person and will (v. 15), which He progressively gives us through God's Word and His Holy Spirit. The more fully we receive and understand His revelation, the more we will seek to fulfill His desires and commands, and the more we will treasure our friendship with Him.

V. Christ's will gives direction to His branches.

    A. Bear eternal fruit for God.

        ¹⁶ᵃYe have not chosen me, but I have chosen you, and ordained you, that ye should go and bring forth fruit, and that your fruit should remain:

    B. Claim His promises in prayer.

        ¹⁶ᵇthat whatsoever ye shall ask of the Father in my name, he may give it you.

    C. Love one another.

        ¹⁷These things I command you, that ye love one another.

In conclusion, Christ summarized some of the principal requirements for (and also the fruits of) abiding in Him. Each of these is a command in its own right (v. 17) that is impossible to keep without abiding in Him. He has ordained us for His service (v. 16a), has given us the resources to perform it (v. 16b), and has provided fellow believers for our mutual encouragement and fellowship (v. 17). Our progress in these crucial areas is a measure of our progress in abiding in Him.

Other Pictures of Spiritual Fruit

The nature of any fruit is determined by the kind of seed that is sown. Similarly, the quantity and the quality of that fruit are determined by the care and nourishment the seedling receives. So it is in the spiritual realm. What is sown is reaped, is reaped in abundance, and is reaped for eternity. The following pictures of spiritual fruit, and of the seeds that produce it, illustrate some of the ways we should or should not bear fruit. (Most of these passages are also included under other topics, as indicated.)

    I. Salvation produces good fruit, and many-fold.

        A. The fruit of repentance and conversion.

            LK 3:8 Bring forth therefore fruits worthy of [consistent with] repentance, and begin not to say within yourselves, We have Abraham to [as] our father: for I say unto you, That God is able of these stones to raise up children unto Abraham.

        B. The fruit of abundant spiritual life.

            MT 13:23 But he that received seed [God's Word] into the good ground is he that heareth the word, and understandeth it; which also beareth fruit, and bringeth forth, some an hundredfold, some sixty, some thirty.

C. The fruit of the Spirit within one's life.

LK 8:15 . . . the good ground are they, which in an honest and good heart, having heard the word, keep it, and bring forth fruit with patience.

In LK 3, John the Baptist challenged the Pharisees to produce spiritual fruit in their lives that would evidence repentance from sin and saving faith in God, as did Abraham. (See Sec. V on p. 386.) Christ used a similar analogy in His parable of the seed and the soils. Matthew's account highlights the abundance of that fruit; Luke focuses on the nature and quality of that fruit, especially as they relate to the believer's character and conduct. (See Sec. IV.D on p. 409.)

II. Evangelism yields eternal fruit, with rewards for its reapers.

JN 4:35 Say not ye, There are yet four months, and then cometh harvest? behold, I say unto you, Lift up your eyes, and look on the fields; for they are white already to harvest.

³⁶And he that reapeth receiveth wages, and gathereth fruit unto life eternal: that both he that soweth and he that reapeth may rejoice together.

The fruit gathered "unto life eternal" includes both (1) the souls that are "harvested" unto eternal salvation through the diligent efforts of God's workers and (2) the eternal rewards and eternal rejoicing that both sowers and reapers will experience as God honors their faithful labors. In many of God's fields, others have already sown the seed of the gospel. The harvest is ready, and reapers are urgently needed to bring in the sheaves. (See Sec. VIII on p. 6.)

III. Self-denial brings abundant fruit that remains forever.

JN 12:24 Verily, verily, I say unto you, Except a corn [kernel] of wheat fall into the ground and die, it abideth alone: but if it die, it bringeth forth much fruit.

²⁵He that loveth his life shall lose it; and he that hateth his life in this world shall keep it unto life eternal.

By dying in the ground of self-denial and self-sacrifice, a believer will "bring forth much fruit." This includes the fruit of the Spirit in his own life, the fruit of salvation in others' lives, and the fruit of eternal rewards in the next life.

IV. The mouth bears definitive fruit that reveals the heart.

MT 12:33 Either make [consider] the tree good, and his fruit good; or else make [consider] the tree corrupt, and his fruit corrupt: for the tree is known by his fruit.

³⁴O generation of vipers, how can ye, being evil, speak good things? for out of the abundance of the heart the mouth speaketh.

In rebuking the Pharisees who accused Him of serving Satan, Christ declared that one cannot consider a tree "corrupt" if its fruit is "good," or vice versa (v. 33). Both must be either one or the other. Because the fruit of Christ's ministry was genuinely good (which the Pharisees could not deny), then He Himself was "good" and was who He claimed to be. He added that a critical fruit by which anyone can be evaluated is the fruit of his mouth. That fruit invariably will soon reveal the true condition of his heart, whether it is good or bad (v. 34). (See Sec. VII on p. 444.)

> V. Worldly cares prevent fruit, by choking its growth.
> **MK 4:7 And some [seed] fell among thorns, and the thorns grew up, and choked it, and it yielded no fruit. . . .**
> **¹⁸And these are they which are sown among thorns; such as hear the word,**
> **¹⁹And the cares of this world, and the deceitfulness of riches, and the lusts of other things entering in, choke the word, and it becometh unfruitful.**

In the parable of the seed and the soils, some people initially responded to God's Word with seeming new life and growth. The "thorns," however, of worldly lusts and materialism (which were already present when the seed was sown) soon outgrew the effects of the good seed and choked it to the point of preventing it from bearing any visible fruit. In such cases, only God knows whether the fruit of salvation ever occurred. Others can only observe that the fruit of the Spirit and the fruit of obedient service are not evident in that life. If, by all appearances, there is no fruit, there probably is no life. (See Sec. IV.C on p. 409.)

> VI. False religion bears worthless fruit, to be chopped and burned.
> **MT 7:16 Ye shall know them [false prophets] by their fruits. Do men gather grapes of thorns, or figs of thistles?**
> **¹⁷Even so every good tree bringeth forth good fruit; but a corrupt tree bringeth forth evil [worthless, rotten] fruit.**
> **¹⁸A good tree cannot bring forth evil fruit, neither can a corrupt tree bring forth good fruit.**
> **¹⁹Every tree that bringeth not forth good fruit is hewn down, and cast into the fire.**
> **²⁰Wherefore by their fruits ye shall know them.**

False religion cannot produce any good fruit of any kind (v. 18). Regardless of what label it bears (including "Christian"), it can only produce thorns and thistles in the hearts and lives of its adherents and purveyors (v. 16). No matter how appealing its teachings and activities may appear, all of its fruit in God's sight is worthless and rotten to the core (v. 17). Verse 20 gives believers both the means and the responsibility for inspecting each professed prophet's fruit (e.g., his doctrine and his deeds) for determining whether that "tree" is good or corrupt. (See Sec. I on p. 383.)

VII. Israel lacked fruit and lost God's kingdom.

    A. Christ tended the tree, but it bore no fruit.

        LK 13:6 He spoke also this parable; A certain man had a fig tree planted in his vineyard; and he came and sought fruit thereon, and found none.

        ⁷Then said he unto the dresser [gardener] of his vineyard, Behold, these three years I come seeking fruit on this fig tree, and find none: cut it down; why cumbereth it the ground?

        ⁸And he answering said unto him, Lord, let it alone this year also, till I shall dig about it, and dung [fertilize] it:

        ⁹And if it bear fruit, well: and if not, then after that thou shalt cut it down.

    B. God gives His kingdom to those who bear its fruit.

        MT 21:42 Jesus saith unto them [the religious leaders], Did ye never read in the scriptures, The stone which the builders rejected, the same is become the head of the corner: this is the Lord's doing, and it is marvelous in our eyes?

        ⁴³Therefore say I unto you, The kingdom of God shall be taken from you, and given to a nation bringing forth the fruits thereof.

The parable of the fruitless fig tree is explained in Section IV on p. 4. Because Israel did not bear the fruits of repentance, salvation, godliness, and service that God desired and that Christ worked to obtain, the nation was "cut down" in terms of its role in God's kingdom during this age. That role (i.e., promoting His kingdom) has been taken from Israel and given to another "nation," which is Christ's church of all true believers. The church now is as responsible to bear God's desired fruit as Israel was previously. (See Sec. III on p. 58.)

The Groom and His Attendants

In the Old Testament, God pictured Israel as His wife. He told her, "thy Maker is thine husband" (Isa. 54:5). He loved her perfectly and faithfully provided everything she needed. She repeatedly, however, played the harlot and pursued other lovers. Israel's spiritual estrangement continued through Christ's time, and she forfeited her golden opportunity to be His bride. In God's eternal plan, therefore, Christ would marry another. On several occasions, He spoke of His coming wedding and of those who would participate in it. He left hidden, however, the identity of His bride — until He revealed it through His apostles after His ascension. The following passages picture Christ as the Groom and portray others involved in His wedding.

I. John the Baptist was the Groom's best man.

A. John was not the Groom but His herald.

JN 3:26 And they came unto John [the Baptist], and said unto him, Rabbi, he that was with thee beyond Jordan, to whom thou barest witness, behold, the same baptizeth, and all men come to him.
[27]John answered and said, A man can receive nothing, except it be given him from heaven.
[28]Ye yourselves bear me witness, that I said, I am not the Christ, but that I am sent before him.

Some of John's disciples noted that the crowds increasingly were following Jesus rather than John. His response in verse 27 implies: "I can only receive whatever ministry and followers God gives me." His answer also implies: "Any followers that Jesus receives are given to Him by God [and who can object to that?]." John's task was to herald the coming of the Messiah (v. 28) and to prepare the people to receive Him. That people were turning to Jesus indicated that John was fulfilling his task.

B. John rejoiced to be the Groom's friend.

[29]He that hath the bride is the bridegroom: but the friend of the bridegroom, which standeth and heareth him, rejoiceth greatly because of the bridegroom's voice: this my joy therefore is fulfilled.
[30]He must increase, but I must decrease.

John's goal was not to obtain a bride of his own but to see Christ receive His God-given bride. He rejoiced at the privilege (desired by Jews for centuries) of being in the Groom's presence and hearing His voice (v. 29). As the Groom's herald and "best man," John readily accepted the fact that Christ "must increase" in honor and attention and in receiving His bride, while he "must decrease," having fulfilled his role in God's plan for Christ's marriage.

Verse 29 is the only reference to Christ's bride in the Gospels. John does not explicitly identify the bride but suggests that she is comprised of those who in some special way belong to Christ. The epistles later reveal that Christ's bride is all those who believe in Him for salvation. Thus, believers are "married to another [rather than to a legalistic system], even to Him who is raised from the dead" (Rom. 7:4). Also, Christ and His church are likened to a husband and his wife in Ephesians 5:22-32. In the Gospels, however, the focus is on the Groom as He makes the preparations for His wedding.

II. Christ's disciples were His groomsmen.

A. They "ate and drank" while with the Groom.

LK 5:33 [MK 2:18] And they [the Jews] said unto him, Why do the disciples of John fast often, and make prayers, and likewise the disciples of the Pharisees; but thine eat and drink?

³⁴And he said unto them, Can ye make the children of the bridechamber [the groom's attendants] fast, while the bridegroom is with them? {As long as they have the bridegroom with them, they cannot fast.}

B. They would fast when He had left.

³⁵But the days will come, when the bridegroom shall be taken away from them, and then shall they fast in those days.

As the Groom's attendants who were helping with preparations for His wedding, Christ's disciples would not logically fast at that time (v. 34). Fasting was more a sign of sorrow or mourning; not something appropriate for a time of rejoicing while they were with the Groom. Alluding to His coming crucifixion and the sorrow it would bring His disciples, Christ said, "Then shall they fast" (v. 35).

III. Christ's guests will be at His marriage.

A. The King planned a marriage for His Son.

MT 22:1 And Jesus answered and spake unto them again by parables, and said,

²The kingdom of heaven is like unto a certain king, which made a marriage for his son,

B. Those notified before were asked to come first.

³And sent forth his servants to call them that were bidden to the wedding: and they would not come.

⁴Again, he sent forth other servants, saying, Tell them which are bidden, Behold, I have prepared my dinner: my oxen and my fatlings are killed, and all things are ready: come unto the marriage.

Jewish custom was to announce a wedding and invite the guests well in advance, and then "call" the same guests when "all things are ready" (v. 4). For about 2,000 years, God had notified the Jewish people of the Messiah's coming and urged them to prepare for it. Now the time had arrived, and God sent His servants (including John the Baptist and Christ's disciples) "to call them that were bidden to the wedding" (v. 3). But "they would not come."

C. They rejected the King's invitation and His messengers.

⁵But they made light of it, and went their ways, one to his farm, another to his merchandise:

⁶And the remnant took his servants, and entreated them spitefully, and slew them.

⁷But when the king heard thereof, he was wroth: and he sent forth his armies, and destroyed those murderers, and burned up their city.

Many of the Jews simply disregarded God's invitation and went about their business as usual (v. 5). Others, led by the religious leaders, were openly hostile to God's messengers and violently persecuted them. God, therefore, sent His armies (the Romans in A.D. 70) and "destroyed those murderers and burned up their city."

> D. The invitation was opened to all, both good and bad.
> **⁸Then saith he to his servants, The wedding is ready, but they which were bidden were not worthy.**
> **⁹Go ye therefore into the highways, and as many as ye shall find, bid to the marriage.**
> **¹⁰So those servants went out into the highways, and gathered together all as many as they found, both bad and good: and the wedding was furnished with guests.**

Because those bidden first "were not worthy," God extended His invitation to whoever could be found, both good and bad, far and wide (i.e., upright people and vile sinners; Jews and Gentiles). This time, many guests came and filled the King's banquet hall.

> E. Only those properly clothed may take part.
> **¹¹And when the king came in to see the guests, he saw there a man which had not on a wedding garment:**
> **¹²And he saith unto him, Friend, how camest thou in hither not having a wedding garment? And he was speechless.**
> **¹³Then said the king to the servants, Bind him hand and foot, and take him away, and cast him into outer darkness; there shall be weeping and gnashing of teeth.**
> **¹⁴For many are called, but few are chosen.**

These guests had been invited on short notice and did not have time to dress appropriately for the occasion. Although not stated, it is understood that the King provided a "wedding garment" to each one. This explains His expectation that every guest be properly attired, as well as the one guest's inability to justify his shortcoming. He evidently thought his own clothes were good enough and therefore declined the King's provision. As a result, he was "cast . . . into outer darkness."

Several Old Testament passages should have helped Christ's audience understand the nature of God's required wedding garments. For example, "He [God] hath clothed me with the garments of salvation, he hath covered me with the robe of righteousness, as a bridegroom decketh himself with ornaments, and as a bride adorneth herself with her jewels (Isa. 61:10). In contrast, our own "spiritual clothing" is completely unfit for God's presence. "All our righteousnesses are as filthy rags" (Isa. 64:6). Our only hope is to be clothed by God Himself with Christ's righteousness, which is received as a gift of God's grace through faith in His Son.

IV. The Groom still is coming for His marriage.

A. He is coming soon, but many are unprepared.

MT 25:1 Then shall the kingdom of heaven be likened unto ten virgins, which took their lamps, and went forth to meet the bridegroom. ²And five of them were wise, and five were foolish. ³They that were foolish took their lamps, and took no oil with them: ⁴But the wise took oil in their vessels with their lamps.

B. He has tarried a while but will suddenly appear.

⁵While the bridegroom tarried, they all slumbered and slept. ⁶And at midnight there was a cry made, Behold, the bridegroom cometh; go ye out to meet him.

The parable is from Christ's Olivet Discourse (see p. 423 ff) in which He foretells conditions on earth that will precede His return. Three key aspects of His coming are indicated here: (1) He will "tarry" for a time (almost 2,000 years now); (2) He will come suddenly when not expected ("at midnight"); and (3) He will receive only those who are ready to meet Him. (Comments here relate primarily to the coming Groom; the wise and foolish virgins are discussed in Sec. III on p. 436 ff.)

C. Each guest must prepare in advance.

⁷Then all those virgins arose, and trimmed their lamps. ⁸And the foolish said unto the wise, Give us of your oil; for our lamps are gone out. ⁹But the wise answered, saying, Not so; lest there be not enough for us and you: but go ye rather to them that sell, and buy for yourselves.

D. The Groom will judge who takes part in His wedding.

¹⁰And while they went to buy, the bridegroom came; and they that were ready went in with him to the marriage: and the door was shut. ¹¹Afterward came also the other virgins, saying, Lord, Lord, open to us. ¹²But he answered and said, Verily I say unto you, I know you not. ¹³Watch therefore, for ye know neither the day nor the hour wherein the Son of man cometh.

The door of opportunity to participate in Christ's marriage will be shut when He returns (v. 10). At His marriage feast in heaven (after the rapture of His church), believers in Christ will "be glad and rejoice, and give honor to Him:

for the marriage of the Lamb is come . . . Blessed are they which are called unto the marriage supper of the Lamb" (Rev. 19:7, 9).

V. The Groom will honor His faithful servants.
> **LK 12:35 Let your loins be girded about, and your lights burning;**
> **³⁶And ye yourselves like unto men that wait for their lord, when he will return from the wedding; that when he cometh and knocketh, they may open unto him immediately.**
> **³⁷Blessed are those servants, whom the lord when he cometh shall find watching: verily I say unto you, that he shall gird himself, and make them to sit down to meat, and will come forth and serve them.**
> **³⁸And if he shall come in the second watch, or come in the third watch, and find them so, blessed are those servants.**

The Groom will return to earth after His wedding in heaven (v. 36), and believers who had prepared for His coming will be honored in His kingdom. Though Christ will come as the majestic King of kings and Lord of lords, He will "gird Himself" as a servant (v. 37) and graciously serve those who were ready for His return.

Girding the loins in verse 35 refers to tieing up and tucking in the long, flowing robes worn in that day, so that the robes would not hinder rapid movement or energetic work. The command means, "Be unencumbered and fully prepared to meet your Lord." Similarly, "Let your lamps be burning" pictures His servants' continual readiness for His imminent return.

The Lord and His Brothers

"Brothers" in scripture may refer to (1) siblings or kinfolk, (2) friends and associates, (3) one's fellow man, or (4) spiritual kindred who are fellow children of God. Christ used each of these meanings on different occasions. Early in His ministry, such as in the Sermon on the Mount, He equated "brother" primarily with "friend" or "fellow man" (MT 5:22-24; 7:3-5). He began referring later to spiritual brothers, and did so increasingly as His departure drew near. This section focuses primarily on passages where "brother" pictures the spiritual kinship that believers have with their Savior and with each other.

I. True brothers share more than physical bonds.

A. Jesus had several physical brothers.
> **MT 13:54 [MK 6:1] And when he was come into his own country, he taught them in their synagogue, insomuch that they were astonished, and said, Whence hath this man this wisdom, and these mighty works?**

⁵⁵Is not this the carpenter's son? is not his mother called Mary? and his brethren, James, and Joses, and Simon, and Judas [Jude]?

⁵⁶And his sisters, are they not all with us? Whence then hath this man all these things?

⁵⁷And they were offended in him. But Jesus said unto them, A prophet is not without honour, save in his own country, {and among his own kin,} and in his own house.

B. His physical brothers were not His spiritual brothers.

JN 7:1 After these things Jesus walked in Galilee: for he would not walk in Jewry, because the Jews sought to kill him.

²Now the Jews' feast of tabernacles was at hand.

³His brethren therefore said unto him, Depart hence, and go into Judaea, that thy disciples also may see the works that thou doest.

⁴For there is no man that doeth any thing in secret, and he himself seeketh to be known openly. If thou do these things, shew thyself to the world.

⁵For neither did his brethren believe in him.

After Christ's virgin birth, Mary and Joseph had at least four sons (named in MT 13) and two or more daughters. Although His half-brothers and sisters observed His perfect sinless life firsthand (with its marked contrast to their own sinful nature), they did not believe He was the Messiah, the Son of God (JN 7). At least two of Christ's brothers, however, also became His spiritual brothers after His crucifixion. James became an apostle (Gal. 1:19) and authored the epistle bearing His name. Jude ("Judas" in MT 13:55) penned the book bearing his name, and identified himself as the brother of James. Neither author traded on his physical kinship to Christ; both humbly referred to themselves merely as His servants (v. 1 in each book).

II. Christ's brothers are those who do God's will.

MT 12:46 While he yet talked to the people, behold, his mother and his brethren stood without, desiring to speak with him.

⁴⁷Then one said unto him, Behold, thy mother and thy brethren stand without, desiring to speak with thee.

⁴⁸But he answered and said unto him that told him, Who is my mother? and who are my brethren?

⁴⁹And he stretched forth his hand toward his disciples, and said, Behold my mother and my brethren!

⁵⁰For whosoever shall do the will of my Father which is in heaven, the same is my brother, and sister, and mother.

LK 8:21b [the same occasion] My mother and my brethren are these which hear the word of God, and do it.

This is Christ's first major reference to His spiritual brothers. It followed the full rejection of His Messiahship by the national leaders (earlier in the same chapter) and accompanied His increasing call for individuals to enter a personal relationship with Him. ("Disciples" in v. 49 refers to all His earnest followers, not just the twelve.) At that point, to "do the will of my Father" (v. 50) was primarily to acknowledge Christ as the Messiah and to obey His teaching and the Mosaic law. Today, it is to trust in Christ as personal Savior, heed God's completed Word, and follow His Spirit's leading.

III. Christ further identified His spiritual brothers.

A. His disciples became His spiritual brethren.

JN 20:16 [On resurrection morn] Jesus saith unto her, Mary. She turned herself, and saith unto him, Rabboni; which is to say, Master. ⁱ⁷Jesus saith unto her, Touch me not; for I am not yet ascended to my Father: but go to my brethren, and say unto them, I ascend unto my Father, and your Father; and to my God, and your God.

MT 28:9 And as they [the women at His tomb] went to tell his disciples, behold, Jesus met them, saying, All hail. And they came and held him by the feet, and worshipped him. ¹⁰Then said Jesus unto them, Be not afraid: go tell my brethren that they go into Galilee, and there shall they see me.

Three days earlier, after the Last Supper, Christ had elevated the eleven from being primarily His "servants" to being His "friends" (JN 15:15). Now, following His resurrection, Christ referred to them for the first time specifically as "my brothers." They remained, of course, His servants and friends; but through His finished work on the cross, they received a deeper, family relationship with Him. God was now fully their "Father," they were His sons, and Christ was their divine brother. They did not at first comprehend the far-reaching implications of these exalted relationships. Indeed, it will take all eternity for any believer to appreciate fully the glorious position he holds as God's son and Christ's brother.

B. Every believer is Christ's spiritual brother.

MT 25:37 [When Christ judges the nations,] Then shall the righteous answer him, saying, Lord, when saw we thee an hungred, and fed thee? or thirsty, and gave thee drink? ³⁸When saw we thee a stranger, and took thee in? or naked, and clothed thee? ³⁹Or when saw we thee sick, or in prison, and came unto thee? ⁴⁰And the King shall answer and say unto them, Verily I say unto you, Inasmuch as ye have done it unto one of the least of these my brethren, ye have done it unto me.

Shortly before His death, Christ prophesied that, when He returns, He will separate His righteous sheep from the unrighteous goats. (See Sec. VIII on p. 444 ff for the full passage.) He will commend and reward these believers for their compassionate care of His "brethren" (v. 40) — their fellow believers, and particularly Jewish believers — who were suffering greatly during the Tribulation. Even "the least" among those who believe in Christ is His full-fledged spiritual brother.

IV. Believers are brothers to one another.

A. All believers are brothers through Christ.
MT 23:8 But be not ye called Rabbi ["honored teacher"]: for one is your Master [Teacher and Leader], even Christ; and all ye are brethren.

It logically follows that if Christ is the brother of every believer, then all believers are brothers of each other. Christ emphasized the reality and importance of that relationship, rather than leaving it merely implicit or theoretical. Verse 8 indicates that participation in that brotherhood depends on each member first making Christ his own Master. There is only one Master, but many brothers. Christ warned believers not to seek recognition and honor from one another, but humbly to love and serve Him and each other.

B. Faithful believers will gain many more brothers.
MK 10:28 Then Peter began to say unto him, Lo, we have left all, and have followed thee.
²⁹And Jesus answered and said, Verily I say unto you, There is no man that hath left house, or brethren, or sisters, or father, or mother, or wife, or children, or lands, for my sake, and the gospel's,
³⁰But he shall receive an hundredfold now in this time, houses, and brethren, and sisters, and mothers, and children, and lands, with persecutions; and in the world to come eternal life.

Though the members of a believer's physical family may desert him because of his faithful testimony for Christ, Jesus promised these believers that they will gain "an hundredfold" more brothers and spiritual family members who will fellowship with them in their faith and service. Further, these "brothers in Christ" will be gained "now in this time" (v. 30), and not only in heaven.

C. Strong believers should strengthen their brothers.
LK 22:31 And the Lord said, Simon, Simon, behold, Satan hath desired to have you, that he may sift you as wheat:
³²But I have prayed for thee, that thy faith fail not: and when thou art converted, strengthen thy brethren.

A few hours earlier, Christ told Peter he would deny Him three times. Here, He warns Peter that Satan desires to "sift [him] as wheat." Christ's prayer request for Peter (v. 32) may be understood: "I have prayed for you that your faith would not utterly fail; and when you have returned [to confessing me as the Son of God], strengthen your brothers [by strengthening their faith in me]."

    D. Offended believers should forgive and restore their brothers.

        MT 18:15 [To His disciples] Moreover if thy brother shall trespass against thee, go and tell him his fault between thee and him alone: if he shall hear thee, thou hast gained thy brother. . . .

        ²¹Then came Peter to him, and said, Lord, how oft shall my brother sin against me, and I forgive him? till seven times?

        ²²Jesus saith unto him, I say not unto thee, Until seven times: but, Until seventy times seven. . . .

        ³⁵So likewise shall my heavenly Father do also unto you [with firm discipline], if ye from your hearts forgive not every one his brother their trespasses.

Unity in God's family is crucial. God created that unity initially when He placed each believer in His family, but believers must work to maintain it (Eph. 4:3). Christ stressed, therefore, the necessity of forgiving trespasses (v. 35) and restoring broken relationships (v. 15) among believers. Unwillingness to do so will incur God's chastisement and withheld blessing. (See Sec. III on p. 215.)

    V. Believers are brothers as children of God.

        A. Those who receive God's Son are born into God's family.

        JN 1:11 He came unto his own, and his own received him not.

        ¹²But as many as received him, to them gave he power [the right] to become the sons of God, even to them that believe on his name:

        ¹³Which were born, not of blood, nor of the will of the flesh, nor of the will of man, but of God.

To receive Christ as Savior requires a voluntary, submissive act of the will (v. 12). The ultimate will behind our receiving Christ, however, is that of God Himself who works within us to draw us to Christ (v. 13). He alone produces our spiritual birth and places us in His family as His son and as Christ's brothers. (See Sec. I on p. 81.)

        B. Those who reflect God's nature are "the children of [their] Father."

        MT 5:44 But I say unto you, Love your enemies, bless them that curse you, do good to them that hate you, and pray for them which despitefully use you, and persecute you;

        ⁴⁵That ye may be the children of your Father which is in heaven: for he maketh his sun to rise on the evil and on the good, and sendeth rain on the just and on the unjust.

LK 6:35 But love ye your enemies, and do good, and lend, hoping for nothing again; and your reward shall be great, and ye shall be the children of the Highest: for he is kind unto the unthankful and to the evil.

For a believer to present a clear picture of godly character and behavior to those around him, he must live as Christ would live and do what He would do. The most telling of such actions and responses are those shown toward "enemies" and "them that hate you" (v. 44). Right responses will demonstrate outwardly what is true inwardly, namely, that the godly believer is a child of his Father in heaven, who is kind even to unjust and evil despisers of His grace.

C. Those who spread God's peace are "the children of God."

MT 5:9 Blessed are the peacemakers: for they shall be called the children of God.

True "peacemakers" not only promote peace among men on earth, but also peace between men and their Creator in heaven. (Christ's next statement was: "Blessed are they which are persecuted for righteousness' sake," clearly including those persecuted for sharing the gospel of peace with the opponents of God.) Such peacemakers will be known among men as "children of God." More importantly, God Himself will acknowledge and honor them as His own children.

D. Those who believe God's Word are His children forever.

LK 20:34 [MT 22:29] And Jesus answering said unto them, {Ye do err, not knowing the scripture, nor the power of God.} The children of this world marry, and are given in marriage:
[35]But they which shall be accounted worthy to obtain that [future] world, and the resurrection from the dead, neither marry {in the resurrection}, nor are given in marriage:
[36]Neither can they die any more: for they are equal unto the angels; and are the children of God, being the children of the resurrection.

In refuting the Sadducees' attempt to discredit the Biblical doctrine of resurrection, Christ confirmed that believers who die will be raised from the dead, never to "die any more." (See Sec. I on p. 440 ff for the full passage.) God will then elevate His children even beyond their present lofty status as Christ's brothers. They will be "glorified together" with Christ as "heirs of God and joint heirs with Christ" (Rom. 8:17), ruling and reigning with Him in His glorious millennial kingdom.

8

Character Sketches of True Believers

(From the Sermon on the Mount)

The Sermon on the Mount is called the greatest of all sermons. It was the first of Christ's major recorded addresses, and it previewed the principal themes He developed throughout His ministry. In it, Christ crystallized the essence of Old Testament precepts and expanded them as elevated standards of personal godliness. It also contains a collage of sketches and vignettes that illustrate many of the issues, choices, and results involved in living as a true believer. Many of these sketches are included in the following pages; others are shown in other chapters.

Jesus of Nazareth is the only person who fully met the perfect standards of righteousness and love He presents here. He requires, however, that His followers evidence, and to an increasing degree, these essential traits and patterns of conduct. Christ pictured true believers as good trees that bear good fruit, and unbelievers as corrupt trees with bad fruit. To distinguish between them, He declared: "By their fruits ye shall know them" (MT 7:20).

Christ most likely preached variations of His principal messages to different audiences in different locales. Although the material varies, many commentators consider the Sermon on the Mount in MT 5-7 and the shorter account in LK 6 to be from the same sermon. The two accounts are presented here, therefore, as a conflation, combining both into one text. Luke's wording is in braces ({ . . . }) when inserted in Matthew's text.

Sketches of Blessed Believers

The principal thrust of being "blessed" in the Bible is that of being "spiritually prosperous." It includes (1) true happiness and joy that do not depend on external circumstances and (2) a flourishing productive life, measured in terms of spiritual values. Christ made it clear that only an obedient believer who is trusting fully in God's guidance and provision can be spiritually prosperous. Beginning with the Beatitudes (below), He sketched the basic profiles of such believers. Later in the message, He filled in many of their features in greater detail. Thus, blessed believers will evidence the following essential traits.

I. They focus on spiritual needs and eternal values.

A. They are keenly aware of their spiritual poverty.
MT 5:3 Blessed are the poor in spirit [the spiritually impoverished]: for theirs is the kingdom of heaven.
⁴Blessed are they that mourn [for their spiritual condition]: for they shall be comforted.
⁵Blessed are the meek [the humble and gentle]: for they shall inherit the earth.

The first step toward spiritual prosperity is an honest recognition of our abject spiritual poverty apart from God (v. 3). This includes a candid admission of our complete inability to improve our standing before God in our own strength. When accompanied by humble contrition (v. 4) for having gone our own selfish and rebellious way, God's forgiveness, restoration, and comfort — the beginnings of spiritual prosperity — immediately follow.

B. They "hunger and thirst" to be godly.
⁶Blessed are they which do hunger and thirst after righteousness: for they shall be filled.

Believers become increasingly prosperous in their spirit as they earnestly hunger and thirst to be righteous in God's eyes. God declared them eternally righteous in Christ at the moment of their salvation, and He works thereafter to create within them both the yearning and the ability to become increasingly righteous in their daily lives. Christ promised that such hunger and thirst will be fully satisfied.

II. They reflect God's character in their lives.
⁷Blessed are the merciful: for they shall obtain mercy.
⁸Blessed are the pure in heart: for they shall see God.
⁹Blessed are the peacemakers: for they shall be called the children of God.

As blessed believers are *filled* by God (v. 6), they become more *like* God. They continually receive God's undeserved mercy and thus should show mercy to others, including to the undeserving. They were made pure by God's forgiveness of their sin at salvation, and they should seek to be pure in both heart and life as they walk with God each day. They have both peace *with* God and the peace *of* God, and they should share and promote such peace in the lives of others. As they increasingly evidence these godly traits, God will multiply their spiritual prosperity abundantly.

III. They bear persecution for Christ's sake.

A. They willingly bear His reproach.

¹⁰Blessed are they which are persecuted for righteousness' sake: for theirs is the kingdom of heaven.

¹¹Blessed are ye, when men shall revile you, and persecute you, {and when they shall separate you from their company, and shall reproach you,} and shall say all manner of evil against you falsely, for my sake.

B. They anticipate the joy that will follow.

¹²Rejoice {in that day, and leap for joy}, and be exceeding glad: for great is your reward in heaven: for so persecuted they the prophets which were before you.

To many of those present, Christ's "revolutionary" message must have breached the limits of credibility when He ascribed blessing to those being hated and persecuted for His sake. The Jews generally believed that the more one exhibited prescribed religious behavior, the more honor and commendation he should receive. They must have thought, "What kind of righteousness results in persecution; and how can persecution bring blessing, and particularly joy?" Only the "poor in spirit" and "pure in heart" who are meek, merciful, and peaceable can understand this seeming contradiction. They will receive God's blessing in the midst of persecution (v. 11), and even more so in heaven (v. 12).

IV. They trust God for all the needs of life.

A. They trust Him through trials and troubles.

LK 6:20 And he lifted up his eyes on his disciples, and said, Blessed be ye poor: for yours is the kingdom of God.

²¹Blessed are ye that hunger now: for ye shall be filled. Blessed are ye that weep now: for ye shall laugh.

Blessed believers continually rely on God to meet their needs and overcome their difficulties. The blessed *poor* disciples in Luke's account (v. 20) include those who forgo earthly goods and comfort to follow and serve Christ. God not only obligates Himself to feed these believers, but He makes them full beneficiaries of His kingdom. "Ye that weep now" (v. 21) include those who grieve over things that displease God, whether failures and weaknesses in their own lives and in others' lives, or sinful conditions in the world at large. Their response will be as joyous laughter when God ultimately makes all things right.

   B. They trust Him for their physical needs.

   MT 6:31 Therefore take no thought [be not anxious or worried], saying, What shall we eat? or, What shall we drink? or, Wherewithal shall we be clothed?

   [32](For after all these things do the Gentiles seek:) for your heavenly Father knoweth that ye have need of all these things.

   [33]But seek ye first the kingdom of God, and his righteousness; and all these things shall be added unto you.

By giving God, His kingdom, and His righteousness first priority in their lives, believers can confidently expect that God will provide all their physical necessities. Unbelievers ("the Gentiles" in v. 32) spend virtually all of their time and effort seeking more and more of these earthly things. Believers should not be like them, but rely instead on the One who knows what they need and wants to bless them by providing it. (For the full passage, MT 6:19-34, see "Your Master" on p. 250.)

V. They worship God sincerely and "in secret."

   A. They give in secret and are blessed openly.

   MT 6:1 Take heed that ye do not your alms before men, to be seen of them: otherwise ye have no reward of your Father which is in heaven. . . .

   [3]But when thou doest alms, let not thy left hand know what thy right hand doeth:

   [4]That thine alms may be in secret: and thy Father which seeth in secret himself shall reward thee openly.

   B. They pray in secret and are blessed openly.

   MT 6:6 But thou, when thou prayest, enter into thy closet, and when thou hast shut thy door, pray to thy Father which is in secret; and thy Father which seeth in secret shall reward thee openly.

   C. They fast in secret and are blessed openly.

   MT 6:17 But thou, when thou fastest, anoint thine head, and wash thy face;

   [18]That thou appear not unto men to fast, but unto thy Father which is in secret: and thy Father, which seeth in secret, shall reward thee openly.

God promises to bless every believer who worships Him humbly and sincerely. True worship flows from the "secret" recesses of the heart and is never performed to impress others. God rewards such worship in many ways — some "openly" and publicly, and others "secretly" and privately. (For a fuller discussion of the passage, see Sec. I on pp. 163-164.)

VI. They build their lives on a rock, not on sand.

A. They submit to the lordship of Christ.

LK 6:46 And why call ye me, Lord, Lord, and do not the things which I say?

B. Their obedience to His Word provides a firm foundation.

MT 7:24 [LK 6:47] Therefore whosoever heareth these sayings of mine, and doeth them, I will liken him unto a wise man, which built his house {and digged deep, and laid the foundation} upon a rock:

C. They withstand all assaults on their faith.

25And the rain descended, and the floods came, and the winds blew, and beat {vehemently} upon that house {and could not shake it}; and it fell not: for it was founded upon a rock.

D. Foolish people build without God's foundation.

26And every one that heareth these sayings of mine, and doeth them not, shall be likened unto a foolish man, which built his house {without a foundation} upon the sand:

E. The storms of life bring their fall and ruin.

27And the rain descended, and the floods came, and the winds blew, and beat {vehemently} upon that house; and {immediately} it fell: and great was the fall {and the ruin} of it.

Both the wise man and the foolish man *heard* Christ's message. The difference was in how they *responded* to it. The wise man implemented Christ's teaching; the foolish man ignored it. The difference between them was not whether they professed to follow Christ, because LK 6:46 suggests that both builders called Him "Lord." Only the obedient builder's *house* (his entire spiritual life) was blessed with stability, safety, and security when the storms of life assailed it.

This parable applies as much, if not more, to each believer's ongoing obedience as it does to his initial salvation. Erring believers who fail to heed God's Word are building on sand in some respects as unbelievers are. Like the foolish man, they too will suffer the consequences of wrong responses and wrong choices. In contrast, obedient believers who are "doers of the Word, and not hearers only" can withstand the stormy trials of life. They are firmly founded on the Rock of Christ and His unfailing Word.

The Old Way and the New
(MT 5:17-48; LK 5:36-39)

Christ often contrasted the "new way" of salvation and life that He was offering to the "old way" of religious ritual to which the people had become accustomed. Initially, the old way (the Old Covenant God made with Israel through Moses) was good and perfect. The problem was that no one was able to live up to its standard of perfect holiness and righteous behavior. Worse yet, the religious leaders of Christ's day had so thoroughly perverted the old way that it no longer represented what God originally intended. They gutted the moral heart of the law and effectively legalized much of the wrong behavior God had prohibited. In the process, they made their version of the old way even more difficult to keep by adding to it a multitude of picayune regulations. Much of the Sermon on the Mount, therefore, deals with the major differences between the Jews' "old way" and Christ's "new way" of salvation and life.

I. Christ fulfilled the "Old" Covenant, and introduced the "New."

A. He met all of the Old Covenant's requirements.

MT 5:17 Think not that I am come to destroy the law, or the prophets: I am not come to destroy, but to fulfil.

¹⁸For verily I say unto you, Till heaven and earth pass, one jot or one tittle [the smallest letter and part of a letter] shall in no wise pass from the law, till all be fulfilled.

"The law and the prophets" refers to the Old Testament (the Old Covenant). Christ fulfilled that Covenant in four major respects. First, He met all of its requirements for personal holiness and righteous behavior — and did so perfectly every day of His life. He had no sin of His own, therefore, that separated Him from God. Second, as our perfect substitute, He voluntarily paid the law's prescribed penalty of death for every person who ever sinned. Third, He completed the revelation of God's essence and of His love for mankind, including God's plan for our salvation. Fourth, as the Messiah whose coming was foretold throughout the Old Testament, He fulfilled its prophecies, including establishing the "New Covenant" that God promised in Jeremiah 31:31.

B. God's moral laws in the Old are included in the New.

¹⁹Whosoever therefore shall break one of these least commandments, and shall teach men so, he shall be called the least in the kingdom of heaven: but whosoever shall do and teach them, the same shall be called great in the kingdom of heaven.

Although Christ's "new way" replaced the Old Covenant after His passion and ascension, the moral principles on which the Old was based are eternal. The

Beatitudes that precede the above passage and the "new" standards of right-eousness that follow it (beginning in Sec. III below) are based on those eternal principles. Present-day believers are to "do and teach them" (v. 19), as were Old Testament believers.

C. The New demands more than was achievable under the Old.
²⁰For I say unto you, That except your righteousness shall exceed the righteousness of the scribes and Pharisees, ye shall in no case enter into the kingdom of heaven.

The only way a person's righteousness can "exceed that of the scribes and Pharisees" is if he abandons the old way of trying to earn his salvation by keep-ing God's laws, and comes Christ's new way by accepting His perfect righteous as a gift of God by faith. (The full revelation of Christ's new way came later, after His ascension.)

II. The New Way is brand new material, not just a patch for the Old.

A. New salvation requires a whole new garment.
LK 5:36 And he spake also a parable unto them; No man putteth a piece of a new garment upon an old; if otherwise, then both the new maketh a rent, and the piece that was taken out of the new agreeth not with the old.

B. New faith must reside in a new vessel.
³⁷And no man putteth new wine into old bottles [old wineskins]; else the new wine will burst the bottles, and be spilled, and the bottles shall perish.
³⁸But new wine must be put into new bottles; and both are preserved.

This parable helps explain both why and how a true believer's righteousness must exceed that of the scribes and Pharisees. The "why" is that the New is incompatible with the Old, and mixing them will only make matters worse. The "how" is that the New must be placed in a "whole new vessel," a converted heart. This way, "both are preserved," and forever.

C. Many prefer the Old Way of working for salvation.
³⁹No man also having drunk old wine straightway [immediately] desireth new: for he saith, The old is better.

Those addicted to the old way typically will not leave it immediately or easily in favor of the New. In their mind, "The old is better." This was borne out by the very small number of Pharisees that believed in Christ while He ministered on earth. Even the general populace was so accus-tomed to the old way that it took a mighty working of God's Holy Spirit after Christ's ascension to persuade very many of them to leave the old way for the New.

The above parable also illustrates why the Jews' old standards of behavior (addressed individually in the following sections) are unacceptable to God and must be replaced by new and higher standards of godliness (that are achievable only through Christ).

III. The Old forbids murder; the New, anger also.

A. Anger is tantamount to murder and warrants similar punishment.
MT 5:21 Ye have heard that it was said by them of old time, Thou shalt not kill; and whosoever shall kill shall be in danger of the judgment [punishment by death]:
²²But I say unto you, That whosoever is angry with his brother without a cause shall be in danger of the judgment: and whosoever shall say to his brother, Raca [you empty head!], shall be in danger of the council [a death sentence by the highest court]: but whosoever shall say, Thou fool, shall be in danger of hell fire.

B. Conflicts among believers negate their worship of God.
²³Therefore if thou bring thy gift to the altar, and there rememberest that thy brother hath ought [any grievance] against thee;
²⁴Leave there thy gift before the altar, and go thy way; first be reconciled to thy brother, and then come and offer thy gift.

C. Conflicts must be resolved quickly before they get out of control.
²⁵Agree [settle] with thine adversary quickly, whiles thou art in the way with him; lest at any time the adversary deliver thee to the judge, and the judge deliver thee to the officer, and thou be cast into prison.
²⁶Verily I say unto thee, Thou shalt by no means come out thence, till thou hast paid the uttermost farthing [the last cent].

Those "of old time" (ancient religious leaders) rightly quoted God's commandment against murder. They, and those in Christ's day, however, did not take the commandment far enough. They left it unsaid that the sinful anger that leads to hatred and murderous thoughts is tantamount to murder in God's sight. Christ emphasized the spirit of God's commands, in contrast to the Jew's efforts to interpret them either as narrowly or as permissively as possible, depending upon their own desires in each case. Hence, Christ urged that conflicts be settled promptly lest they result in broken fellowship both with a brother and with God Himself (v. 24) and bring serious, long-term harm to ourself (v. 25).

IV. The Old bans adultery; the New, lust as well.

   A. Lust commits adultery in the heart.

     [27]Ye have heard that it was said by them of old time, Thou shalt not commit adultery:

     [28]But I say unto you, That whosoever looketh on a woman to lust after her hath committed adultery with her already in his heart.

   B. It is better to lose a part of your body than all of it.

     [29]And if thy right eye offend thee [draws you into sin], pluck it out, and cast it from thee: for it is profitable for thee that one of thy members should perish, and not that thy whole body should be cast into hell.

     [30]And if thy right hand offend thee, cut it off, and cast it from thee: for it is profitable for thee that one of thy members should perish, and not that thy whole body should be cast into hell.

Again, the Jews correctly quoted God's commandment against adultery, but they did not properly interpret and apply it. "Looking with lust" is committing adultery "already in the heart" (v. 28). Christ's prescribed cure in verses 29-30 in most cases is not to be taken literally because He just said the real problem is in the heart, not in the body. Because of the seriousness of the offense, however, (in thought as well as deed), drastic preventive action is necessary by those so tempted. Cut yourself off, therefore, from the source of temptation. Avoid it, discard it, destroy it — whatever is necessary to overcome it.

   V. The Old allows divorce; the New requires greater fidelity.

     [31]It hath been said, Whosoever shall put away his wife, let him give her a writing [certificate] of divorcement:

     [32]But I say unto you, That whosoever shall put away his wife, saving for the cause of fornication [her infidelity]), causeth [encourages] her to commit adultery: and whosoever shall marry her that is divorced committeth adultery.

The Jews seized upon Moses' narrowly-worded exception to the permanence of marriage in Deuteronomy 24:1-4 and interpreted it to permit divorce for any reason. Christ here corrects their evil interpretation. Later, He put God's original command and Moses' regulation in their proper light, saying, "For the hardness of your heart he [Moses] wrote you this precept. . . . What therefore God hath joined together, let not man put asunder" (MK 10:5-9). (See Sec.II on p. 237.)

VI. The Old accepts broken vows; the New demands integrity.

A. The Jews devised vows to evade their commitments.

³³Again, ye have heard that it hath been said by them of old time, Thou shalt not forswear [perjure] thyself, but shalt perform unto the Lord thine oaths:

³⁴But I say unto you, Swear not at all; neither by heaven; for it is God's throne:

³⁵Nor by the earth; for it is his footstool: neither by Jerusalem; for it is the city of the great King.

³⁶Neither shalt thou swear by thy head, because thou canst not make one hair white or black.

B. God requires complete truthfulness.

³⁷But let your communication be, Yea, yea; Nay, nay: for whatsoever is more than these cometh of evil.

As with divorce, the Jews created gaping loopholes in God's laws regarding the sanctity of vows (i.e., of keeping solemn promises). They cleverly differentiated between vows sworn "unto the Lord" (v. 33), which had to be kept, and those invoking another name or place, which could be evaded (see MT 23:16-22). Christ cut through their system of subterfuge and commanded: "Let your `yes' be yes and your `no' be no — period!"

VII. The Old permits revenge; the New seeks peaceful relationships.

A. The Old Way gets even; the New "turns the other cheek."

³⁸Ye have heard that it hath been said, An eye for an eye, and a tooth for a tooth:

³⁹But I say unto you, That ye resist not evil: but whosoever shall smite thee on thy right cheek, turn to him the other also.

B. The New Way is kind, and "goes the extra mile."

⁴⁰And if any man will sue thee at the law, and take away thy coat, let him have thy cloak also.

⁴¹And whosoever shall compel thee to go a mile, go with him twain.

⁴²Give to him that asketh thee, and from him that would borrow of thee turn not thou away.

Again, the Pharisees twisted God's original command in Exodus 21:22-25, which gave instructions to judges in civil proceedings for meting out punishment commensurate with each offense (v. 38). The Jews wrongly used that command as an excuse for *personal* revenge and retribution, which God specifically prohibited. Christ not only corrected their faulty thinking but went much further. He called for responses of kindness, gentleness, forbearance, and even generosity to those who abused them.

VIII. The Old perpetuates enmity; the New requires love.

A. Love your enemies and seek their good.

⁴³Ye have heard that it hath been said, Thou shalt love thy neighbor, and hate thine enemy.

⁴⁴But I say unto you, Love your enemies, bless them that curse you, do good to them that hate you, and pray for them which despitefully use you, and persecute you;

B. Do so because that is how God treats them.

⁴⁵That ye may be the children of your Father which is in heaven: for he maketh his sun to rise on the evil and on the good, and sendeth rain on the just and on the unjust.

C. Otherwise, you are no better than despised sinners.

⁴⁶For if ye love them which love you, what reward have ye? do not even the publicans [tax collectors] {and sinners} the same?

⁴⁷And if ye salute your brethren only, what do ye more than others? do not even the publicans so?

Up to this point, Christ's criticism of the "old way" dealt with commands that either were rightly quoted but too narrowly applied (III-IV above) or that were both misquoted and wrongly applied (V-VII above). In verse 43, He addresses their so-called "command" that was little more than a man-made fabrication to permit classifying anyone as an enemy and treating him accordingly.

The Jews gave their spurious command a semblance of validity by incorporating into it "love thy neighbor" from Leviticus 19:18. That verse, however, teaches just the opposite of "hate your enemy." It reads: "Thou shalt not avenge, nor bear any grudge against the children of thy people, but thou shalt love thy neighbor as thyself: I am the Lord." (See "The Golden Rule" on p. 150.)

IX. New life in Christ fulfills God's eternal law.

⁴⁸Be ye therefore perfect, even as your Father which is in heaven is perfect.

This command may be understood: "Be complete in your spirit and character, just as your heavenly Father is complete in all of His being." It summarizes the entire "Old Law" as God intended it to be understood and practiced. In it, Christ combined two "old" commands: "Thou shalt be perfect with [before] the Lord thy God" (Deut. 18:13), and "Ye shall be holy: for I the Lord your God am holy" (Lev. 19:2). He did not mean that sinless perfection is achievable in this life, but that God's children should always pursue godliness as their goal. Every believer should live as "the children of your Father which is in heaven" (v. 45).

Applying the Golden Rule

Israel in Christ's time seethed with animosity and strife. The Jews hated the Romans, despised the Samaritans, and scorned the Gentiles. Religious Jews shunned secular Jews and abhorred "publicans and sinners." The Pharisees, Sadducees, and Herodians disliked and distrusted each other; and Judeans disdained Galileans. Into this cauldron, Christ introduced the Golden Rule with its preamble "Love your enemies . . . bless them that curse you." His message reflected timeless Old Testament principles, but not the way they were being taught and practiced. To the Jews, Christ was prescribing an entirely new way of thinking and behaving.

Christ did not give the Golden Rule in isolation or without clear guidelines for how it should be applied. LK 6:27-38 (presented below) gives both its expanded content and its expansive context. These are pictured in the many applications that accompany it, and they apply to every relationship and circumstance — not just those we wish to cultivate or exploit. The foundation for the Golden Rule is the love that God extended to us while we were still *His* enemies. He demonstrated that love as His first step in reconciling us to Himself. We should show similar love to "our enemies" and seek to be reconciled with them. As we do so, Christ declared, "ye shall be the children of the Highest."

I. Show God's love to those who oppose you.

    A. Reflect God's goodness to those who hate you.
        LK 6:27 But I say unto you which hear, Love your enemies, do good to them which hate you,

    B. Pray God's blessing on those who revile you.
        [28]Bless them that curse you, and pray for them which despitefully use you.

    C. Extend God's grace to those who abuse you.
        [29]And unto him that smiteth thee on the one cheek offer also the other; and him that taketh away thy cloak forbid not to take thy coat also.
        [30]Give to every man that asketh of thee; and of him that taketh away thy goods ask them not again.

The principal characteristic of genuine love is that it gives generously and unselfishly, expecting nothing in return. The ultimate test of such love is how it responds to those who treat it with contempt and hatred. God's love for us is never diminished or withdrawn because of our failure to respond in kind to His overtures. Our love for others should be equally enduring and unshakable, even to those who mistreat us. Humanly, there are limits (too often with low thresholds) to the abuse we will bear before angrily rejecting the abuser. Christ commanded, however, not that we raise these thresholds, but that we remove them altogether. We can only do so sincerely, effectively, and consistently as we permit Him to duplicate His own loving responses in and through us.

Christ personally demonstrated each of the above expressions of unselfish love throughout His ministry — including under the most extreme circumstances just before His death. Thus, He restored the severed ear of an assailant in the garden (LK 22:51); He took the slaps to His face when condemned by the Sanhedrin (MK 14:65); He prayed on the cross for His killers' forgiveness, while soldiers took His garments (LK 23:34); and He gave salvation to the thief who earlier reviled Him (LK 23:43).

II. Follow this Rule in all relationships.

A. Treat everyone as you would like to be treated.
LK 6:31 And as ye would that men should do to you, do ye also to them likewise.

B. This is the essence of God's law.
MT 7:12 Therefore all things whatsoever ye would that men should do to you, do ye even so to them: for this is the law and the prophets.

The Golden Rule is commonly quoted as "Do unto others as you would have them do unto you." This closely approximates the wording in both Luke and Matthew. Note, however, the important addition in Matthew regarding the Rule's basis and authority — "for this is the law and the prophets." The Golden Rule encapsules all of the Old Testament's teaching regarding our attitudes toward and relationships with everyone else.

III. Do good even to those who do not reciprocate.

A. Be kind and generous to all.
LK 6:32 For if ye love them which love you, what thank have ye? for sinners also love those that love them.
33And if ye do good to them which do good to you, what thank have ye? for sinners also do even the same.
34And if ye lend to them of whom ye hope to receive, what thank have ye? for sinners also lend to sinners, to receive as much again.

B. Treat others as God treats both them and you.
35But love ye your enemies, and do good, and lend, hoping for nothing again; and your reward shall be great, and ye shall be the children of the Highest: for he is kind unto the unthankful and to the evil.
36Be ye therefore merciful, as your Father also is merciful.

Even most "sinners" repay kindness for kindness. Where their kind responses end, however, a believer's kindness should be only beginning. Our example and standard is our Heavenly Father, who "is kind to the unthankful and the evil" (v. 35). Thus, our motivation for practicing the Golden Rule is not to get what we want from others, but to be as much like our Heavenly Father as possible and in that way represent Him before others.

IV. Trust God to reward your right responses.

A. Forgive others, and God will forgive you.
³⁷Judge not, and ye shall not be judged: condemn not, and ye shall not be condemned: forgive, and ye shall be forgiven:

See the following pages for the full teaching in the Sermon on the Mount regarding "Judge not."

B. Give to others, and God will give through others to you.
³⁸Give, and it shall be given unto you; good measure, pressed down, and shaken together, and running over, shall men give into your bosom. For with the same measure that ye mete withal [i.e., that you measure with] it shall be measured to you again.

Although Christ gave "as you would that men should do to you" as the guideline for our behavior, He does not promise that others will always respond to us in that way. He does promise, however, that our right responses will be rewarded (implying: in the appropriate way at the appropriate time, as God knows best). Some of God's rewards will be channeled to us through others ("men will give into your bosom," i.e., "into the pouch of your robe" for you to carry home), while other rewards will come directly from Him. Either way, they will bountifully exceed whatever we have given (v. 38).

In the context of the Golden rule, verse 38 deals primarily with our responsibility to give specifically and directly to other people, especially those with unmet needs. (The giving of tithes and offerings through a church is not the issue here.) Christ indicated in MT 25:34-45 that a believer's giving to others (and particularly to His "brethren") is tantamount to presenting those gifts to Christ Himself. Believers are to give generously to God, therefore, both through their church and through other people. God more than repays all such giving.

To Judge or Not to Judge

The Bible uses *to judge* in several different senses. One is "to try a case, as in a court of law." A second is "to criticize another in a censorious manner," as used in Section II below. A third is "to evaluate objectively and spiritually"; for example, "Judge not according to the appearance, but judge righteous judgment" (JN 7:24). Another is "to correct a fault and effect restoration": "For if we would judge ourselves, we should not be judged" (I Cor. 11:31). Thus, believers are commanded to judge in some ways and not to judge in others. Knowing when and how to judge or not judge is often a difficult and serious problem. Christ dealt with both sides of that question in the following verses.

I. Correct your own blind spots before correcting others.

A. Do not fall into the same ditch yourself.

LK 6:39 And he spake a parable unto them, Can the blind lead the blind? shall they not both fall into the ditch?

B. Make sure that you follow and imitate Christ.

⁴⁰The disciple is not above his master: but every one that is perfect shall be as his master.

At first glance, verse 39 appears to be much like Christ's condemnation of the Pharisees as "blind leaders of the blind" in MT 15:14. Here, however, the context of both the preceding and the following verses deals with character traits to be evidenced in the lives of Christ's disciples. This implies that a believer can be blind to serious shortcomings in his life and his relationship to Christ, and that such blindness can cause him to lead others astray as well. The solution is offered in verse 40: focus continually on Christ, submit to Him as Master, and strive to be like Him in all aspects of your life. With this prerequisite, the next two verses in LK 6 (which parallel MT 7:3-5 below) then deal with proper versus improper judgment of others.

II. Do not exercise censorious judgment.

A. Expect to be measured by your own critical yardstick.

MT 7:1 Judge not, that ye be not judged.
²For with what judgment ye judge, ye shall be judged: and with what measure ye mete, it shall be measured to you again.

B. Remove your own plank before tackling another's speck.

³And why beholdest thou the mote [speck or splinter] that is in thy brother's eye, but considerest not the beam [large plank or log] that is in thine own eye?
⁴Or how wilt thou say to thy brother, Let me pull out the mote out of thine eye; and, behold, a beam is in thine own eye?
⁵Thou hypocrite, first cast out the beam out of thine own eye; and then shalt thou see clearly to cast out the mote out of thy brother's eye.

Christ condemned censorious criticism and judgment of one's "brothers," whether they be fellow believers or simply fellow men. Implicit in His warning are these principles: (1) authoritative judgment of another person's heart and motives is reserved to God alone; (2) we are incapable of making fully objective and equitable judgment because of incomplete information and distorted perceptions; and (3) we are often disqualified as judges because of "beams" in our own eyes that cloud or block our vision of others' needs. When we properly deal with our own problems, we are better prepared spiritually (with God's direction and assistance) to help our brothers with the "specks" in their lives.

C. Forgive, rather than judge and condemn.

LK 6:37 Judge not, and ye shall not be judged: condemn not, and ye shall not be condemned: forgive, and ye shall be forgiven:

Rather than censure and denounce others, we are to have a merciful and forgiving spirit. A major reason given here is that our own being forgiven (by others in some cases, but primarily by God according to MT 6:15) depends on our willingness to forgive others. (See Sec. III on p. 215.)

III. Exercise cautious judgment regarding unbelievers.

A. Don't expose holy treasures to "dogs" and "swine."

MT 7:6 Give not that which is holy unto the dogs, neither cast ye your pearls before swine, lest they trample them under their feet, and turn again and rend you.

After commanding His followers not to judge censoriously, Christ also commanded them not to do certain things with "dogs" and "swine" — referring to certain kinds of people. This obviously requires judging in the sense of making an objective spiritual evaluation. "That which is holy" and "your pearls" include precious and intimate treasures involving God's person, His Word, and our relationship with Him. "Dogs" and "swine" are hardened scoffers who look for opportunities to oppose and ridicule the things of God. Believers must exercise spiritual judgment and discretion in determining how to respond (including when to be silent or withdraw) in such encounters.

B. Don't be fooled by wolves in sheep's clothing.

MT 7:15 Beware of false prophets, which come to you in sheep's clothing, but inwardly they are ravening wolves.
16Ye shall know them by their fruits. Do men gather grapes of thorns, or figs of thistles? . . .
20Wherefore by their fruits ye shall know them.

Christ also commanded believers to exercise spiritual discernment and judgment with respect to false prophets. These religious charlatans often are dressed in "sheep's clothing," and it is up to believers to ascertain whether in fact they are "ravening wolves." The objective standard Christ specified for making this determination is "their fruits." If their lives and ministry do not produce genuine good fruit (when tested in the light of God's Word), "ye shall know them" for the dangerous imposters they really are. (See "False Prophets" on p. 383.)

    IV. Be honest and objective in judging others and yourself.

        A. Examine the fruit in judging the tree.

LK 6:42b Thou hypocrite, cast out first the beam out of thine own eye, and then shalt thou see clearly to pull out the mote that is in thy brother's eye.

⁴³For a good tree bringeth not forth corrupt fruit; neither doth a corrupt tree bring forth good fruit.

⁴⁴For every tree is known by his own fruit. For of thorns men do not gather figs, nor of a bramble bush gather they grapes.

        B. Appraise the treasure in judging its source.

⁴⁵A good man out of the good treasure of his heart bringeth forth that which is good; and an evil man out of the evil treasure of his heart bringeth forth that which is evil: for of the abundance of the heart his mouth speaketh.

In MT 7:15-20 (Sec. III.B, above), the purpose in evaluating someone's "fruit" was primarily to unmask false religious leaders. In contrast, the emphasis in the parallel passage in LK 6:43-44 (as shown by its context) is as much on our making sure that we ourselves are good trees and are bearing good fruit, as on our properly evaluating someone else's fruit. The same dual application can be made with verse 45. One's words reveal what he treasures in his heart, and this applies as much to our words as to anyone else's. As in Sections I and II above, we must first deal honestly and humbly with our own shortcomings in these areas before we can effectively assist others with their problems.

9

Steps in Walking with God

Merely the possibility of finite and fallible people walking in close communion with Almighty God stretches the limits of human understanding. God, however, not only desires such an intimate relationship with each of His children, He has made all of the arrangements necessary for its reality. Thus Christ often addressed the steps that believers must take to stay close to God's side.

Although walking with God must always be on His terms and not our own, He gives us considerable freedom and latitude within His path in the ways that we show our devotion to Him. Thus, He has established principles and guidelines for our personal worship, while leaving its expression to each believer's heart and soul. Similarly, God has made astounding promises regarding the exercise of our faith in Him, but He commits to us its daily practice. God has prepared the path; now He declares, "This is the way, walk ye in it" (Isa. 30:21).

The Nature of Worship

Most of us define "worship" too narrowly. Worship certainly includes reverent participation in church services and other spiritual gatherings and in personal devotions. It also takes many forms, such as praise, prayer, giving, and singing. In its full sense, however, Biblical worship is loving and revering God with all of one's being. It encompasses all of the positive thoughts about God, close communion with God, and ready responses to God that flow from a heart full of love for Him.

Every proper activity in which a believer engages can be a vehicle for honoring and glorifying God and thus can contribute to worship of Him. Such "living worship" is pictured in Romans 12:1: "I beseech you therefore, brethren, by the mercies of God, that ye present your bodies a living sacrifice, holy, acceptable unto God, which is your reasonable service [your spiritual service of worship]." The following passages illustrate the worship that God desires and deserves.

I. Worship is the essence of "the first commandment."

A. Worship is loving God as your only Lord.
MK 12:28 And one of the scribes came, and having heard them reasoning together, and perceiving that he had answered them well, asked him, Which is the first [the greatest] commandment of all?
²⁹And Jesus answered him, The first of all the commandments is, Hear, O Israel; The Lord our God is one Lord:
³⁰And thou shalt love the Lord thy God with all thy heart, and with all thy soul, and with all thy mind, and with all thy strength: this is the first commandment.

The scribes identified 613 separate statutes in the Mosaic law and continually debated their relative importance. Christ replied that the greatest commandment is the one in Deuteronomy 6:4-5, which He quoted above. Because of who and what God is, and because He loves His people without reservation, He expects them to love Him similarly in return. Such love for God is the essence of worship. True worship also acknowledges God as the only Lord and Master of your life. It is expressed through reverential devotion to Him in your innermost being ("all of your heart, soul, and mind") and through devoted service ("all of your strength").

B. Worship of God includes loving others.
³¹[MT 22:39-40] And the second is like {it}, namely this, Thou shalt love thy neighbor as thyself. There is none other commandment

greater than these. {On these two commandments hang all the law and the prophets.}

Love for God and love for all those God loves (both believers and unbelievers) are inseparable. "He that loveth not his brother, whom he hath seen, how can he love God, whom he hath not seen?" (I John 4:20b). Also, "Love your enemies . . . and ye shall be the children of the Highest (LK 6:35). These two commandments (vv. 30 and 31, above) are not only the greatest commandments, they are also the foundation and guiding principle for all of the other commandments (MT 22:40).

C. Worship is more than religious ritual.

³²And the scribe said unto him, Well, Master, thou hast said the truth: for there is one God; and there is none other but he:
³³And to love him with all the heart and with all the understanding, and with all the soul, and with all the strength, and to love his neighbor as himself, is more than all whole burnt offerings and sacrifices.
³⁴And when Jesus saw that he answered discreetly [intelligently], he said unto him, Thou art not far from the kingdom of God. And no man after that durst ask him any question.

This particular scribe (more than his fellows) seemed to grasp Christ's message that there is much more to worshipping God than merely complying with the law's religious rituals and regulations. With this requisite understanding, he was "not far" from entering God's kingdom. He was not yet there but was on the right track.

II. Worship must be "in spirit and in truth."

A. Worship is not restricted to holy places.

JN 4:19 The [Samaritan] woman saith unto him, Sir, I perceive that thou art a prophet.
²⁰Our fathers worshipped in this mountain; and ye say, that in Jerusalem is the place where men ought to worship.
²¹Jesus saith unto her, Woman, believe me, the hour cometh, when ye shall neither in this mountain, nor yet at Jerusalem, worship the Father.

The Samaritan and Jewish religions each had its principal center of worship — Mt. Garizim and Jerusalem respectively. Christ declared, however, that the geographic locale of worship soon would be unimportant. That time arrived when God Himself tore the veil of the temple in Jerusalem from top to bottom as Christ died on the cross. He thus signified that entrance into His presence is now available to everyone everywhere who comes to Him through Christ.

B. True worship requires true revelation about the true God.

²²Ye worship ye know not what: we know what we worship: for salvation is of the Jews.

All false religions "know not what they worship" because they are not based on an accurate knowledge of God and His *one way* of salvation. This salvation "is of the Jews" in that they were chosen and used by God (1) to receive and transmit His verbal revelation of Himself and the way of salvation He gave through His prophets and the scriptures; (2) to experience and testify of His miraculous power, loving care, and merciful deliverance on their behalf; and (3) to see and hear the Messiah firsthand as He lived and ministered in their midst.

C. God must be worshipped as He is and as He says.

²³But the hour cometh, and now is, when the true worshippers shall worship the Father in spirit and in truth: for the Father seeketh such to worship him.

²⁴God is a Spirit: and they that worship him must worship him in spirit and in truth.

Christ declared that God was implementing a new means of worshipping Him (v. 23). "True worshippers," which God would "seek out" through Christ, would be able to worship Him more perfectly than was possible under the old covenant. Because God's essence is spirit, the essence of worship must be spiritual, not physical. Worship, therefore, must flow from a person's spirit, i.e., from his heart, soul, and mind, as in the "first commandment" above. Outward acts of true worship will naturally accompany or follow such inner responses to God.

Worship must also be "in truth"; that is, in accordance with God's truth, His Word. Our worship, therefore, must be consistent with and reflect God's revelation about Himself and how we are to approach Him through Christ. We must worship God as He is ("in spirit") and as He prescribes ("in truth"). Anything else is not true worship.

III. Worship must be to God alone.

MT 4:8 Again, the devil taketh him up into an exceeding high mountain, and showeth him all the kingdoms of the world, and the glory of them;

⁹And saith unto him, All these things will I give thee, if thou wilt fall down and worship me.

¹⁰Then saith Jesus unto him, Get thee hence, Satan: for it is written, Thou shalt worship the Lord thy God, and him only shalt thou serve.

Satan's goal is to overthrow God and receive the worship and service of God's created beings. Christ overcame Satan's all-out attempt to obtain His worship in exchange for "all the kingdoms of the world." He replied, "Worship God, and Him only!" Most believers today are not tempted to worship Satan directly, but are often tempted to put material things, various activities, and other desires above God in their lives. Satan uses these ersatz gods to solicit our effective worship and service. To resist these temptations as Christ did requires filling our minds with God's Word and drawing upon it when temptation first appears. Also, by worshipping and serving God with all of our heart, soul, mind, and strength, we leave little room for Satan's enticement through his broad array of idols and false gods. (See Sec. II under "The Adversary" on p. 360 for the full passage.)

IV. Worship of God must be through Christ.
JN 14:6 Jesus saith unto him [a disciple], I am the way, the truth, and the life: no man cometh unto the Father, but by me.

JN 5:22 For the Father judgeth no man, but hath committed all judgment unto the Son:
²³That all men should honor the Son, even as they honor the Father. He that honoreth not the Son honoreth not the Father which hath sent him.

Jesus Christ is "the way," and the only way, to God, whether for salvation or for worship (see Sec. VII on p. 10). He declared that anyone who does not "honor" (i.e., revere, exalt, and worship) Him in the same way and to the same degree that he claims to honor the Father does not honor or worship God at all.

V. Worship of Christ must revere Him as God.

A. The wise men worshipped Christ fittingly.
MT 2:1 Now when Jesus was born in Bethlehem of Judaea in the days of Herod the king, behold, there came wise men from the east to Jerusalem,
²Saying, Where is he that is born King of the Jews? for we have seen his star in the east, and are come to worship him. . . .
¹¹And when they were come into the house, they saw the young child with Mary his mother, and fell down, and worshipped him: and when they had opened their treasures, they presented unto him gifts; gold, and frankincense, and myrrh.

What the wise men understood about God and about Christ, beyond His being "King of the Jews," is not revealed. Their *purpose* in seeking Christ, however, is clearly stated, namely, "to worship Him." This they did in a manner thoroughly befitting the divine King of the Jews. Gold in scripture often is associated with royalty (e.g., Psalm 21:1-3); frankincense, with the worship of Jehovah (Ex. 30:34-38); and myrrh, with human life and death (MK 15:23; JN

19:39-40). Thus, the wise men's gifts were appropriate pictures of Christ's sovereignty, deity, and humanity.

B. A healed man worshipped Christ readily.

JN 9:35 Jesus heard that they had cast him out [the blind man Christ healed had been excommunicated]; and when he had found him, he said unto him, Dost thou believe on the Son of God?

³⁶He answered and said, Who is he, Lord, that I might believe on him?

³⁷And Jesus said unto him, Thou hast both seen him, and it is he that talketh with thee.

³⁸And he said, Lord, I believe. And he worshipped him.

The word translated *worship* in these passages means to kneel and bow to the earth or to prostrate oneself in giving homage. Some of those Christ healed and who responded to Him with "worship" and thanksgiving probably did not understand that He was God incarnate and was deserving of worship as God. This formerly blind man, however, had sufficient evidence and understanding of Christ's deity (even though elementary and newly received) to render Him genuine and full worship. Christ accepted it as readily as it was given.

C. Believers worshipped Christ wholeheartedly.

MT 14:33 Then they [His disciples] that were in the ship [when He calmed the storm] came and worshipped him, saying, Of a truth thou art the Son of God.

MT 28:9 And as they [the women leaving His empty tomb] went to tell his disciples, behold, Jesus met them, saying, All hail. And they came and held him by the feet, and worshipped him.

MT 28:16 Then [later after His resurrection] the eleven disciples went away into Galilee, into a mountain where Jesus had appointed them.

¹⁷And when they saw him, they worshipped him: but some doubted.

LK 24:51 And it came to pass, while he blessed them, he was parted from them, and carried up into heaven.

⁵²And they worshipped him, and returned to Jerusalem with great joy:

⁵³And were continually in the temple, praising and blessing God. Amen.

These passages recount the worship of Christ that His closest followers earnestly and fervently gave Him. MT 14:33 followed a rapid series of astounding miracles (including feeding the 5,000, walking on the sea, and calming the storm). Overwhelmed with awe at His unlimited power, the disciples fell at His feet in adoration and worship.

In MT 28:9, the added elements of joy and thanksgiving for Christ's victory over death and the grave are evident in the women's worship. His disciples' worship in MT 28:16 includes their submission and rededication to the risen Lord they previously had deserted. Following Christ's ascension in LK 24, the disciples' worship included "great joy" and public praise to God. Immediate reasons for their worship included Christ's promised return, their new understanding of Old Testament passages regarding the Messiah and salvation, and Christ's promise of His Holy Spirit to empower them to live and witness for Him.

Principles and Precepts for Worship

Worship that pleases and honors God includes the earnest and sincere exercise of practices that Christ commanded or commended in the Gospels. These include faithful attention to God's Word and prayer, the joyful giving of praise and offerings for God's goodness, and reverential attendance in God's house. Outward acts of worship must reflect, of course, right views of their meaning, right motives for their practice, and right conduct in their exercise.

I. Worship includes humble sincerity before God.

A. Don't parade your worship before men.

MT 6:1 Take heed that ye do not your alms [religious exercises] before men, to be seen of them: otherwise ye have no reward of your Father which is in heaven.

Verse 1a may be understood: "Be careful not to practice your religious service and worship before men to attract their attention to your performance." The problem is not that others may see our good works; what is wrong is a desire to draw attention and glory to ourselves rather than to God. Christ had just stressed, "Let your light so shine before men, *that they may see your good works, and glorify your Father* which is in heaven" (MT 5:16). Those who "show off their worship" before others receive their reward only from human observers, not from God.

B. Don't "blow your horn" when giving.

²Therefore when thou doest thine alms [here, meaning charitable giving], do not sound a trumpet before thee, as the hypocrites do in the synagogues and in the streets, that they may have glory [admiration] of men. Verily I say unto you, They have their reward.
³But when thou doest alms, let not thy left hand know what thy right hand doeth:
⁴That thine alms may be in secret: and thy Father which seeth in secret himself shall reward thee openly.

Those who advertise their giving are called "hypocrites" because their intent is to deceive those who observe them. They pretend to give to God, but their primary goal is to *receive* praise and esteem from men. Verse 3 implies, "do not even tell yourself what a good thing you are doing." "Giving in secret" (unadvertised and for God's glory alone) pleases God, and He will reward you both "openly" (publicly) and "in secret" (privately).

C. "Enter your closet" to pray.

> **⁵And when thou prayest, thou shalt not be as the hypocrites are: for they love to pray standing in the synagogues and in the corners of the streets, that they may be seen of men. Verily I say unto you, They have their reward [in full].**
> **⁶But thou, when thou prayest, enter into thy closet, and when thou hast shut thy door, pray to thy Father which is in secret; and thy Father which seeth in secret shall reward thee openly.**

Christ is not teaching that praying in public is wrong. He encouraged group prayer in MT 18:19-20 and commended the tax collector's prayer in the temple in LK 18:10-14. Rather, personal prayer is for solemn, intimate communication with God, not for public display. Praying in "your closet" (any private place) helps remove that temptation to impress others. It also aids concentration, freedom of thought, and openness with God. Christ promised that the Father, who sees in the secret recesses of your heart, as well as in your secret place of prayer, will reward such private communion with Him. (See Sec. IV on p. 191 and Sec. I.B on p. 192 for subsequent verses in MT 6 on prayer.)

D. Don't make a sad face when fasting.

> **¹⁶Moreover when ye fast, be not, as the hypocrites, of a sad countenance: for they disfigure their faces, that they may appear unto men to fast. Verily I say unto you, They have their reward.**
> **¹⁷But thou, when thou fastest, anoint thine head, and wash thy face;**
> **¹⁸That thou appear not unto men to fast, but unto thy Father which is in secret: and thy Father, which seeth in secret, shall reward thee openly.**

The only regularly-scheduled fast that God commanded in the Old Testament was for the annual Day of Atonement (Lev. 16:29 ff.). The Jewish people also fasted (either individually or collectively) at other times and for various reasons, such as when sorrowing for sin or a calamity, for concentrating on a critical spiritual task, or for solemn meditation on an important event or experience. Christ supported appropriate fasting by saying *"when ye fast."* He condemned, however, hypocritical and showy fasting, just as He condemned pretentious and self-exalting prayer. God rewards only that fasting that is humble, sincere, and directed toward Him.

II. Worship includes reverent attention to God's Word.

LK 10:38 Now it came to pass, as they went, that he entered into a certain village: and a certain woman named Martha received him into her house.

³⁹And she had a sister called Mary, which also sat at Jesus' feet, and heard his word.

⁴⁰But Martha was cumbered about much serving, and came to him, and said, Lord, dost thou not care that my sister hath left me to serve alone? bid her therefore that she help me.

⁴¹And Jesus answered and said unto her, Martha, Martha, thou art careful and troubled about many things:

⁴²But one thing is needful: and Mary hath chosen that good part, which shall not be taken away from her.

Mary adored Christ as Israel's (and her own) Messiah, and attended His every word. He declared that her reverent attention was "needful" and "good" (v. 42). What she learned from Christ and His Word would benefit her long after He, and Martha's meal, were gone. As a result of her careful and thoughtful listening, Mary later evidenced a greater understanding of His approaching death than even His twelve disciples when she anointed His body for burial (see Sec. I on p. 63).

III. Worship includes joyful praise for God's goodness.

A. Praise is central to worship.

LK 17:12 And as he entered into a certain village, there met him ten men that were lepers, which stood afar off:

¹³And they lifted up their voices, and said, Jesus, Master, have mercy on us.

¹⁴And when he saw them, he said unto them, Go show yourselves unto the priests. And it came to pass, that, as they went, they were cleansed.

¹⁵And one of them, when he saw that he was healed, turned back, and with a loud voice glorified God,

B. Thankfulness is essential in worship.

¹⁶And [he] fell down on his face at his feet, giving him thanks: and he was a Samaritan.

¹⁷And Jesus answering said, Were there not ten cleansed? but where are the nine?

¹⁸There are not found that returned to give glory to God, save this stranger.

C. Faith is prerequisite for worship

¹⁹And he said unto him, Arise, go thy way: thy faith hath made thee whole.

Christ answered the prayer of all ten lepers for healing, but only one (and a Samaritan at that) gave Him thanks and glorified God. Christ accepted his worship and gratitude and commended his faith. He faulted the nine, however, for not giving glory to God for their deliverance. Prayer, faith, praise, and thanksgiving all complement and strengthen each other in worship. There is little worship, however, where there is little gratitude and praise.

IV. Worship includes generous giving to God's causes.

A. Deny yourself, and give sacrificially.

MK 12:41 And Jesus sat over against the treasury, and beheld how the people cast money into the treasury: and many that were rich cast in much.

⁴²And there came a certain poor widow, and she threw in two mites, which make a farthing.

⁴³And he called unto him his disciples, and saith unto them, Verily I say unto you, That this poor widow hath cast more in, than all they which have cast into the treasury:

⁴⁴For all they did cast in of their abundance; but she of her want [poverty] did cast in all that she had, even all her living.

The "treasury" refers to chests located in the court of the temple into which worshippers dropped their tithes and offerings. Although the widow gave only two mites, worth at most a few cents in our currency, Christ declared that her gift was greater than anyone else's. The large gifts the wealthy had given did not significantly cost them, but the poor widow gave all that she had to live on. Christ made it a point to call His disciples to Him and teach them this lesson on sacrificial giving. He similarly observes our giving and wants us to learn the same lesson.

B. Show mercy and compassion, and give generously.

LK 11:41 But rather give alms [to the poor and needy] of such things as ye have; and, behold, all things are clean unto you.

⁴²But woe unto you, Pharisees! for ye tithe mint and rue and all manner of herbs, and pass over judgment [justice] and the love of God: these ought ye to have done, and not to leave the other undone.

MT 9:13 But go ye and learn what that meaneth, I will have [I desire] mercy, and not sacrifice: for I am not come to call the [self]righteous, but sinners to repentance.

In these passages, Christ rebuked the Pharisees who scrupulously tithed all of their gain — even from the herbs in their gardens — but failed to obey the greater commandments in God's Law to show kindness and mercy to their fellow men. Verse 42 may be read: "You give God a tenth of your mint and rue [a plant used medicinally] and all manner of herbs, but you fail to practice justice and the love of God. You should have done these latter things, without omitting the former [i.e., tithing]." Because of their self-centeredness, their tithes and sacrifices were unacceptable, even repugnant, to God. Formalistic Christians can easily commit the same error.

    C. Resolve any offenses, and give obediently.

> **MT 5:23 Therefore if thou bring thy gift to the altar, and there rememberest that thy brother hath ought [something] against thee;**
> **²⁴Leave there thy gift before the altar, and go thy way; first be reconciled to thy brother, and then come and offer thy gift.**

God places a higher priority on restoring and maintaining unity among believers than even on our giving of offerings to Him. We are commanded to give to God, but only after seeking to resolve offenses (whether actual or alleged) with other believers. (See Sec. VI on p. 218.)

    D. Pay your taxes, and give faithfully.

> **MT 22:15 [MK 12:13] Then went the Pharisees, and took counsel how they might entangle him in his talk.**
> **¹⁶And they sent out unto him their disciples with the Herodians, saying, Master, we know that thou art true, and teachest the way of God in truth, neither carest thou for any man: for thou regardest not the person of men.**
> **¹⁷Tell us therefore, What thinkest thou? Is it lawful to give tribute unto Caesar, or not? {Shall we give, or shall we not give?}**
> **¹⁸But Jesus perceived their wickedness, and said, Why tempt ye me, ye hypocrites?**
> **¹⁹Shew me the tribute money. And they brought unto him a penny.**
> **²⁰And he saith unto them, Whose is this image and superscription?**
> **²¹They say unto him, Caesar's. Then saith he unto them, Render therefore unto Caesar the things which are Caesar's; and unto God the things that are God's.**

The *tribute* in verse 17 was a Roman poll tax levied on every adult male. The Pharisees in particular hated it, although the Herodians (Roman-accommodating Jews) generally tolerated it. Both groups joined in an attempt to trick Christ into taking an untenable position on the tax. Whichever answer He gave, the other group would charge Him with treason — either against the Jewish people or against Rome. Christ properly and wisely answered that God's people are to give both God and government their due — including government that is ungodly and oppressive.

IV. Worship includes respectful attendance in God's house.

    A. Christ regularly attended synagogue services.

LK 4:15 And he taught in their synagogues, being glorified of all.
¹⁶And he came to Nazareth, where he had been brought up: and, as his custom was, he went into the synagogue on the sabbath day, and stood up for to read.

As Christ traveled throughout Israel, it was "His custom" to honor His Father by attending a synagogue each sabbath. Similarly, when He was in Jerusalem, He spent much of His time in the temple. Even as a twelve year old boy, when found by His parents in the temple, He asked them, "How is it that ye sought me? wist ye not that I must be about my Father's business?" (LK 2:49).

    B. The "Father's house" must not be a "house of merchandise."

JN 2:13 And the Jews' passover was at hand, and Jesus went up to Jerusalem,
¹⁴And found in the temple those that sold oxen and sheep and doves, and the changers of money sitting:
¹⁵And when he had made a scourge of small cords, he drove them all out of the temple, and the sheep, and the oxen; and poured out the changers' money, and overthrew the tables;
¹⁶And said unto them that sold doves, Take these things hence; make not my Father's house an house of merchandise.
¹⁷And his disciples remembered that it was written, The zeal of thine house hath eaten me up.

    C. "The house of prayer" must not be a "den of thieves."

MT 21:12 And Jesus went into the temple of God, and cast out all them that sold and bought in the temple, and overthrew the tables of the moneychangers, and the seats of them that sold doves,
¹³And said unto them, It is written, My house shall be called the house of prayer; but ye have made it a den of thieves.

These similar incidents occurred three years apart near the first and last Passover feasts during Christ's ministry. They demonstrate that the religious system of the day was neither inwardly revived nor outwardly reformed during the three years He intensively proclaimed the essence of true worship. In both cases, Christ condemned inappropriate activity in God's house. Clearly, making merchandise of religion and allowing "a den of thieves" to operate in "the house of prayer" are contrary to basic principles of worship. Using church today to conduct personal business or seek financial gain is just as offensive to God as the dealings of these merchants and thieves.

Signs and Symbols in Baptism

Baptism as practiced in the Gospels was outwardly similar to believers' baptism today, but it differed from present baptism in both purpose and pictorial representation. These differences are often misunderstood, in part because of the terminology and the historical contexts involved. For example, *baptize* and *baptism* are based on Greek words that are not translated in our English Bibles. Rather, they have been borrowed and transliterated, i.e., spelled with English letters to look like English words. Their common meaning in Greek is "immerse" or "dip."

Well before John the Baptist came, the Pharisees baptized their Gentile proselytes to symbolize the latter's (supposed) spiritual purification as well as their identification with Judaism. The Pharisees also greatly expanded Old Testament practices regarding ceremonial washings of all sorts. These included frequent "baptisms," i.e., ritual bathing by self-immersion, to achieve absolution from moral impurity.

Even villages too small to have a synagogue (which required at least ten married men) generally had a rectangular public pool designed for ritual baptisms. Upper-class Jews often had such pools in their homes. The Jewish people, therefore, readily understood both the mode and the meaning of John's baptism as a symbol of moral cleansing and as a sign of one's embrace of his particular teaching. Beginning with Christ's "great commission" and in Acts and the epistles, however, the pictures conveyed by baptism received substantially greater meaning.

I. John the Baptist's baptism.

A. A sign of preparation for the coming Messiah.
MT 3:1 In those days came John the Baptist, preaching in the wilderness of Judaea,
²And saying, Repent ye: for the kingdom of heaven is at hand.
³For this is he that was spoken of by the prophet Esaias [Isaiah], saying, The voice of one crying in the wilderness, Prepare ye the way of the Lord, make his paths straight.

JN 1:19 And this is the record [witness] of John, when the Jews sent priests and Levites from Jerusalem to ask him, Who art thou?
²⁰And he confessed, and denied not; but confessed, I am not the Christ. . . .
²⁵And they asked him, and said unto him, Why baptizest thou then, if thou be not that Christ, nor Elias, neither that prophet?

> [26]John answered them, saying, I baptize with water: but there standeth one among you, whom ye know not;
> [27]He it is, who coming after me is preferred before me, . . .
> [31]And I knew him not: but that he should be made manifest to Israel, therefore am I come baptizing with water.

God's prophets called the Jewish people to repentance and obedience throughout their history. John's call took on even greater import and urgency with his related declaration that the long-awaited Messianic kingdom was "at hand." With the Messiah's soon arrival, the spiritual preparation of His people to inhabit His fundamentally-spiritual kingdom was of prime importance. Verse 31 ties John's baptizing of the people to that spiritual preparation. Through baptism, they signified their readiness to receive, obey, honor, and serve their coming Messiah.

    B. A sign of repentance and confessed sin.

> MK 1:4 John did baptize in the wilderness, and preach the baptism of repentance for the remission of sins.
> [5]And there went out unto him all the land of Judaea, and they of Jerusalem, and were all baptized of him in the river of Jordan, confessing their sins.

    C. A sign of commitment to righteous living.

> LK 3:10 And the people asked him, saying, What shall we do then?
> [11]He answereth and saith unto them, He that hath two coats, let him impart to him that hath none; and he that hath meat, let him do likewise.
> [12]Then came also publicans [tax-collectors] to be baptized, and said unto him, Master, what shall we do?
> [13]And he said unto them, Exact no more than that which is appointed you.
> [14]And the soldiers likewise demanded of him, saying, And what shall we do? And he said unto them, Do violence to no man, neither accuse any falsely; and be content with your wages.

> MT 3:7 But when he saw many of the Pharisees and Sadducees come to his baptism, he said unto them, O generation of vipers, who hath warned you to flee from the wrath to come?
> [8]Bring forth therefore fruits meet for [in keeping with] repentance:

John proclaimed that the Jewish people, individually and nationally, needed to repent of their sins and live in accordance with God's holy Law. Those who heeded his call gave outward expression, through baptism, of their repentance and their commitment to obey God's commands. The Pharisees, however, incurred John's condemnation because they neglected or willfully disobeyed the spirit of the Law and perverted the practice of its requirements. With hardened hearts, they rejected both John's message and his baptism.

II. John's baptism of Jesus Christ.

A. A symbol of Christ's identification with mankind.

MT 3:13 Then cometh Jesus from Galilee to Jordan unto John, to be baptized of him.

¹⁴But John forbad him, saying, I have need to be baptized of thee, and comest thou to me?

¹⁵And Jesus answering said unto him, Suffer [Permit] it to be so now: for thus it becometh us to fulfil all righteousness. Then he suffered him.

John's initial reluctance to baptize Christ is understandable. Christ had no sin to confess or heart condition that needed to be changed. His answer in verse 15 may be read: "for it is proper for us in this way to comply with every righteous requirement." These "requirements" may include (1) identifying Himself with the sin-laden people who had come to John for baptism; (2) dedicating Himself to His mission as their and our sin-bearer (as in Part B below); and (3) confirming that John's ministry was of God, including his baptizing people to prepare them for the kingdom that was at hand.

B. A symbol of Christ's consecration for God's service.

¹⁶And Jesus, when he was baptized, went up straightway out of the water: and, lo, the heavens were opened unto him, and he saw the Spirit of God descending like a dove, and lighting upon him:

¹⁷And lo a voice from heaven, saying, This is my beloved Son, in whom I am well pleased.

The standard age for entering the priesthood was thirty (Num. 4:3). Luke reports that Jesus, our High Priest, was "about thirty years of age" at this time (3:23). Jesus' baptism served as His public introduction to His earthly ministry and as His public consecration of Himself for that ministry. At that time, the Holy Spirit anointed and empowered Him to that end. The Father also declared His approval of His Son, including His Son's baptism and coming ministry as the Father's representative.

III. Christ's baptism of His early followers.

A. A sign they believed He was the Messiah.

JN 3:22 After these things came Jesus and his disciples into the land of Judaea; and there he tarried with them, and baptized. . . .

> [26]And they [John's disciples] came unto John, and said unto him, Rabbi, he that was with thee beyond Jordan, to whom thou barest witness, behold, the same baptizeth, and all men come to him.
> [27]John answered and said, A man can receive nothing, except it be given him from heaven.
> [28]Ye yourselves bear me witness, that I said, I am not the Christ [the Messiah], but that I am sent before him.

Among its meanings and symbols, baptism was also a sign given by baptized people that they were disciples (followers) of the one who baptized them. This was true of those John baptized, and later it was true of those that Christ's disciples baptized on His behalf. John fully expected that his followers would follow Christ when they realized that He was the Messiah whom John had heralded.

B. A source of conflict with the Pharisees.

> JN 4:1 When therefore the Lord knew how the Pharisees had heard that Jesus made and baptized more disciples than John,
> [2](Though Jesus himself baptized not, but his disciples,)
> [3]He left Judaea, and departed again into Galilee.

> LK 7:29 And all the people that heard [Christ's teaching] and the publicans, justified God, being [having been] baptized with the baptism of John.
> [30]But the Pharisees and lawyers rejected the counsel of God against themselves, being not baptized of him [John].

Luke notes that, in general, those who accepted John's baptism also initially followed Christ, while those who rejected it also rejected Him. The Pharisees, still incensed at John's condemnation of them, now heard that the One whom John proclaimed to be the Messiah was baptizing more disciples than John baptized. To avoid provoking a premature crisis with them, Christ left their stronghold of Judea for Galilee.

IV. Christ's baptism of believers with the Holy Spirit.

A. Foretold by John before Christ's ministry.

> MK 1:7 And [John] preached, saying, There cometh one mightier than I after me, the latchet of whose shoes I am not worthy to stoop down and unloose.
> [8]I indeed have baptized you with water: but he shall baptize you with the Holy Ghost.

> JN 1:33 And I knew him not: but he that sent me to baptize with water, the same said unto me, Upon whom thou shalt see the Spirit

descending, and remaining on him, the same is he which baptizeth with the Holy Ghost.

³⁴And I saw, and bare record that this is the Son of God.

B. Promised by Christ at the end of His ministry.

ACTS 1:4 And, being assembled together with them, [Jesus] commanded them that they should not depart from Jerusalem, but wait for the promise of the Father, which, saith he, ye have heard of me.

⁵For John truly baptized with water; but ye shall be baptized with the Holy Ghost not many days hence. . . .

⁸But ye shall receive power, after that the Holy Ghost is come upon you: and ye shall be witnesses unto me both in Jerusalem, and in all Judaea, and in Samaria, and unto the uttermost part of the earth.

Scripture identifies two simultaneous spiritual baptisms that are eternal realities of which water baptism is a shadow. Both are performed by God alone and occur at the moment of every believer's salvation. One is cited here: Christ's baptism of believers with the Holy Spirit. This refers to Christ's bestowal of the Holy Spirit upon each believer to dwell within him forever (see Sec. IV.A under "the Holy Spirit" on p. 351.) The other spiritual baptism is that of every believer by the Holy Spirit into Christ and into His body of all true believers (see Sec. V.B below).

V. Christ's command to make and baptize disciples.

A. A sign of their personal faith in Him.

MK 16:15 And he said unto them, Go ye into all the world, and preach the gospel to every creature.

¹⁶He that believeth and is baptized shall be saved; but he that believeth not shall be damned.

The essential elements of the gospel and "belief in Christ" for salvation became abundantly clear after His crucifixion and resurrection. Before that, references to people who "believed in Him" related primarily to those who recognized Jesus as the Messiah and (in varying degrees) followed Him as such. Now, the gospel is "that Christ died for our sins according to the scriptures; and that he was buried, and that he rose again the third day according to the scriptures;" I Cor. 15:1-4).

Baptism does not contribute toward anyone's salvation, but is to be a public testimony that the person being baptized has placed his faith in Christ as his personal Savior from his sin. The sequence in scripture, therefore, is always belief in Christ first, then baptism. A prior baptism, such as by John the Baptist, was not a substitute for baptism after salvation (see Acts 19:1-5).

B. A sign of their union with Christ and allegiance to Him.

MT 28:19 Go ye therefore, and teach [make disciples of] all nations, baptizing them in the name of the Father, and of the Son, and of the Holy Ghost:

20Teaching [instructing] them to observe all things whatsoever I have commanded you: and, lo, I am with you alway, even unto the end of the world. Amen.

Baptizing all believers is a major element of the Great Commission. Being baptized, therefore, is one of a believer's initial steps of obedience in following Christ. It also signifies his identification with Christ and allegiance to Him as his personal Savior and Lord.

In summary, baptism presents the following solemn and precious pictures of every believer's salvation: (1) It portrays Christ's death, burial, and resurrection, on which anyone's salvation must be based. (2) It illustrates the believer's own "dying to himself" and to his own agenda, and his "rising to a new life" of service for Christ as his Lord and Master. (3) It reflects the believer's baptism by the Holy Spirit, who at the moment of his salvation placed him fully and eternally into Christ and into His universal body of all true believers (i.e., His church), of which Christ is the head.

These pictures presented by baptism are combined in Romans 6:3-6: "Know ye not, that as many of us as were baptized into Jesus Christ [by the Holy Spirit] were baptized into his death? Therefore we are buried with him by baptism into death: that like as Christ was raised up from the dead by the glory of the Father, even so we also should walk in newness of life. For if we have been planted together in the likeness of his death, we shall be [raised] also in the likeness of his resurrection: knowing this, that our old man [our sinful nature] is crucified with him, that the body of sin might be destroyed, that henceforth we should not serve sin."

Lessons on Living by Faith

Both Testaments declare, "The just shall live by faith" (Hab. 2:4, Rom. 1:17, et al.). Believers are not only saved through faith, they must also live by faith day by day. Christ often taught this principle — to individuals, to His disciples, and to the crowds at large. Many of these lessons on practical, functioning faith were in response to personal crises that people faced. They often included miracles that demonstrated both man's utter helplessness and God's infinite capability to provide whatever is needed. Whether their faith was strong or weak, Christ met them where they were, dealt with their need, and encouraged them toward greater faith in Him.

I. A Roman centurion's great faith.

    A. The centurion's plight and plea.

      MT 8:5 [LK 7:1] And when Jesus was entered into Capernaum, there came unto him a centurion, beseeching him,

      ⁶And saying, Lord, my servant lieth at home sick of the palsy, grievously tormented {and ready to die}.

    B. His commendable life and deeds.

      LK 7:4 And when they [the Jewish elders] came to Jesus, they besought him instantly, saying, That he was worthy for whom he should do this:

      ⁵For he loveth our nation, and he hath built us a synagogue.

      MT 8:7 And Jesus saith unto him, I will come and heal him.

    C. His genuine submission and faith.

      ⁸The centurion answered and said, Lord, {trouble not thyself} I am not worthy that thou shouldest come under my roof: but speak the word only, and my servant shall be healed.

      ⁹For I {also} am a man under authority, having soldiers under me: and I say to this man, Go, and he goeth; and to another, Come, and he cometh; and to my servant, Do this, and he doeth it.

The centurion's statement may be understood: "Being under the authority of a commanding officer myself, and also having soldiers under my authority, I recognize the authority and power that God has given you. Just as my soldiers and servants obey my commands immediately and fully, I know that if you speak the word only, my servant shall be healed promptly and completely."

    D. Christ's commendation of his faith.

      ¹⁰When Jesus heard it, he marvelled, and said to them that followed, Verily I say unto you, I have not found so great faith, no, not in Israel.

    E. Christ's comparison of his faith.

      ¹¹And I say unto you, That many shall come from the east and west, and shall sit down with Abraham, and Isaac, and Jacob, in the kingdom of heaven.

      ¹²But the children of the kingdom shall be cast out into outer darkness: there shall be weeping and gnashing of teeth.

    F. Christ's fulfillment of his faith.

      ¹³And Jesus said unto the centurion, Go thy way; and as thou hast believed, so be it done unto thee. And his servant was healed in the selfsame hour.

Christ was amazed at this Roman officer's "great faith" — a faith greater than any He found in all Israel. He foretold that many people around the world would exhibit similar faith, and would participate in His millennial kingdom. (In contrast, faithless Jews will be excluded from His kingdom because they failed to recognize and accept Him as their Messiah.) Christ honored the centurion's faith by commending it and gladly fulfilling it — by healing his servant as requested.

II. A Gentile woman's persistent faith.

A. The woman's plight and plea.

MT 15:21 [MK 7:24] Then Jesus went thence, and departed into the coasts of Tyre and Sidon.

²²And, behold, a woman of Canaan came out of the same coasts {and fell at his feet}, and cried unto him, saying, Have mercy on me, O Lord, thou son of David; my daughter is grievously vexed with a devil.

B. Christ's testing of her faith.

²³But he answered her not a word. And his disciples came and besought him, saying, Send her away; for she crieth after us.

²⁴But he answered and said, I am not sent but unto the lost sheep of the house of Israel.

C. The woman's unshakable faith.

²⁵Then came she and worshipped him, saying, Lord, help me.

²⁶But he answered and said, {Let the children first be filled;} It is not meet [right] to take the children's bread, and to cast it to dogs.

²⁷And she said, Truth, Lord: yet the dogs eat of the crumbs which fall from their masters' table.

D. Christ's honoring of her faith.

²⁸Then Jesus answered and said unto her, O woman, great is thy faith: be it unto thee even as thou wilt {the devil is gone out of thy daughter}. And her daughter was made whole from that very hour.

This needy Gentile woman in a Gentile region somehow recognized Christ as the Messiah ("Son of David") and reverently called Him "Lord" (v. 22). For her greater benefit, He delayed answering her at first. When He did respond, He likened granting her plea to giving the (Jewish) children's bread to lowly (Gentile) dogs. Her humble and reverent reply that even the Master's dogs benefit from crumbs spilled from His table demonstrated the strength and depth of her faith that Christ would meet her need. He commended her "great faith" and gladly granted her request.

III. A diseased woman's humble faith.

A. The woman's plight and plan.

LK 8:43 [MK 5:25-34] And a woman having an issue of blood

twelve years, which had spent all her living upon physicians, neither
could be healed of any,

⁴⁴Came behind him, and touched the border of his garment: and
immediately her issue of blood stanched. {For she said, If I may
touch but his clothes, I shall be whole.}

    B. Christ's awareness of her faith.

⁴⁵And Jesus said, Who touched me? When all denied, Peter and
they that were with him said, Master, the multitude throng thee and
press thee, and sayest thou, Who touched me?

⁴⁶And Jesus said, Somebody hath touched me: for I perceive that
virtue [power] is gone out of me.

    C. The woman's confession of her faith.

⁴⁷And when the woman saw that she was not hid, she came trembling, and falling down before him, she declared unto him before
all the people for what cause she had touched him, and how she
was healed immediately.

    D. Christ's approval of her faith.

⁴⁸And he said unto her, Daughter, be of good comfort: thy faith
hath made thee whole; go in peace.

Christ asked, "Who touched me?" to bring the woman forward so that He
could further strengthen her faith. He wanted to comfort and encourage her
personally as well as give her an opportunity to tell the others what He had
done for her. He wanted the crowd to learn what had happened and to hear
directly from the woman the background and nature of His unseen miracle.
Then, in everyone's hearing, He attributed her healing to her faith in Him.

    IV. Two blind men's sufficient faith.

      A. The men's plight and plea.

MT 9:27 And when Jesus departed thence, two blind men followed
him, crying, and saying, Thou son of David, have mercy on us.

      B. Christ's test of their faith.

²⁸And when he was come into the house, the blind men came to
him: and Jesus saith unto them, Believe ye that I am able to do this?
They said unto him, Yea, Lord.

      C. Christ's reward for their faith.

²⁹Then touched he their eyes, saying, According to your faith be it
unto you.

³⁰And their eyes were opened; and Jesus straitly charged them,
saying, See that no man know it.

³¹But they, when they were departed, spread abroad his fame in all that country.

By addressing Christ as "son of David," the blind men acknowledged Him as the Messiah. He delayed responding to their pleas while in public, but asked them in private concerning their faith in His power. He then healed them "according to their faith." Although faith in Christ was not a prerequisite for all or even most of His miracles, Christ honored those who exhibited such faith. At times, however, He withheld His miraculous power when unbelief was prevalent. His command not to tell anyone (v. 30) was to prevent the crowds from clamoring to make Him their king and physical benefactor (rather than coming to Him with personal repentance and faith for salvation).

V. A nobleman's growing faith.

A. The man's plight and plea.

JN 4:46 So Jesus came again into Cana of Galilee, where he made the water wine. And there was a certain nobleman, whose son was sick at Capernaum.

⁴⁷When he heard that Jesus was come out of Judaea into Galilee, he went unto him, and besought him that he would come down, and heal his son: for he was at the point of death.

B. The man's minimal faith.

⁴⁸Then said Jesus unto him, Except ye see signs and wonders [attesting and amazing miracles], ye will not believe.

⁴⁹The nobleman saith unto him, Sir, come down ere my child die.

⁵⁰ªJesus saith unto him, Go thy way; thy son liveth.

This "nobleman," an official in Herod's court, lived in Capernaum, 16 miles from Cana. Christ had recently performed a number of miracles in Jerusalem and had just returned to Galilee to start His major ministry there. The nobleman apparently had heard of or seen these miracles, and he begged Christ to come and heal his son. Christ knew that he did not recognize His deity or appreciate the extent of His power. (The man assumed that Christ had to be present to heal, and had to heal his son before he died). After reproving his minimal faith, Christ healed his son anyway — fully, instantly, and from 16 miles away.

C. The man's maturing faith.

⁵⁰ᵇAnd the man believed the word that Jesus had spoken unto him, and he went his way.

⁵¹And as he was now going down [to Capernaum], his servants met him, and told him, saying, Thy son liveth.

⁵²Then enquired he of them the hour when he began to amend. And they said unto him, Yesterday at the seventh hour [7 p.m.] the fever left him.

⁵³So the father knew that it was at the same hour, in the which Jesus said unto him, Thy son liveth: and himself believed, and his whole house.

In response to Christ's rebuke, and before he left for home, the man put his faith in Christ's *word*, not just what he could see with his eyes. His growing faith was strengthened by his servants' report, and he believed more fully in Christ. The testimony of his encounter with Christ led "his whole house" (family and servants) to believe in Him also.

VI. The disciples' weak faith.

A. The disciples' plight and plea.

MT 8:23 [MK 4:36; LK 8:22] And when he was entered into a ship, his disciples followed him,

²⁴And, behold, there arose a great tempest in the sea, insomuch that the ship was covered with the waves: but he was asleep.

²⁵And his disciples came to him, and awoke him, saying, Lord, save us: we perish. {carest thou not that we perish?}

B. Christ's rebuke of their missing faith.

²⁶And he saith unto them, Why are ye fearful, O ye of little faith? {How is it that ye have no faith?} {Where is your faith?} Then he arose, and rebuked the winds and the sea; and there was a great calm.

²⁷But the men marvelled, saying, What manner of man is this, that even the winds and the sea obey him!

Earlier in MT 8, Christ healed several people who evidenced faith (including "great faith"; see Part I) in His miraculous power. His own disciples, however, soon became preoccupied with their adverse circumstances and failed to exercise any faith in Christ when they faced their test. (See also Sec. III on p. 296.)

VII. The disciples' ineffective faith.

A. A father's plight and plea.

MT 17:14 [MK 9:14; LK 9:37] And when they were come to the multitude, there came to him a certain man, kneeling down to him, and saying,

¹⁵Lord, have mercy on my son: for he is lunatic [epileptic], and sore vexed . . . {and, lo, a spirit taketh him, and he suddenly crieth out; and it teareth him that he foameth again, and bruising him hardly departeth from him}.

B. The disciples' lack of faith.

LK 9:40 And I besought thy disciples to cast him out; and they could not.
⁴¹And Jesus answering said, O faithless and perverse generation, how long shall I be with you, and suffer [put up with] you? Bring thy son hither.

This incident immediately followed Christ's transfiguration, and the disciples in verse 16 were the nine not with Him on the mount. At the beginning of the chapter in Luke, Christ gave His disciples "power and authority over all demons" (v. 1). Now, however, they were "faithless" (unbelieving) and "perverse" ("turned from the right way") and could not cast out the demon out of the boy.

C. The father's desire for faith.

MK 9:21 And he asked his father, How long is it ago since this came unto him? And he said, Of a child.
²²And ofttimes it hath cast him into the fire, and into the waters, to destroy him: but if thou canst do any thing, have compassion on us, and help us.
²³Jesus said unto him, If thou canst believe, all things are possible to him that believeth.
²⁴And straightway the father of the child cried out, and said with tears, Lord, I believe; help thou mine unbelief.

The father pleaded with Christ, "*If you* can do anything . . . help us" (v. 22). Christ replied "*If you* can believe, all things are possible." The limiting factor was not what Christ could do, but what the man believed Christ *would* do. Desperately desiring to meet Christ's condition, but acutely aware of his limited faith, the father cried, "I believe; help my unbelief."

D. Christ's support of his faith.

LK 9:42 . . . and Jesus rebuked the unclean spirit, and healed the child, and delivered him again to his father.

E. Christ's promise for our faith.

MT 17:19 Then came the disciples to Jesus apart, and said, Why could not we cast him out?
²⁰And Jesus said unto them, Because of your unbelief: for verily I say unto you, If ye have faith as a grain of mustard seed, ye shall say unto this mountain, Remove hence to yonder place; and it shall remove; and nothing shall be impossible unto you.

Christ plainly stated that their unbelief prevented the disciples from overcoming the demon's power. If they only had faith as small as a mustard seed, they could "move mountains" (i.e., remove overwhelming obstacles to their spiritual growth and service). As He told the distraught father, "All things are possible to him that believeth" (MK 9:23 above). (See Sec. III on p. 189.)

VIII. Peter's denials of faith.

A. Peter's plight and peril.

LK 22:31 And the Lord said, Simon, Simon, behold, Satan hath desired to have you, that he may sift you as wheat:

B. Christ's prayer for his faith.

³²But I have prayed for thee, that thy faith fail not: and when thou art converted, strengthen thy brethren.

C. Peter's self-based faith.

³³And he said unto him, Lord, I am ready to go with thee, both into prison, and to death.
³⁴And he said, I tell thee, Peter, the cock shall not crow this day, before that thou shalt thrice deny that thou knowest me.

Satan desired to put Peter and the other disciples "through the mill" ("you" in v. 31 is plural). Verse 32 may be understood: "But I prayed for you [singular] in particular, that your faith would not utterly fail. And when you return [to full faith in me], strengthen your brothers [in their faith in me]." At the moment, however, Peter's faith was more in his own steadfastness than in God's sustaining power (v. 33). Christ foretold his coming denials and how he would know when his misplaced faith had utterly failed (v. 34).

D. His initial denials of faith.

⁵⁴Then took they him [they arrested Jesus], and led him, and brought him into the high priest's house. And Peter followed afar off.
⁵⁵And when they had kindled a fire in the midst of the hall [court-yard], and were set down together, Peter sat down among them.
⁵⁶But a certain maid beheld him as he sat by the fire, and earnestly looked upon him, and said, This man was also with him.
⁵⁷And he denied him, saying, Woman, I know him not.
⁵⁸And after a little while another saw him, and said, Thou art also of them. And Peter said, Man, I am not.

E. His third denial of faith.

⁵⁹And about the space of one hour after, another confidently affirmed, saying, Of a truth this fellow also was with him: for he is a Galilean.
⁶⁰And Peter said, Man, I know not what thou sayest. {Then began he to curse and to swear, saying, I know not the man. [MT 26:74]} And immediately, while he yet spake, the cock crew.

> [61]And the Lord turned, and looked upon Peter. And Peter remembered the word of the Lord, how he had said unto him, Before the cock crow, thou shalt deny me thrice.
> [62]And Peter went out and wept bitterly.

When the cock crowed and Christ looked at Peter with sorrow and pity, Peter knew instantly that both his faith in himself and his faith in Christ had failed miserably.

IX. Peter's renewed faith.

A. Christ's restoration of his faith.

> LK 24:12 [Hearing that Christ had risen,] Then arose Peter, and ran unto the sepulchre; and stooping down, he beheld the linen clothes laid by themselves, and departed, wondering in himself at that which was come to pass. . . .
> [33b][Later that day,] the eleven gathered together, and them that were with them,
> [34]Saying, The Lord is risen indeed, and hath appeared to Simon [Peter].

B. Christ's employment of his faith.

> JN 21:15 So when they had dined, Jesus saith to Simon Peter, Simon, son of Jonas, lovest thou me more than these? He saith unto him, Yea, Lord; thou knowest that I love thee. He saith unto him, Feed my lambs.
> [16]He saith to him again the second time, Simon, son of Jonas, lovest thou me? He saith unto him, Yea, Lord; thou knowest that I love thee. He saith unto him, Feed my sheep.
> [17]He saith unto him the third time, Simon, son of Jonas, lovest thou me? Peter was grieved because he said unto him the third time, Lovest thou me? And he said unto him, Lord, thou knowest all things; thou knowest that I love thee. Jesus saith unto him, Feed my sheep.
> [19b]And . . . He saith unto him, Follow me.

Scripture does not record the details of Christ's appearance to Peter on the day He arose. It is noteworthy, however, that He appeared first and privately to Peter before appearing to the other disciples. Similarly (in JN 21), Christ focused first on Peter's love and service for Him before giving His Great Commission to all the disciples. Peter, whose failure was the most complete and most visible, received in turn the fullest measure of Christ's love, mercy, and encouragement. Thereafter, Peter demonstrated the "great faith" that eluded him previously. Beginning on Pentecost, he also "strengthened his brothers" in their faith, as Christ had commanded him. (See Sec. IX on p. 302 and Sec. IV on p. 265 for the full passage in JN 21).

10

Portrayals of Effective Prayer

When asked to identify the weakest link in their spiritual lives, many Christian leaders cite the realm of prayer. Most admit they fail to pray for many particular needs or to pray effectively for the matters they do address in prayer. If consistent, effectual prayer seems difficult for spiritual leaders, how can ordinary Christians succeed in this vital area?

Christ knew the obstacles we would face to having an effective prayer life, and He provided the solutions for overcoming them. Through both His preaching and His practice, He showed how we should approach and communicate with God. He described the basis and prerequisites of prayer, including the heart attitudes and expectations with which we should come before God. He gave patterns and examples of subjects for prayer and how our petitions should be presented to God. He pictured God's answers to prayer and how these answers should be received and understood.

By God's grace, the prayers of a new believer can be just as effective as those of a seasoned veteran. Every believer, therefore, has the same opportunity to enjoy a meaningful and productive prayer life. As shown in the following pages, developing and deepening our personal communication with God is a lifelong process. It grows, prayer by prayer and day by day, until we talk face to face with Him in glory.

Parables on Prayer

In teaching us to pray, Christ began by illustrating the simple fact that we all have inherent needs we are unable to meet on our own. God created us to be dependent on Him, and He alone can meet our needs. We must use, of course, the abilities and resources God has given us, and He meets many of our needs through these endowments. At times, however, God reminds each of us that we are completely helpless without His gracious intervention and provision on our behalf. The following parables each picture some aspect of our dependency on God and His provision through our prayer. Specific needs may vary and God's responses may vary, but prayer is always a connecting link.

I. A needy man and his reluctant friend.

A. Some needs require outside help.

LK 11:5 And he said unto them [His disciples], Which of you shall have a friend, and shall go unto him at midnight, and say unto him, Friend, lend me three loaves;

⁶For a friend of mine in his journey is come to me, and I have nothing to set before him?

B. Some help requires persistent pleading.

⁷And he from within shall answer and say, Trouble me not: the door is now shut, and my children are with me in bed; I cannot rise and give thee.

⁸I say unto you, Though he will not rise and give him, because he is his friend, yet because of his importunity [persistence] he will rise and give him as many as he needeth.

C. God responds to persistent prayer.

⁹And I say unto you, Ask, and it shall be given you; seek, and ye shall find; knock, and it shall be opened unto you.

¹⁰For every one that asketh receiveth; and he that seeketh findeth; and to him that knocketh it shall be opened.

In the parable, the man's need resulted from an unexpected event and/or inadequate preparation. Many of our needs fall into this category (e.g., sickness, accidents, financial problems, etc.). Often in such cases, we must call upon a source outside of ourselves to provide what we cannot. In verses 9 and 10, God promises, "Ask me, and I will meet your needs." Christ's progressively intensive commands to "ask, seek, and knock" underscore our helplessness in facing our needs, the urgency of bringing them before God, and God's desire and ability to meet them through prayer. These commands also suggest that we are to persevere in praying for such matters until God clearly answers.

II. A dependent son and his loving father.

A. Good parents readily give good things to their children.

LK 11:11 If a son shall ask bread of any of you that is a father, will he give him a stone? or if he ask a fish, will he for a fish give him a serpent? 12Or if he shall ask an egg, will he offer him a scorpion?

B. God gives much more to His children who pray.

13[MT 7:11] If ye then, being evil, know how to give good gifts unto your children: how much more shall your heavenly Father give the Holy Spirit {give good things} to them that ask him?

A loving father readily gives his dependent child what the child needs for health, strength, and well-being. The child, knowing his father loves him, implicitly trusts his father to provide what he needs. The parable does not say that a father gives his son whatever he wants. It emphasizes, rather, that a good father will not give bad things to his son, but only wholesome things for the son's ultimate good.

"How much more" will God give exactly what is needed — in the right amount and at the right time — "to them that ask Him." He accomplishes this provision through His Holy Spirit (v. 13). The Holy Spirit and the "good things" (MT 7:11) God gives His children are so closely associated in each believer's life that the Gospel writers refer to these divine gifts interchangeably. Our responsibility is to "ask Him" in simple, trusting, child-like prayer.

III. A persistent widow and an unjust judge.

A. Repeated prayer for unmet needs is appropriate.

**LK 18:1 And he spake a parable unto them to this end, that men ought always to pray, and not to faint [lose heart];
2Saying, There was in a city a judge, which feared not God, neither regarded man:
3And there was a widow in that city; and she came unto him, saying, Avenge me of [Give me justice regarding] mine adversary.
4And he would not for a while: but afterward he said within himself, Though I fear not God, nor regard man;
5Yet because this widow troubleth me, I will avenge her, lest by her continual coming she weary me.**

B. God may delay His answer — but answer He will, and justly.

**6And the Lord said, Hear what the unjust judge saith.
7And shall not God avenge his own elect, which cry day and night unto him, though he bear long with them?
8I tell you that he will avenge them speedily [suddenly]. Nevertheless, when the Son of man cometh, shall he find faith on the earth?**

After a long delay, the aggrieved widow's persistent pleas for justice were finally granted. The parable follows Christ's description of conditions on earth just before His return, and its principal application is to the extended pleading of persecuted believers for God's justice and deliverance. A broader application, however, is also suggested; namely, that persistent prayer for any biblically-based unanswered request is entirely appropriate — until God provides a clear indication, one way or another, of His will in the matter. If a self-centered, unjust judge would finally respond to persistent pleading, how much more will the all-loving and perfectly just God of heaven answer the repeated cries of His own children.

Verses 7-8 may be understood: "And shall not God execute justice for His own chosen people, who cry day and night to Him, even though He delays responding for a long while? I tell you that He will execute justice for them suddenly [when Christ returns]. Nevertheless, when the Son of man comes again, will He find on earth that enduring faith [demonstrated by the persistent widow]?"

IV. A repentant sinner and a merciful God.

A. Some confess their sinfulness; others feign righteousness.

LK 18:9 And he spake this parable unto certain which trusted in themselves that they were righteous, and despised others:

¹⁰Two men went up into the temple to pray; the one a Pharisee, and the other a publican.

¹¹The Pharisee stood and prayed thus with himself, God, I thank thee, that I am not as other men are, extortioners, unjust, adulterers, or even as this publican.

¹²I fast twice in the week, I give tithes of all that I possess.

¹³And the publican, standing afar off, would not lift up so much as his eyes unto heaven, but smote upon his breast, saying, God be merciful to me a sinner.

B. God forgives only the penitent and exalts only the humble.

¹⁴I tell you, this man went down to his house justified rather than the other: for every one that exalteth himself shall be abased; and he that humbleth himself shall be exalted.

Although last in Luke's order of the four parables, this one pictures God's first requirement for answered prayer; namely, that we recognize our absolute unworthiness and complete dependence on His mercy and grace to receive anything from His hand. We cannot trust in ourselves or our own righteousness (v. 9) to produce anything but our downfall (v. 14).

Our greatest need is to be "justified" (v. 14), i.e., declared righteous by God through His forgiveness of our sinful nature and the multitude of sins it has spawned. God meets this need with eternal forgiveness when we call upon Him in prayer for salvation. Thereafter, as believers, we must continue to call on God for daily cleansing from new sins, including all wrongdoing and failures to do what is right. "If we confess our sins, He is faithful and just to forgive us our sins, and to cleanse us from all unrighteousness" (I John 1:9). Whether for salvation or for subsequent cleansing, our prayer must always include the thought, "God be merciful to me a sinner."

Prescriptions and Promises for Prayer

Christ provided enough instruction to enable every believer to pray effectively and to do so consistently. Even so, most believers fail to maintain an active and productive prayer life. Does our failure stem from insufficient knowledge of how to pray? or from insufficient time spent in prayer? Does it reflect a mechanical approach or casual attitude toward prayer? or impatience with unanswered prayer? Does our lack of results stem from a lack of faith? or from unconfessed sin? or from wrong motives in prayer? Is our problem as basic as not adequately understanding our relationship with God? The following passages illustrate how these and other impediments to effective prayer can be overcome.

I. Prayer and abiding in Christ "bears fruit."

   A. Abide and pray, and bear "much fruit."

      JN 15:5 I am the vine, ye are the branches: He that abideth in me, and I in him, the same bringeth forth much fruit: for without me ye can do nothing. . . .

      ⁷If ye abide in me, and my words abide in you, ye shall ask what ye will, and it shall be done unto you.

      ⁸Herein is my Father glorified, that ye bear much fruit; so shall ye be my disciples.

Abiding in Christ is both a prerequisite and a guarantee of a fruitful prayer life. (To abide in Christ is to maintain close, intimate communion with Him; see Sec. II on p. 122.) Christ promised that those who abide in Him will "bear much fruit" to the glory of God. The more we abide in Him, the more our prayers will be in line with God's will, and the more fruit He will produce in our lives.

   B. Serve and pray, and bear "lasting fruit."

      JN 15:16 Ye have not chosen me, but I have chosen you, and ordained you, that ye should go and bring forth fruit, and that your fruit should remain: that whatsoever ye shall ask of the Father in my name, he may give it you.

Christ has "ordained" (commissioned) us to "go and bring forth fruit." One of the principal resources He has given us for accomplishing that service is direct access to the Father through prayer. In particular, prayer that is related to service for Christ will bear lasting fruit. That fruit is not specifically identified here, but we know from other scripture that it includes the fruit of the Spirit in our own lives (Gal. 5:22-23) and the fruit of evangelism in the lives of others (JN 4:35-36). It also includes the fruit of good works in activities that please and honor God (MT 7:17-18). Each of these lasting fruits is nourished and brought to fruition with the aid of faithful, fervent prayer.

II. Prayer in Christ's name does "great works."

A. Its outcome will glorify the Father and the Son.

JN 14:12 Verily, verily, I say unto you, He that believeth on me, the works that I do shall he do also; and greater works than these shall he do; because I go unto my Father.

[13]And whatsoever ye shall ask in my name, that will I do, that the Father may be glorified in the Son.

[14]If ye shall ask any thing in my name, I will do it.

Praying "in Christ's name" includes prayer that is in His stead (what He Himself would request), for His glory (for His benefit more than our own), through His office (as our heavenly High Priest), with His authority (as our sovereign Lord), invoking His power (as the all-wise and all-powerful Son of God), and as His representative (in His earthly service). Christ promised to answer such prayers in such a way "that the Father may be glorified in the Son" (v. 13).

Everything we request, therefore, must be consistent with (and submissive to) God's will for that matter. He will answer such requests perfectly and completely — even accomplishing through our prayers "greater works" than the miracles Christ Himself performed on earth (v. 12). The latter is possible in that God's answers to such prayers will produce eternal spiritual benefits (such as the salvation of the lost and changed lives of believers) that are of greater value than the temporal physical benefits of Christ's miracles.

B. Its answer will cause "your joy [to] be full."

JN 16:24 Hitherto have ye asked nothing in my name: ask, and ye shall receive, that your joy may be full.

[25]These things have I spoken unto you in proverbs: but the time cometh, when I shall no more speak unto you in proverbs, but I shall show you plainly of the Father.

[26]At that day ye shall ask in my name: and I say not unto you, that I will pray the Father for you:

²⁷For the Father himself loveth you, because ye have loved me, and have believed that I came out from God.

The joy of seeing God mightily respond to our prayers is one of the great blessings of a faithful prayer life. In this passage, Christ told His disciples that after His departure they would have direct access to the Father through prayer in His name. What they so request, they would receive. God readily answers such prayers out of His great love for His children and in response to their love for Christ (v. 27).

C. Its request "shall be done" when sought collectively.

MT 18:19 Again I say unto you, That if two of you shall agree on earth as touching any thing that they shall ask, it shall be done for them of my Father which is in heaven.
²⁰For where two or three are gathered together in my name, there am I in the midst of them.

Christ promised to be "in the midst" of faithful believers who unite together in prayer. This suggests that He will so aid in the formulation of their petitions that a positive response from heaven is assured. The verses that precede this passage suggest that the "two or three" mentioned here are earnest believers who have joined to seek God's will for resolving an issue between other believers (see Sec. VII on p. 219 for the full passage). Based on the above sections, however, believers who are abiding in Christ and who jointly pray in His name may claim this promise for prayers that relate to other matters as well.

III. Prayer with faith "moves mountains."

A. Faith in God's power works miracles.

MT 21:18 [MK 11:20] Now in the morning as he returned into the city, he hungered.
¹⁹And when he saw a fig tree in the way, he came to it, and found nothing thereon, but leaves only, and said unto it, Let no fruit grow on thee henceforward for ever. And presently the fig tree withered away.
²⁰And when the disciples saw it, they marvelled, saying, How soon is the fig tree withered away!
²¹Jesus answered and said unto them, {Have faith in God.} Verily I say unto you, If ye have faith, and doubt not, ye shall not only do this which is done to the fig tree, but also if ye shall say unto this mountain, Be thou removed, and be thou cast into the sea; it shall be done.

B. Faith with prayer accomplishes "all things."

²²[MK 11:23] And all things, whatsoever ye shall ask in prayer, believing, ye shall receive. {For verily I say unto you, That whosoever . . . shall not doubt in his heart, but shall believe that those

things which he saith shall come to pass; he shall have whatsoever he saith. Therefore I say unto you, What things soever ye
desire, when ye pray, believe that ye receive them, and ye shall
have them.}

C. Faith as small as a mustard seed works the impossible.

LK 17:5 And the apostles said unto the Lord, Increase our faith.

⁶And the Lord said, If ye had faith as a grain of mustard seed, ye
might say unto this sycamine [black mulberry] tree, Be thou plucked up
by the root, and be thou planted in the sea; and it should obey you.

MT 17:20b . . . verily I say unto you, If ye have faith as a grain of
mustard seed, ye shall say unto this mountain, Remove hence to
yonder place; and it shall remove; and nothing shall be impossible
unto you.

As in the preceding section, these astounding promises are for believers who
are abiding in Christ and praying in His name. There may not be many
instances where actually removing physical trees or mountains would accomplish God's will, but there are many mountainous obstacles to our spiritual
growth and service that God wants to remove from our lives or paths. Prayer
with faith in His infinite power can remove these just as decisively and miraculously as with any physical mountain. With such prayer, "nothing shall be
impossible [for] you" (MT 17:20).

IV. Prayer "in your closet" brings God's reward.

A. God sees "in secret" behind closed doors.

MT 6:5 And when thou prayest, thou shalt not be as the hypocrites
are: for they love to pray standing in the synagogues and in the cor-
ners of the streets, that they may be seen of men. Verily I say unto
you, They have their reward.

⁶But thou, when thou prayest, enter into thy closet, and when thou
hast shut thy door, pray to thy Father which is in secret; and thy
Father which seeth in secret shall reward thee openly.

With the great privileges, promises, and power that God gives believers
through prayer, it is easy to begin thinking that these result, at least in part,
from our goodness or faithfulness or some other measure of our worthiness.
The wickedness of such thoughts is demonstrated by how quickly they seek
validation through recognition and praise from others (v. 5). As shown in Sec.
I on p. 158 ff, similar traps exist in every area of worship and spiritual service.
Christ commanded, therefore, that we consciously avoid drawing attention to
ourselves when we pray. If necessary, withdraw to your "closet" and pray to
God "in secret" behind closed doors. God honors and rewards such humble,
personal prayer in many ways, both privately and openly.

B. God knows our needs before we ask.

7But when ye pray, use not vain repetitions, as the heathen do: for they think that they shall be heard for their much speaking.
8Be not ye therefore like unto them: for your Father knoweth what things ye have need of, before ye ask him.

"Vain repetitions" (e.g., empty recitations of religious phrases and cliches) can infect both private and public prayers. Avoiding such pitfalls requires a humble spirit, simple faith, and candid honesty. Prayers that express godly desires and that flow from the heart will not be vain repetitions. Wonderfully, God knows exactly what we need, and exactly how and when to supply it, even before we ask Him (v. 8). When we pray as Christ taught, our prayers will accomplish great works, move mountains, and bear much fruit. Thus God answers our prayers that please and honor Him.

Patterns for Prayer

Christ's disciples keenly sensed their inadequacy in prayer. They asked Him, therefore, "Teach us to pray." Certainly they knew the traditional practices and procedures of prayer. From childhood, they had been exposed to Old Testament teaching and examples of prayer, and they often observed the religious leaders in prayer. Yet they asked Jesus, "Teach us to pray." As earnest believers, they wanted their prayers to be more than mechanical recitations that lack vitality and bear few results. They desired to pray purposefully and effectively, with assurance that their prayers would be heard and answered by God.

I. Patterns for prayer that God will answer.

A. The Lord's pattern prayer for His disciples.

LK 11:1 And it came to pass, that, as he was praying in a certain place, when he ceased, one of his disciples said unto him, Lord, teach us to pray, as John also taught his disciples.
2And he said unto them, When ye pray, say,

Our Father which art in heaven,
Hallowed be thy name.
Thy kingdom come.
Thy will be done, as in heaven, so in earth.
3Give us day by day our daily bread.
4And forgive us our sins;
for we also forgive every one that is indebted to us.
And lead us not into temptation;
but deliver us from evil [the evil one].

Christ gave this "disciples' prayer" as a model for their and our instruction. It is an example for all believers (who alone may call God "Father"), showing what our priorities should be in prayer and the spirit in which we should present our petitions. It is remarkable for its simplicity and brevity, its breadth, and its balance. As a pattern, it was not given primarily to be recited by rote, and Christ varied its wording on another occasion (see below). It may be prayed verbatim, however, if done so thoughtfully and sincerely with reverence and understanding.

        B. A similar prayer from the Sermon on the Mount.
          MT 6:9 After this manner therefore pray ye:
          Our Father which art in heaven,
          Hallowed be thy name.
          [10]Thy kingdom come.
          Thy will be done in earth, as it is in heaven.
          [11]Give us this day our daily bread.
          [12]And forgive us our debts,
          as we forgive our debtors.
          [13]And lead us not into temptation,
          but deliver us from evil [the evil one]:
          For thine is the kingdom, and the power, and the glory, for ever.
          Amen.

The first three petitions (vv. 9-10) recognize and relate to God's proper position in our thoughts, our lives, and our environment. His "name" represents His entire being, as revealed by His attributes, purposes, and actions. "Hallowed" means "made holy." Although God is infinitely and eternally holy without any contribution from finite, sinful people, we need to "make Him holy" in our minds and lives, and to present Him as holy to others. This is one of the ways in which His kingdom (kingship) will come, i.e., be furthered and increased.

God's kingdom in this context includes both His rule in individual human hearts in this age and His millennial worldwide rule through Christ in the age to come. (See also "The Kingdom" on p. 398 ff.) His will is always done completely and perfectly "in heaven" through the full, instant, and joyful obedience of the angels who serve at His throne. So should it be done "on earth" by those who claim to serve Him here. (In any event, His sovereign plan will be accomplished, in both heaven and earth, with or without the voluntary submission of His created beings.)

The second three petitions deal with basic human needs. These are (1) our dependence on God for daily sustenance; (2) our reliance on God for forgiveness and cleansing; and (3) our deliverance by God from sin and Satan. Each of these needs should make us humble in our attitudes and thinking, faithful in our conduct and practice, and thankful for God's supply in their fulfillment.

"Our daily bread" pictures everything we require (but not everything we want), as we trust God for today and leave the future in His sovereign care. His daily forgiveness of our sins (now promised in advance and guaranteed by Christ's atonement) should foster in us an increasing willingness to forgive those who sin against us. God will never "lead us into temptation" (see James 1:13); rather, the last petition is a plea that He will direct us away from temptation, which He does through His Word, His Spirit, and His providence (I Cor. 10:13). As we trust and obey Him, He will deliver us from both evil and the evil one.

II. Particular prayers God desires to answer.

A. Prayer for victory over temptation and weakness.

MT 26:41 [to His disciples in Gethsemane] Watch and pray, that ye enter not into temptation: the spirit indeed is willing, but the flesh is weak.

LK 22:45 And when he rose up from prayer, and was come to his disciples, he found them sleeping for sorrow,
⁴⁶And said unto them, Why sleep ye? rise and pray, lest ye enter into temptation.

Vigilant praying that we not succumb to temptation will remind us of (1) the ever-present reality and dangerous character of temptation; (2) our inherent weakness and inability to overcome it in our own strength; and (3) God's enabling power that is always available for gaining the victory over it.

B. Prayer for forgiveness and for a forgiving spirit.

MK 11:25 And when ye stand praying, forgive, if ye have ought against any: that your Father also which is in heaven may forgive you your trespasses.

Christ commanded believers to be willing to forgive whenever we have anything against anybody (v. 25). A forgiving spirit is essential both for effective prayer in general and specifically for receiving God's cleansing and restoration when we sin ourselves. (See also Sec. III on p. 215.)

C. Prayer for God's blessing on those who hate you.

MT 5:44 But I say unto you, Love your enemies, bless them that curse you, do good to them that hate you, and pray for them which despitefully use you, and persecute you;

> **⁴⁵That ye may be the children of your Father which is in heaven: for he maketh his sun to rise on the evil and on the good, and sendeth rain on the just and on the unjust.**

This command goes well beyond forgiving our enemies; it requires that we also pray sincerely for their blessing. The reason is at least twofold: (1) it develops God-like character in us (v. 45), and (2) it opens an avenue for God's mercy and grace to flow to those who clearly need God to work in their lives. (See "the Golden Rule" on p. 150.)

D. Prayer for workers and the reaping of God's "harvest."

> **MT 9:37 Then saith he unto his disciples, The harvest truly is plenteous, but the laborers are few;**
> **³⁸Pray ye therefore the Lord of the harvest, that he will send forth laborers into his harvest.**

This command indicates the importance and urgency of praying for the spread of the gospel. Such prayer heightens our awareness of (1) the plight of the unsaved in the largely untended and waiting harvest; (2) our own responsibility to labor diligently in God's world-wide field; (3) our complete dependence on "the Lord of the harvest" for bringing in any part of His harvest; and (4) the praise and worship that God deserves from all of His created beings. (See also Sec. VIII on p. 6.)

E. Prayer for readiness for Christ's return.

> **MK 13:32 But of that day and that hour knoweth no man, no, not the angels which are in heaven, neither the Son, but the Father.**
> **³³Take ye heed, watch and pray: for ye know not when the time is.**

> **LK 21:34 And take heed to yourselves, lest at any time your hearts be overcharged with surfeiting, and drunkenness, and cares of this life, and so that day come upon you unawares.**
> **³⁵For as a snare shall it come on all them that dwell on the face of the whole earth.**
> **³⁶Watch ye therefore, and pray always, that ye may be accounted worthy to escape all these things that shall come to pass, and to stand before the Son of man.**

Nothing in life is more important than being "accounted worthy . . . to stand before the Son of man" when He comes again. Although our salvation depends entirely on Christ's atonement, our readiness for His return requires our diligence in both preparation and prayer. Constant prayer to this end ("pray always," v. 36) is crucial because there are so many temptations and "cares of this life" (v. 34) that can divert our focus from Christ's imminent return and our standing before Him for judgment and rewards. (See also "Mankind's Judgment" in Secs. VI-IX on p. 444 ff.)

Christ's Example in Prayer

In preceding sections, Christ taught the people (and especially His disciples) through pictures and precepts pertaining to prayer. In this and the following section, He taught them through His personal practice of prayer. Prayer played a major role in His life and ministry, and His example in prayer illustrates the place it should have in our lives and ministries. In calling us to prayer, as in calling us for service, Christ commands, "Follow me."

I. Christ prayed frequently throughout His ministry.

A. At His baptism, at the beginning of His ministry.

LK 3:21 Now when all the people were baptized, it came to pass, that Jesus also being baptized, and praying, the heaven was opened, [22]And the Holy Ghost descended in a bodily shape like a dove upon him, and a voice came from heaven, which said, Thou art my beloved Son; in thee I am well pleased.

B. In times of strenuous service.

LK 5:15 But so much the more went there a fame abroad of him: and great multitudes came together to hear, and to be healed by him of their infirmities. [16]And he withdrew himself into the wilderness, and prayed.

MK 1:34 And he healed many that were sick of divers diseases, and cast out many devils; and suffered not the devils to speak, because they knew him. [35]And in the morning, rising up a great while before day, he went out, and departed into a solitary place, and there prayed.

MT 14:23 And when he had sent the multitudes away [after feeding the 5,000], he went up into a mountain apart to pray: and when the evening was come, he was there alone.

C. When feeding the multitudes.

JN 6:11 And Jesus took the loaves; and when he had given thanks, he distributed to the disciples, and the disciples to them that were set down [5,000 men, plus women and children]; and likewise of the fishes as much as they would.

MT 15:36 And he took the seven loaves and the fishes, and gave thanks, and brake them, and gave to his disciples, and the disciples to the multitude [4,000 men, plus women and children].

D. At His transfiguration.

LK 9:28 And it came to pass about an eight days after these sayings, he took Peter and John and James, and went up into a mountain to pray.

²⁹And as he prayed, the fashion of his countenance was altered, and his raiment was white and glistering [glistening].

As this and following sections show, Christ prayed frequently and in a variety of circumstances. He undoubtedly prayed more often than is specifically reported, but the instances that are reported are informative. Sections A and D above indicate that He prayed at major junctures in His ministry, recognizing His dependence on the Father for accomplishing His ordained work and seeking God's blessing on it. Section B reveals the strain, both physically and emotionally, that Christ's demanding work placed on His human capacities. He needed regular strengthening and refreshing, and these were provided through precious times alone with His Father in prayer. Section C indicates that Christ prayed before meals, recognizing God as the source of all of earthly blessings and thanking Him for His goodness and bounty.

II. Christ prayed earnestly for His disciples.

A. Before calling His chosen twelve.

LK 6:12 And it came to pass in those days, that he went out into a mountain to pray, and continued all night in prayer to God.

¹³And when it was day, he called unto him his disciples: and of them he chose twelve, whom also he named apostles;

B. When teaching them to pray.

LK 11:1 And it came to pass, that, as he was praying in a certain place, when he ceased, one of his disciples said unto him, Lord, teach us to pray, as John also taught his disciples. [The Lord's Prayer followed; see p. 191.]

C. When preparing them for His coming death.

LK 9:18 And it came to pass, as he was alone praying, his disciples were with him: and he asked them, saying, Whom say the people that I am?

¹⁹They answering said, John the Baptist; but some say, Elias; and others say, that one of the old prophets is risen again.

²⁰He said unto them, But whom say ye that I am? Peter answering said, The Christ of God.

²¹And he straightly charged them, and commanded them to tell no man that thing;

²²Saying, The Son of man must suffer many things, and be rejected of the elders and chief priests and scribes, and be slain, and be raised the third day.

D. In supporting Peter's weak faith.
LK 22:31 And the Lord said, Simon, Simon, behold, Satan hath desired to have you, that he may sift you as wheat:
³²But I have prayed for thee, that thy faith fail not: and when thou art converted [returned to full faith in me], strengthen thy brethren.

E. In sending them the Holy Spirit.
JN 14:16 And I will pray the Father, and he shall give you another Comforter, that he may abide with you for ever;
¹⁷Even the Spirit of truth; whom the world cannot receive, because it seeth him not, neither knoweth him: but ye know him; for he dwelleth with you, and shall be in you.

Christ was acutely aware of His disciples' weaknesses and limitations. He knew these required faithful prayer, including His own on their behalf. He knew the many trials they would face and how often they would fail. As a result, He spent all night in prayer before selecting the Twelve. To equip them for their own ministry, Christ taught His disciples to pray. Several teaching opportunities arose when they observed Him in prayer. He set the example in every area of service He expected them to fulfill, including that of diligent prayer.

III. Christ prayed graciously for people's needs.

A. For little children, that God would bless them.
MT 19:13 Then were there brought unto him little children, that he should put his hands on them, and pray: and the disciples rebuked them.
¹⁴But Jesus said, Suffer little children, and forbid them not, to come unto me: for of such is the kingdom of heaven.

MK 10:15 Verily I say unto you, Whosoever shall not receive the kingdom of God as a little child, he shall not enter therein.
¹⁶And he took them up in his arms, put his hands upon them, and blessed them.

B. For "babes in Christ," that they would know Him more fully.
LK 10:21 In that hour Jesus rejoiced in spirit, and said, I thank thee, O Father, Lord of heaven and earth, that thou hast hid these things from the wise and prudent, and hast revealed them unto babes: even so, Father; for so it seemed good in thy sight.
²²All things are delivered to me of my Father: and no man knoweth who the Son is, but the Father; and who the Father is, but the Son, and he to whom the Son will reveal him.

C. For Lazarus' mourners, that they would believe in Him.

JN 11:41 Then they took away the stone from the place where the dead was laid. And Jesus lifted up his eyes, and said, Father, I thank thee that thou hast heard me.

⁴²And I knew that thou hearest me always: but because of the people which stand by I said it, that they may believe that thou hast sent me.

⁴³And when he thus had spoken, he cried with a loud voice, Lazarus, come forth.

⁴⁴And he that was dead came forth, bound hand and foot with graveclothes: and his face was bound about with a napkin. Jesus saith unto them, Loose him, and let him go.

Christ was always conscious of the particular needs of the people around Him. He was also in constant communication with His Father with respect to meeting those needs. In the above examples, Christ prayed for various people, invoking God's grace on their behalf. Three broad categories of people are represented here. Section A pictures those who need to hear the message of salvation and to come to Christ in simple child-like faith. Section B represents "babes in Christ" who responded to Him in simple, humble faith, and now need to grow in their relationship with Him. Section C illustrates unbelievers who have not responded to prior invitations to receive Christ, but to whom God continues to provide opportunities to trust in Him. In each case, Christ brought the people and their particular needs before His Father in prayer.

IV. Christ prayed submissively regarding His death.

A. That God would be glorified through His death.

JN 12:27 Now is my soul troubled; and what shall I say? Father, save me from this hour: but for this cause came I unto this hour.

²⁸Father, glorify thy name. Then came there a voice from heaven, saying, I have both glorified it, and will glorify it again.

B. For the new covenant established by His death.

LK 22:19 And he took bread, and gave thanks, and brake it, and gave unto them, saying, This is my body which is given for you: this do in remembrance of me.

²⁰Likewise also the cup after supper, saying, This cup is the new testament in my blood, which is shed for you.

C. For accepting God's will concerning His death.

LK 22:39 And he came out, and went, as he was wont [accustomed], to the mount of Olives; and his disciples also followed him.

⁴⁰And when he was at the place, he said unto them, Pray that ye enter not into temptation.

⁴¹And he was withdrawn from them about a stone's cast, and kneeled down, and prayed,

⁴²Saying, Father, if thou be willing, remove this cup from me: nevertheless not my will, but thine, be done.

D. For bearing the pain and grief of His death.

⁴³And there appeared an angel unto him from heaven, strengthening him.

⁴⁴And being in an agony he prayed more earnestly: and his sweat was as it were great drops of blood falling down to the ground.

⁴⁵And when he rose up from prayer, and was come to his disciples, he found them sleeping for sorrow,

⁴⁶And said unto them, Why sleep ye? rise and pray, lest ye enter into temptation.

In praying publicly in JN 12, with His disciples in LK 22, and then privately later in LK 22, Christ subjected His personal desires to the Father's will regarding His death. As a man, He dreaded the horrible, excruciating torture and death He knew was just ahead. As the Son of God, He also knew that bearing our sin on the cross would bring full separation from the Father (see below). These issues had been settled in eternity past in the immutable counsels of God; yet Christ as a man needed to reaffirm His complete self-denial and submission to the Father's will alone. (See Sec. IV on p. 53.)

Christ's full submission to the Father's will was demonstrated clearly when He refused to pray for deliverance from His captors a few minutes later. "Then said Jesus unto him [Peter], Put up again thy sword into his place; . . . Thinkest thou that I cannot now pray to my Father, and he shall presently give me more than twelve legions of angels? But how then shall the scriptures be fulfilled, that thus it must be?" (MT 26:52-54).

V. Christ prayed selflessly while dying on the cross.

A. For mercy for those who crucified Him.

LK 23:33 And when they were come to the place, which is called Calvary, there they crucified him, and the malefactors, one on the right hand, and the other on the left.

³⁴Then said Jesus, Father, forgive them; for they know not what they do. And they parted his raiment, and cast lots.

B. When forsaken by God while bearing our sin.

MT 27:45 Now from the sixth hour there was darkness over all the land unto the ninth hour.

46And about the ninth hour Jesus cried with a loud voice, saying, Eli, Eli, lama sabachthani? that is to say, My God, my God, why hast thou forsaken me?

C. In sacrificing Himself for our salvation.

LK 23:45 And the sun was darkened, and the veil of the temple was rent in the midst.

46And when Jesus had cried with a loud voice, he said, Father, into thy hands I commend my spirit: and having said thus, he gave up the ghost.

Christ's prayers on the cross demonstrate how fully and selflessly He submitted to God's plan for our salvation. His prayer of intercession sought God's mercy for those who were putting Him to death. His prayer of anguish as God forsook Him indicated the horrible separation from God He experienced as He bore our death and hell in our place. His final prayer of committal conveyed His very life, with all it represented, into the Father's hands in satisfaction of the sin-debt of all mankind. "He gave up the ghost [His spirit]" may be understood: "He voluntarily breathed out His life" — for you and me.

Christ's Heart Revealed in Prayer
(John Chapter 17)

On the eve of His crucifixion, Christ prayed two very different prayers. In Gethsemane, He prayed, "If it be possible, let this cup pass from me: nevertheless, not as I will, but as thou wilt" (MT 26:39). That prayer revealed the great internal struggle He experienced as a man in irrevocably submitting His body, soul, and spirit to the Father's will for His death on the cross. In contrast, Christ prayed earlier that evening more as God the Son addressing God the Father, speaking as God with God. The Son maintained His submission to the Father throughout, but their perfect union and complete harmony are evident in every phrase. This is truly "the Lord's prayer" — Christ's petition that God's glory be manifested and magnified on earth through His work and through the lives of His followers until He returns.

I. Christ's prayer that The Father and The Son be glorified.

A. In the Son's "hour" of death.

JN 17:1 These words spake Jesus, and lifted up his eyes to heaven, and said, Father, the hour is come; glorify thy Son, that thy Son also may glorify thee:

B. In those the Father has given Him.

2As thou hast given him power over all flesh, that he should give eternal life to as many as thou hast given him.

³**And this is life eternal, that they might know thee the only true God, and Jesus Christ, whom thou hast sent.**

C. In The Son's restored eternal glory.

⁴**I have glorified thee on the earth: I have finished the work which thou gavest me to do.**

⁵**And now, O Father, glorify thou me with thine own self with the glory which I had with thee before the world was.**

The Jews previously wanted to kill Christ, but "His hour was not yet come" (JN 7:30, 8:20). Now His hour had arrived. It was, however, an hour of glorification, not an hour of defeat. Both Father and Son were (and are) glorified through the cross, as it magnified their love, justice, mercy, and grace. They were also glorified through the empty tomb, as it acclaimed their immutable plan and promises and their infinite power. And they were glorified through Christ's ascension to God's throne, as it exalted their eternal majesty, glory, and sovereignty over all creation.

II. His prayer that His followers be kept steadfast and secure.

A. In God's message and in His Messenger.

⁶**I have manifested thy name unto the men which thou gavest me out of the world: thine they were, and thou gavest them me; and they have kept thy word.**

⁷**Now they have known that all things whatsoever thou hast given me are of thee.**

⁸**For I have given unto them the words which thou gavest me; and they have received them, and have known surely that I came out from thee, and they have believed that thou didst send me.**

B. In God's Name and in His care.

⁹**I pray for them: I pray not for the world, but for them which thou hast given me; for they are thine.**

¹⁰**And all mine are thine, and thine are mine; and I am glorified in them.**

¹¹**And now I am no more in the world, but these are in the world, and I come to thee. Holy Father, keep through thine own name those whom thou hast given me, that they may be one, as we are.**

¹²**While I was with them in the world, I kept them in thy name: those that thou gavest me I have kept, and none of them is lost, but the son of perdition; that the scripture might be fulfilled.**

Christ distinguished clearly between those *of the Word* and those *of the world* (vv. 6, 9, 14-16). The former both *keep* the Word and are *kept* by the Word. He prayed that the Father would "keep through thine own name" all those the Father had given Him (v. 11). The Father's "name" refers to His essential being, attributes, character, and purposes. He reveals these to believers through His

Word and through His works on their behalf. Being kept through His name means being made secure by all that God is.

C. In Christ's joy and in God's Word.

¹³And now come I to thee; and these things I speak in the world, that they might have my joy fulfilled in themselves.

¹⁴I have given them thy word; and the world hath hated them, because they are not of the world, even as I am not of the world.

D. In spite of attacks by an evil world.

¹⁵I pray not that thou shouldest take them out of the world, but that thou shouldest keep them from the evil [the evil one].

¹⁶They are not of the world, even as I am not of the world.

Christ prayed that believers would be filled with His joy — in spite of unhappy and trying circumstances. He did not pray that they would be taken "out of the world" — neither out of the physical world nor out from among the world of unbelievers to whom they are sent as witnesses. He did pray, however, that God would preserve and protect them "from the evil" (or, "from the evil one"), including from the godless world system.

III. His prayer that believers be sanctified and unified.

A. As God's representatives in the world.

¹⁷Sanctify them through thy truth: thy word is truth.

¹⁸As thou hast sent me into the world, even so have I also sent them into the world.

¹⁹And for their sakes I sanctify myself, that they also might be sanctified through the truth.

B. As one united body in the world.

²⁰Neither pray I for these alone, but for them also which shall believe on me through their word;

²¹That they all may be one; as thou, Father, art in me, and I in thee, that they also may be one in us: that the world may believe that thou hast sent me.

C. As proof of God's love for the world.

²²And the glory which thou gavest me I have given them; that they may be one, even as we are one:

²³I in them, and thou in me, that they may be made perfect in one; and that the world may know that thou hast sent me, and hast loved them, as thou hast loved me.

Sanctify means "set apart" or "make holy" for God's purpose or use. In verse 19, Christ "set Himself apart" to be our Savior and Lord so that we might be "made holy and set apart" for God's service in the world. God's Word is the means with which He sanctifies us. The sanctification of believers leads to unity among believers — not merely outward unity, but unity of spirit, love, and purpose, as exists between the Father and the Son (v. 21). Such unity is necessary if unbelievers are to become convinced that God sent Christ into the world, and that He loves them and wants to save them (v. 23).

IV. His prayer that believers will experience Him fully.

A. Through their glorious presence with Him in heaven.

²⁴Father, I will that they also, whom thou hast given me, be with me where I am; that they may behold my glory, which thou hast given me: for thou lovedst me before the foundation of the world.

B. Through His loving presence with them on earth.

²⁵O righteous Father, the world hath not known thee: but I have known thee, and these have known that thou hast sent me.

²⁶And I have declared unto them thy name, and will declare it: that the love wherewith thou hast loved me may be in them, and I in them.

The great desire and longing of Christ's heart is that all those who believe in Him be with Him in glory. This is the "inheritance" given to Him by the Father and is "the joy that was set before Him," for which He "endured the cross" (Heb. 12:2). Until then, He declares the Father's name to those the Father has given Him (i.e., He reveals God's nature, purposes, etc. to them, as in v. 11 above). He also showers on His own the same infinite love the Father bestowed on Him. His loving presence within every believer (v. 26) assures their future presence with Him in heaven forever.

11

Reflections of God in Believers

God created man in His own likeness (Gen. 5:1), but that likeness was fatally marred when Adam sinned (Rom. 5:12). One of God's purposes in "re-creating" those who receive Christ as their Savior is that they bear His likeness and "be conformed to the image of His Son" (Rom. 8:29). Christ taught, therefore, that we are to be like our heavenly Father and reflect His nature in our attitudes and behavior. We are to be kind and merciful as He is kind and merciful (LK 6:35-36); to love and give as He loves and gives (MT 5:44-45); and to help and serve others as He (through Christ) helps and serves us (MT 20:26-28). In summary, "Be ye therefore perfect [i.e., complete; lacking nothing], even as your Father which is in heaven is perfect" (MT 5:48).

Although God's commands alone should be sufficient to evoke obedient responses from His children on any matter, He often couples His commands with promises to bless those who obey Him. This is true in every major area of the Christian life. Christ not only commanded, for example, that we put away pride and selfishness, He promised rewards for those who are humble and graciously serve others. He also accompanied His commands with instructions and illustrations for how to implement them. This chapter reviews some of the principal ways in which we are to portray God in our lives by reflecting His character in our own.

Examples of Love and Giving

"God so loved . . . that He gave." Infinite loving and infinite giving are among God's principal characteristics — and the most welcome by needy people. In the New Testament, God's love is described primarily with the Greek word *agape*. Agape is unilateral, unconditional, and unlimited love. It is based solely on the deliberate choice of the one extending it. Such love is not diminished by a lesser response from its intended recipient or by any other factor or circumstance. (The *form* of its expression, though, may vary greatly depending on the situation, including reproof and chastisement when necessary.)

Above all, agape is love that gives. It gives of itself for the good of another — it gives generously and sacrificially, willingly and even eagerly. This is how God loves and gives to us, and it is how we are to love and give to Him, and also to one another.

I. "God is love."

A. "Herein is love . . . that He loved us, and sent His Son."
JN 3:16 For God so loved the world, that he gave his only begotten Son, that whosoever believeth in him should not perish, but have everlasting life.
¹⁷For God sent not his Son into the world to condemn the world; but that the world through him might be saved.

B. "We have known and believed the love that God hath to us."
JN 17:23 [Christ prayed:] . . . thou hast sent me, and hast loved them, as thou hast loved me. . . .
²⁶And I have declared unto them thy name, and will declare it: that the love wherewith thou hast loved me may be in them, and I in them.

These and the following verses from John's Gospel (and the headings from his first epistle, in 4:7-19) declare the infinite love that God has for all mankind (JN 3) and the particular love He has for those who receive Christ as their Savior (JN 17). Words cannot describe such love or express the overwhelming sense of thanksgiving and praise within those who receive it.

C. "We love Him because He first loved us."
JN 15:9 As the Father hath loved me, so have I loved you: continue ye in my love.

D. "He that dwelleth in love dwelleth in God, and God in him."
JN 14:23b If a man love me, he will keep my words: and my Father will love him, and we will come unto him, and make our abode with him.

As God's love for us is unchanging and eternal, our love for Him should be steadfast and unceasing. Christ reveals in JN 15 how we are to continue and grow in His love (see Sec. III on p. 123). Our continuing relationship with Christ, and with the Father through Him, is based on their perfect love for us and our responding in love to them. All the while, the Father, the Son, and the Holy Spirit all make their abode within us (JN 14:17-23) and continually demonstrate their love to us.

II. God shows His love through manifold giving.

God's love for us is clearly declared in the Gospels (especially in John). It is also demonstrated there by the many gifts and benefits He abundantly bestows on His children. The following brief passages illustrate the variety and scope of the invaluable gifts God freely gives every believer through His Son and His Holy Spirit.

A. God gives us the Bread of Life from heaven.

JN 6:32 Then Jesus said unto them, Verily, verily, I say unto you, Moses gave you not that bread from heaven; but my Father giveth you the true bread from heaven.

33For the bread of God is he which cometh down from heaven, and giveth life unto the world.

B. God gives us eternal life through Christ.

JN 10:27 My sheep hear my voice, and I know them, and they follow me:

28And I give unto them eternal life; and they shall never perish, neither shall any man pluck them out of my hand.

29My Father, which gave them me, is greater than all; and no man is able to pluck them out of my Father's hand.

C. God gives us living water to quench our souls' thirst.

JN 4:10 Jesus answered and said unto her, If thou knewest the gift of God, and who it is that saith to thee, Give me to drink; thou wouldest have asked of him, and he would have given thee living water. . . .

14But whosoever drinketh of the water that I shall give him shall never thirst; but the water that I shall give him shall be in him a well of water springing up into everlasting life.

D. God gives us sonship in His family.

JN 1:12 But as many as received him, to them gave he power [the right] to become the sons of God, even to them that believe on his name:

13Which were born, not of blood, nor of the will of the flesh, nor of the will of man, but of God.

No greater gift has ever been given than God's gift of His Son for our salvation. Some of that gift's many facets are indicated in the above verses, including eternal life, security in His care, satisfaction of our souls' hunger and thirst, and placement as full-fledged sons in His family. "Thanks be unto God for His unspeakable gift!" (II Cor. 9:15).

E. God gives us His Word to guide and strengthen us.

JN 17:8 For I have given unto them the words which thou gavest me; and they have received them, and have known surely that I came out from thee, and they have believed that thou didst send me. . . .

[17]Sanctify them through thy truth: thy word is truth.

F. God gives us His Spirit to abide within us.

JN 14:16 And I will pray the Father, and he shall give you another Comforter, that he may abide with you for ever;

[17]Even the Spirit of truth; whom the world cannot receive, because it seeth him not, neither knoweth him: but ye know him; for he dwelleth with you, and shall be in you.

G. God gives us "good things" in answer to our prayers.

MT 7:7 Ask, and it shall be given you; seek, and ye shall find; knock, and it shall be opened unto you: . . .

[11]If ye then, being evil, know how to give good gifts unto your children, how much more shall your Father which is in heaven give good things to them that ask him?

God has given us the three inexhaustible resources cited above to enable us to live abundantly and productively as His children. These are (1) His Word, which reveals Himself and His will to us, and prepares (sanctifies) us to live for Him; (2) His Holy Spirit, who indwells us to guide our understanding and application of His Word and to mold us into the image of His Son; and (3) prayer, through which we can approach Him with our needs and concerns and enlist His infinite power on our (and others') behalf. "His divine power hath given unto us all things that pertain unto life and godliness, through the knowledge of Him that hath called us to glory and virtue" (II Peter 1:3).

H. God gives us rest, peace, and joy.

MT 11:28 Come unto me, all ye that labor and are heavy laden, and I will give you rest.

JN 14:27 Peace I leave with you, my peace I give unto you: not as the world giveth, give I unto you. Let not your heart be troubled, neither let it be afraid.

JN 15:11 These things have I spoken unto you, that my joy might remain in you, and that your joy might be full.

I. God gives us our daily provision.

LK 11:3 Give us day by day our daily bread.

LK 12:29 And seek not ye what ye shall eat, or what ye shall drink, neither be ye of doubtful mind. . . .
³¹But rather seek ye the kingdom of God; and all these things shall be added unto you.

J. God gives us an eternal heavenly kingdom.

LK 12:32 Fear not, little flock; for it is your Father's good pleasure to give you the kingdom.

God gives us everything we need to sustain us in this life and to prepare us for our life to come. For our souls, He provides rest, peace, and joy in the midst of the troubles and trials of life. For our bodies, He provides the food, clothing, shelter, and strength we need each day to do His will for our lives. For our spirits, He provides the assurance of our relationship with Him, His continuing presence with us, and our future eternal home with Him in heaven. "My God shall supply all your need according to his riches in glory by Christ Jesus" (Phil. 4:19).

III. Believers show love for Christ by obeying Him.

A. Through loving obedience, we know Christ more fully.

JN 14:15 If ye love me, keep my commandments.. . .
²¹He that hath my commandments, and keepeth them, he it is that loveth me: and he that loveth me shall be loved of my Father, and I will love him, and will manifest myself to him.

B. Through loving obedience, we abide in Christ continually.

JN 15:10 If ye keep my commandments, ye shall abide in my love; even as I have kept my Father's commandments, and abide in his love.

The principal test of our love for Christ is whether we obey His commands. These commands (God's entire Word) cover every area of life, either explicitly or implicitly, through precepts, principles, examples, and illustrations. Our obedience also must be constant and complete, not selective or sporadic. Consistent obedience, however, is possible only through the enabling power of the Holy Spirit and our submission to His leading. (God's forgiveness is readily available for our confessed failures, but we dare not presume on His mercy and grace.)

IV. Believers show love for Christ by loving each other.

A. It demonstrates we are Christ's disciples.

JN 13:34 A new commandment I give unto you, That ye love one another; as I have loved you, that ye also love one another.

³⁵By this shall all men know that ye are my disciples, if ye have love one to another.

B. It replicates the love Christ has for us.

JN 15:12 This is my commandment, That ye love one another, as I have loved you.

¹³Greater love hath no man than this, that a man lay down his life for his friends.

In both of these passages, Christ's standard for our love for other believers is that it be "as I have loved you" — i.e., the same in nature and to the same degree. In our own strength, this is as impossible as "keeping His commandments" in Sec. III above. We can only love others in the way Christ requires as we allow Him to love them through us. As with His other commandments, He provides the ability and direction for showing such love through His Holy Spirit. Seeing such a love among believers, others will know that we are Christ's disciples — for His honor and glory.

V. Believers give to God by giving to His children.

A. They give help and encouragement to Christ's needy "brethren."

MT 25:31 When the Son of man shall come in his glory, . . .

³⁴Then shall the King say unto them on his right hand, Come, ye blessed of my Father, inherit the kingdom prepared for you from the foundation of the world:

³⁵For I was an hungered, and ye gave me meat: I was thirsty, and ye gave me drink: I was a stranger, and ye took me in:

³⁶Naked, and ye clothed me: I was sick, and ye visited me: I was in prison, and ye came unto me.

³⁷Then shall the righteous answer him, saying, Lord, when saw we thee an hungered, and fed thee? or thirsty, and gave thee drink? . . .

⁴⁰And the King shall answer and say unto them, Verily I say unto you, Inasmuch as ye have done it unto one of the least of these my brethren, ye have done it unto me.

A distinguishing feature of those who belong to Christ is the loving and gracious assistance they give His needy brethren (v. 40). That assistance often is rendered simply because the recipient is a brother in Christ and a fellow member of God's family. These verses do not teach that anyone is either saved or lost on the basis of his good works (see Sec. VIII on p. 444 for the full passage). They do teach, however, that those who love God and give generously to His children are giving to God Himself.

B. They give hospitality and support to Christ's faithful servants.

MT 10:40 He that receiveth you [Christ's disciples] receiveth me, and he that receiveth me receiveth him that sent me.

⁴¹**He that receiveth a prophet in the name of a prophet [i.e., because he is a prophet] shall receive a prophet's reward; and he that receiveth a righteous man in the name of [because he is] a righteous man shall receive a righteous man's reward.**

Christ promised that believers who aid and support God's faithful servants in their ministries will share in the eternal rewards those servants will receive. Paul thanked Philippian believers who generously gave to support his ministry, "Not because I desire a gift: but I desire fruit that may abound *to your account*" (4:17).

C. They give aid and assistance to Christ's humble children.

MT 10:42 And whosoever shall give to drink unto one of these little ones a cup of cold water only in the name of [because he is] a disciple, verily I say unto you, he shall in no wise lose his reward.

MK 9:41 For whosoever shall give you a cup of water to drink in my name, because ye belong to Christ, verily I say unto you, he shall not lose his reward.

God is impartial and "no respecter of persons" (Acts 10:34). His children likewise should extend just as much love and kindness to Christ's little-known followers as they would to recognized "prophets" and notable "righteous men." *Little ones* in verse 42 include new and dependent converts of all ages as well as seemingly lowly or unimposing believers who also need loving help and encouragement. In each of the above passages, Christ promises eternal rewards to every believer who helps meet the needs of other believers.

VI. Believers must give with a loving spirit.

A. Give willingly to those who need your help.

LK 6:30 Give to every man that asketh of thee; and of him that taketh away thy goods ask them not again.
³¹**And as ye would that men should do to you, do ye also to them likewise.**

B. Give graciously even to those who hate you.

³²**For if ye love them which love you, what thank have ye? for sinners also love those that love them. . . .**
³⁵**But love ye your enemies, and do good, and lend, hoping for nothing again; and your reward shall be great, and ye shall be the children of the Highest: for he is kind unto the unthankful and to the evil.**

C. Give generously to others without partiality.

³⁸**Give, and it shall be given unto you; good measure, pressed down, and shaken together, and running over, shall men give into**

your bosom. For with the same measure that ye mete withal it shall be measured to you again.

Much of the context in which Christ gave the "Golden Rule" (v. 31) relates to the manner of our giving and its recipients (see p. 150 ff for the full passage.). The gracious and generous spirit with which we give to all types of people will be a public indication that we are "children of the Highest" (v. 35). Just as He is kind to the unthankful and the evil, so must we be in our responses and giving to others. When we give with such a spirit, Christ promised that God will cause other people (including those unrelated to the matter at hand) to give generously to us in return.

    D. Give charitably to the poor and unfortunate.

    LK 12:33 Sell that ye have, and give alms [to the poor]; provide yourselves bags which wax not old, a treasure in the heavens that faileth not, where no thief approacheth, neither moth corrupteth. ³⁴For where your treasure is, there will your heart be also.

    E. Give unselfishly to those who cannot reciprocate.

    LK 14:1 And it came to pass, as he went into the house of one of the chief Pharisees to eat bread on the sabbath day, that they watched him. . . .

    ¹²Then said he also to him that bade him, When thou makest a dinner or a supper, call not thy friends, nor thy brethren, neither thy kinsmen, nor thy rich neighbors; lest they also bid thee again, and a recompense be made thee.

    ¹³But when thou makest a feast, call the poor, the maimed, the lame, the blind:

    ¹⁴And thou shalt be blessed; for they cannot recompense thee: for thou shalt be recompensed at the resurrection of the just.

Believers should be generous not only with friends and loved ones, but also with those normally overlooked or left out. In the above passages, Christ commanded that we focus our giving on those who are unable to return the favor or respond in any like manner. When we so give, God obligates Himself to be our rewarder, with compensation far greater than what we have given or what any person could ever give us in return.

Lessons on Forgiveness and Reconciliation

Who should we forgive, and when, and how often? Also, what should we do when we have offended someone else? Questions like these bothered the disciples and have troubled believers in all ages. Christ addressed these issues with several unusual (and unusually strong) commands and comparisons. He condemned the limits and conditions that people commonly impose on their willingness to forgive, and He made God's example our standard and guide. What He taught by precept, He lived in practice and fulfilled on the cross. Our part is to obey His instruction and follow His example — by portraying His forgiving spirit with our own.

I. Be willing to forgive without limit.

    A. Forgive your brother "seventy times seven" times.

MT 18:21 Then came Peter to him, and said, Lord, how oft shall my brother sin against me, and I forgive him? till seven times?

22Jesus saith unto him, I say not unto thee, Until seven times: but, Until seventy times seven.

    B. Forgive him even "seven times in a day."

LK 17:3 Take heed to yourselves: If thy brother trespass against thee, rebuke him; and if he repent, forgive him.

4And if he trespass against thee seven times in a day, and seven times in a day turn again to thee, saying, I repent; thou shalt forgive him.

Peter apparently wanted Christ to set an upper limit beyond which he no longer had to forgive an offending brother. Christ's answer, although framed in Peter's numerical format, clearly indicates that forgiveness is not to be meted out in limited quantities. Rather, His followers are to grant a virtually unlimited series of full pardons, and do so from a willing, merciful heart. The parallel passage in Luke adds the offended person's responsibility to confront the offender graciously, and the latter's responsibility to repent sincerely.

II. Forgive others, as a much-forgiven debtor.

    A. Everyone is accountable to God, with debts that are unpayable.

MT 18:23 Therefore is the kingdom of heaven likened unto a certain king, which would take account of [settle accounts with] his servants.

24And when he had begun to reckon, one was brought unto him, which owed him ten thousand talents [millions of dollars].

25But forasmuch as he had not to pay, his lord commanded him to be sold, and his wife, and children, and all that he had, and payment to be made.

    B. Those who rightly seek God's mercy receive it.

26The servant therefore fell down, and worshipped him, saying, Lord, have patience with me, and I will pay thee all.

27Then the lord of that servant was moved with compassion, and loosed him, and forgave him the debt.

This parable is part of Christ's answer to Peter's question in Sec. I.A, and it illustrates why a believer's willingness to forgive must be virtually unlimited.

The servant pictures our position as a sinner indebted to God far beyond our ability to repay. (Ten thousand talents would equal at least several million dollars today — many times what any servant could earn, let alone repay, in his lifetime.) Justice demanded the loss of *everything* the servant had. The kindly king, however, had compassion for the helpless servant and readily forgave the entire debt.

C. Some who are forgiven will not forgive in turn.

> ²⁸But the same servant went out, and found one of his fellowservants, which owed him an hundred pence [denarii]: and he laid hands on him, and took him by the throat, saying, Pay me that thou owest.
> ²⁹And his fellowservant fell down at his feet, and besought him, saying, Have patience with me, and I will pay thee all.
> ³⁰And he would not: but went and cast him into prison, till he should pay the debt.

This debt, about four month's wages for a laborer, was a tiny fraction (less than one-fourth of one percent) of the debt the first servant had been forgiven. But while his own pardon still echoed in the background, he callously refused to give any leeway to his minor debtor. The ratio of the two debts depicts the magnitude of our sins against God (and also of His forgiveness) in comparison with any offense that anyone may commit against us.

D. Those who are forgiven must also be forgiving.

> ³¹So when his fellowservants saw what was done, they were very sorry, and came and told unto their lord all that was done.
> ³²Then his lord, after that he had called him, said unto him, O thou wicked servant, I forgave thee all that debt, because thou desiredst me:
> ³³Shouldest not thou also have had compassion on thy fellowservant, even as I had pity on thee?

The principal message of the parable is that those whom God has forgiven should readily and graciously forgive those who genuinely seek their forgiveness — especially when the offender is a "fellow servant" of the Lord. An application of verse 31 is that those who observe the wrong treatment of one believer by another should respond with godly sorrow and intercessory prayer. Their earnest desire should be for restoration and reunion, not rejection or retribution.

E. Refusing to forgive will incur God's judgment.

> ³⁴And his lord was wroth, and delivered him to the tormentors, till he should pay all that was due unto him.
> ³⁵So likewise shall my heavenly Father do also unto you, if ye from your hearts forgive not every one his brother their trespasses.

Because of the wicked servant's unforgiving spirit, the king withdrew his clemency and imposed the well-deserved sentence. These verses do not imply that a believer can lose his salvation; rather, they show that refusal to forgive (and from the *heart*) is a serious offense that deserves severe judgment. Here again, the parable applies primarily to believers because of their undeserved and unlimited forgiveness by God. God's judgment can take many forms and may fall at any time; its principal purposes are (1) to produce repentance in the sinning believer's heart and restoration in his relationships and (2) to serve as a warning to other believers of the consequences of an unforgiving spirit.

III. Forgive others, and enjoy God's blessing.

A. Forgiving others is required by God.

MT 6:9 [LK 11:2-4] After this manner therefore pray ye: . . .
¹²And forgive us our debts, as we forgive our debtors. {And forgive us our sins; for we also forgive every one that is indebted to us.} . . .
¹⁴For if ye forgive men their trespasses, your heavenly Father will also forgive you:
¹⁵But if ye forgive not men their trespasses, neither will your Father forgive your trespasses.

Christ's atonement obtained the full forgiveness of all of our sins — past, present, and future. Our forgiving others, therefore, cannot merit our forgiveness by God. These verses (and those below), however, clearly indicate that a ready and willing disposition to forgive others is an indispensable characteristic of those whom God has forgiven. A believer's assurance of his own forgiveness and his ongoing experience of the joys and blessings of salvation depend heavily on his obedience to God's commands — high on the list of which is that he forgive others as he has been forgiven (Eph. 4:32).

B. Forgiving others is a prerequisite for answered prayer.

MK 11:24 Therefore I say unto you, What things soever ye desire, when ye pray, believe that ye receive them, and ye shall have them.
²⁵And when ye stand praying, forgive, if ye have ought against any: that your Father also which is in heaven may forgive you your trespasses.
²⁶But if ye do not forgive, neither will your Father which is in heaven forgive your trespasses.

One of the conditions for answered prayer is that we not hold any thing against anybody (v. 25). A believer who refuses to forgive and be reconciled to someone who has offended him cannot have the assurance that God will answer his prayers — including prayers for his own forgiveness and cleansing from his sin.

C. Forgiving others develops God-like character.

LK 6:36 Be ye therefore merciful, as your Father also is merciful.
³⁷Judge not, and ye shall not be judged: condemn not, and ye shall not be condemned: forgive, and ye shall be forgiven:

Our forgiveness of others should follow the pattern God established in forgiving us — namely, to forgive willingly, graciously, fully, and permanently (never raising the offense again). An ongoing readiness to so forgive will develop in us the God-like qualities of being merciful and kind, will honor and glorify God before others, and will multiply His blessing on our lives as well.

IV. Follow Christ's example of forgiving others.

A. He sought forgiveness for His enemies.

LK 23:33 And when they were come to the place, which is called Calvary, there they crucified him, and the malefactors, one on the right hand, and the other on the left.
³⁴Then said Jesus, Father, forgive them; for they know not what they do. And they parted his raiment, and cast lots.

Christ interceded not only for the Roman soldiers, but also for the Jewish leaders who orchestrated His death, the mob that demanded it, and the nation that rejected Him as its Messiah. Inherent in His prayer for their forgiveness was His longing that they acknowledge and repent of their sin and accept Him as their Savior. God substantially answered His prayer when thousands of Jews, including many priests, trusted in Christ for salvation beginning on Pentecost some 50 days later.

B. He gave forgiveness to the penitent thief.

³⁹And one of the malefactors which were hanged railed on him, saying, If thou be Christ, save thyself and us.
⁴⁰But the other answering rebuked him, saying, Dost not thou fear God, seeing thou art in the same condemnation?
⁴¹And we indeed justly; for we receive the due reward of our deeds: but this man hath done nothing amiss.
⁴²And he said unto Jesus, Lord, remember me when thou comest into thy kingdom.
⁴³And Jesus said unto him, Verily I say unto thee, To day shalt thou be with me in paradise.

Matthew and Mark report that, at first, *both* thieves reviled Jesus on the cross. One, however, later recognized his own guilt and Christ's innocence. Repenting of his sin, he asked Christ simply but effectively to remember him in His future kingdom. Christ graciously gave Him more than he dared request. That same day, he entered Christ's glorious presence in heaven itself.

C. He grants forgiveness to repentant sinners.

1. Some condemn too quickly or harshly.
JN 8:3 And the scribes and Pharisees brought unto him a woman taken in adultery; and when they had set her in the midst,
⁴They say unto him, Master, this woman was taken in adultery, in the very act.
⁵Now Moses in the law commanded us, that such should be stoned: but what sayest thou?
⁶This they said, tempting him, that they might have to accuse him. But Jesus stooped down, and with his finger wrote on the ground, as though he heard them not.

2. He knows the repentant from the recalcitrant.
⁷So when they continued asking him, he lifted up himself, and said unto them, He that is without sin among you, let him first cast a stone at her.
⁸And again he stooped down, and wrote on the ground.
⁹And they which heard it, being convicted by their own conscience, went out one by one, beginning at the eldest, even unto the last: and Jesus was left alone, and the woman standing in the midst.

3. He forgives and restores completely.
¹⁰When Jesus had lifted up himself, and saw none but the woman, he said unto her, Woman, where are those thine accusers? hath no man condemned thee?
¹¹She said, No man, Lord. And Jesus said unto her, Neither do I condemn thee: go, and sin no more.

Christ did not excuse the woman's sin or relax the Law's command. Although unstated, He knew that in her heart she repented of her wicked deed and longed for God's forgiveness. His challenge to the Pharisees in verse 7 turned their attention to their own sin and to their deserved judgment. With smitten consciences or the realization that Christ had foiled their attempt to trick Him, they slinked away one by one.

Christ graciously forgave the penitent woman and assured her that her deserved condemnation had been removed. Both as a command and a warning, however, He admonished her to forsake forever such sinful behavior. She went her way relieved, restored, and no doubt reformed.

V. Seek and grant forgiveness, as did the prodigal and his father.

A. Repentance requires contrition and confession.
LK 15:17 And when he [the prodigal son] came to himself, he said, How many hired servants of my father's have bread enough and to spare, and I perish with hunger!

> [18]I will arise and go to my father, and will say unto him, Father, I have sinned against heaven, and before thee,
> [19]And am no more worthy to be called thy son: make me as one of thy hired servants.
> [20a]And he arose, and came to his father.

The son recognized he had sinned not only against his father but "against heaven" (see Sec. IV on p. 93 for the full parable). All wrongs, both of commission and omission, are first and foremost against God. Confession and repentance before God, therefore, is the first step in seeking forgiveness for a wrong against others. A confession to his father also was necessary, and the son set out to ask his father's forgiveness.

B. Forgiveness includes compassion and consolation.

> [20b]But when he was yet a great way off, his father saw him, and had compassion, and ran, and fell on his neck, and kissed him.
> [21]And the son said unto him, Father, I have sinned against heaven, and in thy sight, and am no more worthy to be called thy son.

C. Restoration brings communion and celebration.

> [22]But the father said to his servants, Bring forth the best robe, and put it on him; and put a ring on his hand, and shoes on his feet:
> [23]And bring hither the fatted calf, and kill it; and let us eat, and be merry:
> [24]For this my son was dead, and is alive again; he was lost, and is found. And they began to be merry.

The loving and forgiving father pictures God in the parable. Our response to those who have offended us should be like this father's (and like God's with us). He obviously was prepared in advance to forgive his son, and he looked expectantly for the opportunity to do so. At the first sign of the son's desire to deal with his wrong, the father did everything in his power to accept both the son and his confession and to effect their full reconciliation.

VI. Seek reconciliation when you may be in the wrong.

A. When someone believes you have wronged him.

> **MT 5:23 Therefore if thou bring thy gift to the altar, and there rememberest that thy brother hath ought against thee;**
> [24]**Leave there thy gift before the altar, and go thy way; first be reconciled to thy brother, and then come and offer thy gift.**

Without regard to who may be at fault (thereby avoiding disputes and closing possible loopholes), Christ addressed every instance in which a believer knows or suspects that a brother holds a grievance against him. Even when the alleged offender honestly believes he has committed no wrong, he is to follow the procedure Christ prescribed above. Through humble, objective, and gracious discussion of the alleged offense, the two brothers should seek reconciliation. If an offense existed, confession should be made and forgiveness given. Each brother may then worship and serve God with a clear conscience and a clean slate.

> B. When someone accuses or opposes you.
>> [25]**Agree with thine adversary quickly, whiles thou art in the way with him; lest at any time the adversary deliver thee to the judge, and the judge deliver thee to the officer, and thou be cast into prison.**
>> [26]**Verily I say unto thee, Thou shalt by no means come out thence, till thou hast paid the uttermost farthing.**

This command deals with cases in which an allegedly aggrieved party becomes an adversary against a believer. To the extent possible within scriptural limits, the believer should quickly and honorably make peace with his adversary. Otherwise, the believer's financial and physical well-being may be in jeopardy, as well as his reputation and testimony. Promptly resolving such disputes may also increase the believer's ability to influence an unbelieving adversary with the gospel.

> VII. Resolve offenses within Christ's body.

> A. Settle problems promptly and privately.
>> **MT 18:15 Moreover if thy brother shall trespass against thee, go and tell him his fault between thee and him alone: if he shall hear thee, thou hast gained thy brother.**

Prompt and private resolution of offenses involving believers is the best procedure with the best outcome. One may ask, who should take the first step toward reconciliation — the offended brother (as in this verse), or the offending brother (as in 5:23 above)? These passages make it clear that *each* of the parties should assume full responsibility for seeking reconciliation with the other. Each should be conscious of how much he has been forgiven by God and be willing to forgive as he has been forgiven. Their God-given love for fellow believers should draw them toward each other and facilitate their full reconciliation.

> B. Obtain, if necessary, the aid of godly believers.
>> [16]**But if he will not hear thee, then take with thee one or two more, that in the mouth of two or three witnesses every word may be established.**
>> [17]**And if he shall neglect to hear them, tell it unto the church: but if he neglect to hear the church, let him be unto thee as an heathen man and a publican.**

The goal in verse 16, and again in 17a, still is reconciliation of the alienated brothers. The seriousness of this process and the expanding involvement of other believers should help impress the offender to repent and confess his wrongdoing. Although bringing the matter before the local church is to be the last resort, taken only after all other patient, prayerful efforts have failed, it must be taken when there is stubbornly-held sin in the body of Christ.

C. Decide the matter in Christ's presence with His authority.
¹⁸Verily [assuredly] I say unto you, Whatsoever ye shall bind [or, forbid] on earth shall be bound [shall have been forbidden] in heaven: and whatsoever ye shall loose [or, permit] on earth shall be loosed [shall have been permitted] in heaven.
¹⁹Again I say unto you, That if two of you shall agree on earth as touching any thing that they shall ask, it shall be done for them of my Father which is in heaven.
²⁰For where two or three are gathered together in my name, there am I in the midst of them.

Christ promised that when a church rightly follows His prescribed procedure for dealing with unresolved offenses in its midst, what it concludes and either "forbids" or "permits" in the matter has already been confirmed in heaven itself. In this context, the "two or three" praying believers in verses 19-20, may well refer to the "two or three witnesses" in verse 16 who carefully and prayerfully examined the alleged offense and reported their findings to the church. Christ promised to be present among even the smallest group of such believers and to answer their prayers regarding such matters. (See also Sec. II.C on collective prayer on p. 189.)

This passage (vv. 15-20) immediately preceded and led to Peter's question on forgiveness in Section I and Christ's parable on the subject in Section II.

Pictures of Humility and Service to Others

Self-centeredness is mankind's common trait, and self-satisfaction its common goal. These characteristics brought about man's fall into sin in Eden, and they remain a principal hindrance to both salvation and Christian growth. By the same token, true humility and sacrificial service to others are totally contrary to human nature. Christ, therefore, often proclaimed God's will for these vital areas. He repeatedly stressed that whoever exalts himself will be humbled, but whoever humbles himself will be exalted (MT 23:12). This basic principle applies both to our attitudes and responses toward God (LK 18:14) and to our attitudes and responses toward other people (LK 14:11).

I. Object lessons with little children. (MT 18; MK 9; LK 9)

  A. Humility precedes honor, and service precedes prominence.

LK 9:46 Then there arose a reasoning [dispute] among them [the disciples], which of them should be greatest.

MT 18:1 At the same time came the disciples unto Jesus, saying, Who is the greatest in the kingdom of heaven?

MK 9:35 And he sat down, and called the twelve, and saith unto them, If any man desire to be first, the same shall be last of all, and servant of all {for he that is least among you all, the same shall be great}.

The disciples frequently strove over which of them would hold the highest positions in the Messiah's kingdom. Their selfish desires for prestige and personal power clashed head-on with the entire thrust of Christ's ministry. Rather than justly rebuking them, however, He demonstrated His own servant's heart by patiently exhorting them to put their own desires last and become "servants of all." Only with genuine humility and submissive service would they "be great" in God's sight and in His kingdom.

  B. Humility includes child-like faith and submission.

MT 18:2 And Jesus {perceiving the thought of their heart,} called a little child unto him, and set him in the midst of them, {and when he had taken him in his arms,}
³[He] said, Verily I say unto you, Except ye be converted, and become as little children, ye shall not enter into the kingdom of heaven.
⁴Whosoever therefore shall humble himself as this little child, the same is greatest in the kingdom of heaven.

Using a small child as an object lesson, Christ admonished His disciples to "be converted" ("turned around") from the selfish way they were headed and to humble themselves "as little children." The childlike characteristics God requires include pure, simple faith in His Word, full dependence on His loving care, and prompt obedience to His calls and commands. Godly childlikeness also includes a true concern for those in need; it is shown in unselfish acts of giving and kindness to others.

  C. Responses to "little ones" are responses to God Himself.

⁵And whoso shall receive [shall welcome] one such little child in my name receiveth me {and whosoever shall receive me receiveth him that sent me}.
⁶But whoso shall offend one of these little ones which believe in me, it were better for him that a millstone were hanged about his neck, and that he were drowned in the depth of the sea. . . .

¹⁰Take heed that ye despise not one of these little ones; for I say unto you, That in heaven their angels do always behold the face of my Father which is in heaven.

God's "little ones" include (1) impressionable children (v. 5) who depend on older people to meet their needs and who imitate their behavior, and (2) new converts and immature Christians ("which believe in me"; v. 6) who similarly are strongly influenced by the attitudes and behavior of older believers. "Offending them" (i.e., causing them to stumble spiritually in any way) is a most serious offense against both them and God Himself. In contrast, warmly welcoming them into fellowship and further discipleship honors both their Savior and their heavenly Father.

"Despise not" in verse 10 covers the full range of possible negative responses from strong dislike to irritation and disdain to indifference and neglect. Christ emphatically commanded, "Take heed" not to treat even one single little one in such a manner. Their angels have constant access to their Father in heaven and are His ministers for their benefit. Their angels also are a potent force to be reckoned with by those who in any way despise one of God's little ones.

> D. Helping God's little ones pleases Him.
>
> **MK 10:13 [MT 19:13] And they brought young children to him, that he should touch them {put his hands on them, and pray}: and his disciples rebuked those that brought them.**
>
> **¹⁴But when Jesus saw it, he was much displeased, and said unto them, Suffer [permit] the little children to come unto me, and forbid them not: for of such is the kingdom of God.**
>
> **¹⁵Verily I say unto you, Whosoever shall not receive the kingdom of God as a little child, he shall not enter therein.**
>
> **¹⁶And he took them up in his arms, put his hands upon them, and blessed them.**

Soon after their lesson in MT 18, the disciples had an opportunity to implement it in MT 19. But they failed completely. They rebuked, rather than welcomed, those who brought children to Christ for His blessing. This time, Christ was "moved with indignation" (v. 14) and said (lit.) "stop hindering them, for to such little children belongs the kingdom of God." Those who love God will develop an increasing love for His "little ones" as they realize how much He loves them and that all believers are God's children and members together in His family.

II. Contrasts between chiefs and servants.

A. Some Christians care more about status than service.

MK 10:37 They [two disciples, James and John] said unto him, Grant unto us that we may sit, one on thy right hand, and the other on thy left hand, in thy glory.

³⁸But Jesus said unto them, . . .

⁴⁰ᵇto sit on my right hand and on my left hand is not mine to give; but it shall be given to them for whom it is prepared.

B. But those who serve are greater in God's sight.

MT 20:24 And when the ten heard it, they were moved with indignation against the two brethren.

²⁵But Jesus called them unto him, and said, Ye know that the princes of the Gentiles exercise dominion [domineering oppression] over them, and they that are great exercise authority [despotic control] upon them.

²⁶But it shall not be so among you: but whosoever will be great among you, let him be your minister [attendant];

²⁷And whosoever will be chief among you, let him be your servant:

Again, the disciples squabbled over their relative status in the coming kingdom. James and John asked for the two highest positions next to Christ's throne, and the others reacted angrily. In response, Christ declared that God seeks and honors submissive service, not self-promotion. Believers must not adopt earthly rulers' typical means of gaining influence and exercising authority, or seek preeminence over others (as James and John had just done). God's "great" ones and "chief" ones are those who attend and serve fellow believers, and who do so with humility, submission, and selflessness.

C. Christ is our example of sacrificial service.

²⁸Even as the Son of man came not to be ministered unto, but to minister, and to give his life a ransom for many.

Christ came specifically to serve people, and to serve sacrificially as our ransom. Originally, a ransom was the price paid to free a slave from bondage. Most slaves were destitute, and the ransom typically had to be paid by another on their behalf. In the ultimate act of sacrificial service, Christ gave His life as a ransom to purchase our redemption and free us from the bondage of sin. With His life and in His death, He set the example of the humble, gracious service He wants all believers to give to one another.

D. God will exalt each humble servant that belongs to Him.

MT 23:11 But he that is greatest among you shall be your servant.

¹²And whosoever shall exalt himself shall be abased; and he that shall humble himself shall be exalted.

In His final recorded address to the Jewish people, Christ again stressed the importance of humbly serving others (v. 11). In the broader context of MT 23, verse 12 clearly includes those who either humble themselves or exalt themselves before God with respect to their need for salvation. These will either be exalted with eternal life or abased with eternal condemnation. Those, however, who humble themselves *before God* for salvation should also humble themselves *before others* in sacrificial Christ-like service. God will further exalt these humble servants in His way and in His time, both in this life and in eternity.

III. The serving Savior and the dining disciples.

A. He served *them* at the *Lord's* Supper.

LK 22:14 And when the hour was come, he sat down, and the twelve apostles with him.

¹⁵And he said unto them, With [great] desire I have desired to eat this passover with you before I suffer: . . .

¹⁹And he took bread, and gave thanks, and brake it, and gave unto them, saying, This is my body which is given for you: this do in remembrance of me.

²⁰Likewise also the cup after supper, saying, This cup is the new testament in my blood, which is shed for you.

B. He even served Judas, who planned to betray Him.

²¹But, behold, the hand of him that betrayeth me is with me on the table. {He it is, to whom I shall give a sop, when I have dipped it. And when he had dipped the sop, he gave it to Judas Iscariot, the son of Simon. (JN 13:26)}

C. Instead of serving, they were striving.

²⁴And there was also a strife among them, which of them should be accounted the greatest.

After three years of hearing and observing Christ's lessons on humility and service, and after having been corrected before for arguing about "which of them should be the greatest," the disciples were at it again! Equally notable is Christ's continued longsuffering and gentleness in repeating these lessons for His stumbling students. On each occasion, He reinforced His teaching with new illustrations of humble service.

D. Diners outrank servers — except among believers.

²⁵And he said unto them, The kings of the Gentiles exercise lordship over them; and they that exercise authority upon them are called benefactors ["well-doers," though they be tyrants].

²⁶But ye shall not be so: but he that is greatest among you, let him be as the younger; and he that is chief, as he that doth serve.

[27]For whether is greater, he that sitteth at meat, or he that serveth? is not he that sitteth at meat? but I am among you as he that serveth.

Christ declared that His "greatest" disciples defer willingly to other believers, as a younger person defers to his seniors (especially in that culture). He also contrasted those who dine in comfort with those who humbly serve their meal. Although diners were considered "greater" than lowly servers, Christ said "I am among you as a server." After serving their supper, He humbly served them further in the following example.

IV. The Master washing His servants' feet.

    A. Christ performed a lowly servant's lowly task.

JN 13:3 Jesus knowing that the Father had given all things into his hands, and that he was come from God, and went to God;
[4]He riseth from supper, and laid aside his garments; and took a towel, and girded himself.
[5]After that he poureth water into a basin, and began to wash the disciples' feet, and to wipe them with the towel wherewith he was girded.

Sandaled feet dirtied quickly on Israel's dusty roads. A servant or a bond-slave, therefore, would wash the feet of arriving guests or a returning master. In the borrowed room used for the Last Supper, no servants were present. None of the disciples (who were arguing about being the greatest) volunteered for this lowly task. Christ removed His cloak and tunic and, wearing only a loincloth as a lowly servant, quietly began washing His disciples' feet. At first, they watched in silence, stunned at what they were seeing.

    B. Peter missed the point of the picture.

[6]Then cometh he to Simon Peter: and Peter saith unto him, Lord, dost thou wash my feet?
[7]Jesus answered and said unto him, What I do thou knowest not now; but thou shalt know hereafter [i.e., after His death and resurrection].
[8]Peter saith unto him, Thou shalt never wash my feet. Jesus answered him, If I wash thee not, thou hast no part with me.

Christ is teaching two lessons simultaneously: (1) the original lesson of humble submission and service to one another, and (2) the deeper lesson of His own sacrifice of Himself for their salvation and spiritual cleansing. Peter missed the point of both. He saw only the incongruity of his Master washing his dirty feet, and he objected strongly. He did not grasp that Christ also was picturing His earthly humiliation that would soon culminate on the cross and the cleansing from sin that His substitutionary death would provide. Verse 8 means, "If I don't wash you [from the defilement of your sin], you will have no part with me."

C. Peter then wanted a full bath.

> ⁹Simon Peter saith unto him, Lord, not my feet only, but also my hands and my head.
>
> ¹⁰Jesus saith to him, He that is washed [bathed] needeth not save to wash his feet, but is clean every whit: and ye are clean, but not all.
>
> ¹¹For he knew who should betray him; therefore said he, Ye are not all clean.

Verse 10 may be read: "He that is bathed does not need further cleansing, except to wash his feet, but is fully clean. You [plural; the disciples] are clean, but not every one of you [not Judas, the son of perdition]." In other words, those already "bathed" (cleansed completely in God's sight through saving faith in Christ) are "fully clean." Each believer, however, "dirties his feet" every day through sins that require God's current forgiveness and cleansing. Peter did not need another bath, but to see his need for daily cleansing.

D. The Lord set the example as their Servant.

> ¹²So after he had washed their feet, and had taken his garments, and was set down again, he said unto them, Know ye [Do you grasp] what I have done to you?
>
> ¹³Ye call me Master and Lord ["Teacher and Master"]: and ye say well; for so I am.
>
> ¹⁴If I then, your Lord and Master [Master and Teacher], have washed your feet; ye also ought to wash one another's feet.
>
> ¹⁵For I have given you an example, that ye should do as I have done to you.
>
> ¹⁶Verily, verily, I say unto you, The servant is not greater than his lord; neither he that is sent greater than he that sent him.
>
> ¹⁷If ye know these things, happy are ye if ye do them.

Christ returns now to the original lesson, namely that they should humble themselves and serve one another, as He had served them. Heretofore, they apparently viewed Christ more as their "Teacher" (v. 13) than as their "Lord" (in the full sense of the latter term). In response, Christ reversed the order, stressing the priority of His full Lordship. This heightened the impact of the lesson: "If I, your *Lord*, have washed your feet," and "the servant is not greater than his lord," then "do as I have done to you." Christ's promise accompanies His command: "You will be happy [blessed; spiritually prosperous] if you practice these things."

V. The parable of a true neighbor.

A. Love God supremely, and "thy neighbor as thyself."

> LK 10:25 And, behold, a certain lawyer stood up, and tempted him, saying, Master, what shall I do to inherit eternal life?

²⁶He said unto him, What is written in the law? how readest thou? ²⁷And he answering said, Thou shalt love the Lord thy God with all thy heart, and with all thy soul, and with all thy strength, and with all thy mind; and thy neighbor as thyself.

B. People define *neighbor* too narrowly.

²⁸And he [Jesus] said unto him, Thou hast answered right: this do, and thou shalt live. ²⁹But he, willing [seeking] to justify himself, said unto Jesus, And who is my neighbor?

The lawyer gave the right answer (v. 27) but his motives were wrong and his knowledge therefore was of little value. His intent was not to "inherit eternal life" but to trip up Jesus (v. 25). When Christ told him to act in accordance with his knowledge, he tried get to off the hook by raising a question that was controversial among the Jews, namely, "Who is (and who is not) my neighbor?" Christ answered that question with the following parable.

C. Some religious people ignore their neediest neighbors.

³⁰And Jesus answering said, A certain man went down from Jerusalem to Jericho, and fell among thieves, which stripped him of his raiment, and wounded him, and departed, leaving him half dead. ³¹And by chance there came down a certain priest that way: and when he saw him, he passed by on the other side. ³²And likewise a Levite, when he was at the place, came and looked on him, and passed by on the other side.

The priest and Levite most likely were returning to Jericho after serving or worshipping in the temple. With God's Word and presence so recently on their minds (supposedly), they suddenly encountered an excellent opportunity to share God's mercy and grace with a fellow countryman in desperate need. But they merely looked and passed by.

D. Being a neighbor involves compassion and sacrificial service.

³³But a certain Samaritan, as he journeyed, came where he was: and when he saw him, he had compassion on him, ³⁴And went to him, and bound up his wounds, pouring in oil and wine, and set him on his own beast, and brought him to an inn, and took care of him. ³⁵And on the morrow when he departed, he took out two pence, and gave them to the host, and said unto him, Take care of him; and whatsoever thou spendest more, when I come again, I will repay thee.

The Jews hated the Samaritans as unclean heretical half-breeds. Here, a Samaritan had compassion on a helpless Jew and freely gave of his resources, time, and effort in caring for the needy man. He walked so that the wounded could ride, and he cared for him when they arrived at the inn. When the Samaritan had to leave the next day, he prepaid the innkeeper two denarii (two day's wages) and promised to reimburse him for any additional cost of caring for the convalescing Jew.

E. Your "neighbor" is any needy person you can help.
> ³⁶**Which now of these three, thinkest thou, was neighbor unto him that fell among the thieves?**
> ³⁷**And he said, He that showed mercy on him. Then said Jesus unto him, Go, and do thou likewise.**

Again, the lawyer answered correctly. Again, Christ told him to act in accordance with his knowledge. He commanded, in essence: "Go, and help *your* neighbor." We have the same knowledge as the lawyer, and therefore the same responsibility. As the parable indicates, anyone with a need that we can help meet is our neighbor.

Christ's application of the parable contains an even more fundamental message. The lawyer originally asked, "Who is my neighbor?" as if qualifying for that designation were up to the other person. Christ turned his question around in verse 36 and, by implication, asked him, "To whom can *you* be a neighbor?" Being a neighbor to others is our own responsibility. We are the ones who should take the initiative in finding and ministering to those who need a neighbor.

Examples of Humble Service to God

A believer's service to other people, rendered in the right spirit and with right motives, is also service to God. Some forms of service, however, are primarily for God Himself, even when other people are major beneficiaries. These include the dissemination of God's Word, prayer for God's ministries, and giving tithes and offerings for God's work. To please God, such service must be from the heart. It should flow from a deep love and appreciation for Him and a strong desire to please and honor Him. The following examples illustrate devoted service to God.

I. The parable of a humble, selfless servant.
> **LK 17:7 But which of you, having a servant [slave] plowing or feeding cattle, will say unto him by and by, when he is come from the field, Go and sit down to meat [your meal]?**
> ⁸**And will not rather say unto him, Make ready wherewith I may sup [eat], and gird thyself, and serve me, till I have eaten and drunken; and afterward thou shalt eat and drink?**

⁹Doth he thank that servant because he did the things that were commanded him? I trow [think] not.

¹⁰So likewise ye, when ye shall have done all those things which are commanded you, say, We are unprofitable servants: we have done that which was our duty to do.

The parable warns against believing, even when we think we have done "everything that was commanded" (v. 9), that God somehow owes us His approval and a reward. We never can come close to doing all that He commands; and even if we could, we would only be doing our minimal duty. Any approval and rewards that God may give are solely by His grace, with nothing earned by our merit. Realizing this, our attitude can only be "We are unworthy servants; we are merely doing our duty."

II. The example of John the Baptist

A. He recognized Christ's preeminence and his own unworthiness.

JN 1:26 [MT 3:11] John answered them [the Pharisees], saying, I baptize with water: but there standeth one among you, whom ye know not; {He shall baptize you with the Holy Ghost and with fire:}
²⁷He it is, who coming after me is preferred before me, whose shoe's latchet I am not worthy to unloose.

B. He recognized Christ's deity and his own humanity.

JN 1:29 The next day John seeth Jesus coming unto him, and saith, Behold the Lamb of God, which taketh away the sin of the world.
³⁰This is he of whom I said, After me cometh a man which is preferred before me: for he was before me.

C. He recognized Christ's righteousness and his own sinfulness.

MT 3:13 Then cometh Jesus from Galilee to Jordan unto John, to be baptized of him.
¹⁴But John forbad him, saying, I have need to be baptized of thee, and comest thou to me?
¹⁵And Jesus answering said unto him, Suffer it to be so now: for thus it becometh us to fulfil all righteousness. Then he suffered him.

D. He recognized Christ's lordship and his own servanthood.

JN 3:28 Ye yourselves bear me witness, that I said, I am not the Christ, but that I am sent before him.
²⁹He that hath the bride is the bridegroom: but the friend of the bridegroom, which standeth and heareth him, rejoiceth greatly because of the bridegroom's voice: this my joy therefore is fulfilled.
³⁰He must increase, but I must decrease.

Throughout his ministry, John was widely recognized as a prophet and was followed by many. He was always conscious, however, of his limited status and subordinate role as a forerunner and herald of the coming King. He boldly confronted the sinful religious leaders of the day, but he humbly submitted to his Master and Messiah. In the passages above, John's example shows four major reasons why all believers should humbly submit to Christ and selflessly serve Him as their Lord and King. Our credo too should be "He must increase, but I must decrease."

III. John's steadfast service in life and death.

A. His unwavering stand for righteousness.

MAT 14:3 For Herod had laid hold on John, and bound him, and put him in prison for Herodias' sake, his brother Philip's wife.

⁴For John said unto him, It is not lawful for thee to have her.

⁵And when he would have put him to death, he feared the multitude, because they counted him as a prophet.

B. His ultimate sacrifice for God.

⁶But when Herod's birthday was kept, the daughter of Herodias danced before them, and pleased Herod.

⁷Whereupon he promised with an oath to give her whatsoever she would ask.

⁸And she, being before instructed of her mother, said, Give me here John Baptist's head in a charger.

⁹And the king was sorry: nevertheless for the oath's sake, and them which sat with him at meat, he commanded it to be given her.

¹⁰And he sent, and beheaded John in the prison.

¹¹And his head was brought in a charger, and given to the damsel: and she brought it to her mother.

¹²And his disciples came, and took up the body, and buried it, and went and told Jesus.

John's faithfulness and boldness in denouncing sin and upholding righteousness led to his imprisonment and execution. He never shrank from his calling or compromised his message. The "voice crying in the wilderness" (JN 1:23) did not live to see the fulfillment of the kingdom that he faithfully proclaimed, but his work for that kingdom was all that God desired.

IV. Christ's portrayal of John's service.

A. He was "a burning and a shining light."

JN 5:33 [Christ said to the Jews,] Ye sent unto John, and he bare witness unto the truth. . . .

³⁵**He was a burning and a shining light: and ye were willing for a season to rejoice in his light.**

³⁶**But I have greater witness than that of John: for the works which the Father hath given me to finish, the same works that I do, bear witness of me, that the Father hath sent me.**

John was a *light* in that He faithfully proclaimed God's message that the Messiah's kingdom was imminent. The Pharisees "rejoiced in his light" for a while, gladly anticipating that kingdom's physical benefits. They soon rejected John's light, however, because of his insistence that they meet God's spiritual requirements for receiving His kingdom and for serving His King.

B. He was no "flimsy reed" or "preening prince."

LK 7:24 And when the messengers of John were departed, he [Christ] began to speak unto the people concerning John, What went ye out into the wilderness for to see? A reed shaken with the wind?

²⁵**But what went ye out for to see? A man clothed in soft raiment? Behold, they which are gorgeously apparelled, and live delicately, are in kings' courts.**

Although John began to wonder while in prison if Jesus was the Christ (see Sec. I on p. 311), Jesus told the people that John was no flimsy reed swayed by the winds of adversity. John had served God faithfully in spite of strong opposition from the nation's leaders, and Christ commended his godly character and steadfast testimony. Similarly, John was no kowtowing yes man, as were those in Herod's court where obsequious service was rewarded with fine clothing and sumptuous banquets. Clothed instead with camel's hair and living off the land, John staunchly proclaimed God's truth and condemned wickedness.

C. He was "more than a prophet," and none was greater.

²⁶**But what went ye out for to see? A prophet? Yea, I say unto you, and much more than a prophet.**

²⁷**This is he, of whom it is written, Behold, I send my messenger before thy face, which shall prepare thy way before thee.**

²⁸**For I say unto you, Among those that are born of women there is not a greater prophet than John the Baptist: but he that is least in the kingdom of God is greater than he.**

The prophecy Christ quoted in verse 27 is from Malachi 3:1, which foretells a coming herald for the Messiah. He declared that John was that herald (thereby indicating that He was the Messiah) and that no greater prophet had ever been born than John. He then made the amazing statement that even the lowliest citizen in God's kingdom is greater than John. John died without witnessing fully the kingdom of God that Christ offered the people. Those who hear and accept Christ's message of salvation are "greater" (more privileged) than John and prior prophets who "desired to see those things which ye see, and have not seen them" (LK 10:24).

      D. He was "Elijah" but was not received as such.

> **MT 17:10 And his disciples asked him, saying, Why then say the scribes that Elias [Elijah] must first come [before the establishment of Christ's kingdom]?**
>
> **¹¹And Jesus answered and said unto them, Elias truly shall first come, and restore all things.**
>
> **¹²But I say unto you, That Elias is come already, and they knew him not, but have done unto him whatsoever they listed [whatever they wished]. Likewise shall also the Son of man suffer of them.**
>
> **¹³Then the disciples understood that he spake unto them of John the Baptist.**
>
> **MT 11:12 And from the days of John the Baptist until now the kingdom of heaven suffereth violence, and the violent take it by force.**
>
> **¹³For all the prophets and the law prophesied until John.**
>
> **¹⁴And if ye will receive it, this is Elias [he is Elijah], which was for to come.**
>
> **¹⁵He that hath ears to hear, let him hear.**

The Old Testament ended with Malachi's prophecy: "Behold, I will send you Elijah the prophet before the coming of the great and dreadful day of the Lord" (4:5). The Jews were looking, therefore, not only for the Messiah, but also for His forerunner, Elijah. John the Baptist came "in the spirit and power of Elijah" (LK 1:17), but the religious leaders refused to receive him as such.

Commentators differ on the meaning of 11:12 (above). It may refer to the violent rejection of God's kingdom by the Jewish leaders as it was proclaimed and offered to them by both John and Jesus. Alternatively, it may mean "The kingdom of heaven is advancing forcefully, and strong and resolute people are eagerly embracing it." In either case, Christ indicated that John served as Elijah, God's promised herald for that kingdom.

     V. The example of Mary, Jesus' mother.

      A. Mary's chaste and upright life.

> **LK 1:26 And in the sixth month [of Elisabeth's pregnancy] the angel Gabriel was sent from God unto a city of Galilee, named Nazareth,**
>
> **²⁷To a virgin espoused to a man whose name was Joseph, of the house of David; and the virgin's name was Mary.**
>
> **²⁸And the angel came in unto her, and said, Hail, thou that art highly favored, the Lord is with thee: blessed art thou among women.**

²⁹And when she saw him, she was troubled at his saying, and cast in her mind what manner of salutation this should be.

³⁰And the angel said unto her, Fear not, Mary: for thou hast found favor with God.

B. Her unique and great God-given role.

³¹And, behold, thou shalt conceive in thy womb, and bring forth a son, and shalt call his name JESUS.

³²He shall be great, and shall be called the Son of the Highest: and the Lord God shall give unto him the throne of his father David:

³³And he shall reign over the house of Jacob for ever; and of his kingdom there shall be no end.

C. Her humble, selfless submission to God.

³⁴Then said Mary unto the angel, How shall this be, seeing I know not a man?

³⁵And the angel answered and said unto her, The Holy Ghost shall come upon thee, and the power of the Highest shall overshadow thee: therefore also that holy thing which shall be born of thee shall be called the Son of God.

³⁶And, behold, thy cousin Elisabeth, she hath also conceived a son in her old age: and this is the sixth month with her, who was called barren.

³⁷For with God nothing shall be impossible.

³⁸And Mary said, Behold the handmaid of the Lord; be it unto me according to thy word. And the angel departed from her.

Mary was a young lady of humble social status living in a small, unremarkable town in largely-rural Galilee. Although a needy sinner like everyone else, her upright and noble character was known and appreciated by God. In spite of her understandable puzzlement at the meaning of the angel's announcements, she humbly accepted and submitted to whatever God desired for her. She knew that becoming pregnant before completion of her promised marriage to Joseph would open her to criticism, derision, and possible stoning. Yet she readily trusted in God's infinite wisdom, power, and grace to accomplish His amazing plan for her life and for His eternal glory.

D. Her active, submissive faith in Christ.

JN 2:1 And the third day there was a marriage in Cana of Galilee; and the mother of Jesus was there:

²And both Jesus was called, and his disciples, to the marriage.

³And when they wanted wine, the mother of Jesus saith unto him, They have no wine.

⁴Jesus saith unto her, Woman, what have I to do with thee? mine hour is not yet come.

> [5]His mother saith unto the servants, Whatsoever he saith unto you, do it.

It appears that Mary was involved with the marriage feast because she knew they were out of wine before the manager learned of the shortage. Also, the servants followed her instructions to do whatever Christ asked. She knew that Christ as the Son of God could meet any need, and she believed that He would meet this need in particular. She simply mentioned it to Christ and trusted Him to do what was best. Mary practiced her faith by encouraging the servants to submit to Christ's will as she had. (See Sec. I on p. 294 for Christ's miracle.)

VI. Christ's submission and service to His Father.

With every deed and every word, Christ submissively served His Father. All of the Gospels testify to that service, but the following passages from John highlight its breadth and depth.

A. He did His Father's will, not His own.

> JN 6:38 For I came down from heaven, not to do mine own will, but the will of him that sent me.

> JN 4:34 Jesus saith unto them, My meat [food] is to do the will of him that sent me, and to finish his work.

> JN 5:30 I can of mine own self do nothing: as I hear, I judge: and my judgment is just; because I seek not mine own will, but the will of the Father which hath sent me.

> JN 8:29 And he that sent me is with me: the Father hath not left me alone; for I do always those things that please him.

Christ *always* did His Father's will. His *food* (4:34) was that which satisfied the hunger of His heart, namely, doing His Father's will. That food also motivated and energized His service for God. In 5:30, Christ said He was unable to do anything by Himself (i.e., independently of the Father). Because His nature and will were identical to the Father's, it was impossible for Christ to do anything contrary to the Father's will. He perfectly obeyed and fulfilled all that the Father desired.

B. He honored His Father, not Himself.

> JN 7:18 He that speaketh of himself seeketh his own glory: but he that seeketh his glory that sent him, the same is true, and no unrighteousness is in him.

> JN 8:48 Then answered the Jews, and said unto him, Say we not well that thou art a Samaritan, and hast a devil [demon]?

⁴⁹Jesus answered, I have not a devil; but I honor my Father, and ye do dishonor me.

⁵⁰And I seek not mine own glory: there is one that seeketh and judgeth.

The Jews accused Jesus of seeking His own glory and honoring Himself. In fact, He always exalted the Father, with perfect submission, dedication, and faithfulness to Him. In everything Christ intended and accomplished, He gave all the honor and glory to His Father.

C. He displayed His Father's nature completely.

JN 12:45 And he that seeth me seeth him that sent me.

JN 14:7 If ye had known me, ye should have known my Father also: and from henceforth ye know him, and have seen him.

⁸Philip saith unto him, Lord, show us the Father, and it sufficeth us.

⁹Jesus saith unto him, Have I been so long time with you, and yet hast thou not known me, Philip? he that hath seen me hath seen the Father; and how sayest thou then, Show us the Father?

"For in Him [Christ] dwelleth all the fullness of the Godhead bodily" (Col. 2:9); "for it pleased the Father that in Him should all fullness dwell" (Col. 1:19); "being the brightness of [God's] glory, and the express image [exact representation] of His person" (Heb. 1:3).

D. He credited His Father for His message and doctrine.

JN 7:16 Jesus answered them [the Jews], and said, My doctrine is not mine, but his that sent me.

¹⁷If any man will [desires to] do his will, he shall know of the doctrine, whether it be of God, or whether I speak of myself.

JN 12:49 For I have not spoken of myself; but the Father which sent me, he gave me a commandment, what I should say, and what I should speak.

⁵⁰And I know that his commandment is life everlasting: whatsoever I speak therefore, even as the Father said unto me, so I speak.

E. He credited His Father for His deeds and miracles.

JN 14:10 Believest thou not that I am in the Father, and the Father in me? . . . the Father that dwelleth in me, he doeth the works.

11. Believe me that I am in the Father, and the Father in me: or else believe me for the very works' sake.

F. He credited His Father for our salvation.

JN 6:44a No man can come to me, except the Father which hath sent me draw him: . . .

> [37]All that the Father giveth me shall come to me; and him that
> cometh to me I will in no wise cast out. . . .
> [40]And this is the will of him that sent me, that every one which seeth
> the Son, and believeth on him, may have everlasting life: and I will
> raise him up at the last day.

Christ gave all the honor and glory to the Father for everything He taught, performed, and achieved while on earth. In His speaking, He was the Father's faithful spokesman. In His work, He was the Father's obedient servant. In salvation, He was the Father's submissive sacrifice. In every realm, Christ acknowledged the Father as the sole source and the principal beneficiary of all His purposes, His power, and His accomplishments.

> G. He glorified His Father and finished His work.
> JN 17:1 These words spake Jesus, and lifted up his eyes to heaven,
> and said, Father, the hour is come; glorify thy Son, that thy Son also
> may glorify thee: . . .
> [4]I have glorified thee on the earth: I have finished the work which
> thou gavest me to do.

Christ exalted and glorified His Father by doing *everything* the Father gave Him to do. He did so exactly as the Father desired and wholly for the Father's glory. His is the perfect example of the humble, obedient, faithful service that God desires and deserves. Christ's present glory in heaven also pictures the future glory that God's faithful servants will share with Him as joint heirs with Christ. Since God will glorify His servants there, how much more should they seek to glorify Him here.

Applications for the Home

The Old Testament presented God's requirements for husbands, wives, parents, and children, and Christ did not directly address many of these matters. Other than His teaching on the sanctity and permanence of marriage, most of His references to the home and family were made to illustrate other spiritual truths. He taught, for example, that God's goodness to His children is much greater than a loving father's goodness to his children. Similarly, He stressed that faithfulness in following Him requires a devotion to Him that takes precedence over a believer's ties to his loved ones. These references, and their applications for each member of the family, are reviewed below. (The New Testament's principal teaching on family relationships and responsibilities comes later, in the epistles.)

> I. Spiritual unity establishes a home.
> MK 3:25 And if a house be divided against itself, that house cannot stand.

Christ knew that even the blasphemous Pharisees recognized this obvious truth as He refuted their allegations that Satan, not God, was His father (see Sec. III on p. 349). As Christ's unity with His Father and the Holy Spirit was essential for the effectiveness of His ministry, unity in the home is essential for its stability and success. Spiritual unity in particular, which is based on biblical principles and godly relationships, is crucial for any family that desires God's full blessing on their home.

II. Marriage is of God and should be permanent.

A. Husband and wife are "one flesh."

MK 10:6 [MT 19:4] But from the beginning of the creation God made them male and female.

⁷For this cause shall a man leave his father and mother, and cleave to his wife;

⁸And they twain shall be one flesh: so then they are no more twain, but one flesh.

⁹What therefore God hath joined together, let not man put asunder.

After God made the first man, He made a woman and established marriage, because "it is not good that the man should be alone" (Gen. 2:18). In verses 7-8 above, Christ quoted Genesis 2:24 to emphasize both the completeness and the permanence of the marriage union. "One flesh" signifies not only the physical union for which God designed them, but also the spiritual, mental, and emotional union that results as a man "cleave[s] to his wife." God ordained marriage as His means for joining each husband and wife in a complete union that no one should break.

B. Divorce is against God's will.

MK 10:2 [MT 19:3] And the Pharisees came to him, and asked him, Is it lawful for a man to put away his wife {for any cause [i.e., for any reason at all]}? tempting him.

³And he answered and said unto them, What did Moses command you?

⁴And they said, Moses suffered to write a bill of divorcement, and to put her away.

⁵And Jesus answered and said unto them, For the hardness of your heart he wrote you this precept {[and] suffered you to put away your wives: but from the beginning it was not so}.

God "hateth putting away [divorce]" (Mal. 2:16). Divorce apparently was widespread, however, in Israel in Christ's time. In the passage above, the Pharisees tried to trap Christ into taking a position on divorce that would alienate either liberal Jews, who allowed it for any reason, or conservative Jews, who permitted it only for sexual sins. They claimed Moses condoned divorce (based on Deut. 24:1-4), but Christ replied that Moses gave them regulations to govern divorce only because of their rebellious hearts. God's will has always been that marriage be permanent. (Christ's teaching in Sec. A followed that in Sec. B.)

C. Leaving a spouse and marrying another is adultery.

MK 10:10 And in the house his disciples asked him again of the same matter.

[11]And he saith unto them, Whosoever shall put away his wife, and marry another, committeth adultery against her.

[12]And if a woman shall put away her husband, and be married to another, she committeth adultery.

D. Infidelity, however, may permit divorce.

MT 19:9 And I say unto you, Whosoever shall put away his wife, except it be for fornication, and shall marry another, committeth adultery: and whoso marrieth her which is put away doth commit adultery.

These passages clearly prohibit anyone who initiates a divorce, in the absence of "fornication" (moral uncleanness) by his spouse, from marrying another person. Such divorce and remarriage is adultery. Both passages (in MT and MK) condemn divorce, but with different emphases. Matthew was written primarily to Jews who had the Mosaic Law and would recognize the exception for fornication (given twice in MT, including 5:32, but not in MK). Thus, when Joseph apparently thought that Mary's pregnancy resulted from fornication, he "being a just [righteous] man, and not willing to make her a public example, was minded to [divorce her quietly]" (MT 1:19).

Matthew focuses on men who divorce their wives, and not vice versa, because Jewish law did not permit wives to initiate divorce. The first-century Jewish historian Josephus wrote: "It is the husband who is permitted by us to do this." The Jews, therefore, most likely understood MT 19:9 to mean that an upright man who obeyed the Law (such as Joseph) could rightfully divorce an unfaithful wife, but a man who married her would be guilty of adultery with her.

Mark, in contrast, was written primarily to Romans, who were not familiar with Mosaic law and among whom divorces initiated by both husbands and wives for any reason were common. MK 10:11-12 therefore prohibits whichever spouse initiates a divorce (presumably without biblical justification) from remarrying. Neither Mark nor Matthew addresses whether a faithful spouse who was left behind by an unfaithful and unrepentant spouse (through adultery or divorce) may remarry. (Some believe that I Cor. 7:15 and 27-28 permit it in certain cases.) In every culture and circumstance, however, God hates divorce and condemns adultery.

E. Not everyone can "receive this saying."

¹⁰**His disciples say unto him, If the case of the man be so with his wife, it is not good to marry.**

¹¹**But he said unto them, All men cannot receive this saying, save they to whom it is given.**

¹²**For there are some eunuchs, which were so born from their mother's womb: and there are some eunuchs, which were made eunuchs of men: and there be eunuchs, which have made themselves eunuchs for the kingdom of heaven's sake. He that is able to receive it, let him receive it.**

The disciples were surprised by the restrictions Christ placed on divorce and remarriage. They said, in effect, "If that's the case, it's better never to marry!" Christ's reply in verse 11 seems to acknowledge that not everyone is able to maintain his or her marriage (such as a person left by an adulterous spouse who remarries). This was not to excuse or lessen the sinfulness of divorce but to deal mercifully and practically with its tragic consequences, as Moses did previously. (See God's merciful provision for certain divorced women in Lev. 22:12-13.) Some believe that verse 11 refers primarily to those in verse 12 who remain single "for the kingdom of heaven's sake," to serve God with greater devotion and concentration.

III. Parents and children should portray spiritual relationships.

A. Parents should meet their children's needs, as God meets theirs.

MT 7:9 [LK 11:11] Or what man is there of you, whom if his son ask bread, will he give him a stone?

¹⁰**Or if he ask a fish, will he give him a serpent? {Or if he shall ask an egg, will he offer him a scorpion?}**

¹¹**If ye then, being evil, know how to give good gifts unto your children, how much more shall your Father which is in heaven give good things to them that ask him?**

In teaching on prayer, Christ cited a father's natural desire to satisfy his son's hunger with wholesome food. Loving parents not only meet their children's needs in beneficial ways, but they also withhold and shield them from things that are inappropriate and worthless (v. 9) or harmful and dangerous (v. 10). Parents (and fathers in particular) are to picture the heavenly Father to their children in the way they care for them and provide for their needs.

B. Children should submit to their parents, as Christ did to His.

LK 2:51 And he went down with them [His parents], and came to Nazareth, and was subject unto them: . . .

⁵²**And Jesus increased in wisdom and stature, and in favor with God and man.**

As a 12-year old boy in LK 2 above, Jesus set the example for all children as He was subject unto His parents. He perfectly fulfilled God's command (written later): "Children, obey your parents in all things: for this is well pleasing unto the Lord" (Col. 3:20).

C. Children should honor their parents as they would honor God.

MT 15:3 [MK 7:9] But he answered and said unto them, Why do ye also transgress the commandment of God by your tradition?

⁴For God commanded, saying, Honor thy father and mother: and, He that curseth father or mother, let him die the death.

⁵But ye say, Whosoever shall say to his father or his mother, It is a gift [dedicated to God], by whatsoever thou mightest be profited by me;

⁶And honor not his father or his mother, he shall be free. {And ye suffer him no more to do ought [permit him not to do anything] for his father or his mother;} Thus have ye made the commandment of God of none effect by your tradition.

Christ rebuked the Pharisees for overriding God's commandments with their traditions. They circumvented, for example, the commandment "Honor thy father and thy mother" (Ex. 20:12) by allowing adult children to avoid caring for needy parents by declaring (probably falsely) that their resources were dedicated to God and were not available for their parents' needs. Christ indicated they should honor their parents first, even before making voluntary offerings to God.

D. Families should foster close relationships, as God's family should.

MT 12:49And he stretched forth his hand toward his disciples, and said, Behold my mother and my brethren!

⁵⁰For whosoever shall do the will of my Father which is in heaven, the same is my brother, and sister, and mother.

Christ drew upon the crowd's common knowledge that a loving and faithful family member would seek to please and benefit the other members of his family. So should it be in God's family. All believers should gladly do the Father's will, which includes serving and encouraging their brothers and sisters in Christ. (See Sec. II on p. 134 for the full passage.)

IV. Devotion to Christ should have first priority.

A. Follow Him even if loved ones do not.

MT 10:37 He that loveth father or mother more than me is not worthy of me: and he that loveth son or daughter more than me is not worthy of me.

> MK 10:28 Then Peter began to say unto him, Lo, we have left all, and have followed thee.
>
> ²⁹And Jesus answered and said, Verily I say unto you, There is no man that hath left house, or brethren, or sisters, or father, or mother, or wife, or children, or lands, for my sake, and the gospel's,
>
> ³⁰But he shall receive an hundredfold now in this time, houses, and brethren, and sisters, and mothers, and children, and lands, with persecutions; and in the world [age] to come eternal life.

There is no greater privilege and no greater responsibility than to belong to Christ and to follow and serve Him. Even the closest and dearest relationships with loved ones must be subordinated to a believer's allegiance to Christ and his obedience to His commands. Following Him means being willing to leave everything and everybody else behind if need be. Although it is much easier and more pleasant when families serve Christ together, many of His followers have had to leave (or have been left by) parents, spouse, or children "for His sake and the gospel's." The temporal cost may be great, but the eternal reward is greater. (See Sec. I on p. 278.)

> B. Expect opposition from carnal kin.
>
> MK 6:4 But Jesus said unto them, A prophet is not without honor, but in his own country, and among his own kin, and in his own house.
>
> LK 12:51 Suppose ye that I am come to give peace on earth? I tell you, Nay; but rather division:
>
> ⁵²For from henceforth there shall be five in one house divided, three against two and two against three.
>
> ⁵³The father shall be divided against the son, and the son against the father; the mother against the daughter, and the daughter against the mother; the mother-in-law against her daughter-in-law, and the daughter-in-law against her mother-in-law.
>
> MT 10:36 And a man's foes shall be they of his own household.

Christ often warned His disciples that they would be subject to opposition, and at times to extreme persecution, when they openly and devotedly lived for Him. Although the gospel brings God's peace to individual hearts, it also brings sharp division between Christ's followers and those who reject its claims. That opposition often is most intense and that division most painful when it comes from unbelieving loved ones who spurn and mock the Savior. Other relatives who claim to be Christians also may seek to diminish a believer's wholehearted dedication to Christ and His service. (See Sec. III on p. 274.)

Examples of opposition from professing believers would include a selfish or doubting spouse who refuses to join the other in doing God's will, and possessive and controlling parents who object to their children (and/or grandchildren) "moving far away" or "living in deprivation" in the Lord's service. Although the pain and heartache from such opposition are very real, God promises that His grace will be sufficient in these difficult cases.

12

Pictures of Money and Masters

Those who dislike sermons on money and giving would have been most uncomfortable in Christ's audiences. He frequently talked about money and material possessions, and He made their place in our lives a key measure of our relationship with God. He declared that we either worship and serve God with our money or we worship and serve our money to the exclusion of God.

Even in teaching spiritual principles not directly related to money, Christ often drew parallels between the two. The people were so occupied with material pursuits that illustrations based on money should have made the spiritual lessons abundantly clear. Typically, though, they reacted with the same negative response or deaf ear that materialistic people react with today. In contrast, those who heed Christ's teaching wisely "lay up [their] treasures in heaven" — knowing that is the only way to multiply and retain for eternity the resources God gives us.

Pictures of Two Masters — God and Materialism

God and materialism vie for control in the lives of both believers and unbelievers. For the latter, materialism often raises a major obstacle to their salvation, and the battle for their souls may be fought on this front. Believers, too, often find materialism's pull hard to resist; many find it easier to trust God for salvation than for meeting their daily needs. In every life, either God or materialism will have the preeminence. The following pictures highlight this fundamental conflict.

I. The impossibility of serving two masters.

A. A master demands exclusive allegiance.

LK 16:13 No servant can serve two masters: for either he will hate the one, and love the other; or else he will hold to the one, and despise the other. Ye cannot serve God and mammon [money; materialism].

The master/servant relationship was well understood by the Jews. They knew it was impossible, both logically and practically, for anyone to serve two competing masters. Christ declared that the same is true in the spiritual realm. Serving God requires selfless devotion to Him alone and willing sacrifice for His glory. Serving materialism inherently fosters selfishness and self-aggrandizement. These two masters cannot coexist in one life.

B. Many esteem materialism, but God abhors it.

¹⁴And the Pharisees also, who were covetous, heard all these things: and they derided him.
¹⁵And he said unto them, Ye are they which justify yourselves before men; but God knoweth your hearts: for that which is highly esteemed among men is abomination in the sight of God.

Although materialism is "highly esteemed among men" and covetousness (craving possessions) is the norm, God despises them as idolatry (Col. 3:5). The Pharisees sought to earn material blessing from God through pious and legalistic behavior; thus, they were *covetous*. They could not deny that they "esteemed mammon"; instead, they ridiculed Christ for saying they could not also serve God with equal dedication and fidelity. They may have convinced others that their covetous lives were "spiritually correct," but God knew their hearts (v. 15).

II. The hard choice in choosing your master.

A. Man's common desire — having eternal life.

MK 10:17 [MT 19:16; LK 18:18] And when he was gone forth into the way, there came one {a certain ruler} running, and kneeled to

him, and asked him, Good Master, what {good thing} shall I do that
I may inherit eternal life?

B. Man's common error — missing Christ and trusting works.
   ¹⁸And Jesus said unto him, Why callest thou me good? there is
none good but one, that is, God; {but if thou wilt enter into life, keep
the commandments.}

The ruler probably was an official in the local synagogue. He also was relatively young (MT 19:22) and very rich (LK 18:23). Although he seemingly had
a good lot in life, he knew there was a void in his soul. He sincerely desired
eternal life, but his opening question revealed two major misconceptions
regarding it. The first was his limited assessment of Jesus as a "good teacher"
rather than as God incarnate. That failing was common among the people, and
Christ responded: "Only God is good." He implied: "If I am truly and fully
good, that is evidence I am God." The man's second error was thinking that he
could do some "good thing" to inherit eternal life. Again, his views mirrored
those of the people at large. To expose that fallacy, Christ gave him an essential
but impossible order: "Keep the commandments."

C. God's eternal standard — perfect holiness.
   ¹⁹{He saith unto Him, Which? Jesus said,} Thou knowest the commandments, Do not commit adultery, Do not kill, Do not steal, Do
not bear false witness, Defraud not, Honour thy father and mother:
{and, Thou shalt love thy neighbor as thyself}.

The ruler was headed down the wrong track of trying to earn his salvation
through moral behavior. Christ tried to show him the futility of that route by
holding up God's standard of perfect holiness. If the ruler perfectly kept every one
of God's commandments all of his life (past, present, and future), then he could
"inherit eternal life." But that is impossible. No one has ever come close to meeting God's requirement of perfect holiness — except Christ Himself. He alone
earned eternal life, so that He could give it as a gift to those who accept His sacrificial payment for their failure to keep God's commandments.

D. Man's typical self-appraisal — "I'm basically good."
   ²⁰And he answered and said unto him, Master, all these have I
observed from my youth: {what lack I yet?}

The ruler should have said, "I have tried to keep the commandments but I
can't. At one time or another, I have broken all of them in thought, word, or
deed." He could not be saved and receive eternal life until he realized he was a
sinner and hopelessly lost.

E. Christ's loving invitation — "Forsake all and follow Me."

²¹Then Jesus beholding him loved him, and said unto him, One thing thou lackest: {If thou wilt be perfect [complete; pleasing to God],} go thy way, sell whatsoever thou hast, and give to the poor, and thou shalt have treasure in heaven: and come, take up the cross, and follow me.

F. The ruler's sad choice — goods before God.

²²And he was sad at that saying, and went away grieved: for he had great possessions {he was very rich}.

In spite of the ruler's major misconceptions, Jesus "loved him." He kindly told him, "Your riches occupy the place in your life that God alone deserves. Shed these and take up the cross of self-denial and follow me." Had he done so, he would have learned that Christ was infinitely more than a "good teacher" and that through faith in Him he could inherit the eternal life he greatly desired. But the ruler, sad and grieved, clung to his possessions and left Christ.

G. Christ's observation — wealth hinders salvation.

²³And Jesus looked round about, and saith unto his disciples, How hardly shall they that have riches enter into the kingdom of God!
²⁴And the disciples were astonished at his words. But Jesus answereth again, and saith unto them, Children, how hard is it for them that trust in riches to enter into the kingdom of God!

H. Christ's illustration — a camel through a needle's eye.

²⁵It is easier for a camel to go through the eye of a needle, than for a rich man to enter into the kingdom of God.
²⁶And they were astonished out of measure, saying among themselves, Who then can be saved?
²⁷And Jesus looking upon them saith, With men it is impossible, but not with God: for with God all things are possible.

The disciples' astonishment reflected the Jews' common belief that physical prosperity was a natural result of spirituality. The two were often related in the Old Testament, with material blessings given to those who faithfully kept God's precepts. The Jews reversed the analysis, thinking that if a person was rich (and not obviously bad), he must be "good" and have found favor with God. Christ replied, however, that wealth can severely hinder salvation rather than facilitate it. Verse 27 indicates that achieving salvation through human effort is impossible, regardless how rich and seemingly good a person may be. With God, however, anyone's salvation is possible. Even a rich person can be saved if he trusts solely in God and not in his riches.

III. The folly of making mammon your master.

   A. Life should not be measured in material terms.

LK 12:13 And one of the company [crowd] said unto him, Master, speak to my brother, that he divide the inheritance with me.

¹⁴And he said unto him, Man, who made me a judge or a divider over you?

¹⁵And he said unto them, Take heed, and beware of covetousness: for a man's life consisteth not in the abundance of the things which he possesseth.

Christ warned the petitioner and the surrounding crowd not to be deceived by covetousness. It dupes many into believing that the quality of life is measured by the quantity of things they consume or accumulate on earth. The folly of covetousness is evident in the irony of the present-day maxim: "He who dies with the most toys, wins." What has he won? What good are "things" when he dies? The following parable illustrates Christ's warning.

   B. God blesses (and tests) some with abundance.

¹⁶And he spake a parable unto them, saying, The ground of a certain rich man brought forth plentifully:

¹⁷And he thought within himself, saying, What shall I do, because I have no room where to bestow [store] my fruits?

   C. Some trust wealth to satisfy their soul.

¹⁸And he said, This will I do: I will pull down my barns, and build greater; and there will I bestow all my fruits and my goods.

¹⁹And I will say to my soul, Soul, thou hast much goods laid up for many years; take thine ease, eat, drink, and be merry.

There was nothing wrong with this man's being rich. His bumper crops resulted from his diligent work and God's blessing. He failed, however, to acknowledge God as the source of his bounty and credited only himself (note the *I*s and *my*s). Also, he thought only of his own comfort and enjoyment and not the needs of others. Farthest from his mind was honoring God with his wealth. Then he boasted, "Soul, you have many goods stored up," as though physical goods could meet the needs of his spiritual soul. He added, "for many years," expecting to live indefinitely.

   D. Materialists soon will lose everything.

²⁰But God said unto him, Thou fool, this night thy soul shall be required of thee: then whose shall those things be, which thou hast provided?

²¹So is he that layeth up [hoards] treasure for himself, and is not rich toward God.

God suddenly called the rich fool into account, and he entered eternity empty-handed. All that he worked for was lost in an instant. Everything he hoarded was left to others. Christ foretold the same end for anyone who selfishly keeps his God-given resources for his own purposes rather than using them to honor God and to lay up treasure in heaven.

IV. The end result of serving mammon.

    A. The pleasures of wealth end at death.

> LK 16:19 There was a certain rich man, which was clothed in purple and fine linen, and fared sumptuously every day:
> ²⁰And there was a certain beggar named Lazarus, which was laid at his gate, full of sores, . . .
> ²²And it came to pass, that the beggar died, and was carried by the angels into Abraham's bosom: the rich man also died, and was buried;

    B. Mammon is utterly worthless in hell.

> ²³And in hell he lift up his eyes, being in torments, and seeth Abraham afar off, and Lazarus in his bosom.
> ²⁴And he cried and said, Father Abraham, have mercy on me, and send Lazarus, that he may dip the tip of his finger in water, and cool my tongue; for I am tormented in this flame.

    C. Choices in life last for eternity.

> ²⁵But Abraham said, Son, remember that thou in thy lifetime receivedst thy good things, and likewise Lazarus evil [bad] things: but now he is comforted, and thou art tormented.
> ²⁶And beside all this, between us and you there is a great gulf fixed: so that they which would pass from hence to you cannot; neither can they pass to us, that would come from thence.

The parable presupposes that Lazarus trusted in God for salvation, while the rich man trusted in his wealth. The latter served materialism all his life, and now he reaped its consequences. When he died, the results of his choice were as irrevocably "fixed" as the "great gulf" that separated him from God forever. (The full parable is presented in Section I on p. 447.)

    D. Mammon's reward is in this life only.

> LK 6:24 Woe unto you that are rich [in earthly wealth alone]! for ye have received your consolation.
> ²⁵Woe unto you that are full [physically but not spiritually]! for ye shall hunger. Woe unto you that laugh now [in selfish pleasure]! for ye shall mourn and weep.
> ²⁶Woe unto you, when all men shall speak well of you [solely for your earthly success]! for so did their fathers to the false prophets.

Christ overturned traditional Jewish thinking that success and wealth were signs of God's approval and that poverty and sorrow indicated His punishment. In this passage from the Sermon on the Mount, He pronounced judgment and woe on those who live for earthly pleasures and pursuits. The wealth they accumulate and the enjoyment they experience in this life are the only consolation they will ever receive.

V. Choosing Christ over mammon.

A. Wealthy people need Christ like everyone else.

LK 19:1 And Jesus entered and passed through Jericho.

²And, behold, there was a man named Zacchaeus, which was the chief among the publicans [tax collectors], and he was rich. . . .

⁵And when Jesus came to the place, he looked up, and saw him, and said unto him, Zacchaeus, make haste, and come down; for to day I must abide at thy house.

⁶And he made haste, and came down, and received him joyfully. . . .

B. Salvation changes material values as well as spiritual values.

⁸And Zacchaeus stood, and said unto the Lord; Behold, Lord, the half of my goods I give to the poor; and if I have taken any thing from any man by false accusation, I restore him fourfold.

⁹And Jesus said unto him, This day is salvation come to this house, forsomuch as he also is a son of Abraham [i.e., through faith].

¹⁰For the Son of man is come to seek and to save that which was lost.

Zacchaeus, a chief tax-collector, was rich but lost. He sought to see Jesus, but Jesus sought and saved him. One of the ways he evidenced his new salvation was by gladly making restitution to those he had cheated. Depending on the nature and circumstances of dishonest gain, Mosaic law required repayment of from 120% (Lev. 6:1-5) to 500% (Ex. 22:1-4) of the original value. Zacchaeus' repayment probably exceeded the law's requirement — and he also gave half of his wealth to the poor. (See Sec. V on p. 15 for the full passage.)

VI. Which Master will you serve — Christ or mammon?

A. The Savior's call.

MK 8:34 And when he had called the people unto him with his disciples also, he said unto them, Whosoever will come after me, let him deny himself, and take up his cross, and follow me.

Christ issued this challenge (then and now) both to the people at large and to His disciples. The former need to make Him their Master for salvation; the latter, their Master for service. His threefold call is (1) deny yourself (i.e., forsake your personal desires and ambitions, and submit wholly to Christ as the Lord of your life); (2) take up *your* cross (your personal and particular sacrificial service for Christ); and (3) follow Him, both now and from now on.

   B. The servant's choice.

> ³⁵**For whosoever will [desires to] save his life shall lose it; but whosoever shall lose his life for my sake and the gospel's, the same shall save it.**

Christ framed His call to follow and serve Him in the context of the life or death issues involved. For "the people," the issue is everlasting life versus everlasting death. For His disciples, it is a worthwhile and enduring life versus an empty and wasted life. Whoever vainly pursues a self-centered, materialistic life certainly will lose everything at death. In contrast, those who make Christ their Master and "lose their life for His sake" (i.e., surrender it fully and sacrificially to Him), will preserve forever all that He accomplishes in and through their lives and service.

   C. The soul's cost.

> ³⁶**For what shall it profit a man, if he shall gain the whole world, and lose his own soul?**
> ³⁷**Or what shall a man give in exchange for his soul?**

   D. The Son's coming.

> ³⁸**Whosoever therefore shall be ashamed of me and of my words in this adulterous and sinful generation; of him also shall the Son of man be ashamed, when he cometh in the glory of his Father with the holy angels.**

Christ added that whoever lives for himself, even if he temporarily "gain[s] the whole world," will not only lose whatever he gained, but his own soul as well. No conceivable loss of any kind could be greater. In contrast, those who forsake the world's ways and allures and heed Christ's call to follow and serve Him will gain eternal rewards that are infinitely greater than whatever they "lost" on earth. Christ Himself will be the judge and rewarder of our "losing and gaining" when He comes again as King.

Sketches that Identify Your Master
(MT 6:19-34 and LK 12:22-34)

In the following collage of simple sketches, Christ pictures the issues and consequences everyone faces in choosing to serve either God or materialism. These drawings raise and explore this basic question: Is your paramount desire to honor, serve, and please God with your possessions — or, to honor, serve, and please yourself? The issue is far broader than how much you should give to God versus spend on yourself. It extends to all of your attitudes and purposes regarding everything you possess. The answers to the following questions will readily reveal who or what is your master.

I. What is really important to you?

A. Will your treasure be eaten by moths and rust?

MT 6:19 Lay not up for yourselves treasures upon earth, where moth and rust doth corrupt, and where thieves break through and steal:
²⁰But lay up for yourselves treasures in heaven, where neither moth nor rust doth corrupt, and where thieves do not break through nor steal:
²¹For where your treasure is, there will your heart be also.

Christ literally commanded, "*Stop* laying up treasures on earth." He was not just encouraging His listeners to make right choices in the future; they were already making wrong choices. Earthly treasures are perishable and vulnerable, but heavenly treasures are permanent and secure. Verse 21 means that whichever treasure (heavenly or earthly) we truly desire, our life will be absorbed in pursuing it, loving it, and sacrificing the other treasure (earthly or heavenly) to achieve it.

B. Do your eyes fill your life with light?

²²The light [lamp] of the body is the eye: if therefore thine eye be single [healthy], thy whole body shall be full of light.
²³But if thine eye be evil [defective], thy whole body shall be full of darkness. If therefore the light that is in thee be darkness, how great is that darkness! {Take heed therefore that the light which is in thee be not darkness. If thy whole body therefore be full of light, having no part dark, the whole shall be full of light, as when the bright shining of a candle doth give thee light [LK 11:35-36].}

Verses 22-23a may be understood: "Your eye receives light to guide your body. If your eye is healthy, your whole body receives good direction. But if your eye is defective, your whole body will be misled." In context, verse 23b and LK 11:35-36 can be interpreted: "If your focus is on earthly treasures, you are living in darkness, and how great is that darkness! Take heed, therefore, that your eyes do not become focused on the things of darkness. If, however, you seek heavenly treasures, with no conflicting earthly desires, your whole life will be full of light and will shine as brightly as a burning lamp."

C. Which master do you love and serve?

²⁴No man can serve two masters: for either he will hate the one, and love the other; or else he will hold to the one, and despise the other. Ye cannot serve God and mammon.

> [25]Therefore I say unto you, Take no thought [Be not anxious; do not worry] for your life, what ye shall eat, or what ye shall drink; nor yet for your body, what ye shall put on. Is not the life more than meat, and the body than raiment?

Christ declared again that no one can divide his devotion, loyalty, and service between two masters — especially masters as all-encompassing and mutually exclusive as God and materialism. Only one of these can be the master in any life. He indicated (in v. 25) that God will meet the basic material needs of those who make Him their Master. Many people, however, seek to indulge well beyond their needs as though material things were the essence of life. Christ asked, in effect, "Are food and clothing (and by extension, all material things) ends in themselves? Isn't there more to life than mere consumption?"

II. In whom do you trust to meet your needs?

A. Will God feed the sparrows and not you?

> MT 6:26 Behold the fowls of the air: for they sow not, neither do they reap, nor gather into barns; yet your heavenly Father feedeth them. Are ye not much better than they? {Are not two sparrows sold for a farthing? and one of them shall not fall on the ground without [the will of] your Father. But the very hairs of your head are all numbered. Fear ye not therefore, ye are of more value than many sparrows [MT 10:29-31].}

Another reason to make God your master, rather than mammon, is God's all-sufficient loving care for His own. If He cares and provides for lowly sparrows, will He not do much more for His children, whom He created in His own image? He is the sparrows' sustainer, but He is "your heavenly *Father*."

B. Who controls the "cubits" of your life?

> [27]Which of you by taking thought can add one cubit unto his stature? {If ye then be not able to do that thing which is least, why take ye thought for [worry about] the rest? [LK 12:26].}

One cubit is about 18 inches, an incredibly-large increment to anyone's height. Christ, however, said that adding a cubit would be doing "that which is least." The likely explanation is that the word translated "stature" can also mean "age" or "life-span." Adding 18 inches to the cumulative length of one's lifelong travels would be a minuscule increase indeed. But even that is impossible through human thought and effort. Our impotence, even in "that which is least," is further reason for making God our master, rather than trusting in mammon and self-effort.

C. Will God clothe the lilies and not you?

> ²⁸And why take ye thought for raiment? Consider the lilies of the field, how they grow; they toil not, neither do they spin:
>
> ²⁹And yet I say unto you, That even Solomon in all his glory was not arrayed like one of these.
>
> ³⁰Wherefore, if God so clothe the grass of the field, which to day is, and to morrow is cast into the oven, shall he not much more clothe you, O ye of little faith?

The choice of either God or mammon as your master is primarily a matter of *faith*. Simply put, are you trusting God for your needs, or are you trusting in your own abilities and resources? Christ called those who fret and churn over obtaining material things "ye of little faith." God amply demonstrates His faithful care of all creation every day. Will He not do *much more* for you (v. 30)?

D. Do you worry as those with no heavenly Father?

> ³¹Therefore take no thought, saying, What shall we eat? or, What shall we drink? or, Wherewithal shall we be clothed? {neither be ye of doubtful mind.}
>
> ³²(For after all these things do the Gentiles {the peoples of the world} seek:) for your heavenly Father knoweth that ye have need of all these things.

"The peoples of the world" do not trust God for their needs but are preoccupied with materialistic pursuits. Believers are to be different — because they have a heavenly Father who is all knowing, all loving, and all sufficing. They can have full confidence He will readily and suitably meet their needs, as they trust each day in His loving care.

III. Are you living for the present? Or for eternity?

A. Whose "kingdom" are you seeking to advance?

> MT 6:33 But seek ye first the kingdom of God, and his righteousness; and all these things shall be added unto you.
>
> ³⁴Take therefore no thought for the morrow: for the morrow shall take thought for the things of itself. Sufficient unto the day is the evil [trouble or adversity] thereof.

These admonitions may be understood: "Seek continually and primarily to enthrone God as King [in your life and in others' lives] and to magnify His righteousness in every sphere and realm. Then, all that you need will be provided for you. Do not worry, therefore, about what may happen tomorrow, for tomorrow will take care of its own affairs. Each day has enough of its own trouble and adversity."

B. Will your "bags wear out" or your "treasure run out?"

LK 12:32 Fear not, little flock; for it is your Father's good pleasure to give you the kingdom.

³³Sell that ye have, and give alms; provide yourselves bags [purses] which wax not old [never wear out], a treasure in the heavens that faileth not [never runs out], where no thief approacheth, neither moth corrupteth.

³⁴For where your treasure is, there will your heart be also.

In MT 6:33 the "kingdom of God and His righteousness" refers primarily to the *kingship of God* among people currently on earth. In LK 12:32, however, "the kingdom" is the heavenly kingdom (including the Messianic kingdom) the Father will give His children in the future. Because both their daily provision and their heavenly inheritance are assured, God's children should give generously of their earthly possessions to needy people and worthy causes (12:33). In so doing, they provide for themselves "purses" full of eternal heavenly wealth. They send, as it were, their earthly treasure ahead of them to heaven where it becomes imperishable and secure. As they do so, their affections and desires also will be directed (along with their treasure) toward their eternal dwelling with God (v. 34).

Parables about the Master's Stewards

A steward manages another's property or business. He holds that property in trust and manages it within parameters established by the owner. Stewardship involves the exercise of delegated authority and includes full accountability to the owner for the safety and/or productivity of the entrusted property. "Moreover it is required in stewards that a man be found faithful" (I Corinthians 4:2).

Christ drew frequently on the Jews' understanding of stewardship to picture spiritual truth. Each of the following parables uses some aspect of material stewardship to portray the spiritual stewardship that God assigns every believer. In each case, something of great spiritual value is entrusted to the steward, instructions are given regarding its use, and an accounting is required in the future. Earthly stewardship often includes rewards for faithful performance, but these pale in comparison with the great eternal rewards that Christ promises His faithful stewards.

I. Christ made every believer His steward until He returns.

A. His stewards are to care for "His house" (His work and ministry).

MK 13:34 For the Son of man is as a man taking a far journey, who left his house, and gave authority to his servants, and to every man his work, and commanded the porter to watch.

³⁵**Watch ye therefore: for ye know not when the master of the house cometh, at even, or at midnight, or at the cockcrowing, or in the morning:**
³⁶**Lest coming suddenly he find you sleeping.**
³⁷**And what I say unto you I say unto all, Watch.**

B. His stewards are to care for "His household" (other believers).

MT 24:45 Who then is a faithful and wise servant, whom his lord hath made ruler over his household, to give them meat [food] in due season?
⁴⁶**Blessed is that servant, whom his lord when he cometh shall find so doing.**
⁴⁷**Verily I say unto you, That he shall make him ruler over all his goods.**

The lessons taught in these parables include: (1) *every* servant of the Lord is to do "his [own assigned] work" while the Master is gone; (2) that work is related in some specific way to the Master's "house" (His work and ministry on earth) and His "household" (His family of all believers, who need to be given spiritual food at appropriate times); and (3) the Master has given each servant all the authority and ability he needs to do his particular work. (See Secs. I and II on p. 434 ff.)

II. Christ will judge and reward each steward's *faithfulness*.

A. Each believer is uniquely endowed for God's service.

MT 25:14 For the kingdom of heaven is as a man travelling into a far country, who called his own servants, and delivered unto them his goods.
¹⁵**And unto one he gave five talents, to another two, and to another one; to every man according to his several ability; and straightway took his journey.**

In this parable, each servant was given a particular endowment "according to his several [individual; distinct] ability." Thus, the number of "talents" entrusted to them varied greatly from one servant to another. (A talent was a large amount of money, as much as 20 years' wages for a laborer.)

B. Each steward decides how he will use his talents.

¹⁶**Then he that had received the five talents went and traded with the same, and made them other five talents.**
¹⁷**And likewise he that had received two, he also gained other two.**
¹⁸**But he that had received one went and digged in the earth, and hid his lord's money.**

C. Each steward faces a reckoning at Christ's return.

> [19] After a long time the lord of those servants cometh, and reckoneth with them.

D. Each steward will be rewarded according to his faithfulness.

> [20] And so he that had received five talents came and brought other five talents, saying, Lord, thou deliveredst unto me five talents: behold, I have gained beside them five talents more.
> [21] His lord said unto him, Well done, thou good and faithful servant: thou hast been faithful over a few things, I will make thee ruler over many things: enter thou into the joy of thy lord.

Each servant's output was determined by a combination of his initial endowment (for which the Master was fully responsible) and his faithfulness in employing that endowment (for which the servant was responsible). A servant's faithfulness "over a few things" will result in rewards involving "many things." More importantly, he will eternally experience the joy of the Lord's presence and approval.

E. Stewards faithful with lesser endowments still receive a full reward.

> [22] He also that had received two talents came and said, Lord, thou deliveredst unto me two talents: behold, I have gained two other talents beside them.
> [23] His lord said unto him, Well done, good and faithful servant; thou hast been faithful over a few things, I will make thee ruler over many things: enter thou into the joy of thy lord.

It is most encouraging that servants who faithfully employ seemingly lesser talents (according to human standards of measurement) in their Master's service will receive the same supreme commendation and reward as those who faithfully employ "greater" talents. (Verses 21 and 23 are identical.)

F. Unfaithful stewards neglect their talents.

> [24] Then he which had received the one talent came and said, Lord, I knew thee that thou art an hard man, reaping where thou hast not sown, and gathering where thou hast not strawed:
> [25] And I was afraid, and went and hid thy talent in the earth: lo, there thou hast that is thine.

G. They will lose their talents, with no reward.

> [26] His lord answered and said unto him, Thou wicked and slothful servant, thou knewest that I reap where I sowed not, and gather where I have not strawed:
> [27] Thou oughtest therefore to have put my money to the exchangers, and then at my coming I should have received mine own with usury [interest].

²⁸**Take therefore the talent from him, and give it unto him which hath ten talents.**

The "wicked servant" apparently was no servant at all. Although he knew what the lord required, he never submitted to his lordship. His supposed service, therefore, was of no value and he received no reward. Accordingly, he was condemned and banished from the lord's presence forever (see v. 30 below).

H. Faithful stewards will be given greater stewardship.

²⁹**For unto every one that hath shall be given, and he shall have abundance: but from him that hath not shall be taken away even that which he hath.**

³⁰**And cast ye the unprofitable servant into outer darkness: there shall be weeping and gnashing of teeth.**

Verse 29 may be understood: "Everyone who bears fruit in faithful service will be given additional opportunities for greater service and greater rewards, and he will have both in abundance. But the one who does not faithfully use what he has received, from him will be taken even those opportunities for service and rewards that he initially had."

III. Christ will judge and reward each steward's *productivity*.

A. The Lord went away, but He will return.

LK 19:11 And as they heard these things, he added and spake a parable, because he was nigh to Jerusalem, and because they thought that the kingdom of God should immediately appear.

¹²**He said therefore, A certain nobleman went into a far country to receive for himself a kingdom, and to return.**

B. All stewards receive the same endowment and same instructions.

¹³**And he called his ten servants, and delivered them ten pounds, and said unto them, Occupy [do business] till I come.**

In this parable, each servant received one pound (about three months' wages for a laborer.) The identical endowments represent a responsibility for service that all believers receive equally. The gospel message that Christ entrusts to every believer for investing and multiplying in others' lives fits this parameter. The lord's instruction, "Occupy till I come," is the parable's equivalent of Christ's Great Commission to all believers for this present age.

C. Most people reject the Lord.

¹⁴**But his citizens hated him, and sent a message after him, saying, We will not have this man to reign over us.**

This verse introduces a second group of people who were not in the parable on the talents, and these are presented in sharp contrast to the Lord's servants.

Their reaction is a warning to His servants at the outset that most people will reject Christ and the message of the gospel.

D. Each steward faces a reckoning at Christ's return.

> [15]And it came to pass, that when he was returned, having received the kingdom, then he commanded these servants to be called unto him, to whom he had given the money, that he might know how much every man had gained by trading.

E. Their rewards will be in proportion to their productivity.

> [16]Then came the first, saying, Lord, thy pound hath gained ten pounds.
> [17]And he said unto him, Well [done], thou good servant: because thou hast been faithful in a very little, have thou authority over ten cities.
> [18]And the second came, saying, Lord, thy pound hath gained five pounds.
> [19]And he said likewise to him, Be thou also over five cities.

The Lord will reward His faithful servants when He has "received the kingdom" at His second coming (v. 15). Authority "over cities" probably represents positions of honor and responsibility in that kingdom. These will be given in proportion to evangelistic service of all kinds (direct and indirect, including prayer, giving, and training other servants), as God alone can measure and evaluate it. Compared with God's pervasive role in anyone's salvation, His servants' efforts will seem as "very little" (v. 17).

F. No steward can excuse inactivity and negligence.

> [20]And another came, saying, Lord, behold, here is thy pound, which I have kept laid up in a napkin:
> [21]For I feared thee, because thou art an austere man: thou takest up that thou layedst not down, and reapest that thou didst not sow.
> [22]And he saith unto him, Out of thine own mouth will I judge thee, thou wicked servant. Thou knewest that I was an austere man, taking up that I laid not down, and reaping that I did not sow:
> [23]Wherefore then gavest not thou my money into the bank, that at my coming I might have required mine own with usury [interest]?

G. Unproductive stewards will lose all they had.

> [24]And he said unto them that stood by, Take from him the pound, and give it to him that hath ten pounds.
> [25](And they said unto him, Lord, he hath ten pounds.)
> [26]For I say unto you, That unto every one which hath shall be given; and from him that hath not, even that he hath shall be taken away from him.
> [27]But those mine enemies, which would not that I should reign over them, bring hither, and slay them before me.

As in the prior parable, the Lord calls this wholly unproductive steward a "wicked servant" (v. 22), indicating he was no servant at all. The parable's application in verse 26 may be understood in the same way as MT 25:29 in Section II.H above. Finally, the rebellious populace that rejected the Lord will be justly condemned. Their judgment and the steward's failure call to mind God's warning through Ezekiel: "[If you fail] to warn the wicked from his wicked way, to save his life; the same wicked man shall die in his iniquity; but his blood will I require at thine hand" (2:18).

IV. Christ will judge and reward each steward's *preparation for eternity.*

A. An unfaithful steward is called into account.

LK 16:1 And he said also unto his disciples, There was a certain rich man, which had a steward; and the same was accused unto him that he had wasted his goods.

²And he called him, and said unto him, How is it that I hear this of thee? give an account of thy stewardship; for thou mayest be no longer steward.

³Then the steward said within himself, What shall I do? for my lord taketh away from me the stewardship: I cannot dig; to beg I am ashamed.

The steward apparently was guilty as charged and was fired from his job. His master ordered him to give a final accounting of the assets he had managed in preparation for turning over the books to another steward. While preparing for that accounting, the unfaithful steward agonized over how he would survive in the future. (In contrast to the prior parables, the "lord" here does not picture Christ, nor does the steward represent believers.)

B. He devises a shrewd, dishonest scheme.

⁴I am resolved what to do, that, when I am put out of the stewardship, they may receive me into their houses.

⁵So he called every one of his lord's debtors unto him, and said unto the first, How much owest thou unto my lord?

⁶And he said, An hundred measures of oil. And he said unto him, Take thy bill, and sit down quickly, and write fifty.

⁷Then said he to another, And how much owest thou? And he said, An hundred measures of wheat. And he said unto him, Take thy bill, and write fourscore.

The steward sought to ingratiate himself to his former master's debtors so that they would at least give him lodging while he was out of a job. His scheme was thoroughly crooked (and required the collaboration of crooked debtors) but he pursued it vigorously.

C. He was wiser than many believers by preparing for his future.

⁸And the lord [the former master] commended the unjust steward, because he had done wisely: for the children of this world are in their generation wiser than the children of light.

Verse 8a may be understood: "The master commended the unjust steward because he had acted shrewdly [in preparing for his future]." Christ then made the observation (in v. 8b) that unbelievers in this age often are "wiser" in dealing with their fellows regarding their own future than are God's "children of light" who fail to prepare for their eternal dwelling by laying up treasure in heaven.

D. Wise believers use their resources to prepare for heaven.

⁹And I say unto you, Make to yourselves friends of the mammon of unrighteousness; that, when ye fail [or, when *it* fails], they may receive you into everlasting habitations.

Verse 9 may be understood: "Use the mammon of unrighteousness [your material resources] to make yourselves spiritual friends [through evangelizing the lost and aiding believers]; so that, when your resources have been used in this way, those friends may welcome you [with thankful appreciation] to your eternal home."

E. How we use mammon indicates how we would handle "true riches."

¹⁰He that is faithful in that which is least [the use of his money] is faithful also in much: and he that is unjust in the least is unjust also in much.

¹¹If therefore ye have not been faithful in [your use of] the unrighteous mammon, who will commit to your trust the true riches?

¹²And if ye have not been faithful in that which is another man's [that which belongs to God], who shall give you that which is your own?

How we use money is a spiritual indicator. It reveals how faithful and obedient we likely are (or will be) in the truly valuable matters of life (v. 10). If we do not heed God's commands and principles in managing our money, how can we expect God to entrust to us His true (greater and permanent) riches (v. 11)? Similarly, since everything we possess really belongs to God and we are only His stewards, how can we expect Him to give us anything of our own (heavenly rewards) if we are not faithful in managing His resources in this life? (v. 12).

13

Profiles of the Lord's Disciples

Christ invited everyone to come to Him for "life," "bread," "drink," and "rest" with only one proviso — that they trust fully in Him. He stressed, however, and in the strongest terms, that those who receive His life must give evidence of having it. Similarly, He tied believing in Him to following Him; receiving His rest to taking His yoke; and being in Him to bearing fruit for Him. To whom He is Savior, He must be Lord.

Christ never distinguished between true believers on the one hand and faithful disciples on the other. The two should be one and the same. Although many fair-weather believers and temporary disciples appear in the Gospels, these probably were neither true believers nor real disciples. We do find in the epistles (and, sadly, in our churches) saved people who are not walking closely with their Savior. Christ, however, did not provide for such a dichotomy. He calls every believer to wear His name, care for His work, bear his own cross, and (ultimately) share in His glory.

The Disciples' Calling

Disciple means "follower" and "pupil or learner," an apt description of those who followed Christ during His ministry. (A parallel today is a tradesman's apprentice.) The term is not limited to the twelve that Christ chose; it applies to all who follow Him (then and now) with an earnest desire to learn of Him and do His will. Discipleship, however, is more than earnestly learning and faithfully doing certain things. At its heart, it is reproducing Christ's life — His character, purposes, principles, and ways — in every area of our lives and also in the lives of others. It is continually living and teaching "*all things* whatsoever I have commanded you" (MT 28:20). Christ called every believer to be His disciple and to make disciples of others. The following pictures illustrate this calling.

I. The crux of discipleship.

A. Be "light" in a dark world.

> **MT 5:14 Ye are the light of the world. A city that is set on an hill cannot be hid.**
> **¹⁵Neither do men light a candle [lamp], and put it under a bushel, but on a candlestick [lampstand]; and it giveth light unto all that are in the house.**
> **¹⁶Let your light so shine before men, that they may see your good works, and glorify your Father which is in heaven.**

Christ Himself is *the* Light of the world (see Sec. IV on p. 8.). Believers, however, who walk closely with Him will reflect His light in their lives and thereby become "the light of the world" also. In verse 14, believers *collectively* are the light of the world — as a Mideastern city of many buildings clustered on a hill, brightly reflecting the sunlight off their white-washed walls. Such a city "cannot be hid." Even in the darkness of night, the city's lights proclaim its location and profile.

In verse 15, believers *individually* are to be the light of the world — as a lamp that gives light to everyone in the house. Their light is to be conspicuous (not "under a bushel"), considerate (given generously and graciously), constructive (dispelling darkness), and consistent (shining faithfully to all around it). Both collectively and individually, believers should "so shine" (as the city and the lamp) through godly lives that those who see them will glorify God for His greatness and goodness.

B. Be "salt" in a decaying world.

> **MT 5:13 Ye are the salt of the earth: but if the salt have lost his savor, wherewith shall it be salted? it is thenceforth good for nothing, but to be cast out, and to be trodden under foot of men.**

MK 9:50 Salt is good: but if the salt have lost his saltness, wherewith will ye season it? Have salt in yourselves and have peace one with another.

Salt's principal uses include preserving and flavoring foods. As the "salt of the earth," a believer's Christ-like life and testimony should serve to retard moral corruption and decay in his surrounding community. It should also enhance the flavor of his own life and of other believers' lives as he encourages them in their walk with the Lord.

Both believers and salt must maintain their distinctive savor or saltiness to be of any value and accomplish their intended purpose. Christ asked rhetorically, "If salt has lost its savor, how can its savor be restored?" (v. 13). That it can become "good for nothing but to be cast out" implies a warning: "Don't lose your saltiness among men and your place in God's service." Believers are to "have salt continuously within themselves" (v. 50), in the form of gracious speech and behavior (Col. 4:6) and peaceful fellowship with other believers.

II. The challenge of discipleship.

   A. Be "fishers of men" for the Savior.

MT 4:18 And Jesus, walking by the sea of Galilee, saw two brethren, Simon called Peter, and Andrew his brother, casting a net into the sea: for they were fishers.

¹⁹And he saith unto them, Follow me, and I will make you fishers of men.

²⁰And they straightway left their nets, and followed him.

Peter and Andrew were followers of Christ before He called them to become "fishers of men" (see JN 1:35-42). This new call, therefore, was to closer association, deeper commitment, and more active service. They immediately left their nets and followed Him. Not until after Christ's resurrection, however, did they fully grasp what fishing for men really meant and how they should go about doing it. (The full sequence of Christ's calling of these men is given on p. 282 ff.)

   B. Be reapers in God's harvest.

JN 4:35 Say not ye, There are yet four months, and then cometh harvest? behold, I say unto you, Lift up your eyes, and look on the fields; for they are white already to harvest.

³⁶And he that reapeth receiveth wages, and gathereth fruit unto life eternal: that both he that soweth and he that reapeth may rejoice together.

³⁷And herein is that saying true, One soweth, and another reapeth.

³⁸I sent you to reap that whereon ye bestowed no labor: other men labored, and ye are entered into their labors.

> **MT 9:37** Then saith he unto his disciples, The harvest truly is plenteous, but the laborers are few;
> ³⁸Pray ye therefore the Lord of the harvest, that he will send forth laborers into his harvest.

> **JN 15:16** Ye have not chosen me, but I have chosen you, and ordained you, that ye should go and bring forth fruit, and that your fruit should remain: that whatsoever ye shall ask of the Father in my name, he may give it you.

These passages highlight several aspects of our calling to work in God's harvest field. First, the harvest is "the Lord's harvest," not ours, and Christ has commissioned us to bring in His harvest. Second, now is the time to work — not in four months, or in four years, or whenever we think that we and/or the harvest field will be better prepared. (Even when long-term preparation is necessary for certain tasks, there is much work to do in the meantime and along the way.)

Third, harvest work is team work. Some sow, some reap, but all rejoice together after the harvest. Fourth, the harvest is greater than the available workers can handle. We are to pray earnestly, therefore, that God will commission and empower more workers (including ourselves) for His service. Finally, the yield of the harvest is eternal. The "fruit" of evangelism is eternal, the workers' "wages" are eternal, and the rejoicing of the workers with the Lord of the harvest is eternal.

III. The criteria of discipleship.

On different occasions, Christ cited in succinct statements the following separate criteria by which His true disciples can readily be identified — both by themselves and by others. These measures of discipleship are reviewed in greater detail on the pages indicated.

A. Deny yourself and put Christ first in everything.
> **LK 14:27** And whosoever doth not bear his cross, and come after me, cannot be my disciple. . . .
> ³³So likewise, whosoever he be of you that forsaketh not all that he hath, he cannot be my disciple. [See "Cross," Sec. IV, on p. 272.]

B. Live continually in obedience to God's Word.
> **JN 8:31** Then said Jesus to those Jews which believed on him, If ye continue in my word, then are ye my disciples indeed;
> ³²And ye shall know the truth, and the truth shall make you free. [See "Salvation," Sec. II, on p. 88.]

C. Demonstrate love for all believers.

JN 13:34 A new commandment I give unto you, That ye love one another; as I have loved you, that ye also love one another.
35By this shall all men know that ye are my disciples, if ye have love one to another. [See "Love," Sec. IV, on p. 206.]

D. Bear fruit for God's glory.

JN 15:5 I am the vine, ye are the branches: He that abideth in me, and I in him, the same bringeth forth much fruit: for without me ye can do nothing. ...
8Herein is my Father glorified, that ye bear much fruit; so shall ye be my disciples. [See "Vine" on p. 121.]

Each of the above distinguishing characteristics of Christ's true disciples includes continuing positive action. They may be understood as follows: be carrying your cross and coming after me; remain continually in my word; constantly be loving one another; abide continually in me; be bearing much fruit. When these qualities are in evidence, "so shall ye be my disciples" (JN 15:8). The reverse of each test is also true: i.e., if one does not "follow me," "continue in my word," "love one another," etc., then he "cannot be my disciple" (LK 14:33).

IV. The compulsion of discipleship.

A. Love Christ preeminently, as He desires and deserves.

JN 21:14 This is now the third time that Jesus showed himself to his disciples, after that he was risen from the dead.
15So when they had dined, Jesus saith to Simon Peter, Simon, son of Jonas, lovest thou me more than these? He saith unto him, Yea, Lord; thou knowest that I love thee. He saith unto him, Feed my lambs.

The compelling force in every disciple's service for Christ must be an unlimited and unwavering love for Him. Such love must surpass the love in all other relationships and attachments — including family, friends, career, possessions, and personal desires. Peter had previously told his colleagues, "I'm going back to fishing," and they went with him. (See Sec. IX on p. 302 for the preceding verses.) Christ focused on the key issue facing Peter and asked him, "Do you love me more than these [i.e., these fish on which you plan to rely for your sustenance]? If so, feed my lambs [rather than pursue your own objectives]."

B. Love Christ completely, without reservation.

16He saith to him again the second time, Simon, son of Jonas, lovest thou me? He saith unto him, Yea, Lord; thou knowest that I love thee. He saith unto him, Feed my sheep.

> ¹⁷He saith unto him the third time, Simon, son of Jonas, lovest thou me? Peter was grieved because he said unto him the third time, Lovest thou me? And he said unto him, Lord, thou knowest all things; thou knowest that I love thee. Jesus saith unto him, Feed my sheep.

Twice (v. 15 and v. 16), Christ asked Peter for *agapao* love (Greek for unreserved, unconditional, unwavering love) — the kind of love, for example, used in JN 3:16 to describe how "God so loved the world that He gave His only begotten Son." Still plagued by his three denials of Christ, Peter was understandably reluctant to use such a strong word as *agapao* to describe his commitment to the Lord. Instead, he replied with a lesser term, *phileo*, meaning "fondness, as between friends." The third time Jesus asked, "Lovest thou me?," He used Peter's term *phileo*. Christ graciously accepted the measure of love Peter was able to give and express at that time.

Christ previously pictured Himself as the Good Shepherd (see p. 114). Here, He commissioned Peter (and by extension, all who truly love Him) as His undershepherds to care for His sheep. Each time He asked, "Lovest thou me?," He followed it with a command: "Feed my sheep" or "Feed my lambs." Some undershepherds may be responsible for a large flock; others may have only one or two lambs to nurture. But all disciples are to feed Christ's sheep, with the same loving care that He Himself would give.

C. Follow Christ faithfully, whatever the cost.

> ¹⁸Verily, verily, I say unto thee, When thou wast young, thou girdedst thyself, and walkedst whither thou wouldest: but when thou shalt be old, thou shalt stretch forth thy hands, and another shall gird thee, and carry thee whither thou wouldest not.
> ¹⁹This spake he, signifying by what death he should glorify God. And when he had spoken this, he saith unto him, Follow me.

Using a picture of crucifixion, Christ revealed to Peter how he would die. He also indicated that Peter would live to an old age, giving him many opportunities to feed His sheep and lambs. According to early church writers, Peter was crucified with his head downward (the latter at his request, to contrast his crucifixion with Christ's).

D. Obey Christ singlemindedly, without regard to others' roles.

> ²⁰Then Peter, turning about, seeth the disciple whom Jesus loved following [i.e., John]; which also leaned on his breast at supper, and said, Lord, which is he that betrayeth thee?
> ²¹Peter seeing him saith to Jesus, Lord, and what shall this man do?
> ²²Jesus saith unto him, If I will that he tarry till I come, what is that to thee? follow thou me.

In answering Peter's question regarding John's future ministry, Christ indicated that one disciple's service, and its earthly end, may differ markedly from another's (v. 22). Each disciple must be faithful to his own calling, regardless of how it compares with that of others. Christ concluded His commission with the same command He gave His disciples three years earlier when He first called them to discipleship: "Follow me."

The Disciples' Commission

When Christ first called His disciples to be fishers of men and reapers in God's harvest, He gave them little instruction at the time regarding how, when, and where they were to fulfill these tasks. He simply said, in effect, "Follow me, and I will make you what I call you to be." Their instructions would become clear as they followed Him. Following Christ included both learning from His teaching and emulating His example. For the next two or three years, His disciples received the most intensive discipleship training course ever given.

Twice Christ commissioned His disciples to go out and proclaim His gospel message. Their first mission was to the Jewish people, to announce that their Messiah and His kingdom were at hand. Their second was to all the world, to proclaim that Christ gives eternal life to all who trust in Him. In sending them to herald His kingdom, He outlined (in Secs. I-IV below) the basic content and responsibilities of discipleship for all of His followers, then and now. This passage from MT 10 is a good checklist that every believer can use to evaluate his own commitment and progress as Christ's disciple.

I. Reproduce Christ in your life and service.

 A. Submit as a slave to your Master.
 MT 10:24 The disciple is not above his master [teacher], nor the servant [slave] above his lord.

 B. Strive to be like your Teacher and Lord.
 ²⁵ᵃIt is enough for the disciple that he be [exactly] as his master, and the servant [exactly] as his lord.

Christ pictured His disciples as His bond-slaves. In that day, a slave was owned by his master as a piece of property. He served solely at his master's pleasure and for his benefit, and he was expected to do everything exactly as told. Such is the level of submission and obedience that Christ expects of His disciples. Their service, however, is to be rendered in love, adoration, and thanksgiving, not in craven fear or grudging resignation. His slaves and students are to reproduce His character, priorities, and service in their lives, and be like Him in all respects (v. 25a).

II. Proclaim Christ's message clearly and boldly.

A. Expect and endure spiritual opposition.

²⁵ᵇIf they have called the master of the house Beelzebub [prince of demons], how much more shall they call them of his household? ²⁶Fear them not therefore: for there is nothing covered, that shall not be revealed; and hid, that shall not be known.

B. Stay true to His Word and true to your calling.

²⁷What I tell you in darkness, that speak ye in light: and what ye hear in the ear, that preach ye upon the housetops. ²⁸And fear not them which kill the body, but are not able to kill the soul: but rather fear him [God alone] which is able to destroy both soul and body in hell.

People may kill a disciple's body, but they cannot touch his soul. Christ exhorted His followers, therefore, not to restrict their witness for God out of fear of negative reactions from people. He counselled, "Fear God," not men. The fear of God includes a keen awareness of His absolute holiness and awesome power. For unbelievers, this should be a frightening thought. For believers, however, the fear of God is a reverential awe for His infinite being, coupled with grateful appreciation for His love and mercy (although it also includes a fear of offending Him and of incurring His chastisement). A proper fear of God produces submission to Him, worship of Him, and service for Him.

C. Trust God to uphold you at all times.

²⁹Are not two sparrows sold for a farthing [assarion, a few cents]? and one of them shall not fall on the ground without your Father. {and not one of them is forgotten before God. [LK 12:6]} ³⁰But the very hairs of your head are all numbered. ³¹Fear ye not therefore, ye are of more value than many sparrows.

To encourage His disciples to be bold and fearless in proclaiming the gospel, Christ cited His Father's detailed care of all creation — even for each little sparrow. Nothing can happen to a sparrow, much less to one of Christ's disciples, without the Father specifically willing it so. The extent of God's involvement in our lives is pictured by His numbering every hair on our heads. No believer has an excuse for fearing or failing to speak out for Christ.

D. Identify openly with Christ and His cause.

³²Whosoever therefore shall confess me before men, him will I confess also before my Father which is in heaven. ³³But whosoever shall deny me before men, him will I also deny before my Father which is in heaven.

To confess Christ before men means to acknowledge Him openly in both word and deed as your personal Savior and Lord of your life. To deny Him means to fail to so acknowledge Him. Those who never confess Him in this basic way simply do not know Him, and He will not confess them as His own before His Father in heaven.

    III. Serve Christ above all, regardless of the cost.

        A. Expect the sword of conflict and division.

> **³⁴Think not that I am come to send peace on earth: I came not to send peace, but a sword.**
>
> **³⁵For I am come to set a man at variance against his father, and the daughter against her mother, and the daughter in law against her mother in law.**
>
> **³⁶And a man's foes shall be they of his own household.**

        B. Put allegiance to Christ above family ties.

> **³⁷He that loveth father or mother more than me is not worthy of me: and he that loveth son or daughter more than me is not worthy of me.**

        C. "Lose your life" for Christ's sake.

> **³⁸And he that taketh not his cross, and followeth after me, is not worthy of me.**
>
> **³⁹He that findeth his life shall lose it: and he that loseth his life for my sake shall find it.**

Christ warned that wholehearted commitment to Him and to spreading the gospel would be as a sword that sunders close personal relationships. The most cutting and painful sword thrusts would come from uncommitted family members who openly oppose the disciple's total dedication to his Lord. Although Christ's disciples would have His unfailing presence and peace in their souls, they should not expect to have peace on earth (v. 34). (See "The Disciples' Cross," Sec. III, on p. 274.)

    IV. Support those who trust and serve God.

        A. Receive other believers as you would Christ.

> **⁴⁰He that receiveth [welcomes] you receiveth me, and he that receiveth me receiveth him that sent me.**

        B. Encourage and support God's servants.

> **⁴¹He that receiveth a prophet in the name of [because he is] a prophet shall receive a prophet's reward; and he that receiveth a righteous man in the name of [because he is] a righteous man shall receive a righteous man's reward.**

C. Attend the needs of Christ's "little ones."

⁴²And whosoever shall give to drink unto one of these little ones a cup of cold water only in the name of [because he is] a disciple, verily [truly] I say unto you, he shall in no wise lose his reward.

Faithful disciples will face strong opposition and many adversaries. They each, therefore, should encourage and support one another in their faith, godly living, service, and physical needs. Even giving a cup of cold water to one of Christ's "little ones" (a lowly and needy believer), simply because he is a fellow disciple, is guaranteed an eternal reward. (See "Crowns," Sec. III.C and D, on p. 282.)

V. Heed Christ's commands and follow His example.

MT 11:1 And it came to pass, when Jesus had made an end of commanding his twelve disciples, he departed thence to teach and to preach in their cities.

Christ's instructions in MT 10 are clear *commands* (11:1), not just recommendations for optional behavior. Also, He not only *told* His followers to do His will, but He set the example by going out and performing the same service He expected of them. Discipleship includes the faithful performance of Christ's work, and doing it in Christlike ways.

VI. Fulfill Christ's Great Commission.

In the forty days between His resurrection and His ascension, Christ gave His disciples their final instructions regarding their future service for Him. These included His Great Commission, given in different ways and on different occasions, as reported in each of the Gospels and in Acts (below). This commission was much broader in many respects than their first commission in MT 10 above. It was also based on a deeper relationship with Him and on greater promises from Him.

A. Go with Christ's authority, His message, and His presence.

MT 28:18 And Jesus came and spake unto them, saying, All power [authority] is given unto me in heaven and in earth.

¹⁹Go ye therefore, and teach [make disciples of] all nations, baptizing them in the name of the Father, and of the Son, and of the Holy Ghost:

²⁰Teaching them to observe all things whatsoever I have commanded you: and, lo, I am with you alway, even unto the end of the world. Amen.

God vested *all* authority in Christ — over every created being and thing in both heaven and earth. Nothing is excluded from His jurisdiction. From this absolutely supreme position, Christ delegated to His disciples both the responsibility and the authority to proclaim His message throughout the world, to make and baptize additional disciples, and to teach the latter to "observe all things" that He had taught them.

B. Go to everyone everywhere, giving them the gospel.

MK 16:15 And he said unto them, Go ye into all the world, and preach the gospel [the good news] to every creature.

The disciples' first commission in MT 10 was "to the lost sheep of Israel" and specifically excluded Gentiles and Samaritans. Now, the "good news" is to be taken "to every creature" in "all the world." The first commission also was temporary (and probably in effect only a few weeks). The new commission remains in force as long as anyone remains who has not heard the good news — or until Christ returns and our opportunities to fulfill it are ended.

C. Go proclaiming salvation through the crucified and risen Christ.

LK 24:46 And [Jesus] said unto them, Thus it is written, and thus it behoved Christ to suffer, and to rise from the dead the third day:
⁴⁷And that repentance and remission of sins should be preached in his name among all nations, beginning at Jerusalem.
⁴⁸And ye are witnesses of these things.

The assigned message in the first commission was that the promised Messiah and His kingdom were "at hand." The new message is that the Messiah (the Christ) has already come, and that He suffered, died, and rose again. It further declares that He forgives the sins of all who repent and trust in Him ("in His name") for salvation. The disciples had witnessed these things first hand; now they must proclaim "among all nations" what they have seen and heard.

D. Go with the same dedication and commitment Christ exhibited.

JN 20:21 Then said Jesus to them again, Peace be unto you: as my Father hath sent me, even so send I you.

Christ commissioned His disciples "even as" (in the same way) His Father had commissioned Him in sending Him to earth — that is, with the same divine authority, the same essential message (the gospel), and the same ultimate purpose (the salvation of all who will believe in Him). Christ also expects His "sent ones" to exhibit the same dedication and commitment He exhibited in fulfilling His commission. After Pentecost, His disciples are referred to more as apostles (sent ones) than as disciples (followers/pupils). They were apostles-in-training in MT 10. Now they are to be full-fledged apostles — as fully as Christ was His Father's apostle.

E. Go as Christ's witnesses, in the power of the Holy Spirit.

ACTS 1:6 When they therefore were come together, they asked of him, saying, Lord, wilt thou at this time restore again the kingdom to Israel?

⁷And he said unto them, It is not for you to know the times or the seasons, which the Father hath put in his own power.

⁸But ye shall receive power, after that the Holy Ghost is come upon you: and ye shall be witnesses unto me both in Jerusalem, and in all Judaea, and in Samaria, and unto the uttermost part of the earth.

⁹And when he had spoken these things, while they beheld, he was taken up; and a cloud received him out of their sight.

In MT 28, Christ gave His disciples the responsibility and the authority to go everywhere and enlist, baptize, and train disciples for Him. Here, He adds the indispensable ingredient for any spiritual task, namely, the power of the Holy Spirit. They would receive His power when the Holy Spirit Himself "came upon them" to indwell them and equip them for Christ's service. When He finished arranging for everything they needed to accomplish their task, "He was taken up . . . out of their sight."

The Disciples' Cross

To those under Roman rule, the cross was a despised and feared instrument of horrible death by public execution. It symbolized the ultimate in humiliation and shame. The Romans used it primarily for rebels against their authority, conquered enemies, vile criminals, and runaway slaves. When Christ said that each of His followers must bear his own cross, He pictured the complete self-denial and death to personal ambition that being His disciple entailed. Those contemplating becoming His disciples faced a serious decision regarding their willingness to make such a commitment. For many early Christians, bearing their cross was not only figurative, but also a literal experience, as they sacrificed their lives for their Savior.

I. The cost of discipleship.

A. Forsake treasure on earth for treasure in heaven.

MK 10:17 And when he was gone forth into the way, there came one running, and kneeled to him, and asked him, Good Master, what shall I do that I may inherit eternal life? . . .

²¹Then Jesus beholding him loved him, and said unto him, One thing thou lackest: go thy way, sell whatsoever thou hast, and give to the poor, and thou shalt have treasure in heaven: and come, take up the cross, and follow me.

²²And he was sad at that saying, and went away grieved: for he had great possessions.

For many prospective disciples (such as the rich young ruler above), an attachment to or desire for earthly treasure stands in the way of a full commitment to Christ. This tug-of-war may be waged over salvation at the outset, or over greater discipleship later on. In either case, Christ requires an unreserved willingness to shed and forsake all possessions that compete with Him for our allegiance. Among the rewards for those who take up their cross and follow Him are eternal treasures in heaven. (See Sec. II on p. 244 for the full passage.)

>   B. Bear your cross daily and follow Christ.
>
>   **MK 8:34 [LK 9:23] And when he had called the people unto him with his disciples also, he said unto them, Whosoever will come after me, let him deny himself, and take up his cross {daily}, and follow me. {And he that taketh not his cross, and followeth after me, is not worthy of me. [MT 10:38]}**
>
>   **³⁵For whosoever will save his life shall lose it; but whosoever shall lose his life for my sake and the gospel's, the same shall save it.**

A person condemned to be crucified often was forced to take up his cross (usually the cross-bar of a T-shaped cross) and carry it to the site of his execution. There, he was nailed or tied to the cross-bar, which was fastened to a pole, for his slow, excruciating death. Christ said that each of His followers must willingly "take up his cross daily" in complete self-denial and follow Him as the Lord of his life. Anyone not willing to make such a commitment "is not worthy of me." (See Sec. VI on p. 249 under "Materialism" for the full passage in Mark 8.)

>   C. Die to yourself, as a seed in the ground.
>
>   **JN 12:24 Verily, verily, I say unto you, Except a corn [kernel] of wheat fall into the ground and die, it abideth alone: but if it die, it bringeth forth much fruit.**
>
>   **²⁵He that loveth his life shall lose it; and he that hateth his life in this world shall keep it unto life eternal.**

Before a seed can bear any fruit, it must die in the ground. Each disciple similarly must die to his personal desires and to control over his life. He must bury himself deep in the fertile ground of submission to Christ if he is to bear any fruit acceptable to God. Those who so die will "bring forth much fruit," and their fruit will remain "unto life eternal." Those who love their life and refuse to die will "abide alone," useless and barren, losing all fruit and their own life as well.

>   II. The conditions of discipleship
>
>   A. Allegiance to Christ means "leaving your nest."
>
>   **LK 9:57 And it came to pass, that, as they went in the way, a certain man said unto him, Lord, I will follow thee whithersoever thou goest.**

[58]And Jesus said unto him, Foxes have holes [dens], and birds of the air have nests; but the Son of man hath not where to lay his head.

In this encounter and the two that follow, some aspiring disciples approached Christ with seemingly sincere desires to follow Him. He did not, however, welcome them with open arms. Rather, He cautioned each one regarding the full commitment He required. Christ knew perfectly what was in their hearts and minds and what weaknesses or higher priorities each would have to overcome to become a true disciple. For this first applicant, it appears that leaving the comforts of home would be a major hurdle, especially in exchange for a sacrificial life with no nest or den where he could retreat and rest when weary.

B. Obedience to Christ "leaves the dead to the dead."

[59]And he said unto another, Follow me. But he said, Lord, suffer me first to go and bury my father.
[60]Jesus said unto him, Let the dead bury their dead: but go thou and preach the kingdom of God.

Jewish custom was to bury the dead with minimal delay, giving funeral arrangements high priority over other obligations. It appears, therefore, that this man's father had not yet died, else the man would have been involved with the funeral rather than watching Jesus' heal the sick (MT 8:16-22). His father may have been aged and ill, leading to his excuse for not immediately following Jesus. Christ's answer may be understood: "Let the spiritually dead bury their own dead: but you go and preach the kingdom of God [and spiritual life]."

C. Dedication to Christ "keeps plowing ahead."

[61]And another also said, Lord, I will follow thee; but let me first go bid them farewell, which are at home at my house.
[62]And Jesus said unto him, No man, having put his hand to the plough, and looking back [to what he left behind], is fit for the kingdom of God.

Christ evidently knew that this man would have serious difficulty subordinating his family ties to following Him. Either he would succumb to their initial pleas not to leave them, or he would soon drop out through homesickness or concern for their affairs. No plowman can plow straight furrows and properly till a field if he keeps looking behind him rather than focusing constantly on the task ahead.

III. The conflict in discipleship.

A. Expect opposition from carnal relatives.

LK 12:51 Suppose ye that I am come to give peace on earth? I tell you, Nay; but rather division:

⁵²For from henceforth there shall be five in one house divided, three against two and two against three.

⁵³The father shall be divided against the son, and the son against the father; the mother against the daughter, and the daughter against the mother; the mother in law against her daughter in law, and the daughter in law against her mother in law.

Christ warned His disciples that some of their greatest opposition would come from members of their own families. These include non-Christians with no comprehension of what it means to follow Christ, and also carnal Christians not willing to make the sacrifices involved in full discipleship. These relatives' antagonism toward a disciple's commitment and service to Christ can seriously divide and trouble his household and family relationships. (See the parallel passage in Sec. III on p. 269.)

B. Expect "the world" to hate you.

JN 15:18 If the world hate you, ye know that it hated me before it hated you.

¹⁹If ye were of the world, the world would love his own: but because ye are not of the world, but I have chosen you out of the world, therefore the world hateth you.

²⁰Remember the word that I said unto you, The servant [slave] is not greater than his lord. If they have persecuted me, they will also persecute you; if they have kept my saying, they will keep yours also.

²¹But all these things will they do unto you for my name's sake, because they know not him that sent me.

"The world" in scripture is used in three principal ways: (1) The *physical earth* created by God; (2) *All people* in the world (whom God "so loved" that He sent His Son); and (3) The prevailing *world system* of godless values and behavior which unbelievers, under Satan's influence, have instituted in opposition to everything related to God and His will. The latter is "the world" that hates Christ (v. 18) and will hate His disciples also (v. 19). Christ called His disciples "out of the world," which they must renounce and leave behind to follow Him. "Therefore the world hateth you" and will "persecute you . . . for my name's sake."

C. Expect persecution in the name of religion.

JN 16:1 These things have I spoken unto you, that ye should not be offended [stumble and fall].

²They shall put you out of the synagogues: yea, the time cometh, that whosoever killeth you will think that he doeth God service.

³And these things will they do unto you, because they have not known the Father, nor me.

Much of the persecution directed at God's faithful servants throughout scripture, and against Christ Himself, came from perverters of true religion and purveyors of false religion. Christ's disciples should expect the same treatment from the same sources. These workers of iniquity even think they do God service by killing His servants (v. 2). Their contempt for Christ's representatives prove that they do not know God at all.

D. Expect attacks from worldly wolves.

MT 10:16 Behold, I send you forth as sheep in the midst of wolves: be ye therefore wise as serpents, and harmless as doves.

¹⁷But beware of men: for they will deliver you up to the councils, and they will scourge you in their synagogues;

¹⁸And ye shall be brought before governors and kings for my sake, for a testimony against them and the Gentiles.

The wolves will attack Christ's sheep with every means at their disposal. As indicated before, they especially use the cloaks and tools of institutional religion (v. 17) and ungodly government (v. 18). These two pillars of the "world system" often combine their perverted morals and perverted justice to slander and condemn Christ's disciples. In facing such powerful enemies, disciples must be "wise as serpents," considering in advance the potential effects of their actions and responses, without compromising their principles or ministry. Disciples also must be "harmless as doves." They must add no animosity, reprisal, or personal offense to the offense of the cross, but follow the example Christ gave when He endured similar trials and unwarranted persecution.

IV. The commitment in discipleship.

A. The choices involved may hurt.

LK 14:25 And there went great multitudes with him: and he turned, and said unto them,

²⁶If any man come to me, and hate not his father, and mother, and wife, and children, and brethren, and sisters, yea, and his own life also, he cannot be my disciple. {He that loveth father or mother more than me is not worthy of me: and he that loveth son or daughter more than me is not worthy of me. [MT 10:37]}

The requirement to "hate" our closest relatives might be difficult to understand were it not for Christ's similar challenge in MT 10 above. There, the clear sense is "love Christ more than you love them." Scripture commands throughout that we love our family members, other believers, and even our neighbors "as our selves." Our devotion and commitment to Christ, however, must exceed our love in all other relationships to such an extent that the latter seems as hatred in comparison. The separation from loved ones that may result (whether physical or emotional) can be painful and grievous. This comparative hatred must extend to our "own life also," with the painful choices that too will entail.

B. The cross to bear may be heavy.
²⁷And whosoever doth not bear his cross, and come after me, cannot be my disciple.

A disciple is not called to bear Christ's cross, but his own. In other words, the person to die on this cross is the disciple himself. He must die to the appetites and appeals of his old nature and to all other self-centered desires. He must also be his own executioner (Col. 3:5), and die to himself daily (LK 9:23).

C. The cost to build may be high.
²⁸For which of you, intending to build a tower, sitteth not down first, and counteth the cost, whether he have sufficient to finish it?
²⁹Lest haply, after he hath laid the foundation, and is not able to finish it, all that behold it begin to mock him,
³⁰Saying, This man began to build, and was not able to finish.

Christ cautioned prospective disciples to make certain they are willing and able to "pay the full price" and "build the whole building." A disciple who is unable to finish the building or abandons the project mid-stream brings scorn and shame not only on himself but also on the Master Builder and on His entire building program.

D. The conditions of battle may be harsh.
³¹Or what king, going to make war against another king, sitteth not down first, and consulteth whether he be able with ten thousand to meet him that cometh against him with twenty thousand?
³²Or else, while the other is yet a great way off, he sendeth an ambassage, and desireth conditions of peace.
³³So likewise, whosoever he be of you that forsaketh not all that he hath, he cannot be my disciple.

The outnumbered king pictures a person who is debating whether to submit to Christ as His disciple or to reject Christ's rule over his life and rely on his own inferior resources. The only alternative to fighting a losing battle is to surrender to Christ on His terms and willingly follow Him. How much better to surrender early than to squander resources and life itself in a fruitless struggle against the Almighty King.

E. The constancy required may be hard.
³⁴Salt is good: but if the salt have lost his savor, wherewith shall it be seasoned [how can its flavor be restored]?

³⁵**It is neither fit for the land, nor yet for the dunghill; but men cast it out. He that hath ears to hear, let him hear.**

This picture, like the one of the builder, deals with a disciple's staying power. The former relates primarily to his performance; this relates more to his purity. Salt from the ample deposits around the Dead Sea often contained traces of other chemicals that changed its flavor and made it useless. Christ warned that if a disciple becomes contaminated with impurities and loses his distinctive Christlike flavor, he could become unfit for the Lord's service.

Taken together, the above pictures present a high calling indeed. Most of those in Christ's audiences were not willing to make the kind and level of commitment He required. To anyone with willing ears, however, He said "let him hear" and "follow me."

The Disciples' Crowns

Every disciple's principal motivation for following and serving Christ should be a deep, unreserved love for Him as his personal Savior and Lord. Christ added another incentive, however, to further encourage His disciples in faithful service. That is His promise of great rewards — both in this life and the life to come. Although He revealed little of the specific nature of these rewards, He made it clear that they will far outweigh any effort and sacrifice that we make in serving Him here.

I. All faithful disciples will receive rewards.

    A. Peter was concerned about his rewards.

       MT 19:27 Then answered Peter and said unto him, Behold, we have forsaken all, and followed thee; what shall we have therefore?

Peter's claim and related question followed Christ's invitation to the rich young ruler to forsake all and follow Him, and receive "treasure in heaven." Whether innocently or selfishly, Peter wanted to know what specific reward he and the other disciples would receive, since they had "forsaken all" to follow Christ.

    B. Christ promised them thrones in His kingdom.

       ²⁸**And Jesus said unto them, Verily I say unto you, That ye which have followed me, in the regeneration when the Son of man shall sit in the throne of his glory, ye also shall sit upon twelve thrones, judging the twelve tribes of Israel. {I appoint unto you a kingdom, as my Father hath appointed unto me; that ye may eat and drink at my table in my kingdom, and sit on thrones judging the twelve tribes of Israel. [LK 22:29-30]}**

"The regeneration" (meaning renewal or re-creation) refers to the restored earth during Christ's millennial kingdom. At that time, redeemed Israel (including resurrected Old Testament believers) will receive God's particular favor and blessing. The term may also include the "new heaven and new earth" that will follow the millennium (Rev. 21:1). In both cases, Christ "shall sit in the throne of His glory," and His disciples (including His replacement for Judas) will rule Israel with Him as His honored representatives.

C. Selfless disciples will receive multiplied rewards.
²⁹[MK 10:29] And every one that hath forsaken houses, or brethren, or sisters, or father, or mother, or wife, or children, or lands, for my name's sake {and the gospel's}, shall receive an hundredfold {now in this time, houses, and brethren, and sisters, and mothers, and children, and lands, with persecutions; and in the world to come} shall inherit everlasting life.
³⁰But many that are first shall be last; and the last shall be first.

Whatever resources and relationships any disciple sacrifices for Christ's sake will be repaid by Him "a hundred times over" (i.e., immeasurably). God will give these rewards both "now in this time . . . and in the world to come." In context, verse 30 appears to mean: "Many who seem to be foremost in serving Christ, but who do not serve Him fully and with selfless motives, will receive lesser rewards. In contrast, those whose service is less notable from a human viewpoint, but which is truly sacrificial and from the heart, will be among the first in receiving rewards."

II. God is right and good in His rewards.

A. He "hires laborers" for His work on earth.
MT 20:1 For the kingdom of heaven is like unto a man that is an householder, which went out early in the morning to hire laborers into his vineyard.

B. He promises some a specific reward.
²And when he had agreed with the laborers for a penny [denarius] a day, he sent them into his vineyard.

This parable is part of Christ's answer to Peter's question regarding rewards in 19:27 above. The laborers picture believers because no unbeliever can do any compensable work for God. The master's agreement with his workers illustrates the rewards God promises for faithful service. The agreed-upon wage of one denarius was the customary daily pay for common labor.

C. He promises others whatever is right.
³And he went out about the third hour, and saw others standing idle in the marketplace,

> ⁴And said unto them; Go ye also into the vineyard, and whatsoever is right I will give you. And they went their way.
> ⁵Again he went out about the sixth and ninth hour, and did likewise.
> ⁶And about the eleventh hour he went out, and found others standing idle, and saith unto them, Why stand ye here all the day idle?
> ⁷They say unto him, Because no man hath hired us. He saith unto them, Go ye also into the vineyard; and whatsoever is right, that shall ye receive.

The master made the same promise to those hired in the eleventh hour as to those hired in the third hour. All the laborers hired during the workday implicitly trusted him to give them "whatever is right." His reputation and perhaps their prior experience with him gave them all the assurance they needed to rely on his word and his goodness.

D. His rewards will exceed the expectations of many.

> ⁸So when even was come, the lord of the vineyard saith unto his steward, Call the laborers, and give them their hire, beginning from the last unto the first.
> ⁹And when they came that were hired about the eleventh hour, they received every man a penny [denarius].

These workers received a full day's pay. Those hired last, and those hired at the third, sixth, and ninth hours as well, received more than they could have hoped to obtain through prior negotiation. How much better to leave all rewards up to God! This is the principal point of the parable and is the answer to Peter's question.

E. Those who focus selfishly on rewards receive nothing extra.

> ¹⁰But when the first came, they supposed that they should have received more; and they likewise received every man a penny.
> ¹¹And when they had received it, they murmured against the goodman of the house,
> ¹²Saying, These last have wrought but one hour, and thou hast made them equal unto us, which have borne the burden and heat of the day.

Rather than being thankful for the Master's fulfillment of His agreement with them, which He kept perfectly, these workers focused on their relatively greater contribution (as they measured it) and complained that they did not receive more.

G. All God gives is right and good.

> ¹³But he answered one of them, and said, Friend, I do thee no wrong: didst not thou agree with me for a penny?

¹⁴Take that thine is, and go thy way: I will give unto this last, even as unto thee.
¹⁵Is it not lawful for me to do what I will with mine own? Is thine eye evil, because I am good?
¹⁶So the last shall be first, and the first last: for many be called, but few chosen.

Whatever God gives anyone results from His own righteousness and goodness and therefore is perfectly right and good. In bestowing rewards, however, God declares throughout scripture that He takes into account a believer's *faithfulness*. In context, verse 16 seems to mean: "Those whom God calls to service later in life, but who serve faithfully to the extent of their opportunity, shall receive a full reward. Those called earlier, but who serve with less love and appreciation for their Master, will receive lesser rewards. Many are called to whole-hearted service, but few are chosen who actually so serve."

III. Distinctive service will receive special rewards.

In addition to the immeasurable blessings of dwelling with God in heaven, which all believers will enjoy as a result of their salvation, God will reward certain believers for particular service to Him. The following passages briefly identify some of the rewards that Christ promised His faithful disciples.

A. Rewards for leading souls to Christ.
JN 4:36 And he that reapeth [souls for the Lord] receiveth wages, and gathereth fruit unto life eternal: that both he that soweth and he that reapeth may rejoice together.

Although God alone "gives the increase" when a soul trusts Christ as Savior, believers are to sow, water, and reap as laborers in God's harvest field. Christ promised substantial wages and eternal rejoicing for those who faithfully perform such service for Him.

B. Rewards for suffering for Christ's sake.
MT 5:11 [LK 6:22] Blessed are ye, when men shall revile you, and persecute you, and shall say all manner of evil against you falsely, for my sake {and when they shall separate you from their company, and shall reproach you, and cast out your name as evil for the Son of man's sake}.
¹²Rejoice, and be exceeding glad: for great is your reward in heaven: for so persecuted they the prophets which were before you.

Christ warned His followers that they would face hatred and opposition from unbelievers. When that antagonism escalates to outright persecution and they suffer for His sake, their reward escalates commensurately to a *great reward* in heaven.

C. Rewards for supporting God's servants.

MT 10:41 He that receiveth a prophet in the name of [because he is] a prophet shall receive a prophet's reward; and he that receiveth a righteous man in the name of a righteous man shall receive a righteous man's reward.

D. Rewards for helping fellow believers.

⁴²And whosoever shall give to drink unto one of these little ones a cup of cold water only in the name of a disciple, verily I say unto you, he shall in no wise lose his reward.

MK 9:41 For whosoever shall give you a cup of water to drink in my name, because ye belong to Christ, verily I say unto you, he shall not lose his reward.

Christ particularly desires that every believer seek to meet the needs of other believers, including their physical, material, and emotional needs. Those who faithfully show hospitality and give encouragement to His "prophets and righteous men" (10:41) will receive rewards as though they had rendered the same front-line service that these spiritual leaders performed. By the same token, those who help, even in the smallest way, His "little ones" (humble, unnoted believers) also will receive eternal rewards. (See Sec. VIII on p. 444.)

E. Rewards for all faithful service for Christ.

JN 12:26 If any man serve me, let him follow me; and where I am, there shall also my servant be: if any man serve me, him will my Father honor.

MT 16:27 For the Son of man shall come in the glory of his Father with his angels; and then he shall reward every man according to his works.

When Christ returns, He will judge everyone's works (all of his deeds, words, motives, and thoughts). For believers, all works done for Christ and His glory will receive His commendation and reward. The overwhelming importance of that moment, and the magnitude of its eternal consequences, put in perspective the necessity of following and serving Christ while we still have the opportunity.

The First Disciples

Christ called His twelve closest disciples to an ever-closer walk with Him through a series of personal invitations. For some, the time from their first encounter with Christ until His final selection of the twelve was a year or more. This section presents their progressive calling as full disciples. It also illustrates some of the steps and issues we face in the process of becoming and growing as disciples and in making disciples of others.

I. Initial contacts — lessons in personal discipling.

A. John the Baptist points his followers to Christ.

> **JN 1:35** Again the next day after John stood, and two of his disciples;
> ³⁶And looking upon Jesus as he walked, he saith, Behold the Lamb of God!

B. Christ invites them to "come and see."

> ³⁷And the two disciples heard him speak, and they followed Jesus.
> ³⁸Then Jesus turned, and saw them following, and saith unto them, What seek ye? They said unto him, Rabbi, (which is to say, being interpreted, Master,) where dwellest thou?
> ³⁹He saith unto them, Come and see. They came and saw where he dwelt, and abode with him that day: for it was about the tenth hour [10 a.m.].

C. Andrew brings his brother to Christ.

> ⁴⁰One of the two which heard John speak, and followed him, was Andrew, Simon Peter's brother.
> ⁴¹He first findeth his own brother Simon, and saith unto him, We have found the Messias, which is, being interpreted, the Christ.
> ⁴²And he brought him to Jesus. And when Jesus beheld him, he said, Thou art Simon the son of Jona: thou shalt be called Cephas, which is by interpretation, A stone.

Here are examples of personal disciple-making as God intends it. John the Baptist (whose task was to announce the Messiah's arrival) faithfully pointed two of his followers to Christ. The two, Andrew and John, apparently desired to talk privately with Jesus (probably about what John said of Him), and they asked where He was staying. As to all who earnestly seek God's truth, Jesus replied, "Come and see." (John uses Roman time in his Gospel, which counts from midnight or noon as we do today, and the "tenth hour" here is 10 a.m.) Soon thereafter, Andrew excitedly brought his brother Peter to meet his new-found Messiah.

D. Christ calls Philip to be His disciple.

> ⁴³The day following Jesus would go forth into Galilee, and findeth Philip, and saith unto him, Follow me.
> ⁴⁴Now Philip was of Bethsaida, the city of Andrew and Peter.

E. Philip brings his friend to Christ.

⁴⁵Philip findeth Nathanael, and saith unto him, We have found him, of whom Moses in the law, and the prophets, did write, Jesus of Nazareth, the son of Joseph.

⁴⁶And Nathanael said unto him, Can there any good thing come out of Nazareth? Philip saith unto him, Come and see.

F. Nathanael acknowledges Jesus as the Messiah.

⁴⁷Jesus saw Nathanael coming to him, and saith of him, Behold an Israelite indeed, in whom is no guile!

⁴⁸Nathanael saith unto him, Whence knowest thou me? Jesus answered and said unto him, Before that Philip called thee, when thou wast under the fig tree, I saw thee.

⁴⁹Nathanael answered and saith unto him, Rabbi, thou art the Son of God; thou art the King of Israel.

G. Christ promises them "greater things."

⁵⁰Jesus answered and said unto him, Because I said unto thee, I saw thee under the fig tree, believest thou? thou shalt see greater things than these.

⁵¹And he saith unto him, Verily, verily, I say unto you, Hereafter ye shall see heaven open, and the angels of God ascending and descending upon the Son of man.

Philip may also have been a disciple of John the Baptist, as well as a friend of Andrew and Peter (v. 44). When Philip met Christ, he went to his friend Nathanael (probably the disciple called Bartholomew in the other Gospels) and invited him to come meet Jesus. Nathanael could not make a prophetic connection between "Messiah" and "Nazareth" from the Old Testament, and he replied, "Can any good thing (i.e., the Messiah) come out of Nazareth?" Philip was not deterred by Nathanael's doubts, and he encouraged him to "Come and see." Christ personally removed Nathanael's reservations and won him to Himself.

II. Further contacts — Christ's call to greater commitment.

A. Christ calls Peter and Andrew to be "fishers of men."

MK 1:16 Now as he walked by the sea of Galilee, he saw Simon and Andrew his brother casting a net into the sea: for they were fishers.

¹⁷And Jesus said unto them, Come ye after me, and I will make you to become fishers of men.

¹⁸And straightway they forsook their nets, and followed him.

B. Christ calls James and John to follow Him.

¹⁹And when he had gone a little farther thence, he saw James the son of Zebedee, and John his brother, who also were in the ship mending their nets.

²⁰**And straightway he called them: and they left their father Zebedee in the ship with the hired servants, and went after him.**

This calling occurred at the outset of Christ's principal Galilean ministry, perhaps six months after the events of JN 1 above. It also followed the wedding at Cana and Christ's first ministry in Jerusalem where these men saw His miracles and "believed on Him." In response to this call, the four fishermen immediately left their nets and followed Christ. They apparently only stayed with Him for a time, however, and maintained their family and business ties for the time being.

III. Full commitment — Christ's call to full discipleship.

    A. Christ's divine appointment with Peter.

LK 5:1 And it came to pass, that, as the people pressed upon him to hear the word of God, he stood by the lake of Gennesaret [Galilee],
²**And saw two ships standing by the lake: but the fishermen were gone out of them, and were washing their nets.**
³**And he entered into one of the ships, which was Simon's, and prayed him that he would thrust out a little from the land. And he sat down, and taught the people out of the ship.**

    B. Christ's personal challenge to Peter.

⁴**Now when he had left speaking, he said unto Simon, Launch out into the deep, and let down your nets for a draught.**
⁵**And Simon answering said unto him, Master, we have toiled all the night, and have taken nothing: nevertheless at thy word I will let down the net.**

Peter and his partners believed that Jesus was the Messiah well before He came to Peter's boat — but they had not yet left fishing to follow Him full-time. To persuade them to become "fishers of men," Christ would give them a personal sign of His divine power and authority.

    C. Christ's miraculous sign to the men.

⁶**And when they [Peter and Andrew] had this done, they enclosed a great multitude of fishes: and their net brake.**
⁷**And they beckoned unto their partners [James and John], which were in the other ship, that they should come and help them. And they came, and filled both the ships, so that they began to sink.**

    D. Peter's admission of unworthiness.

⁸**When Simon Peter saw it, he fell down at Jesus' knees, saying, Depart from me; for I am a sinful man, O Lord.**
⁹**For he was astonished, and all that were with him, at the draught of the fishes which they had taken:**

^{10a}And so was also James, and John, the sons of Zebedee, which were partners with Simon.

E. Christ's second call to "catch men" for Him.

^{10b}And Jesus said unto Simon, Fear not; from henceforth thou shalt catch men.

¹¹And when they had brought their ships to land, they forsook all, and followed him.

These men recently had witnessed a great many of Christ's miracles in Capernaum (including His healing of Peter's mother-in-law in LK 4), but this miracle struck home more than any before. Faced with Christ's omnipotence and holiness, Peter became acutely aware of his own weakness and sinfulness (v. 8). He tried to distance himself from this powerful, holy Master, but Christ was only beginning to work in Peter's life. He again called him, along with his partners, to "catch men" rather than fish. This time, "*they forsook all*, and followed Him."

F. Christ's call to Matthew to follow Him.

LK 5:27 And after these things he went forth, and saw a publican [tax collector], named Levi [Matthew], sitting at the receipt of custom: and he said unto him, Follow me.

²⁸And he left all, rose up, and followed him.

Matthew apparently had prior exposure to Christ and His message. He was a tax collector in or near Capernaum, where Christ resided between travels and where He had already performed many miracles. Matthew was working at his post when Christ came by and called him to be His disciple. He too "left all" and followed Christ immediately and fully.

IV. Chosen disciples — Christ's selection of the twelve.

A. A matter of intense prayer.

LK 6:12 And it came to pass in those days, that he went out into a mountain to pray, and continued all night in prayer to God.

B. A call to special service.

¹³[MK 3:14] And when it was day, he called unto him his disciples: and of them he chose twelve, whom also he named apostles ["sent ones"]; {And he ordained twelve, that they should be with him, and that he might send them forth to preach, and to have power to heal sicknesses, and to cast out devils:}

C. The twelve that Christ chose.

¹⁴[MT 10:2] {Now the names of the twelve apostles are these;} Simon, (whom he also named Peter,) and Andrew his brother, James {the son of Zebedee} and John {the brother of James; and he

surnamed them Boanerges, which is, the sons of thunder}, Philip and Bartholomew,

¹⁵Matthew {the publican} and Thomas, James the son of Alphaeus, and Simon {the Canaanite} called Zelotes [the Zealot],

¹⁶And Judas {Lebbaeus, whose surname was Thaddeus} the brother of James, and Judas Iscariot, which also was the traitor.

Christ selected twelve men out of a larger group of followers to be His closest disciples. First, "they should be with Him" (MK 3:14) for intensive training. Then, He would "send them forth to preach" as His apostles ("sent ones"). This selection occurred about a year and a half after the beginning of Christ's ministry, and shortly before His Sermon on the Mount (LK 6:20-49) in which He outlined the principles by which all of His disciples are to live.

V. Commissioned disciples — sent to preach and minister.

MT 10:5 These twelve Jesus sent forth, and commanded them, saying, Go not into the way of the Gentiles, and into any city of the Samaritans enter ye not:

⁶But go rather to the lost sheep of the house of Israel.

⁷And as ye go, preach, saying, The kingdom of heaven is at hand.

⁸Heal the sick, cleanse the lepers, raise the dead, cast out devils: freely ye have received, freely give.

After six to nine months of being with Christ full time, He sent the twelve out on their own with the above commission. Many of the objectives, warnings, principles, and promises Christ gave them in connection with their assignment (in the remainder of MT 10) are reviewed in "The Disciples' Commission" on p. 267.

14

Signs from the Wonderful Counselor

When Jesus saw a need, He met it. When there was a problem, He solved it. He provided food for hungry multitudes, deliverance for distressed disciples, and healing for the sick and diseased. Isaiah prophesied 700 years earlier that the coming Messiah would be a "Wonderful Counselor" (Isaiah 9:6). "Wonderful" here means supernatural and includes the idea of "wonder-working." Thus, the Messiah would be a miracle-working teacher. Jesus' miracles fulfilled this prophecy and signaled that the Wonderful Counselor had come.

The people, however, sought Jesus' wonders more than His counsel. Though He abundantly met their physical needs, they declined His provision for their spiritual needs. They gladly received His food in the wilderness but refused to partake of the Bread of Life. They clamored for His healing of their bodies but rejected His cure for their souls. People's priorities are not much different today. For those who receive His wonderful counsel, however, He still works wonders in their hearts and lives.

The Gospels record 35 specific miracles and refer to another dozen or so instances in which Christ healed many people at a time. In total, therefore, Christ performed hundreds if not thousands of miracles during His ministry. Of the 35 specific miracles, 26 involved some form of physical healing, from curing diseases to raising the dead. (Most of the 26 are reviewed in the next chapter on "The Great Physician.") The other nine miracles pertained to phenomena of nature or other tangible things, such as stilling violent storms and changing water to wine. These are reviewed later in this chapter under "Teaching through Miracles."

The Message of Miracles

Jesus' miracles were object lessons that graphically supported the spiritual lessons He taught orally. Their immediate purpose and application varied from miracle to miracle, but their underlying message always included that He was the promised Messiah. They present Him as the omnipotent yet merciful Son of God who came to save sinners and give them spiritual life. By and large, the people marveled at His miracles but missed their message. The following passages (all but one from John's Gospel) address Christ's miracles collectively; subsequent sections present His miracles individually.

I. Jesus' miracles were signs that He was the Messiah.

A. Many initially thought He was the Christ.

JN 2:23 Now when he was in Jerusalem at the passover, in the feast day, many believed in his name [that He was the Messiah], when they saw the miracles which he did.

JN 7:31 And many of the people believed on him, and said, When Christ cometh, will he do more miracles than these which this man hath done?

Jesus performed miracles from the very beginning of His ministry (as in 2:23 above). The word for miracles means "attesting signs." As remarkable and beneficial as these signs were, they were not an end in themselves. Instead, as with any sign, they pointed to something (and to Someone) greater than the signs alone. In particular, Jesus' miracles had *spiritual* significance, pointing to His divine identity and purposes.

B. He knew their belief was superficial.

JN 2:24 But Jesus did not commit [entrust] himself unto them, because he knew all men,
²⁵And needed not that any should testify of man: for he knew what was in man.

Believe in 2:23 and 7:31 above is used in the sense of "mentally acknowledge Him as Messiah." It does not necessarily include "trust in Him for salvation." *Believe* occurs often in John's Gospel, and which of these two very different meanings is intended must be determined by the context. In 2:24, the same word is translated "commit" (i.e., entrust fully). Jesus did not "commit" Himself to the crowds at the feast because He knew they did not fully entrust themselves to Him (they did not "believe" in Him as the means of their salvation).

C. He directed their focus from His works to His words.

> 3:1 There was a man of the Pharisees, named Nicodemus, a ruler of the Jews:
>
> ²The same came to Jesus by night, and said unto him, Rabbi, we know that thou art a teacher come from God: for no man can do these miracles that thou doest, except God be with him.
>
> ³Jesus answered and said unto him, Verily, verily, I say unto thee, Except a man be born again, he cannot see the kingdom of God.

Nicodemus' statement (v. 2) typified the Jews' limited intellectual belief which acknowledged that Jesus' miracles signified that "God was with Him," but not much more. In reply, Jesus indicated that Nicodemus must move on from mere admission of the reality of His miracles to an understanding and acceptance of their implications. That in turn would produce a full belief in Him, and the resulting new birth of salvation.

D. He used His miracles to prove He was the Christ.

> JN 10:24 Then came the Jews round about him, and said unto him, How long dost thou make us to doubt? If thou be the Christ, tell us plainly.
>
> ²⁵Jesus answered them, I told you, and ye believed not: the works that I do in my Father's name, they bear witness of me. . . .
>
> ³⁷If I do not the works of my Father, believe me not.
>
> ³⁸But if I do, though ye believe not me, believe the works: that ye may know, and believe, that the Father is in me, and I in him.
>
> 5:36 But I have greater witness than that of John [the Baptist]: for the works which the Father hath given me to finish, the same works that I do, bear witness of me, that the Father hath sent me.

Jesus knew that His critics would not accept His word that He was the Christ, the Son of God. (Whenever He made such a claim, or intimated as much, they reacted violently, even trying to kill Him.) He cited, therefore, the evidence of His miracles, which they had clearly seen and could not deny. His miracles fulfilled Old Testament prophecies of which they were aware, proved His supernatural power, and demonstrated the Father's approval of His ministry and message.

II. Jesus' miracles revealed His deity and the people's depravity.

> JN 15:24 If I had not done among them the works which none other man did, they had not had sin: but now have they both seen and hated both me and my Father.
>
> ²⁵But this cometh to pass, that the word might be fulfilled that is written in their law, They hated me without a cause.

Verse 24 may be understood: "If I had not done these miracles among the people, works that no one else has ever done, they would not be guilty of the sin of rejecting their Messiah. But in and through my miracles, they have both seen and hated both me and my Father." Christ's miracles illustrated the love, mercy, and grace of God for His people. By rejecting this evidence and the One presenting it, they demonstrated their hatred for both the Father and the Son. Verse 25 refers to Psalm 69, a Messianic Psalm that vividly portrays Christ's rejection and suffering.

III. Jesus was rejected in spite of His miracles.

A. His home region disregarded the message of His miracles.

> **MT 11:20 Then began he to upbraid the cities wherein most of his mighty works were done, because they repented not:**
>
> ²¹**Woe unto thee, Chorazin! woe unto thee, Bethsaida! for if the mighty works, which were done in you, had been done in Tyre and Sidon, they would have repented long ago in sackcloth and ashes.**
>
> ²²**But I say unto you, It shall be more tolerable for Tyre and Sidon at the day of judgment, than for you.**
>
> ²³**And thou, Capernaum, which art exalted unto heaven, shalt be brought down to hell: for if the mighty works, which have been done in thee, had been done in Sodom, it would have remained until this day.**
>
> ²⁴**But I say unto you, That it shall be more tolerable for the land of Sodom, in the day of judgment, than for thee.**

The residents of these Galilean towns together witnessed most of Christ's miracles. Relatively few, however, recognized His deity, their own sinfulness, and their need of repentance. The godless Gentiles in Tyre and Sidon, and even in Sodom, the epitome of wickedness, were not as spiritually hardened as the people of Capernaum (Christ's home base in Galilee) and the neighboring villages. Because the Galileans rejected the clear message of Christ's miracles and refused to repent, their judgment will be greater than that of godless Gentiles who did not have such revelation and opportunity.

B. His own brothers dismissed the message of His miracles.

> **JN 7:1 After these things Jesus walked in Galilee: for he would not walk in Jewry [Judea], because the Jews sought to kill him.**
>
> ²**Now the Jews' feast of tabernacles was at hand.**
>
> ³**His brethren therefore said unto him, Depart hence, and go into Judaea, that thy disciples also may see the works that thou doest.**
>
> ⁴**For there is no man that doeth any thing in secret, and he himself seeketh to be known openly. If thou do these things, show thyself to the world.**

⁵For neither did his brethren believe in him.

Not believing that Jesus was the Messiah, His brothers challenged Him to go to the week-long feast in Judea and "show off" His miraculous power. Whether they simply wanted Him to leave Galilee (considering Him an embarrassment there) or thought the religious leaders in Jerusalem might "put Him in His place," they too rejected Jesus' claims and the evidence of His miracles.

C. The religious leaders despised the message of His miracles.

JN 11:47 Then gathered the chief priests and the Pharisees a council, and said, What do we? for this man doeth many miracles.

⁴⁸If we let him thus alone, all men will believe on him: and the Romans shall come and take away both our place and nation.

⁴⁹And one of them, named Caiaphas, being the high priest that same year, said unto them, Ye know nothing at all,

⁵⁰Nor consider that it is expedient for us, that one man should die for the people, and that the whole nation perish not.

At the same time as the religious leaders admitted the validity of Jesus' "many miracles," they were plotting His death. They were determined to retain their place of prestige and influence among the people (v. 48), rather than let Christ have spiritual preeminence. They would also rather cling to limited control over their nation (under oppressive Roman domination) than permit the Messiah to inaugurate a millennial kingdom that was not to their liking. They determined, therefore, that Jesus "should die for the people," to preserve their place and nation a little longer.

D. The nation disbelieved the message of His miracles.

JN 12:37 But though he had done so many miracles before them, yet they believed not on him:

³⁸That the saying of Esaias the prophet might be fulfilled, which he spake, Lord, who hath believed our report? and to whom hath the arm of the Lord been revealed?

These verses summarize Israel's overall response to Christ as of a few days before His crucifixion. Of all the reasons the people should have recognized and accepted Jesus as their Messiah, none was greater than the compelling evidence of His miracles. Verse 38 quotes Isaiah 53:1, from the great prophetic chapter that foretells Christ's rejection, humiliation, and crucifixion by His own people.

IV. Jesus' miracles were recorded to encourage our faith.

JN 20:30 And many other signs [attesting miracles] truly did Jesus in the presence of his disciples, which are not written in this book:

³¹But these are written, that ye might believe that Jesus is the Christ, the Son of God; and that believing ye might have life through his name.

JN 21:25 And there are also many other things which Jesus did, the which, if they should be written every one, I suppose that even the world itself could not contain the books that should be written. Amen.

The Gospel writers recorded the works and miracles of Jesus for the same reason that He performed these "attesting signs" throughout His ministry. It is that you and I might believe that Jesus is the Christ, the Son of God; and that so believing (fully entrusting ourselves to Him for salvation), we may receive genuine and abundant life, both now and forever. We can only have such life "through His name," that is, on the basis of His merits and through His power, and not by our own.

Teaching Through Miracles

The Master of miracles was simultaneously the Master Teacher. Accordingly, each of His miracles contained spiritual lessons for thoughtful observers. In some cases, the lessons were explicit, such as "Have faith in God." In others, they were implicit, such as man's helplessness versus God's omnipotence. With each miracle, there was a truth to be learned, a response to be given, and a principle to be applied. This section presents Christ's miracles that pertain to nature and material things, in the order of their occurrence. Miracles of healing are reviewed in the following chapter.

I. Water to wine at a wedding.

A. The need of the moment: there was no wine for the feast.
JN 2:1 And the third day there was a marriage in Cana of Galilee; and the mother of Jesus was there:
²And both Jesus was called, and his disciples, to the marriage.
³And when they wanted [ran out of] wine, the mother of Jesus saith unto him, They have no wine.

B. An application: trust Christ for each need, and obey Him.
⁴Jesus saith unto her, Woman, what have I to do with thee? Mine hour is not yet come.
⁵His mother saith unto the servants, Whatsoever he saith unto you, do it.

Jewish wedding celebrations often lasted a week. Mary may have been assisting with the arrangements and known early of the shortage. She also knew that Jesus could meet any shortage. His reply in verse 4 is not disrespectful; it may be understood: "Madam, your concern does not concern me; my time [to act] has not yet come." Mary demonstrated her faith that Jesus would meet the need when she told the servants to do whatever He said.

C. The miracle: Christ turned water into wine.

> ⁶**And there were set there six waterpots of stone, after the manner of the purifying of the Jews, containing two or three firkins [20 to 30 gallons] apiece.**
>
> ⁷**Jesus saith unto them, Fill the waterpots with water. And they filled them up to the brim.**
>
> ⁸**And he saith unto them, Draw out now, and bear unto the governor of the feast. And they bare it.**
>
> ⁹**When the ruler of the feast had tasted the water that was made wine, and knew not whence it was: (but the servants which drew the water knew;) the governor of the feast called the bridegroom,**
>
> ¹⁰**And saith unto him, Every man at the beginning doth set forth good wine; and when men have well drunk, then that which is worse; but thou hast kept the good wine until now.**

In total, the pots held 120-180 gallons of water. Not only did Christ fully meet the need and with perfect timing, He met it with better wine than others could provide. (The word for "wine" in Greek, and also in Hebrew, Latin, and old English, can mean either fresh or fermented grape juice; scholars are divided over which applies here.)

D. The lesson: the Messiah has come, with power and glory.

> ¹¹ᵃ**This beginning of miracles [attesting signs] did Jesus in Cana of Galilee, and manifested forth his glory;**

E. The disciples' response: their faith in Christ increased.

> ¹¹ᵇ**and his disciples believed on him.**

This first recorded "sign" of Jesus' identity, authority, and glory strengthened the nascent faith of His newly-enlisted disciples (probably six of them at that time) that He was the promised Messiah. It also aided in preparing the people of Galilee for His coming ministry.

II. Peter's first great catch of fish.

> **LK 5:5 And Simon answering said unto him, Master, we have toiled all the night, and have taken nothing: nevertheless at thy word I will let down the net.**
>
> ⁶**And when they had this done, they enclosed a great multitude of fishes: and their net brake. . . .**
>
> ¹⁰ᵇ**And Jesus said unto Simon, Fear not; from henceforth thou shalt catch men.**

The full account of this miracle is presented in Section III on p. 285. It highlights (1) Christ's unlimited knowledge, power, and grace, (2) man's inability to meet his needs apart from God, and 3) a believer's convincing grounds for entrusting his life to Christ in submission, sacrifice, and service.

III. Stilling the storm on the sea.

A. The need of the moment: the disciples' lives were in danger.

MT 8:23 [MK 4; LK 8] And when he was entered into a ship, his disciples followed him,

²⁴And, behold, there arose a great tempest in the sea, insomuch that the ship was covered with the waves {so that it was now full}: but he was asleep {in the hinder part of the ship}.

²⁵And his disciples came to him, and awoke him, saying, Lord, save us: we perish {carest thou not that we perish?}.

Because of the region's topography, the Sea of Galilee is susceptible to sudden, violent storms. This storm, however, was extraordinary. The word for "tempest" in verse 24 means "great shaking," as in a strong earthquake. Several disciples were experienced boatmen, yet they feared for their lives and cried out to Christ for deliverance.

B. A lesson: trust in God's protecting care.

²⁶ᵃAnd he saith unto them, Why are ye fearful, O ye of little faith? {Where is your faith?} {How is it that ye have no faith?}

C. The miracle: Christ calmed the raging storm.

²⁶ᵇThen he arose, and rebuked the winds and the {raging of the} sea {and said unto the sea, Peace, be still. And the wind ceased,} and there was a great calm.

D. The disciples' response: they were astounded at His power.

²⁷But the men marvelled {feared exceedingly}, saying, What manner of man is this, that even the winds and the sea obey him!

Before calming the storm, Christ pointedly asked His disciples, "Where is your faith?" Hadn't they just witnessed many miracles of healing and casting out of demons (see the preceding verses in MT 8)? But they failed to trust Christ for *their* need or to apply what they had learned to *this* crisis. When He stilled the storm, they were utterly amazed at His awesome power. He was far greater than they ever imagined.

IV. The feeding of over 5,000 people.

A. The need of the moment: A multitude had nothing to eat.

LK 9:10b [MT 14; MK 6; JN 6] And he took them [His disciples], and went aside privately into a desert place belonging to the city called Bethsaida.

¹¹And the people, when they knew it, followed him: and he received them, and spake unto them of the kingdom of God, and healed them that had need of healing.

¹²And when the day began to wear away, then came the twelve, and said unto him, Send the multitude away, that they may go into the towns and country round about, and lodge, and get victuals {for they have nothing to eat}: for we are here in a desert place.

B. A lesson: let God meet others' needs through you.

MT 14:16 But Jesus said unto them, They need not depart; give ye them to eat. {And they say unto him, Shall we go and buy two hundred penny [denarii] worth of bread, and give them to eat?}

JN 6:5b He saith unto Philip, Whence shall we buy bread, that these may eat?

⁶And this he said to prove him: for he himself knew what he would do.

⁷Philip answered him, Two hundred pennyworth of bread is not sufficient for them, that every one of them may take a little. {He saith unto them, How many loaves have ye? go and see. And when they knew,}

⁸One of his disciples, Andrew, Simon Peter's brother, saith unto him,

⁹There is a lad here, which hath five barley loaves, and two small fishes: but what are they among so many?

It did not occur to the disciples that Christ could miraculously feed all those people, so they urged Him to send them away. But He tested their faith (v. 6) with three statements, each containing a hint of His planned solution. First, He said, "*You* feed them." They answered, "Should we buy 200 denarii [over one thousand dollars] worth of bread?" Then, He asked, "Where can we buy bread for them?" Philip replied that 200 denarii would only buy enough for each person to have a little. Finally, Christ asked, "How many loaves are here?" Andrew answered, "Five, and two small fish: but what are they among so many?" The disciples' understanding and faith do not appear to have progressed much to this point, but Christ still met the people's need with the little His disciples brought Him.

C. The miracle: Christ fed (to the full) over 5,000 people.

¹⁰And Jesus said, Make the men sit down. Now there was much grass in the place. So the men sat down, in number about five thousand {beside women and children}.

¹¹And Jesus took the loaves; and when he had given thanks, he {brake, and} distributed {the loaves} to the disciples, and the disciples to them that were set down; and likewise of the fishes as much as they would.

D. A lesson: take care of all that God provides.

¹²When they were filled, he said unto his disciples, Gather up the fragments that remain, that nothing be lost.

¹³Therefore they gathered them together, and filled twelve baskets with the fragments of the five barley loaves, which remained over and above unto them that had eaten.

E. The crowd's response: "Make him king [to meet our needs]!"

¹⁴Then those men, when they had seen the miracle that Jesus did, said, This is of a truth that prophet that should come into the world.

¹⁵When Jesus therefore perceived that they would come and take him by force, to make him a king, he departed again into a mountain himself alone. . . .

²⁴When the people therefore saw that Jesus was not there, neither his disciples, they also took shipping, and came to Capernaum, seeking for Jesus.

Because Jesus could miraculously meet their physical needs, the people wanted to make Him their king and benefactor — by force if necessary. He had not come, however, to be that kind of king, so He withdrew from them. They surmised (correctly) that Jesus was the Prophet that Moses foretold in Deut. 18:15: "The Lord thy God will raise up unto thee a Prophet from the midst of thee, of thy brethren, like unto me; unto him ye shall hearken." Although Moses wrote of the Messiah, the Jews seem to have anticipated a lesser prophet (see JN 1:19-25) and did not recognize Jesus as the Christ.

F. The principal lesson: Christ Himself is the Bread of Life.

³⁵And Jesus said unto them, I am the bread of life: he that cometh to me shall never hunger; and he that believeth on me shall never thirst. . . .

⁵¹I am the living bread which came down from heaven: if any man eat of this bread, he shall live for ever: and the bread that I will give is my flesh, which I will give for the life of the world.

See "The Bread of Life" on p. 76 ff for the full passage and a discussion of this principal lesson.

V. Walking on the sea.

A. The need of the moment: the disciples again were in danger.

MT 14:22 [MK K; JN 6] And straightway Jesus constrained his disciples to get into a ship, and to go before him unto the other side, while he sent the multitudes away.

²³**And when he had sent the multitudes away, he went up into a mountain apart to pray: and when the evening was come, he was there alone.**

²⁴**But the ship was now in the midst of the sea, tossed with waves: {and he saw them toiling in rowing;} for the wind was contrary.**

B. The first miracle: Christ walked on the sea.

²⁵**And in the fourth watch of the night [between 3 and 6 a.m.] Jesus went unto them, walking on the sea.**

²⁶**And when the disciples saw him walking on the sea, they were troubled, saying, It is a spirit [a ghost]; and they cried out for fear.**

C. A lesson: the Lord is present; do not fear, but trust Him.

²⁷**But straightway Jesus spake unto them, saying, Be of good cheer; it is I; be not afraid.**

Only hours before, the disciples had been taught to trust in God's provision and care when Christ fed the multitude. They toiled in the storm, however, in their own strength, and were getting nowhere. "For they considered not the miracle of the loaves: for their heart was hardened" (MK 6:52). When Christ appeared, they were terrified (as by a ghost), rather than recognizing the Lord. Without rebuke, Christ assured them it was He, with words of comfort and encouragement.

D. The second miracle: Christ enabled Peter to walk on the sea.

²⁸**And Peter answered him and said, Lord, if it be thou, bid me come unto thee on the water.**

²⁹**And he said, Come. And when Peter was come down out of the ship, he walked on the water, to go to Jesus.**

E. A lesson: focus on Christ, not on circumstances.

³⁰**But when he saw the wind boisterous, he was afraid; and beginning to sink, he cried, saying, Lord, save me.**

³¹**And immediately Jesus stretched forth his hand, and caught him, and said unto him, O thou of little faith, wherefore didst thou doubt?**

After a few initial steps of faith, Peter took his eyes off Christ and focused on the surrounding adverse conditions. Immediately, he began to sink. Christ rescued him but rebuked his doubting and insufficient faith. Failure to take Christ at His word and to trust Him to meet their immediate needs was (and is) a recurring problem for His disciples.

F. Further miracles: Christ stilled the storm and brought them to shore.

³²**And when they were come into the ship, the wind ceased {and immediately the ship was at the land whither they went}.**

G. The disciples' response: they worshiped Christ as God.

³³Then they that were in the ship {were sore amazed in themselves beyond measure, and} came and worshipped him, saying, Of a truth thou art the Son of God.

These amazing miracles occurring in rapid succession completely astounded the disciples. Although initially they lacked faith and "their heart was hardened," they soon realized more than before that Christ was God in human flesh. Overwhelmed, they could only fall at His feet and worship Him.

VI. The feeding of over 4,000 people.

A. The need of the moment: another multitude had no food.

MK 8:1 [MT 15:32] In those days the multitude being very great, and having nothing to eat, Jesus called his disciples unto him, and saith unto them,

B. A lesson: have compassion for the needy.

²I have compassion on the multitude, because they have now been with me three days, and have nothing to eat: {I will not send them away fasting, lest they faint in the way.}

C. A lesson: let Christ use whatever you have.

MT 15:33 And his disciples say unto him, Whence should we have so much bread in the wilderness, as to fill so great a multitude?
³⁴And Jesus saith unto them, How many loaves have ye? And they said, Seven, and a few little fishes.

D. The miracle: Christ fed (to the full) over 4,000 people.

³⁵And he commanded the multitude to sit down on the ground.
³⁶And he took the seven loaves and the fishes, and gave thanks, and brake them, and gave to his disciples, and the disciples to the multitude.
³⁷And they did all eat, and were filled: and they took up of the broken meat that was left seven baskets full.
³⁸And they that did eat were four thousand men, beside women and children.

Not long after Christ fed the 5,000, a similar situation arose. This time, He told His disciples up front, "I have compassion for these people; I will not send them away hungry." Along with faith in God's provision and care (a lesson from the first feeding), the disciples needed to have compassion for the needs of others. Instead, they asked in bewilderment, "Where can we ever get that much bread here in the wilderness?" Christ replied in essence, "Let's start with what you have, trust me for the rest, and I will meet their need through you."

VII. Providing money to pay taxes.

A. The need of the moment: the temple tax was due.

MT 17:24 And when they [Jesus and His disciples] were come to Capernaum, they that received tribute money [temple taxes] came to Peter, and said, Doth not your master pay tribute?
²⁵ᵃHe saith, Yes.

The tax due was the "redemption money" prescribed by God through Moses to fund the operation of the tabernacle. He commanded, "then shall they give every man a ransom for his soul unto the Lord . . . an half shekel shall be the offering of the Lord. And thou shalt . . . appoint it for the service of the tabernacle" (Ex. 30:11-16). Peter lived in Capernaum, and Jesus' home base was there, so the local collectors approached Peter about the tax.

B. A lesson: submit to authorities and avoid offenses.

²⁵ᵇAnd when he [Peter] was come into the house, Jesus prevented him [spoke first], saying, What thinkest thou, Simon? of whom do the kings of the earth take custom or tribute? of their own children, or of strangers?
²⁶Peter saith unto him, Of strangers. Jesus saith unto him, Then are the children free [exempt].
²⁷ᵃNotwithstanding, lest we should offend them,

C. The miracle: Christ provided the money through a fish.

²⁷ᵇgo thou to the sea, and cast an hook, and take up the fish that first cometh up; and when thou hast opened his mouth, thou shalt find a piece of money: that take, and give unto them for me and thee.

Jesus previously called the temple "my Father's house." As the Son of God and "greater than the temple," He was rightfully exempt from that tax. However, to avoid offending the tax collectors with even an appearance of disrespect for God's house or God's law, He told Peter how to pay the tax for both of them. The coin in verse 27 was a "stater" — equal in value to one shekel and exactly the tax for two people. Quick-tempered and combative Peter needed to learn to submit to God-ordained authority and to avoid unnecessarily offending those in authority.

VIII. The fruitless and withered fig tree.

A. The needs of the moment: food for Jesus; faith for His disciples.

MT 21:18 [MK 11:12] Now in the morning as he [Jesus] returned into the city, he hungered.
¹⁹ᵃAnd when he saw a fig tree in the way, he came to it, and found nothing thereon, but leaves only,

B. The miracle: Christ caused the fruitless tree to wither.

> [19b]and [He] said unto it, Let no fruit grow on thee henceforward for ever. And presently [immediately] the fig tree withered away.
> [20]And when the disciples saw it, they marvelled, saying, How soon is the fig tree withered away!

This event occurred in early spring before new leaves and figs appear. Fig trees with leaves from the prior year often still had figs. Seeing the leaves, Christ looked for figs also. In contrast, the disciples' need at that time was not for food but faith. With Christ's crucifixion looming later that week, they needed all the spiritual strengthening they could receive to prepare them for their coming trial. Hence, the following lesson on faith.

C. A lesson: "Have faith in God."

> [21]Jesus answered and said unto them, {Have faith in God.} Verily I say unto you, If ye have faith, and doubt not, ye shall not only do this which is done to the fig tree, but also if ye shall say unto this mountain, Be thou removed, and be thou cast into the sea; it shall be done.
> [22]And all things, whatsoever ye shall ask in prayer, believing, ye shall receive.

The lesson on faith is reviewed in Section III under "Prayer with faith" on p. 189. A less explicit but significant lesson from the fig tree relates to Christ's prophecies regarding Israel. (He had likened Israel to a fruitless fig tree in LK 13; see Sec. IV on p. 4.) At the end of His ministry, Israel had the *appearance* of spiritual life (the leaves), but no fruit that satisfied God. The next day, Christ declared that Israel's "house is left desolate" because of its unbelief (MT 23:38). As the fig tree had withered, so would Israel because it had rejected its Messiah. Later, however, in His Olivet Discourse, Christ pictured Israel's future restoration as a newly-budding fig tree that once again will be blessed by God (see Sec. I on p. 430).

IX. Peter's second great catch of fish.

A. The need of the moment:

(1) from Peter's perspective: returning to fishing;

(2) from Christ's perspective: restoring Peter's discipleship.

> JN 21:1 After these things [following His resurrection] Jesus showed himself again to the disciples at the sea of Tiberias [Galilee]; and on this wise showed he himself.

²There were together Simon Peter, and Thomas called Didymus, and Nathanael of Cana in Galilee, and the sons of Zebedee [James and John], and two other of his disciples.

³Simon Peter saith unto them, I go a fishing. They say unto him, We also go with thee. They went forth, and entered into a ship immediately: and that night they caught nothing.

B. The miracle: more fish than Peter could handle.

⁴But when the morning was now come, Jesus stood on the shore: but the disciples knew not that it was Jesus.

⁵Then Jesus saith unto them, Children, have ye any meat? They answered him, No.

⁶And he said unto them, Cast the net on the right side of the ship, and ye shall find. They cast therefore, and now they were not able to draw it for the multitude of fishes.

Dismayed by his denials of Christ, Peter may have felt he no longer could be His disciple. He told his fellows, "I'm going back to fishing." Christ, however, intended to restore Peter and equip him for a greater role than he had previously. He essentially duplicated the miracle that enlisted Peter in full-time discipleship two years before (see Sec. III on p. 285). Again, through a night of fruitless fishing, then a catch too great to manage, Christ demonstrated to Peter the futility of living for himself and the productive, rewarding life He had for him as a fisher of men.

C. Peter's response: returning quickly to Jesus.

⁷Therefore that disciple whom Jesus loved [John] saith unto Peter, It is the Lord. Now when Simon Peter heard that it was the Lord, he girt his fisher's coat unto him, (for he was naked [without his outer cloak]) and did cast himself into the sea.

⁸And the other disciples came in a little ship; (for they were not far from land, but as it were two hundred cubits,) dragging the net with fishes.

D. An object lesson: the omnipotent Lord ministering as a servant.

⁹As soon then as they were come to land, they saw a fire of coals there, and fish laid thereon, and bread.

¹⁰Jesus saith unto them, Bring of the fish which ye have now caught.

¹¹Simon Peter went up, and drew the net to land full of great fishes, an hundred and fifty and three: and for all there were so many, yet was not the net broken.

¹²Jesus saith unto them, Come and dine. And none of the disciples durst ask him, Who art thou? knowing that it was the Lord.

¹³Jesus then cometh, and taketh bread, and giveth them, and fish likewise.

¹⁴**This is now the third time that Jesus showed himself to his disciples, after that he was risen from the dead.**

Although Peter and his partners came to Christ physically, they initially kept their distance spiritually and emotionally. Christ graciously met them where they were and patiently led them back to full discipleship and usefulness. He also gave them an object lesson of the humble service to which He was calling them by preparing and serving their meal as their servant.

E. The principal lesson: love and serve Christ unreservedly.
¹⁵**So when they had dined, Jesus saith to Simon Peter, Simon, son of Jonas, lovest thou me more than these? He saith unto him, Yea, Lord; thou knowest that I love thee. He saith unto him, Feed my lambs.**

By asking Peter to confirm his love for Him, Christ showed him that He genuinely desired his love and wanted him (and the others) to express that love through willing and faithful service. A principal aspect of that service would be "feeding His lambs." For further comments on verse 15 and the following verses, see Section IV on p. 265.

15

Healing by the Great Physician

Whether they came individually with a particular disease or as large crowds with a variety of afflictions, Christ "healed them all" (MT 12:15). He cured lepers, paralytics, the blind, and the deaf, and He even raised the dead. As no one before or since, Christ provided relief and release from all manner of maladies. Besides healing them, He was moved with compassion when He saw people suffering, and their griefs became His own. He treated each patient, therefore, with the utmost gentleness, mercy, and love. He was the Great Physician in every sense of the term.

Christ also used healing as an opportunity to teach and to portray spiritual principles with physical examples. Although the people's greatest needs were spiritual, they focused more on their physical needs. They were incapable, however, of dealing effectively with either type. By healing physically, Christ demonstrated that He is equally able to heal spiritually. The Great Physician cares about and cares for every human being and every human need.

The Physician's Mission

The Old Testament foretold that the Messiah would be a Great Physician with unique power to heal. His kingdom would feature both physical healing and spiritual healing, each perfect and complete. Some of these prophecies appear to include both types of healing without distinguishing between them. For example, the last chapter of the Old Testament promises: "Behold, the day cometh, that . . . unto you that fear my name shall the Sun of righteousness arise with healing in his wings" (Malachi 4:1-2). Christ came as that "Sun of righteousness," with both spiritual and physical healing "in His wings" for all who would receive Him.

I. He healed "all manner of sickness and disease."

MT 4:23 And Jesus went about all Galilee, teaching in their synagogues, and preaching the gospel of the kingdom, and healing all manner of sickness and all manner of disease among the people.

²⁴And his fame went throughout all Syria: and they brought unto him all sick people that were taken with divers [various] diseases and torments, and those which were possessed with devils, and those which were lunatic [epileptics], and those that had the palsy [paralytics]; and he healed them.

MK 6:53 [MT 14:34] And when they had passed over [the Sea of Galilee], they came into the land of Gennesaret, and drew to the shore.

⁵⁴And when they were come out of the ship, straightway they knew him,

⁵⁵And ran through that whole region round about, {and brought unto him all that were diseased}, and began to carry about in beds those that were sick, where they heard he was.

⁵⁶And whithersoever he entered, into villages, or cities, or country, they laid the sick in the streets, and besought him that they might touch if it were but the border of his garment: and as many as touched him were made whole.

There was no malady Christ could not cure nor any defect He could not restore. Other passages similar to these report that Christ healed great numbers of people on many occasions. Christ truly was the Great Physician for the people of Israel.

II. He offered spiritual healing to sin-sick people.

A. He came to heal broken hearts and bruised spirits.

LK 4:16 And he came to Nazareth, where he had been brought up: and, as his custom was, he went into the synagogue on the sabbath day, and stood up for to read.

¹⁷And there was delivered unto him the book [scroll] of the prophet Esaias [Isaiah]. And when he had opened the book, he found the place where it was written,

¹⁸The Spirit of the Lord is upon me, because he hath anointed me to preach the gospel to the poor [the materially poor and the humble in spirit]; he hath sent me to heal the brokenhearted, to preach deliverance to the captives, and recovering of sight to the blind, to set at liberty them that are bruised [and bound, as by sin or disease].

¹⁹To preach the acceptable year of the Lord [the year of God's favor].

Christ read from Isaiah 61:1-2a, which prophesied the Messiah's healing ministry. (Luke uses the Septuagint's Greek translation of the original Hebrew; the inserts reflect the sense of the latter.) Isaiah wrote that the Holy Spirit would empower the Messiah to preach the gospel and heal needy people. This clearly includes spiritual healing as well as physical healing. Christ offered both to the Jewish people in "the year of God's favor."

B. He offered Himself as their Physician and Deliverer.

²⁰And he closed the book, and he gave it again to the minister, and sat down. And the eyes of all them that were in the synagogue were fastened on him.

²¹And he began to say unto them, This day is this scripture fulfilled in your ears.

Christ followed the Jews' order of worship in the synagogue. As did the scribes, He stood to read the scripture and sat to teach. Here, He stopped reading in the middle of a sentence and rolled up the scroll. He ended with "the acceptable year of the Lord" and omitted "and the day of vengeance of our God." Christ announced that Isaiah's prophecy, with its attendant healing, was being fulfilled. "The year of God's grace" extends through our present age; "the day of God's vengeance" awaits Christ's second coming and is for those who refuse His spiritual healing.

C. They took offense at His claims.

²²ᵃ[MK 6:2] And all bare him witness, and wondered at the gracious words which proceeded out of his mouth {and many hearing him were astonished, saying, From whence hath this man these things? and what wisdom is this which is given unto him, that even such mighty works are wrought by his hands?}

²²ᵇAnd they said, Is not this Joseph's son? {Is not this the carpenter, the son of Mary, the brother of James, and Joses, and of Juda, and Simon? and are not his sisters here with us? And they were offended at him.}

The people could not deny Christ's great wisdom and healing power. But for Him to apply Isaiah's prophecy to Himself, thereby claiming to be their Messiah, was more than they could accept. After all, wasn't this the lowly carpenter who grew up in their midst? And weren't His (ordinary and fallible) brothers and sisters still living there? With skepticism and unbelief, "they were offended at Him" (i.e., were unable to acknowledge who and what He was).

    III. He diagnosed their disease of unbelief.

        A. They wanted physical, not spiritual, healing.

            ²³And he said unto them, Ye will surely say unto me this proverb, Physician, heal thyself: whatsoever we have heard done in Capernaum, do also here in thy country.

            ²⁴And he said, Verily I say unto you, No prophet is accepted in his own country {and among his own kin, and in his own house}.

Although the people had heard that Christ had done mighty works in a nearby town, they wanted to see some miracles firsthand before deciding the merits of His Messianic claims. He knew they were thinking: "Physician, heal thyself," i.e., prove your claims with a miracle. But He would not be their puppet. He replied that God's messengers are received the least by their own neighbors and kin.

        B. They were less receptive than the Gentile widow.

            ²⁵But I tell you of a truth, many widows were in Israel in the days of Elias [Elijah], when the heaven was shut up [without rain] three years and six months, when great famine was throughout all the land;

            ²⁶But unto none of them was Elias sent, save unto Sarepta [Zarephath], a city of Sidon, unto a woman that was a widow.

Unbelief was widespread in Israel when God sent Elijah to live in a Gentile widow's home (I Kings 17). When her son died and God answered Elijah's prayer to restore his life, she responded, "Now by this I know that thou art a man of God, and that the word of the Lord in thy mouth is truth" (v. 24). Although a Gentile, she was more receptive to God's messenger, and was more blessed by God as a result, than were God's own people Israel. The Jews of Christ's time were as unreceptive as their ancestors, even though they had seen more miracles than Elijah performed.

        C. They were less receptive than the leprous Syrian.

            ²⁷And many lepers were in Israel in the time of Eliseus [Elisha] the prophet; and none of them was cleansed, saving Naaman the Syrian.

Again, God bypassed the lepers in Israel to show His grace and mercy to a Gentile — the top general of the hated Syrian army no less (II Kings 5). When Naaman was miraculously healed, he said, "Now I know that there is no God in all the earth, but in Israel . . . thy servant will henceforth offer neither burnt offering nor sacrifice unto other gods, but unto the Lord" (vv. 15-17). Naaman's response to God's healing was in sharp contrast to the Jews' response to Christ's healing.

D. Rather than be cured, they attacked the Physician.

²⁸**And all they in the synagogue, when they heard these things, were filled with wrath,**

²⁹**And rose up, and thrust him out of the city, and led him unto the brow of the hill whereon their city was built, that they might cast him down headlong.**

³⁰**But he passing through the midst of them went his way,**

E. By rejecting the Physician, they forfeited His healing.

MK 6:5 And he could there do no mighty work {because of their unbelief}, save that he laid his hands upon a few sick folk, and healed them.

⁶ᵃ**And he marvelled because of their unbelief.**

While on earth, Christ seemingly healed more broken bodies than captive souls and broken hearts. Unbelief prevented the latter and at times also limited the former. Since Calvary, most of Christ's healing has been spiritual, through the proclamation and heeding of God's Word. He remains, however, fully capable of healing both body and soul. In heaven, His own will have perfect bodies with no pain or death as well as perfect souls with no sin. Isaiah's prophecy will then be fulfilled completely.

IV. He prescribed repentance for healing from sin.

A. His patients were sinners aware of their need.

MT 9:10 [MK 2:15] And it came to pass, as Jesus sat at meat in the house, behold, many publicans and sinners came and sat down with him and his disciples {for there were many, and they followed him}.

Among the multitudes that followed Jesus and listened attentively to His teaching were many tax-collectors and known sinners. These social and spiritual outcasts knew they fell short of God's righteous demands for their lives. They also recognized in Jesus one who genuinely cared for them and had solutions for their spiritual needs. He readily received them and ministered to them with loving kindness.

B. His critics were sinners blind to their plight.

¹¹**And when the Pharisees saw it, they said unto his disciples, Why eateth your Master with publicans and sinners?**

> **¹²But when Jesus heard that, he said unto them, They that be whole need not a physician, but they that are sick.**

In contrast to the known sinners, the Pharisees often were Christ's incurable critics. Here, He diagnosed their principal maladies: (1) their failure to recognize their own acute and terminal spiritual condition; (2) their view that publicans and sinners were highly contagious and should be avoided in every way; and (3) their misunderstanding of who the Physician was, why He came, and the kind of cure that He offered.

    C. His prescription was to repent and to show mercy to all.

> **¹³But go ye and learn what that meaneth, I will have mercy, and not sacrifice: for I am not come to call the righteous, but sinners to repentance.**

To the Pharisees in particular, but to all people as well, Christ prescribed: (1) repent of your sin before God and turn from your sinful ways; and (2) be merciful and understanding with others, including those still needing His cure. Verse 13 refers to Hosea 6:6 and may be understood: "I desire that you show mercy to others rather than offer [perfunctory and meaningless] sacrifices to God: because I have not come to call self-righteous people, but admitted sinners to repentance and salvation." (See Sec. II on p. 3.)

    V. He willingly bore our sickness and sin.

> **MT 8:16 When the even was come, they brought unto him many that were possessed with devils: and he cast out the spirits with his word, and healed all that were sick:**
>
>   **¹⁷That it might be fulfilled which was spoken by Esaias the prophet, saying, Himself took our infirmities, and bare our sicknesses.**

Matthew here applies Isaiah 53:4, "Surely he hath borne our griefs, and carried our sorrows," to Christ's ministry of physical healing. Although Isaiah 53 deals primarily with Christ's sacrifice of Himself for mankind's sin and spiritual healing, His sacrifice was for all of our sorrows and griefs. Christ bore our infirmities both through His compassionate healing of the sick and by paying in full for mankind's sin, the initial and underlying cause of all sickness and grief. Isaiah's prophecy will be fulfilled in every respect when Christ returns and removes all the effects of sin forever.

The Physician's Motives

Why did Christ spend so much time and energy healing so many people? In this section, fourteen purposes are identified for these miracles. Several are related to His principal purposes of identifying Himself as the promised Messiah and validating His message of salvation. Others relate to glorifying God and revealing God's values and priorities. Taken together, they reveal God's desire for everyone's salvation, and they show the love, mercy, and grace He has for every needy soul.

    I. To demonstrate that He was the Messiah.

        MT 11:2 Now when John had heard in the prison the works of Christ, he sent two of his disciples,

        ³And said unto him, Art thou he that should come, or do we look for another?

        ⁴Jesus answered and said unto them, Go and show John again those things which ye do hear and see:

        ⁵The blind receive their sight, and the lame walk, the lepers are cleansed, and the deaf hear, the dead are raised up, and the poor have the gospel preached to them.

        ⁶And blessed is he, whosoever shall not be offended in me.

Christ did not often publicly and explicitly announce that He was the Messiah. He often *demonstrated*, however, through both His remarkable teaching and His mighty miracles that He was the promised One. He gave the people more than enough evidence to warrant their recognition of His divine origin and authority and for their acceptance of His message of salvation through faith in Him.

John the Baptist, in prison and soon to be beheaded for his preaching, was understandably disheartened by this apparent setback for the Messianic kingdom he had faithfully proclaimed was at hand. He asked of Jesus, "Are you the one that should come?" Jesus reassured him by pointing to His healing miracles, as prophesied in Old Testament passages familiar to John.

    II. To confirm His deity and divine prerogatives.

        A. He proclaimed God's Word to the people.

        MK 2:1 [MT 9; LK 5] And again he entered into Capernaum after some days; and it was noised that he was in the house.

        ²And straightway many were gathered together, insomuch that there was no room to receive them, no, not so much as about the door: and he preached the word unto them. {and the power of the Lord was present to heal them.}

        B. He pronounced forgiveness to the paralytic.

        ³And they come unto him, bringing one sick of the palsy, {lying on a bed;} which was borne of four.

        ⁴And when they could not come nigh unto him for the press, they uncovered the roof where he was: and when they had broken it up,

they let down {through the tiling} the bed wherein the sick of the palsy lay {into the midst before Jesus}.

⁵When Jesus saw their faith, he said unto the sick of the palsy, Son, {be of good cheer;} thy sins be forgiven thee.

C. He perceived unbelief in the scribes.

⁶But there were certain of the scribes {and the Pharisees} sitting there, and reasoning in their hearts,

⁷Why doth this man thus speak blasphemies? who can forgive sins but God only?

⁸And immediately when Jesus perceived in his spirit that they so reasoned within themselves, he said unto them, Why reason ye these things {Why think ye evil} in your hearts?

⁹Whether is it easier to say to the sick of the palsy, Thy sins be forgiven thee; or to say, Arise, and take up thy bed, and walk?

D. He proved His authority to all.

¹⁰But that ye may know that the Son of man hath power [authority] on earth to forgive sins, (he saith to the sick of the palsy,)

¹¹I say unto thee, Arise, and take up thy bed, and go thy way into thine house.

¹²And immediately he arose, took up the bed, and went forth before them all {glorifying God}; insomuch that they were all amazed {and filled with fear}, and glorified God, {who had given such power unto men} saying, We never saw it on this fashion.

Christ acknowledged the paralytic's faith and publicly declared that his sins were forgiven — before healing his infirmity. He did so to show both the doubting scribes and the curious crowd that He was God incarnate and that as God He had full authority to forgive sins (v. 10). By staking His deity and His divine authority on His ability to heal the paralytic, and then meeting the challenge, Christ proved conclusively that He was all that He claimed to be.

III. To validate His message and doctrine.

MK 1:21 And they went into Capernaum; and straightway on the sabbath day he entered into the synagogue, and taught.

²²And they were astonished at his doctrine: for he taught them as one that had authority, and not as the scribes.

²³And there was in their synagogue a man with an unclean spirit; and he cried out,

²⁴Saying, Let us alone; what have we to do with thee, thou Jesus of Nazareth? art thou come to destroy us? I know thee who thou art, the Holy One of God.

²⁵And Jesus rebuked him, saying, Hold thy peace, and come out of him.

²⁶And when the unclean spirit had torn him, and cried with a loud voice, he came out of him.

²⁷And they were all amazed, insomuch that they questioned among themselves, saying, What thing is this? what new doctrine is this? for with authority commandeth he even the unclean spirits, and they do obey him.

Christ regularly used miracles of healing to support and validate His teaching. His declarations and doctrines were so astounding to the people that most would have rejected them outright if He had not provided incontrovertible evidence of His qualifications and authority to make such claims. His miracles provided that evidence. Similarly, each time He commissioned His disciples to go and preach the gospel (the twelve, the seventy, and the eleven after His resurrection), He also gave them power to heal — to validate their message in the same way He validated His.

IV. To show His supremacy in the spiritual realm.

MT 8:28 And when he was come to the other side into the country of the Gergesenes, there met him two possessed with devils, coming out of the tombs, exceeding fierce, so that no man might pass by that way.

²⁹And, behold, they [the demons] cried out, saying, What have we to do with thee, Jesus, thou Son of God? art thou come hither to torment us before the time [of our final judgment and condemnation]?

³⁰And there was a good way off from them an herd of many swine feeding.

³¹So the devils besought him, saying, If thou cast us out, suffer us to go away into the herd of swine.

³²And he said unto them, Go. And when they were come out, they went into the herd of swine: and, behold, the whole herd of swine ran violently down a steep place into the sea, and perished in the waters.

This passage and the one before it are only two of many that illustrate Christ's supremacy over evil spirits including Satan himself. (See Sec. III on p. 373 for a conflation of the three accounts of this incident.) As this chapter shows, Christ's purposes were primarily spiritual. Similarly, His enemies were primarily spiritual, including hosts of demons that appear to have been especially active during His ministry. Christ often cast demons out of helpless people to link His authority in the physical realm with His authority in the spiritual realm. In doing so, He accomplished other purposes as well (see Sec. X below and "Christ's Defeat of Satan's Host" on p. 371).

V. To glorify God and evoke praise to Him.

A. God permitted infirmity for His glory.

JN 9:1 And as Jesus passed by, he saw a man which was blind from his birth.

²And his disciples asked him, saying, Master, who did sin, this man, or his parents, that he was born blind?

³Jesus answered, Neither hath this man sinned, nor his parents: but that the works of God should be made manifest in him. . . .

⁶When he had thus spoken, he spat on the ground, and made clay of the spittle, and he anointed the eyes of the blind man with the clay,

⁷And said unto him, Go, wash in the pool of Siloam, (which is by interpretation, Sent.) He went his way therefore, and washed, and came seeing.

B. God even permitted death for His glory.

JN 11:4 When Jesus heard that [Lazarus was sick], he said, This sickness is not unto death, but for the glory of God, that the Son of God might be glorified thereby. . . .

¹⁴Then said Jesus unto them [His disciples] plainly, Lazarus is dead.

¹⁵And I am glad for your sakes that I was not there, to the intent ye may believe; nevertheless let us go unto him.

C. God was glorified when people were healed.

MT 15:30 And great multitudes came unto him, having with them those that were lame, blind, dumb, maimed, and many others, and cast them down at Jesus' feet; and he healed them:

³¹Insomuch that the multitude wondered [marveled], when they saw the dumb to speak, the maimed to be whole, the lame to walk, and the blind to see: and they glorified the God of Israel.

God permitted a man's blindness "that the works of God should be made manifest in him." God's works include demonstrations of His love, mercy, and grace on the one hand and His authority, power, and glory on the other. (See Sec. IX below for how He was glorified through this miracle.) Christ similarly declared that Lazarus' sickness and death were "for the glory of God" (see Sec. V on p. 325 for the full account). On many occasions, crowds of witnesses responded to Christ's miracles with praise and thanksgiving to God and "glorified the God of Israel."

VI. To show His love and compassion for people.

MT 14:13b When the people had heard thereof [where Jesus went], they followed him on foot out of the cities.

¹⁴And Jesus went forth, and saw a great multitude, and was moved with compassion toward them, and he healed their sick.

The Gospels record a number of instances where Christ was deeply moved with compassion for people. Some of these relate to His compassion for entire multitudes (such as above); others relate to His compassion for individuals with particular plights or afflictions (see Sec. II on p. 322 for examples of the latter). In every case, Christ acted in response to His compassion by addressing the need at hand — such as healing the many who were sick in this particular multitude.

VII. To warn people of the seriousness of sin.

JN 5:5 And a certain man was there [at the pool of Bethesda in Jerusalem], which had an infirmity thirty and eight years.

⁶When Jesus saw him lie, and knew that he had been now a long time in that case, he saith unto him, Wilt thou be made whole?

⁷The impotent man answered him, Sir, I have no man, when the water is troubled, to put me into the pool: but while I am coming, another steppeth down before me.

⁸Jesus saith unto him, Rise, take up thy bed [mat], and walk.

⁹And immediately the man was made whole, and took up his bed, and walked: and on the same day was the sabbath. . . .

¹⁴Afterward Jesus findeth him in the temple, and said unto him, Behold, thou art made whole: [continue in] sin no more, lest a worse thing come unto thee.

Christ did not say that the man's infirmity was the result of his sin. He clearly indicated, however, that the consequences of unconfessed and unforsaken sin are far worse than those of the disease that had plagued him for 38 years. Christ admonished him, therefore, to continue no longer in a sinful condition. His warning includes the principle that once a person has received God's mercy and grace, he will be held to a higher standard of responsibility and accountability for the way he lives thereafter.

VIII. To expose the fallacy of legalistic religion.

JN 5:10 The Jews therefore said unto him that was cured [in Sec. VII above], It is the sabbath day: it is not lawful for thee to carry thy bed.

¹¹He answered them, He that made me whole, the same said unto me, Take up thy bed, and walk.

¹²Then asked they him, What man is that which said unto thee, Take up thy bed, and walk?

¹⁵. . . [He] told the Jews that it was Jesus, which had made him whole.

¹⁶And therefore did the Jews persecute Jesus, and sought to slay him, because he had done these things on the sabbath day.

¹⁷But Jesus answered them, My [very own] Father worketh hitherto, and I work [together with Him].

¹⁸Therefore the Jews sought the more to kill him, because he not only had broken the sabbath, but said also that God was his Father, making himself equal with God.

Christ often clashed with the religious leaders regarding their overly-restrictive rules for behavior on sabbath days. He did not hesitate to heal on the sabbath, and at times it seems that one of His reasons for such healing was to expose the fallacy and hypocrisy of the Pharisees' self-righteous legalism. They had effectively changed the sabbath from a day of restful meditation on God's goodness and grace to a day of seeking to merit salvation through strict self-denial. The rabbis had listed 39 principal forms of work and 234 lesser forms that were prohibited on the sabbath. To His critics, both Christ's healing and the man's carrying his mat were violations of these rules. Christ demonstrated, however, that activities which relieve and encourage suffering people in ways that glorify God are entirely appropriate for the sabbath. (Six of the miracles presented in these sections were performed on sabbath days; note especially Christ's responses to His critics in Sections X and XI.)

IX. To lead individuals to salvation in Him.

A. A man's unique healing by Christ.

JN 9:13 They brought to the Pharisees him that aforetime was blind. ¹⁴And it was the sabbath day when Jesus made the clay, and opened his eyes. [See Sec. V.A above for the miracle.]

¹⁵Then again the Pharisees also asked him how he had received his sight. He said unto them, He put clay upon mine eyes, and I washed, and do see.

¹⁶Therefore said some of the Pharisees, This man is not of God, because he keepeth not the sabbath day. Others said, How can a man that is a sinner do such miracles? And there was a division among them.

B. The man's initial conception of Christ.

¹⁷They say unto the blind man again, What sayest thou of him, that [or, since] he hath opened thine eyes? He said, He is a prophet. . . .

²⁴Then again called they the man that was blind, and said unto him, Give God the praise: we know that this man is a sinner.

²⁵He answered and said, Whether he be a sinner or no, I know not: one thing I know, that, whereas I was blind, now I see.

Initially in the man's interrogation by the Pharisees he viewed Jesus generally as a prophet. He also said, "Whether He is a sinner or not, I don't know. What I do know is that previously I was blind but now I can see." As his interrogation progressed and intensified, however, he gradually became convinced of Jesus' goodness and righteousness.

C. The man's growing defense of Christ.

²⁶Then said they to him again, What did he to thee? how opened he thine eyes?

²⁷He answered them, I have told you already, and ye did not hear: wherefore would ye hear it again? will ye also be his disciples?

²⁸Then they reviled him, and said, Thou art his disciple; but we are Moses' disciples.

²⁹We know that God spake unto Moses: as for this fellow, we know not from whence he is.

D. The man's courageous stand for Christ.

³⁰The man answered and said unto them, Why herein is a marvelous thing, that ye know not from whence he is, and yet he hath opened mine eyes.

³¹Now we know that God heareth not sinners: but if any man be a worshipper of God, and doeth his will, him he heareth.

³²Since the world began was it not heard that any man opened the eyes of one that was born blind.

³³If this man were not of God, he could do nothing.

³⁴They answered and said unto him, Thou wast altogether born in sins, and dost thou teach us? And they cast him out.

After further reflection, the man concluded that Jesus could not be a sinner but rather was a devout and obedient servant of God. He steadfastly held his ground and refused to succumb to the Pharisees' pressure to disavow Christ. When he honored Him instead, they angrily excommunicated him from the synagogue. (That entailed complete exclusion from all Jewish religious activity, with severe social and economic strictures as well.)

E. The man's full belief in Christ.

³⁵Jesus heard that they had cast him out; and when he had found him, he said unto him, Dost thou believe on the Son of God?

³⁶He answered and said, Who is he, Lord, that I might believe on him?

³⁷And Jesus said unto him, Thou hast both seen him, and it is he that talketh with thee.

³⁸And he said, Lord, I believe. And he worshipped him.

Christ honored the man's steadfast defense of His righteousness (even though he had thought Jesus was only a prophet) by giving him a clear and personal affirmation of His deity. As a result, the man was one of few (out of the many that Christ healed) who came to believe that Jesus was the Son of God. When he grasped Jesus' identity, he worshipped Him as his Lord. This was the principal objective of Christ's ministry — to lead individuals to believe in Him for salvation. He came "to seek and to save that which was lost" (LK 19:10).

X. To free people from Satan's bondage.

    A. Satan has power to afflict with disease.

        LK 13:10 And he was teaching in one of the synagogues on the sabbath.

        ¹¹And, behold, there was a woman which had a [demonic] spirit of infirmity eighteen years, and was bowed together, and could in no wise lift up herself.

    B. Only God can break his hold.

        ¹²And when Jesus saw her, he called her to him, and said unto her, Woman, thou art loosed from thine infirmity.

        ¹³And he laid his hands on her: and immediately she was made straight, and glorified God.

    C. God's priorities should be our priorities.

        ¹⁴And the ruler of the synagogue answered with indignation, because that Jesus had healed on the sabbath day, and said unto the people, There are six days in which men ought to work: in them therefore come and be healed, and not on the sabbath day.

        ¹⁵The Lord then answered him, and said, Thou hypocrite, doth not each one of you on the sabbath loose his ox or his ass from the stall, and lead him away to watering?

        ¹⁶And ought not this woman, being a daughter of Abraham, whom Satan hath bound, lo, these eighteen years, be loosed from this bond on the sabbath day?

        ¹⁷And when he had said these things, all his adversaries were ashamed: and all the people rejoiced for all the glorious things that were done by him.

Satan had bound this woman for 18 years through "a spirit of infirmity," i.e., an evil spirit that caused her affliction (v. 11). Not every disease is caused by Satan or his demons but he does have power (limited by God) to afflict with disease for his evil purposes. In such cases, only divine power is able to break his hold. Christ freed the woman from Satan's bondage and brought glory to God among the people. "For this purpose the Son of God was manifested, that he might destroy the works of the devil" (1 John 3:8), including Satan's work of binding people physically as well as spiritually.

XI. To preserve life and relieve suffering.

    MK 3:1 [MT 12:9; LK 6:6] And he [Jesus] entered again into the synagogue; and there was a man there which had a withered hand.

    ²And they watched him, whether he would heal him on the sabbath day; that they might accuse him.

    ³And he saith unto the man which had the withered hand, Stand forth.

⁴And he saith unto them, {I will ask you one thing;} Is it lawful to do good on the sabbath days, or to do evil? to save life, or to kill {or to destroy it}? {And he said unto them, What man shall there be among you, that shall have one sheep, and if it fall into a pit on the sabbath day, will he not lay hold on it, and lift it out? How much then is a man better than a sheep?} But they held their peace.

⁵And when he had looked round about on them with anger, being grieved for the hardness of their hearts, he saith unto the man, Stretch forth thine hand. And he stretched it out: and his hand was restored whole as the other.

Christ both taught and demonstrated the importance of preserving human life and relieving the burdens of those borne down with physical problems. Physical life is a picture (though marred and imperfect) of spiritual life, and the God who created both cares about both. (See "Life and Death" on p. 107). Christ often showed His concern for the sufferings of afflicted people and readily used God's day "to do good" and "to save life." If someone will rescue a helpless animal, how much more should he come to the aid of a needy person with an eternal soul.

XII. To show mercy and kindness to His enemies.

LK 22:47 [JN 18:3] And while he yet spake, behold a multitude {of men and officers}, and he that was called Judas, one of the twelve, went before them, and drew near unto Jesus to kiss him.

⁴⁸But Jesus said unto him, Judas, betrayest thou the Son of man with a kiss?

⁴⁹When they which were about him saw what would follow, they said unto him, Lord, shall we smite with the sword?

⁵⁰And one of them {Simon Peter having a sword drew it, and} smote the servant of the high priest, and cut off his right ear.

⁵¹And Jesus answered and said, {Put up thy sword into the sheath: the cup which my Father hath given me, shall I not drink it?} Suffer ye thus far. And he touched his ear, and healed him.

Christ's final act of healing was for a man who came to arrest Him and have Him crucified. In the midst of Judas' treachery, the Jews' animosity, His disciples' anxiety, and the servant's own culpability, Christ calmly stopped them all in their tracks while He mercifully and graciously healed the servant's ear. The servant (named Malchus in JN 18:10) is not mentioned again in scripture. One wonders what thoughts went through his mind as he watched Christ on the cross and heard Him say, "Father, forgive them; for they know not what they do" (LK 23:34).

XIII. To answer believers' prayers and encourage their faith.

MK 10:46 **And they came to Jericho: and as he went out of Jericho with his disciples and a great number of people, blind Bartimaeus, the son of Timaeus, sat by the highway side begging.**

[47]**And when he heard that it was Jesus of Nazareth, he began to cry out, and say, Jesus, thou son of David, have mercy on me.**

[48]**And many charged him that he should hold his peace: but he cried the more a great deal, Thou son of David, have mercy on me.**

[49]**And Jesus stood still, and commanded him to be called. And they call the blind man, saying unto him, Be of good comfort, rise; he calleth thee.**

[50]**And he, casting away his garment, rose, and came to Jesus.**

[51]**And Jesus answered and said unto him, What wilt thou that I should do unto thee? The blind man said unto him, Lord, that I might receive my sight.**

[52]**And Jesus said unto him, Go thy way; thy faith hath made thee whole. And immediately he received his sight, and followed Jesus in the way.**

Bartimaeus' faith that Christ could restore his sight was based on his belief that Jesus was the "son of David," the Messiah. Christ rewarded his faith by granting his request, and He attributed his healing to his faith. Although Christ did not limit His healing to those who first expressed such faith, He healed all those in whom He found it. Whether it was the rare person with "great faith" or the man who pleaded "I believe; help thou mine unbelief," Christ nurtured and rewarded whatever faith they had and encouraged them toward an ever-increasing faith in God.

XIV. To free believers for greater service for Him.

MK 1:29 [MT 8:14; LK 4:38] **And forthwith, when they were come out of the synagogue, they entered into the house of Simon [Peter] and Andrew, with James and John.**

[30]**But Simon's wife's mother lay sick of a {great} fever, and anon they tell him of her {they besought him for her}.**

[31]**And he came and {stood over her, and rebuked the fever; and} took her by the hand, and lifted her up; and immediately the fever left her, and she {arose, and} ministered unto them.**

God's grace merits every believer's whole-hearted service. Some believers, however, are unable to serve God as fully as they would like because of severe physical infirmities (either their own or of others for whom they are responsible). God's grace is always sufficient for such cases whether or not it is His will that they be healed. Any healing that He does grant should be taken as an encouragement toward greater service while we have the opportunity and ability to honor Him with it.

The Physician's Manner

Christ described Himself as "meek and lowly in heart," that is, as gentle and humble in nature (MT 11:29). His gentle and gracious manner characterized His healing miracles as markedly as did His mighty power and their amazing results. He knew that within the broken and pain-racked forms He met were anxious minds and down-cast hearts. He ministered to their bodies, therefore, in ways that also encouraged their spirits. With the utmost love and mercy, He "took our infirmities and bore our sicknesses" (MT 8:17).

I. He was kind and gentle to the weak.

A. He graciously healed one and all.

MT 12:14 Then the Pharisees went out, and held a council against him, how they might destroy him.

¹⁵But when Jesus knew it, he withdrew himself from thence: and great multitudes followed him, and he healed them all;

B. He quietly and humbly performed His work.

¹⁶And [He] charged them that they should not make him known:

¹⁷That it might be fulfilled which was spoken by Esaias the prophet, saying,

¹⁸Behold my servant, whom I have chosen; my beloved, in whom my soul is well pleased: I will put my spirit upon him, and he shall show judgment [justice] to the Gentiles.

¹⁹He shall not strive, nor cry [not argue or shout]; neither shall any man hear his voice [ranting] in the streets.

C. He tenderly nurtured "bruised reeds and failing flax."

²⁰A bruised reed shall he not break, and smoking flax [a smoldering wick] shall he not quench, till he send forth judgment [establishes justice] unto victory.

²¹And in his name shall the Gentiles trust.

Matthew paraphrased Isaiah 42:1-4, which pictured the coming Messiah as a gentle, unassuming helper of the weak and lowly. He would not arouse crowds with inflammatory speech; neither would He vehemently quarrel with His opponents. Instead, He would lovingly nurture a lowly "bruised reed" back to health, rather than discard it. Similarly, He would restore a struggling "smoldering wick" so that it could produce useful light. The reed and flax picture the common everyday people who came to Christ for healing and to whom He gave the utmost care. Verse 20b suggests that Christ will continue to heal and restore needy people until He comes again to "establish justice in ultimate victory." Not only Jews, but Gentiles also, will trust in His name and receive both His spiritual and His physical healing.

II. He was compassionate and gracious to the helpless.

A. His compassion for a grieving widow.

> LK 7:11 And it came to pass the day after, that he went into a city called Nain; and many of his disciples went with him, and much people.
>
> ¹²Now when he came nigh to the gate of the city, behold, there was a dead man carried out, the only son of his mother, and she was a widow: and much people of the city was with her.
>
> ¹³And when the Lord saw her, he had compassion on her, and said unto her, Weep not.
>
> ¹⁴And he came and touched the bier: and they that bare him stood still. And he said, Young man, I say unto thee, Arise.
>
> ¹⁵And he that was dead sat up, and began to speak. And he delivered him to his mother.
>
> ¹⁶And there came a fear [awe] on all: and they glorified God, saying, That a great prophet is risen up among us; and, That God hath visited his people.

This is the first of three recorded cases of Christ raising the dead. (The others are reviewed in Sections IV and V below.) No one sought His intervention, probably because everyone assumed the case was hopeless. Christ kindly bade the widow to stop weeping — then He miraculously removed the cause of her sorrow. With tender compassion, He restored the son to his mother.

B. His compassion for a pleading leper.

> MK 1:40 And there came a leper to him, beseeching him, and kneeling down to him, and saying unto him, If thou wilt, thou canst make me clean.
>
> ⁴¹And Jesus, moved with compassion, put forth his hand, and touched him, and saith unto him, I will; be thou clean.
>
> ⁴²And as soon as he had spoken, immediately the leprosy departed from him, and he was cleansed.
>
> ⁴³And he straitly charged him, and forthwith sent him away;
>
> ⁴⁴And saith unto him, See thou say nothing to any man: but go thy way, shew thyself to the priest, and offer for thy cleansing those things which Moses commanded, for a testimony unto them.

Christ was "moved with compassion" in response to the leper's pitiful condition, his earnest pleading, and his simple faith. He sent the cured leper to the priest, as required by Mosaic law (see Leviticus 14), to provide the local religious leaders "a testimony" of His healing power and His righteous nature.

C. His compassion for a deranged demoniac.

> MK 5:18 And when he [Jesus] was come into the ship, he that had been possessed with the devil [demon] prayed him that he might be with him.

¹⁹**Howbeit Jesus suffered him not, but saith unto him, Go home to thy friends, and tell them how great things the Lord hath done for thee, and hath had compassion on thee.**

²⁰**And he departed, and began to publish in Decapolis how great things Jesus had done for him: and all men did marvel.**

While the deranged man was still controlled by demons, Christ had compassion on Him and prepared to free him (see Sec. III on p. 373 for the full passage). Afterward, the man begged to stay with his Deliverer, but Christ sent him home to tell his friends of God's goodness and compassion toward him. The man obeyed and gladly testified throughout the surrounding region of Christ's great mercy and healing power.

III. He was patient and longsuffering with the ignorant.

   A. He healed though most mistook His mission.

MK 7:32 And they bring unto him one that was deaf, and had an impediment in his speech; and they beseech him to put his hand upon him.

³³**And he took him aside from the multitude, and put his fingers into his ears, and he spit, and touched his tongue;**

³⁴**And looking up to heaven, he sighed [groaned deeply], and saith unto him, Ephphatha, that is, Be opened.**

³⁵**And straightway his ears were opened, and the string of his tongue was loosed, and he spake plain.**

³⁶**And he charged them that they should tell no man: but the more he charged them, so much the more a great deal they published it;**

³⁷**And were beyond measure astonished, saying, He hath done all things well: he maketh both the deaf to hear, and the dumb to speak.**

Christ took the afflicted man aside from the thronging crowd — to focus the man's attention on what He was about to do for him and to show the man His personal concern for him. He also groaned deeply before healing him, probably because of the crowd's (and the man's) misunderstanding of the spiritual reasons for His healing ministry. (He similarly groaned when seeing the people sorrowing for Lazarus' death in Sec. V below.) In both this miracle and the one that follows, Christ took unusual steps in performing His healing. Throughout His ministry, He used a great variety of outward means in connection with His miracles. These not only demonstrate His infinite nature but show that He considered each person a unique individual as He personally dealt with the needs of each one.

   B. He healed though most dismissed His message.

MK 8:22 And he cometh to Bethsaida: and they bring a blind man unto him, and besought him to touch him.

²³And he took the blind man by the hand, and led him out of the town; and when he had spit on his eyes, and put his hands upon him, he asked him if he saw ought [anything].

²⁴And he looked up, and said, I see men as trees, walking.

²⁵After that he put his hands again upon his eyes, and made him look up: and he was restored, and saw every man clearly.

²⁶And he sent him away to his house, saying, Neither go into the town, nor tell it to any in the town.

Christ had already condemned Bethsaida and nearby towns for their unbelief in spite of the many miracles He had performed there (MT 11:20-22). He cared enough, however, for this blind man and his plight to lead him "out of the town" and then heal him. Christ forbad him to go back into the town or tell anyone there how he had been healed, because the people had already rejected the message of His words and deeds. Mark follows this account with Christ's question to His disciples, "Whom do men say that I am?" The people generally gave wrong answers because they did not believe that He was the Christ, the Son of God.

IV. He gave comfort and encouragement to the distraught.

A. He readily responded to an urgent request.

MK 5:22 [LK 8:41; MT 9:18] And, behold, there cometh one of the rulers of the synagogue, Jairus by name; and when he saw him, he fell at his feet,

²³And besought him greatly, saying, My little daughter lieth at the point of death: I pray thee, come and lay thy hands on her, that she may be healed; and she shall live.

²⁴And Jesus went with him; and much people followed him . . .

B. He promised relief when all hope was lost.

³⁵While he yet spake, there came from the ruler of the synagogue's house certain which said, Thy daughter is dead: why troublest thou the Master any further?

³⁶As soon as Jesus heard the word that was spoken, he saith unto the ruler of the synagogue, Be not afraid, only believe {and she shall be made whole}.

Jairus pleaded in desperation for Christ to come and heal his only daughter (LK 8:42). As a "ruler of the synagogue," he was one of the elders that oversaw the sabbath services. His synagogue most likely was the one in Christ's own city of Capernaum in which He taught when in town (MT 9:1). When word came that the girl had died, Christ encouraged him to take heart and believe that she would be restored to life.

C. He offered encouragement, while others mocked.

³⁷And he suffered no man to follow him, save Peter, and James, and John the brother of James.

³⁸And he cometh to the house of the ruler of the synagogue, and seeth the tumult, and {the minstrels and} them that wept and wailed greatly.

³⁹And when he was come in, he saith unto them, Why make ye this ado, and weep? the damsel is not dead, but sleepeth.

⁴⁰ᵃAnd they laughed him to scorn {knowing that she was dead}.

D. He restored their joy by restoring her life.

⁴⁰ᵇBut when he had put them all out, he taketh the father and the mother of the damsel, and them that were with him, and entereth in where the damsel was lying.

⁴¹And he took the damsel by the hand, and said unto her, Talitha cumi; which is, being interpreted, Damsel, I say unto thee, arise.

⁴²And straightway {her spirit came again, and } the damsel arose, and walked; for she was of the age of twelve years. And they were astonished with a great astonishment.

⁴³And he charged them straitly [strictly] that no man should know it; and commanded that something should be given her to eat.

The customary hired mourners and "minstrels" (flute players) were already at Jairus' house and were carrying on in a loud and tumultuous fashion. When Christ said the girl was sleeping, they laughed and ridiculed Him. In the private company of her parents and His three closest disciples, Christ tenderly raised the girl from the dead and kindly ordered food for her nourishment.

V. He showed love and sympathy for the sorrowing.

A. He loved His friends in their time of trial.

JN 11:1 Now a certain man was sick, named Lazarus, of Bethany, the town of Mary and her sister Martha.

²(It was that Mary which anointed the Lord with ointment, and wiped his feet with her hair, whose brother Lazarus was sick.)

³Therefore his sisters sent unto him, saying, Lord, behold, he whom thou lovest is sick.

⁴When Jesus heard that, he said, This sickness is not unto death, but for the glory of God, that the Son of God might be glorified thereby.

⁵Now Jesus loved Martha, and her sister, and Lazarus.

B. He knew what was best for each one's need.

⁶When he had heard therefore that he was sick, he abode two days still in the same place where he was.

⁷Then after that saith he to his disciples, Let us go into Judaea again.

[8]His disciples say unto him, Master, the Jews of late sought to stone thee; and goest thou thither again?

[11] . . . he saith unto them, Our friend Lazarus sleepeth; but I go, that I may awake him out of sleep.

C. He nurtured His disciples' weak faith.

[12]Then said his disciples, Lord, if he sleep, he shall do well.

[13]Howbeit Jesus spake of his death: but they thought that he had spoken of taking of rest in sleep.

[14]Then said Jesus unto them plainly, Lazarus is dead.

[15]And I am glad for your sakes that I was not there, to the intent ye may believe; nevertheless let us go unto him.

[16]Then said Thomas, which is called Didymus, unto his fellow disciples, Let us also go, that we may die with him.

[17]Then when Jesus came, he found that he had lain in the grave four days already.

Although Christ especially loved Lazarus and his sisters, His loving response in this case was not to heal Lazarus' disease but to let it take its seemingly tragic toll. He was a day's journey from Bethany and knew that Lazarus had already died before news of his sickness arrived. For the sake of all of His disciples (including Lazarus, his sisters, and many others), He delayed his departure another two days — "to the intent ye may believe" more fully in Him as the Son of God. (See Sec. III.B on p. 101 for vv. 9-10, and Sec. IV on p. 442 for vv. 21-27.)

D. He grieved for people in their sorrow.

[31]The Jews then which were with her [with Mary] in the house, and comforted her, when they saw Mary, that she rose up hastily and went out, followed her, saying, She goeth unto the grave to weep there.

[32]Then when Mary was come where Jesus was, and saw him, she fell down at his feet, saying unto him, Lord, if thou hadst been here, my brother had not died.

[33]When Jesus therefore saw her weeping, and the Jews also weeping which came with her, he groaned in the spirit, and was troubled,

E. He grieved for Lazarus in his death.

[34]And [He] said, Where have ye laid him? They said unto him, Lord, come and see.

[35]Jesus wept.

[36]Then said the Jews, Behold how he loved him!

[37]And some of them said, Could not this man, which opened the eyes of the blind, have caused that even this man should not have died?

[38]Jesus therefore again groaning in himself cometh to the grave. It was a cave, and a stone lay upon it.

Christ was deeply grieved at the sight of Mary's weeping. She was one of His most dedicated believers and her grief was as His own. Though He knew exactly what He would do to replace her sorrow with great joy, He "groaned in His spirit" at how sin's universal curse was afflicting those He particularly loved. He also grieved for the unbelief of the weeping Jews who came with Mary (v. 33). He saw them, not only as subject to physical death, but also as bound in spiritual death. He wept openly at Lazarus' grave as the cumulative effect of everyone's sorrow and suffering weighed heavily on His tender, compassionate soul.

F. He encouraged Martha in her struggling faith.

³⁹Jesus said, Take ye away the stone. Martha, the sister of him that was dead, saith unto him, Lord, by this time he stinketh: for he hath been dead four days.

⁴⁰Jesus saith unto her, Said I not unto thee, that, if thou wouldest believe, thou shouldest see the glory of God?

Christ earlier had told Martha, "Thy brother shall rise again" (in v. 23). In spite of her confession, "thou art the Christ, the Son of God," she found it difficult to apply her faith in this seemingly hopeless situation. He reminded her that, through faith in Him, she would see "the glory of God."

G. He prayed for the Jews in their unbelief.

⁴¹Then they took away the stone from the place where the dead was laid. And Jesus lifted up his eyes, and said, Father, I thank thee that thou hast heard me.

⁴²And I knew that thou hearest me always: but because of the people which stand by I said it, that they may believe that thou hast sent me.

H. He ministered to them all through one great deed.

⁴³And when he thus had spoken, he cried with a loud voice, Lazarus, come forth.

⁴⁴And he that was dead came forth, bound hand and foot with graveclothes: and his face was bound about with a napkin. Jesus saith unto them, Loose him, and let him go.

⁴⁵Then many of the Jews which came to Mary, and had seen the things which Jesus did, believed on him.

⁴⁶But some of them went their ways to the Pharisees, and told them what things Jesus had done.

Most of those present still needed to trust Christ as their Messiah. For their benefit, He talked aloud with His Father in prayer "that they may believe that thou hast sent me." His command to Lazarus to come forth was answered dramatically, and many of the Jews believed on Him. With one great deed, Christ tailored the demonstration of His love for each individual or group that was there, to meet the particular need (whether spiritual, physical, or emotional) that each one had at the time.

This miracle probably was the most crucial and influential of all those that Christ performed. Coming near the end of His ministry, it forced the issue for all Israel of whether or not Jesus was the Messiah and the Son of God. The raising of Lazarus confirmed and strengthened the faith of those who believed in Christ, and it added many more to His fold. In contrast, the miracle only hardened the unbelief of some, and they went to report it to the Pharisees. The latter then plotted with the chief priests to put Christ to death, lest "all men will believe on him" (vv. 47-53).

As news of Lazarus' resurrection spread, more and more Jews believed in Jesus as the Messiah because of it. The chief priests, therefore, sought to put Lazarus to death also (JN 12:9-11). His being raised from the dead also contributed to the formation of the joyous throng that hailed Christ as King on Palm Sunday (12:12-18). Thus God used this miracle in setting the stage for the final events leading to Christ's crucifixion.

16

Images of the Father, Son, and Holy Spirit

The members of the Trinity — Father, Son, and Holy Spirit — have always worked as One in perfect union and harmony. Their respective functions, however, in their dealings with mankind have differed in different eras as they together determined. Some of these differences appeared in the Old Testament, but usually in veiled form that awaited New Testament revelation for our fuller understanding. In the Gospels, many of their individual functions and the interrelationship of these functions are clearly seen for the first time.

For example, the Holy Spirit brought the Son into the world through Mary as "the only begotten of the Father." The Son ministered on earth for the glory of the Father in the power of the Spirit. Before His ascension, the Son commanded His disciples to baptize all believers in the name of the Father, Son, and Holy Spirit. He promised that the Father would give them the Spirit who would glorify the Son by showing them what the Father had given the Son.

All who receive Christ as their Savior, now have His Father as their Father and His Spirit in their spirit. Just as Father, Son, and Spirit have lived together in perfect union from eternity past, they now jointly "make their abode" within every believer. Each One performs His individual, complementary, and perfect work in and through us, for our good and God's glory. This chapter presents images and illustrations of the Father, Son, and Holy Spirit as they are revealed in the Gospels.

Portrayals of Our Heavenly Father

The principal name of the First Person of the Godhead in scripture is *Father*. This name wonderfully pictures His relationship with His Son Jesus Christ and with all of His children who are in Christ. *Father* illustrates the paternal aspects of His nature, purposes, and actions. It especially portrays His boundless loving kindness, His faithful provision and protection, and His merciful forgiving spirit.

Jesus was the first to call Him "Father" in this highly personal way. Although He has always been the Father of all true believers, He was seldom called by that name in the Old Testament. There, when He was identified individually, He typically was given the exalted title of "Lord God Almighty." Through Christ, we can approach Him as our Heavenly Father at any time in proper prayer and worship, and with full assurance of being received with open arms. We must ever be mindful, however, that our loving Heavenly Father is also the infinite Lord God Almighty.

The following brief excerpts from passages reviewed in greater detail elsewhere illustrate some of the many ways in which the Almighty God serves as our Heavenly Father.

I. He is our Mighty Sovereign.

A. He rules over heaven and earth.

MT 6:9 After this manner therefore pray ye: Our Father which art in heaven, Hallowed be thy name.
¹⁰Thy kingdom come. Thy will be done in earth, as it is in heaven. . . .
¹³ᵇFor thine is the kingdom, and the power, and the glory, for ever. Amen.

The Father rules as absolute sovereign *in* heaven and *from* heaven. His will is always done in heaven — immediately, willingly, and fully by all the heavenly host. So *should* it be done on earth by and among mankind. And so *will* it be done throughout His universal kingdom, both now and forever.

B. He governs all mankind.

JN 6:65 And he said, Therefore said I unto you, that no man can come unto me, except it were given unto him of my Father.

MT 18:14 Even so it is not the will of your Father which is in heaven, that one of these little ones should perish.

JN 6:39 And this is the Father's will which hath sent me, that of all [those] which he hath given me I should lose nothing, but should raise it up again at the last day.

MT 15:13 But he answered and said [of unbelievers], Every plant, which my heavenly Father hath not planted, shall be rooted up.

C. He controls time and eternity.

ACTS 1:6 When they therefore were come together, they asked of him, saying, Lord, wilt thou at this time restore again the kingdom to Israel?
⁷And he said unto them, It is not for you to know the times or the seasons, which the Father hath put in his own power.

MT 24:36 But of that day and hour knoweth no man, no, not the angels of heaven, but my Father only.

MT 25:34 Then [after the end of this age] shall the King say unto them on his right hand [true believers], Come, ye blessed of my Father, inherit the kingdom prepared for you from the foundation of the world:

The Father "has given" all believers to Christ for their salvation (JN 6:39) and will root up all those He did not plant. It is not His will, however, that any should perish — not even a single and seemingly insignificant "little one" (MT 18:14). At a predetermined time known only to Him, He will gather together all who believe in Christ to dwell forever in the kingdom He prepared for them "from the foundation of the world."

II. He is our Holy God.

A. He is perfectly holy and righteous.

JN 17:11b. Holy Father, keep through thine own name those whom thou hast given me, that they may be one, as we are.

JN 17:25 O righteous Father, the world hath not known thee: but I have known thee, and these have known that thou hast sent me.

In praying for His disciples, and for all believers after them, Christ addressed the Father as holy and righteous. *Holy* refers to the Father's *essence* — that which makes Him God. It indicates His separateness — His glorious transcendence above and apart from all creation. He declared, "I am God, and not man; the Holy One in the midst of thee" (Hosea 11:9). In spite of His transcendence, God is "in the midst" of those He has separated to Himself (i.e., "made holy" by giving them His nature) through His love and grace.

God's righteousness refers to the absolute rectitude and perfection of His *actions*, all of which are fully consistent with and reflective of His holiness. His righteousness is the means by which He demonstrates His holy character to His created beings. For believers, the Father's holiness and righteousness jointly guarantee that He is working all things together for their ultimate good as He conforms them to the perfect image of His Son (Rom. 8:28-29). (See p. 200 for Christ's full prayer in JN 17.)

> B. He is our divine Father and God.
>
> **JN 20:17 Jesus saith unto her [Mary Magdalene], . . . go to my brethren, and say unto them, I ascend unto my Father, and your Father; and to my God, and your God.**
>
> **MT 23:8 But be not ye called Rabbi: for one is your Master, even Christ; and all ye are brethren.**
> **⁹And call no man your father upon the earth: for one is your Father, which is in heaven.**
>
> C. He deserves and desires our worship.
>
> **JN 4:23 But the hour cometh, and now is, when the true worshippers shall worship the Father in spirit and in truth: for the Father seeketh such to worship him.**

Christ differentiated at times between "the Father," "my Father," and "your Father," as in the above passages. "The Father" generally portrays Him as the eternal God and Lord over all His creation. It is "the Father" who continually seeks those who will worship Him as such (JN 4). Although Christ often used "The Father" and "my Father" interchangeably, He tended toward the latter when indicating His own deity and divine authority.

Christ distinguished more clearly between "my Father" and "your Father" (as in JN 20), underscoring the eternal uniqueness of His own personal relationship with The Father as co-equal members of the Godhead. He never said, "our Father" as pertaining jointly to Himself and believers. (That term in the Lord's Prayer is how believers should address *their* Heavenly Father.) Interestingly, in the Sermon on the Mount, every reference is to "your Father" (except one that deals with false believers), indicating to one and all that the Father (and His Father) also desires to be your Father.

> III. He is our Spiritual Father.
>
> A. He sent Christ as our "Bread from heaven."
>
> **JN 6:32 Then Jesus said unto them, Verily, verily, I say unto you, Moses gave you not that bread from heaven; but my Father giveth you the true bread from heaven.**

[33]For the bread of God is he which cometh down from heaven, and giveth life unto the world.

B. He reveals Jesus as the Christ to His own.

MT 16:16 And Simon Peter answered and said, Thou art the Christ, the Son of the living God.

[17]And Jesus answered and said unto him, Blessed art thou, Simon Bar-jona: for flesh and blood hath not revealed it unto thee, but my Father which is in heaven.

LK 10:21 In that hour Jesus rejoiced in spirit, and said, I thank thee, O Father, Lord of heaven and earth, that thou hast hid these things [the way of salvation] from the wise and prudent, and hast revealed them unto babes: even so, Father; for so it seemed good in thy sight.

C. He draws people to Christ for salvation.

JN 6:44 No man can come to me, except the Father which hath sent me draw him: and I will raise him up at the last day.

[45b]Every man therefore that hath heard, and hath learned of [from] the Father, cometh unto me.

The Father in heaven is every believer's Spiritual Father. He sent His Son from heaven to provide for our spiritual birth and life. He also works in our lives and circumstances to draw us to Christ, and He gives us the desire and ability to receive Christ as our Savior. The Father thereby makes us His children and truly becomes our Father.

IV. He is our Gracious Lord.

A. He gives us His Holy Spirit.

JN 14:26 But the Comforter, which is the Holy Ghost, whom the Father will send in my name, he shall teach you all things, and bring all things to your remembrance, whatsoever I have said unto you.

B. He causes us to bear fruit.

JN 15:1 I am the true vine, and my Father is the husbandman.

[2]Every branch in me that beareth not fruit he taketh away: and every branch that beareth fruit, he purgeth it, that it may bring forth more fruit.

C. He answers our prayers through Christ.

JN 15:16 Ye have not chosen me, but I have chosen you, and ordained you, that ye should go and bring forth fruit, and that your fruit should remain: that whatsoever ye shall ask of the Father in my name, he may give it you.

The Father never ceases His active involvement in the lives of those He has drawn to Christ. Along with giving them His Son, He gives them His Holy Spirit for their teaching and spiritual growth (JN 14). The Father also works continuously, together with His Son and His Spirit, to empower believers for their ordained service, to produce lasting fruit in and through their lives, and to answer their prayers to Him (JN 15).

V. He is our Faithful Provider.

A. He knows our needs in advance.

MT 6:8 Be not ye therefore like unto them [unbelievers]: for your Father knoweth what things ye have need of, before ye ask him.

B. He meets our needs faithfully and fully.

MT 6:26 Behold the fowls of the air: for they sow not, neither do they reap, nor gather into barns; yet your heavenly Father feedeth them. Are ye not much better than they?

LK 12:29 And seek not ye what ye shall eat, or what ye shall drink, neither be ye of doubtful mind.
³⁰For all these things do the nations of the world seek after: and your Father knoweth that ye have need of these things.
³¹But rather seek ye the kingdom of God; and all these things shall be added unto you.

C. He provides abundantly beyond our needs.

MT 7:9 Or what man is there of you, whom if his son ask bread, will he give him a stone?
¹⁰Or if he ask a fish, will he give him a serpent?
¹¹If ye then, being evil, know how to give good gifts unto your children, how much more shall your Father which is in heaven give good things to them that ask him?

Every day, our Faithful Father meets our needs and abundantly more. Meeting their children's needs is a principal role of all fathers, and our Heavenly Father is the perfect example of an ideal father. As these pages demonstrate, He provides for His children spiritually, emotionally, physically, and materially. He embodies all the positive qualities and characteristics that human fathers should seek to develop. Though earthly fathers are frail and fallible and fail us at times, our Heavenly Father and Faithful Provider is always true to His name.

VI. He is our Merciful Master.

A. He is kind to all (as we should be kind).

MT 5:44 But I say unto you, Love your enemies, bless them that curse you, do good to them that hate you, and pray for them which despitefully use you, and persecute you;

⁴⁵That ye may be the children of your Father which is in heaven: for he maketh his sun to rise on the evil and on the good, and sendeth rain on the just and on the unjust.

B. He forgives our sins (as we should forgive others).

MK 11:25 And when ye stand praying, forgive, if ye have ought against any: that your Father also which is in heaven may forgive you your trespasses.
²⁶But if ye do not forgive, neither will your Father which is in heaven forgive your trespasses.

C. He is merciful to His enemies (as we should be merciful).

LK 6:35 But love ye your enemies, and do good, and lend, hoping for nothing again; and your reward shall be great, and ye shall be the children of the Highest: for he is kind unto the unthankful and to the evil.
³⁶Be ye therefore merciful, as your Father also is merciful.

The Father certainly is our Merciful Master in giving us salvation and forgiving all our sins. He was merciful to us even before our salvation by making His sun to rise and His rain to fall on "the evil and unjust" (MT 5). He continues to show us His mercy every day of our lives by encouraging, forgiving, comforting, and helping us as we seek to live for Him. He is not only our Master in these areas but also our Example. We are commanded in each of the above passages to be like Him by showing kindness, mercy, and forgiveness to others. In so doing, we portray His goodness and mercy and demonstrate that we belong to Him.

VII. He is our Loving Companion.

A. He loves us for believing in Christ.

JN 16:26 At that day ye shall ask in my name: and I say not unto you, that I will pray the Father for you:
²⁷For the Father himself loveth you, because ye have loved me, and have believed that I came out from God.

B. He loves us for loving and obeying Christ.

JN 14:21 He that hath my commandments, and keepeth them, he it is that loveth me: and he that loveth me shall be loved of my Father, and I will love him, and will manifest myself to him.

C. He loves us and indwells us with Christ.

JN 14:23 Jesus answered and said unto him, If a man love me, he will keep my words: and my Father will love him, and we will come unto him, and make our abode with him.

That the infinite majestic Father could love finite, frail sinners is beyond comprehension. Equally amazing is that the Father, with His Son and Spirit, would come to us and take up permanent residence within us. All three members of the Trinity are our intimate, life-long companions. The Father demonstrated His great love for us first and foremost through the gift of His Son. We demonstrate our love for Him primarily through faith in Christ and obedience to His will. We have continuing fellowship with the Father through His Word, our prayer, and our worship — because we love His Son and they both love us.

VIII. He is our Vigilant Keeper.

    A. He protects our lives from harm.

        MT 10:29 Are not two sparrows sold for a farthing? and one of them shall not fall on the ground without your Father.
        [30]But the very hairs of your head are all numbered.
        [31]Fear ye not therefore, ye are of more value than many sparrows.

    B. He secures our souls "through His name."

        JN 17:11 And now I am no more in the world, but these are in the world, and I come to thee. Holy Father, keep through thine own name those whom thou hast given me, that they may be one, as we are.

    C. He preserves our souls for eternity.

        JN 10:27 My sheep hear my voice, and I know them, and they follow me:
        [28]And I give unto them eternal life; and they shall never perish, neither shall any man pluck them out of my hand.
        [29]My Father, which gave them me, is greater than all; and no man is able to pluck them out of my Father's hand.

Not even an insignificant sparrow falls to the ground without the Father's knowledge and consent (MT 10). He is the sparrows' maker and provider, but He is your *Loving Father and Eternal Keeper*. He cares far more for each believer than for any number of sparrows. As our watchful guardian, He protects and preserves our physical lives for every moment that He wills that we remain alive. More importantly, He keeps our souls secure in our eternal relationship with Christ. He personally guarantees our eternal salvation, our eternal position as His children, and our eternal home with Him in heaven.

IX. He is our Eternal Rewarder.

    A. He rewards faithful righteous living.

        LK 12:32 Fear not, little flock; for it is your Father's good pleasure to give you the kingdom.

MT 13:43 Then shall the righteous shine forth as the sun in the kingdom of their Father. Who hath ears to hear, let him hear.

B. He rewards humble, sincere worship.

MT 6:1 Take heed that ye do not your alms before men, to be seen of them: otherwise ye have no reward of your Father which is in heaven. . . .

³But when thou doest alms, let not thy left hand know what thy right hand doeth:

⁴That thine alms may be in secret: and thy Father which seeth in secret himself shall reward thee openly.

C. He rewards diligent sacrificial service.

JN 12:26 If any man serve me, let him follow me; and where I am, there shall also my servant be: if any man serve me, him will my Father honor.

Although many of the promised rewards that the Father will give believers for faithful service and worship are indefinite as to their nature and timing, they are absolutely certain as to their eventual bestowal. We also know, both from other scripture and personal observation, that many of these rewards are experienced in varying degrees in this present life. These include all manner of spiritual and physical blessings that the Father showers on us day by day. Some are received inwardly, others outwardly, but all are a preview and a down payment of greater rewards still to come.

X. He is our All in All.

The Lord's Prayer touches upon each of the areas identified in prior sections in which the Father functions and meets our needs as our Father. The titles ascribed to Him there relate to the petitions in the prayer as follows:

A. Our Spiritual Father and Holy God.

MT 6:9 After this manner therefore pray ye: Our Father, which art in heaven, Hallowed be thy name.

B. Our Mighty Sovereign and Gracious Lord.

¹⁰Thy kingdom come. Thy will be done in earth, as it is in heaven.

C. Our Faithful Provider and Merciful Master.

¹¹Give us this day our daily bread.

¹²And forgive us our debts, as we forgive our debtors.

D. Our Loving Companion and Vigilant Keeper.

¹³ᵃAnd lead us not into temptation, but deliver us from evil:

E. Our Almighty God and Eternal Rewarder.
¹³ᵇFor thine is the kingdom, and the power, and the glory, for ever. Amen.

Our Father stands ready to meet every believer's needs in every sphere of life, for our good and His glory. The above prayer is better called "the Disciples' Prayer"; Christ gave it to His followers as an example of (1) how they should approach their Heavenly Father, (2) which petitions are particularly appropriate, and (3) how their requests may reverently be framed. Our Father desires that we frequently bring similar prayers to Him, adding and inserting our own praise, worship, thanksgiving, and requests, as His Holy Spirit directs the thoughts and desires of our hearts toward Him.

Only through Christ can we know "the Father" and "His Father" as "our Father." Christ said, "All things are delivered unto me of my Father: and no man knoweth the Son, but the Father; neither knoweth any man the Father, save the Son, and he to whomsoever the Son will reveal him" (MT 11:27). He also declared, "No man cometh unto the Father, but by me. . . . If ye had known me, ye should have known my Father also: and from henceforth ye know him, and have seen him. . . . He that hath seen me hath seen the Father" (JN 14:6-9). "I and my Father are one" (JN 10:30).

Verbal Crowns for God the Son

"God, who at sundry times and in divers manners spake in time past unto the fathers by the prophets, hath in these last days spoken unto us by His Son, whom He hath appointed heir of all things, by whom also He made the worlds; who being the brightness of His glory, and the express image of His person, and upholding all things by the word of His power, when He had by Himself purged our sins, sat down on the right hand of the Majesty on high" (Hebrews 1:1-3).

Before Christ came, God spoke to His people "in many parts and in different ways." He did so "by the prophets," i.e., in and through their spoken and written words. Now He has spoken fully and finally "by His Son," in and through the Living Word. God also has pictured Himself for us in His Son. Christ is the "radiant shining forth of God's glory" and "the exact representation of His essence" (v. 3 above).

Three simple terms transcribed by the apostle John picture these glorious aspects of God the Son. Each is a majestic crown that illustrates the fullness of His deity. Thus, Christ communicates God's mind and will as "the Word of God," He demonstrates God's essence as the great "I AM," and He radiates God's glory as "the Alpha and Omega." This section presents Christ in these portrayals of His deity.

I. Christ is "the Word of God."

   A. The Word is God eternal.

      JN 1:1 In the beginning was the Word, and the Word was with God, and the Word was God.
      ²The same was in the beginning with God.

   B. The Word is God the Creator.

      ³All things were made by him; and without him was not any thing made that was made.

John's Gospel begins with a clear affirmation of the deity of Jesus Christ — "the Word was God." As The Word, Christ is the full expression of the nature, heart, mind, and will of God. One of the means by which He proclaims God's nature to mankind is through creation. The physical worlds reveal "the invisible things" of God, "even his eternal power and Godhead," so that these "are clearly seen, being understood by [through] the things that are made, so that they [all people] are without excuse" (Rom. 1:20).

   C. The Word is God the Light.

      ⁴In him was life; and the life was the light of men.
      ⁵And the light shineth in darkness; and the darkness comprehended [overcame] it not. . . .
      ⁹That was the true Light, which lighteth every man that cometh into the world.

A second (and the principal) way the Word speaks to mankind is as the Light who reveals the nature of spiritual life and proclaims its availability to those in darkness (see Sec. II on p. 99). The living Word of God and the written Word of God (which presents Him throughout) declare that this life is available only through Christ, the true Light.

A third means by which the Word communicates to people is through man's inherent moral nature and general spiritual awareness. Christ implants this inner light within "every man that cometh into the world" (v. 9). With each of His means of communication, those who respond to their initial light will be given more light. When they fully receive the Word, He gives them true life (v. 4) — eternal spiritual life with God.

   D. The Word is God incarnate.

      ¹⁴And the Word was made flesh, and dwelt among us, (and we beheld his glory, the glory as of the only begotten of the Father,) full of grace and truth.

¹⁵John [the Baptist] bare witness of him, and cried, saying, This was he of whom I spake, He that cometh after me is preferred before me: for he was before me.

That "the Word was made flesh, and dwelt among us" is one of the greatest and most incomprehensible messages of all time. Through His incarnation, perfect life, and atoning death, Christ became God's ultimate communication of Himself to mankind. "The Word . . . was full of grace and truth" (v. 14). Christ demonstrated and extended God's grace (unmerited favor) to all people everywhere in every aspect of His ministry. He also proclaimed, pictured, and fulfilled God's truth as the full reality of that which had previously been foretold through fragmentary prophecies, types, and figures throughout the Old Testament.

E. The Word is God revealed.
¹⁷For the law was given by Moses, but grace and truth came by Jesus Christ.
¹⁸No man hath seen God at any time; the only begotten Son, which is in the bosom of the Father, he hath declared him.

Christ "declared the Father" to mankind through descriptions of His nature, exemplification of His character, and demonstration of His power. As He told Philip, "He that hath seen me hath seen the Father" (JN 14:9); "for in Him [Christ] dwelleth all the fullness of the Godhead bodily" (Col. 2:9).

F. The Word is God rejected.
¹⁰He was in the world, and the world was made by him, and the world knew him not.
¹¹He came unto his own [creation], and his own [people] received him not.

G. The Word is God received.
¹²But as many as received him, to them gave he power [the right] to become the sons of God, even to them that believe on his name:
¹³Which were born, not of blood, nor of the will of the flesh, nor of the will of man, but of God.

Our response to the Word is our response to God. We can either reject Him or receive Him. We receive Him by believing "on His name," i.e., by trusting in (entrusting ourselves to) Jesus Christ as our personal Savior and Lord. (See Sec. I.C on p. 81.)

H. The Word is God the coming King.
REV 19:11 And I saw heaven opened, and behold a white horse; and he that sat upon him was called Faithful and True, and in righteousness he doth judge and make war.

> [12]His eyes were as a flame of fire, and on his head were many crowns; and he had a name written, that no man knew, but he himself. [13]And he was clothed with a vesture dipped in blood: and his name is called The Word of God. . . .
> [16]And he hath on his vesture and on his thigh a name written, KING OF KINGS, AND LORD OF LORDS.

In His first advent, the Word came humbly and obscurely in Bethlehem's manger. He will come again, however, in infinite power and majesty to reign over the entire earth. Although the Word is "the same yesterday, today, and forever" (Heb. 13:8), He reveals God in different ways in different eras. In this age, He is the Word of God (i.e., from and about God) to all mankind — for salvation to unbelievers, and for sanctification to believers. He is also every believer's Word to God, as their High Priest and Advocate with the Father (Heb. 7:25). When He returns as King of kings and Lord of lords, everyone will know and confess that the Word is God and the rightful ruler of heaven and earth.

II. Christ is the great "I AM."

When God called Moses to lead His people out of Egypt, Moses asked, "When I come unto the children of Israel, and shall say unto them, The God of your fathers hath sent me unto you; and they shall say to me, What is his name? what shall I say unto them? And God said unto Moses, I AM THAT I AM: and he said, Thus shalt thou say unto the children of Israel, I AM hath sent me unto you" (Ex. 3:13-14).

"I AM" depicts God's eternal being — without beginning or end — as well as His unchanging character and attributes. It also signifies His self-sufficiency as the eternally self-existent One. When Jesus identified Himself as "I AM" in the following passages, He was claiming no less than that He was the God who delivered His people from Egypt and protected them throughout their history to that very day. ("I AM" is printed here in capital letters as in Ex. 3:14. Also, the "he" that generally follows "I am" in the KJV was supplied by translators and is omitted in this section.)

A. Most did not believe that Jesus is I AM.

> JN 8:23 And he said unto them, Ye are from beneath; I am from above: ye are of this world; I am not of this world.
> [24]I said therefore unto you, that ye shall die in your sins: for if ye believe not that I AM, ye shall die in your sins.
> [25]Then said they unto him, Who art thou? And Jesus saith unto them, Even the same that I said unto you from the beginning.

B. His death and resurrection would prove He is I AM.

²⁶I have many things to say and to judge of you: but he that sent me is true; and I speak to the world those things which I have heard of him.

²⁷They understood not that he spake to them of the Father.

²⁸Then said Jesus unto them, When ye have lifted up the Son of man, then shall ye know that I AM, and that I do nothing of myself; but as my Father hath taught me, I speak these things.

C. They tried to kill Him for claiming to be I AM.

⁵⁶Your father Abraham rejoiced to see my day: and he saw it, and was glad.

⁵⁷Then said the Jews unto him, Thou art not yet fifty years old, and hast thou seen Abraham?

⁵⁸Jesus said unto them, Verily, verily, I say unto you, Before Abraham was, I AM.

⁵⁹Then took they up stones to cast at him: but Jesus hid himself, and went out of the temple, going through the midst of them, and so passed by.

In JN 8, Christ progressively revealed and emphasized that He was the I AM who spoke to Moses and Abraham. The Jews' initial puzzlement at His claim soon turned to outrage, and they tried to kill Him for blasphemy.

Early Old Testament believers, such as Abraham, appear to have had a greater knowledge and understanding of God's person and His program for the ages than is stated in the Old Testament. This seems particularly so regarding the future glorification and reign of Jesus Christ. Verse 56 above is one example. Also, Job, who lived at about the time of Abraham, stated, "I know that my redeemer liveth, and that he shall stand at the latter day upon the earth" (Job 19:25). The writer of Hebrews states of these early believers: "These all died in faith, not having received the promises, but having seen them afar off, and were persuaded of them, and embraced them" (11:13).

D. His disciples would believe He is I AM.

JN 13:18b. I know whom I have chosen: but that the scripture may be fulfilled, He that eateth bread with me hath lifted up his heel against me.

¹⁹Now I tell you before it come, that, when it is come to pass, ye may believe that I AM.

Just before His crucifixion, Christ declared that David's prophetic statement in Psalm 41:9 ("Yea, mine own familiar friend, in whom I trusted, which did eat of my bread, hath lifted up his heel against me") was about to be fulfilled. He also declared that by His announcing its fulfillment in advance, His disciples would believe that He is I AM when it came to pass.

David's prophecy was fulfilled by Judas' seeming close friendship with Christ as His disciple and his sharing many meals with Christ during His ministry. It was pointedly fulfilled when Judas received the morsel of bread ("sop") from Christ at the Last Supper (JN 13:26). When the disciples understood these things after His Passion, they knew assuredly that He was and is I AM.

E. He showed His captors that He is I AM.
 1. His powerful name toppled them.
JN 18:3 Judas then, having received a band of men and officers from the chief priests and Pharisees, cometh thither with lanterns and torches and weapons.
 ⁴Jesus therefore, knowing all things that should come upon him, went forth, and said unto them, Whom seek ye?
 ⁵They answered him, Jesus of Nazareth. Jesus saith unto them, I AM. And Judas also, which betrayed him, stood with them.
 ⁶As soon then as he had said unto them, I AM, they went backward, and fell to the ground.

 2. His mercy did not dissuade them.
 ⁷Then asked he them again, Whom seek ye? And they said, Jesus of Nazareth.
 ⁸Jesus answered, I have told you that I AM: if therefore ye seek me, let these go their way: . . .
 ¹⁰Then Simon Peter having a sword drew it, and smote the high priest's servant, and cut off his right ear. {And Jesus answered and said, Suffer ye thus far. And he touched his ear, and healed him [LK 22:51]}. . . .
 ¹²Then the band and the captain and officers of the Jews took Jesus, and bound him,
 ¹³And led him away . . .

Christ's last use of "I AM" portrayed both His infinite power and His boundless mercy. The power inherent in the name alone struck His would-be captors to the ground. In mercy, however, He spared their lives and asked again, "Whom seek ye?" Again, He declared, "I AM," giving them another opportunity to repent and believe in Him. They persisted, however, in their evil plan. When Peter wielded his sword, Christ demonstrated His complete control of the situation by healing the servant's ear. Instead of using His power as I AM against His enemies, He used it to manifest God's merciful and patient love and grace. And He willingly went to the cross.

III. Christ is "the Alpha and Omega."

Alpha and omega are the first and last letters of the Greek alphabet. In combination, they picture the full range or entire content of a matter, much as we would say "from A to Z." Christ portrayed Himself as the Alpha and Omega in a unique revelation to the Apostle John about 65 years after His ascension. This picture of the glorified Christ is included here because it was painted by the same Master, in the same style, and with the same human hand as His other "I am" self-portraits in John's Gospel.

A. The Alpha and Omega is the Lord Almighty.
> **REV 1:7 Behold, he cometh with clouds; and every eye shall see him, and they also which pierced him: and all kindreds of the earth shall wail because of him. Even so, Amen.**
> **⁸I am Alpha and Omega, the beginning and the ending, saith the Lord, which is, and which was, and which is to come, the Almighty.**

"Alpha and Omega" depicts Christ's infinite person and eternal being. He now is, always was, and is still coming (v. 8). This accords with Isaiah's identification of Christ as "the Everlasting Father," or literally "the Father of Eternities" (9:6). The term also portrays the completeness and perfection of all of His attributes as Almighty God.

B. The Alpha and Omega is the Lord of salvation.
> **REV 21:6 And he said unto me, It is done. I am Alpha and Omega, the beginning and the end. I will give unto him that is athirst of the fountain of the water of life freely.**
> **⁷He that overcometh shall inherit all things; and I will be his God, and he shall be my son.**

"Alpha and Omega, the beginning and the end" also pictures Christ's perfect and complete work of salvation. He is both "the author [the beginning] and finisher [the completer] of our faith" (Heb. 12:2). As the God/Man, "Alpha and Omega" portrays His perfect, sinless life and His full atonement for mankind's sin. It assures the full sufficiency of His gift of the water of life (v. 6) and the perfection of the heavenly inheritance (v. 7) that He as God is preparing for His children.

C. The Alpha and Omega is the Lord of His Church.
> **REV 1:10 I [John] was in the Spirit on the Lord's day, and heard behind me a great voice, as of a trumpet,**
> **¹¹Saying, I am Alpha and Omega, the first and the last: and, What thou seest, write in a book, and send it unto the seven churches which are in Asia;**

"Alpha and Omega, the first and the last" also portrays Christ's preeminent position and authority in His Church. He is "the head of the body, the church; who is the beginning, the first-born from the dead, that in all things he might have the preeminence" (Col. 1:18).

> D. The Alpha and Omega is the Lord of life and death.
> **REV 1:17 And when I saw him [in His glory], I fell at his feet as dead. And he laid his right hand upon me, saying unto me, Fear not; I am the first and the last:**
> **[18] I am he that liveth, and was dead; and, behold, I am alive for evermore, Amen; and have the keys of hell and of death.**

Here, "the first and the last" depicts Christ in His present heavenly majesty as the sovereign Lord over life and death. As the final Judge of all mankind, He holds the keys to both heaven and hell. He alone will determine and declare every person's eternal destiny. By applying "Alpha and Omega, the first and the last" to Himself (in 1:11 and 1:17), Christ further identified Himself as the Jehovah of the Old Testament. "Thus saith the Lord [Jehovah] the King of Israel, and his redeemer the Lord of hosts; I am the first, and I am the last; and beside me there is no God" (Isa. 44:6).

> E. The Alpha and Omega is the Lord of His servants.
> **REV 22:12 And, behold, I come quickly; and my reward is with me, to give every man according as his work shall be.**
> **[13] I am Alpha and Omega, the beginning and the end, the first and the last. . . .**
> **[20] He which testifieth these things saith, Surely I come quickly. Amen. Even so, come, Lord Jesus.**

The Alpha and Omega will "come quickly" and reward each of His servants according to "his work." Their rewards will be based on their faithfulness and their use of their resources for God's glory. (See "Christ's Stewards" on p. 254.) His servants' greatest reward, however, will be to dwell with Him in God's glorious presence for all eternity. Anticipating these things, we earnestly pray with John, "Even so, come, Lord Jesus."

Silhouettes of the Holy Spirit

As with "Father," the name "Holy Spirit" takes on particular meaning beginning with the Gospels. There are many references in the Old Testament to "the Spirit of God," "the Spirit of the Lord," "my Spirit," etc., but it is not clear that Old Testament believers understood that the Holy Spirit is an individual person distinct from the Father and the Son. The Holy Spirit is clearly identified, however, as a distinct being in the angelic announcements to Mary that "the

Holy Ghost shall come upon thee," and to Joseph that "that which is conceived in her is of the Holy Ghost."

Christ variously pictured the Holy Spirit through similes and metaphors, such as invisible wind and living water. These pictures puzzled His hearers, in large part because "the Holy Ghost was not yet given; because Jesus was not yet glorified [i.e., crucified, risen, and ascended]" (JN 9:39). On the eve of His crucifixion, however, Christ portrayed the Holy Spirit much more clearly to His disciples. He promised that "the Spirit of Truth" would be their comforter, teacher, guide, and much more. These promises were fulfilled in Acts and the epistles, and they continue to be fulfilled in the lives of true believers today.

I. Likenesses of the Holy Spirit.

A. Like a dove at Jesus' baptism.

MT 3:16 [LK 3:21] And Jesus, when he was baptized, went up straightway out of the water: and, lo, the heavens were opened unto him, and he saw the Spirit of God descending {in a bodily shape} like a dove, and lighting upon him:

¹⁷And lo a voice from heaven, saying, This is my beloved Son, in whom I am well pleased.

JN 1:32 And John [the Baptist] bare record, saying, I saw the Spirit descending from heaven like a dove, and it abode upon him.

³³And I knew him not: but he that sent me to baptize with water, the same said unto me, Upon whom thou shalt see the Spirit descending, and remaining on him, the same is he which baptizeth with the Holy Ghost.

This is the public introduction of both Jesus the Messiah and the Holy Spirit who anointed Him for His earthly ministry. *Messiah* and *Christ* both mean "the anointed One." It was the Holy Spirit's visible anointing of Jesus "in a bodily shape like a dove" that signaled to John the Baptist that Jesus was the Messiah. Although Christ's divine nature was perfect and complete, His human nature and physical body received the enabling power of the Holy Spirit for the work the Father had given Him (see Sec. II on p. 171). The Holy Spirit's anointing of Jesus, therefore, both commissioned Him for service and empowered Him to fulfill it.

B. Like a mother giving birth.

JN 3:3 Jesus answered and said unto him, Verily, verily, I say unto thee, Except a man be born again, he cannot see the kingdom of God.

⁴Nicodemus saith unto him, How can a man be born when he is old? can he enter the second time into his mother's womb, and be born?

⁵Jesus answered, Verily, verily, I say unto thee, Except a man be born of water and of the Spirit, he cannot enter into the kingdom of God.

⁶That which is born of the flesh is flesh; and that which is born of the Spirit is spirit.

⁷Marvel not that I said unto thee, Ye must be born again.

C. Like a blowing unseen wind.

⁸The wind bloweth where it listeth, and thou hearest the sound thereof, but canst not tell whence it cometh, and whither it goeth: so is every one that is born of the Spirit.

Christ combined these two pictures to illustrate that (1) a complete change in our spiritual nature is required before we can have any hope of heaven; (2) we must be "born again" spiritually through an act of the Holy Spirit, which (as physical birth) is a specific and distinct event; (3) the Holy Spirit's activity in regeneration is as free from human control as the wind; and (4) there will be clear evidence of the new birth, as there is evidence of the wind's presence and power, though neither of these energizing sources is visible.

D. Like rivers of living water.

JN 7:37 In the last day, that great day of the feast, Jesus stood and cried, saying, If any man thirst, let him come unto me, and drink.

³⁸He that believeth on me, as the scripture hath said, out of his belly [innermost being] shall flow rivers of living water.

³⁹(But this spake he of the Spirit, which they that believe on him should receive: for the Holy Ghost was not yet given; because that Jesus was not yet glorified.)

JN 4:10 Jesus answered and said unto her [the woman at the well], If thou knewest the gift of God, and who it is that saith to thee, Give me to drink; thou wouldest have asked of him, and he would have given thee living water. . . .

¹³Jesus answered and said unto her, Whosoever drinketh of this water [from a well] shall thirst again:

¹⁴But whosoever drinketh of the water that I shall give him shall never thirst; but the water that I shall give him shall be in him a well of water springing up into everlasting life.

The Holy Spirit is so involved in and identified with each person's salvation that Christ used the same picture of living water to illustrate both the Spirit and everlasting life. Man cannot live physically without water, and man cannot live spiritually without the living water of the Holy Spirit. Everyone is invited to "drink" of Christ through the Holy Spirit (v. 37), and whoever drinks will never thirst again (v. 14). The Holy Spirit continually supplies each desirous partaker with an abundance of the fresh, living water of everlasting life.

E. Like a breath from God.

> **JN 20:21. Then said Jesus to them [His disciples] again, Peace be unto you: as my Father hath sent me, even so send I you.**
> **²²And when he had said this, he breathed on them, and saith unto them, Receive ye the Holy Ghost:**
> **²³Whose soever sins ye remit, they are remitted unto them; and whose soever sins ye retain, they are retained.**

The principal Hebrew and Greek words for "spirit" in the Bible also mean breath or wind. The *Holy* Spirit is "the Breath of God." For example, Elihu told Job, "The Spirit of God hath made me, and the breath of the Almighty hath given me life" (33:4). The day Christ arose, He "breathed" the Holy Spirit upon His disciples (the eleven plus others who were present) in preparation for their future service. He later told them to wait in Jerusalem "until ye be endued with power from on high" (LK 24:49). His breathing the Spirit on them appears to have been an interim bequest to sustain them spiritually until Pentecost and to enable them to receive His teaching during the days before His ascension. When their full anointing came (50 days later), they powerfully proclaimed the gospel — offering the remission of sins to those who believe it, and declaring the retention of sins by those who reject it (v. 23).

II. Comparisons with the Holy Spirit.

A. Compared with baptism with water.

> **ACTS 1:4 And, being assembled together with them, [Christ] commanded them that they should not depart from Jerusalem, but wait for the promise of the Father, which, saith he, ye have heard of me.**
> **⁵For John truly baptized with water; but ye shall be baptized with the Holy Ghost not many days hence.**

John's baptizing of his followers with water was to demonstrate their repentance for sin in preparation for the coming Messiah. Christ's promised baptizing of His followers with the Holy Spirit would envelop and fill their souls with the Spirit's permanent indwelling presence and divine nature. Since Pentecost, this baptism "with the Holy Ghost" occurs within every believer at the moment of his salvation.

B. Compared with baptism with fire.

> **MT 3:11 I [John the Baptist] indeed baptize you with water unto repentance: but he that cometh after me [Christ] is mightier than I, whose shoes I am not worthy to bear: he shall baptize you with the Holy Ghost, and with fire:**

Christ's baptism of believers with the Holy Spirit is also compared with a "baptism with fire." One of the usages of *fire* in scripture is to picture spiritual purification. Every believer is purified positionally and eternally before God at salvation when he is baptized with the Holy Spirit. (When the Spirit first came upon believers at Pentecost, He came as "cloven tongues of fire," Acts 2:3.) Thereafter, the Holy Spirit continually works within each believer as a purifying fire to purge and refine his life and service for God.

C. Compared with a father's gift to his son.

LK 11:11 [MT 7:9-11] If a son shall ask bread of any of you that is a father, will he give him a stone? or if he ask a fish, will he for a fish give him a serpent?

¹²Or if he shall ask an egg, will he offer him a scorpion?

¹³If ye then, being evil, know how to give good gifts unto your children: how much more shall your heavenly Father give the Holy Spirit {give good things} to them that ask him?

Parents naturally want to give good things to their children. "How much more" the Heavenly Father wants to give good things to His children, which He does through His Holy Spirit. In response to their prayers and obedience to His Word, the Father regularly fills believers with the Holy Spirit. Many "good things" from God accompany the Spirit's working in their lives.

This recurrent filling by the Holy Spirit differs from the once-for-all baptism with the Holy Spirit that occurs at salvation. Whereas baptism with the Spirit is conditioned solely upon saving faith in Christ, filling by the Spirit is conditioned largely upon faithful obedience to God and willing submission to His Spirit's leading. The Spirit's filling *begins* at salvation, but should occur continually throughout a believer's life (Eph. 5:18).

III. Parables regarding the Holy Spirit.

A. Pharisees ascribed Christ's power to Satan.

MT 12:22 [MK 3:22; LK 11:14] Then was brought unto him one possessed with a devil, blind, and dumb: and he healed him, insomuch that the blind and dumb both spake and saw.

²³And all the people were amazed, and said, Is not this the son of David?

²⁴But when the Pharisees heard it, they said, This fellow doth not cast out devils, but by Beelzebub the prince of the devils.

B. But "a divided house cannot stand."

²⁵And Jesus knew their thoughts, and said unto them {in parables, How can Satan cast out Satan?} Every kingdom divided against itself is brought to desolation; and every city or house divided against itself shall not stand:

[26]And if Satan cast out Satan, he is divided against himself; how shall then his kingdom stand?

C. The Holy Spirit gave Christ His power.

[27]And if I by Beelzebub cast out devils, by whom do your children cast them out? therefore they shall be your judges.

[28][LK 11:20] But if I cast out devils by the Spirit of God {with the finger of God}, then {no doubt} the kingdom of God is come unto you.

The Pharisees could not deny Christ's miracles; instead they misconstrued and misrepresented the *source* of His miraculous power. They claimed that Satan, not God, enabled Him to cast out demons. Christ refuted their blasphemy by citing (1) the illogical nature of their assertion that Satan would cast out himself; (2) common knowledge that a divided house or kingdom cannot remain strong; and (3) their claims that their own "children" (i.e., their followers) could cast out demons with power they certainly would not ascribe to Satan. Christ carried His argument to its logical conclusion: "If I cast out demons by the Spirit of God, then the kingdom of God is come to you" (v. 28) — and I truly am the Messiah and King.

In combination, MT 12:28 and LK 11:20 picture the Holy Spirit as "the finger of God." Christ's amazing healing of the blind and dumb man (in MT 12:22) required no more from God than a mere "lifting of His finger" in demonstration of the Holy Spirit's infinite power.

D. Through the Spirit, Christ "bound the strong man."

[29]Or else [i.e., without the Holy Spirit's power] how can one enter into a strong man's house, and spoil his goods, except he first bind the strong man? {But when a stronger than he shall come upon him and overcome him, he taketh away from him all his armor wherein he trusted,} And then he will spoil his house.

This parable affirms that the Holy Spirit was the source of Christ's miraculous power. Thus, He could "bind the strong man" (Satan) in his own house (his earthly realm), remove his armor (demonic power), and take away his spoils (the demon-possessed people that Christ freed). (See "The strong man" on p. 367.)

E. Calling the Spirit a demon is unforgivable blasphemy.

MT 12:30 He that is not with me is against me; and he that gathereth not with me scattereth abroad.

[31]Wherefore I say unto you, All manner of sin and blasphemy shall be forgiven unto men: but the blasphemy against the Holy Ghost shall not be forgiven unto men.

[32]**And whosoever speaketh a word against the Son of man, it shall be forgiven him: but whosoever speaketh against the Holy Ghost, it shall not be forgiven him, neither in this world, neither in the world to come.**

MK 3:30 Because they said, He [Jesus] hath an unclean spirit.

The Holy Spirit is God's principal agent for convicting unbelievers of their sin and need for salvation. When an unbeliever, having learned sufficiently of Christ's sacrifice for his sin, deliberately and defiantly rejects salvation and attributes the Spirit's working to a demon (as in MK 3:30), he "blasphemes against the Holy Spirit."

At some point, the scoffer effectively removes himself from the Holy Spirit's convicting work and forfeits further opportunity to repent and be saved. Others, and perhaps the blasphemer himself, are unable to ascertain when that point has been passed. God alone decides when His Spirit no longer will "strive" with a sinner (Gen. 6:3). All other sin or blasphemy, no matter how wicked or offensive to God, will be fully forgiven when the sinner repents and receives salvation (MT 12:31).

IV. Previews of the Holy Spirit

The night before His crucifixion, Christ gave His disciples His clearest and most detailed portrayals of the coming Holy Spirit. At that point, they were distraught that He said He was leaving and that they would deny Him. Christ assured them, however, that it was to their *benefit* that He leave and send the Holy Spirit in His place. To that end, He gave them these pictures of the Holy Spirit's relation to and working in each believer until He comes again (from JN 14-16).

A. He is the believer's Comforter and Helper.

JN 14:16 And I will pray the Father, and he shall give you another Comforter [Companion and Helper], that he may abide with you for ever;
[17]**Even the Spirit of truth; whom the world cannot receive, because it seeth him not, neither knoweth him: but ye know him; for he dwelleth with you, and shall be in you.**

JN 16:7 Nevertheless I tell you the truth; It is expedient [advantageous] for you that I go away: for if I go not away, the Comforter will not come unto you; but if I depart, I will send him unto you.

Christ promised His disciples "another Comforter" (lit. another helper of the same kind as He) who would never leave them. The word *Comforter* (Paraclete) means "one called alongside to help." Christ would be their Paraclete (translated "Advocate") with their Father in heaven (I JN 2:1); and the Holy

Spirit would be their Paraclete on earth. The Spirit would help them in a host of ways, as summarized below.

In the context of "Let not your heart be troubled" in JN 14:1, Christ focused here on the help and comfort the Holy Spirit would give His disciples while He was gone. More than dwelling *with* them as Christ had, the Holy Spirit would dwell *in* them (v. 17), and would do so *forever* (v. 16). How much better to have the indwelling Holy Spirit than even the physical presence of Christ Himself but without His indwelling Spirit.

> B. He is the believer's Foster Parent and Guardian.
>
> **JN 14:18 I will not leave you comfortless [lit. "orphans"]: I will come to you.**
>
> **19Yet a little while, and the world seeth me no more; but ye see me: because I live, ye shall live also.**

Christ would not leave His disciples as helpless orphans but would "come to them" in the person of His Holy Spirit (v. 18). The Spirit would serve as their spiritual foster parent while they are on earth. Verse 19b may be understood: "but you will see me through my representative, the Holy Spirit: because I live, you too shall live (through the regenerating and enabling power of the Holy Spirit)."

> C. He is the believer's Teacher and Guide.
>
> **JN 14:25 These things have I spoken unto you, being yet present with you.**
>
> **26But the Comforter, which is the Holy Ghost, whom the Father will send in my name, he shall teach you all things, and bring all things to your remembrance, whatsoever I have said unto you.**
>
> **JN 16:12 I have yet many things to say unto you, but ye cannot bear them now.**
>
> **13Howbeit when he, the Spirit of truth, is come, he will guide you into all truth: for he shall not speak of himself; but whatsoever he shall hear, that shall he speak: and he will show you things to come.**
>
> **14He shall glorify me: for he shall receive of mine [i.e., that which pertains to me], and shall show it unto you.**
>
> **15All things that the Father hath are mine: therefore said I, that he shall take of mine, and shall show it unto you.**

A key way in which the Holy Spirit comforts and helps believers is by aiding them in understanding "all truth" (16:13) and "all things" (14:26). When they respond with a willing and obedient spirit, He builds their faith, transforms their lives, blesses them spiritually (in spite of circumstances), and strengthens and equips them for God's service.

D. He is Christ's Witness to and through believers.

JN 15:26 But when the Comforter is come, whom I will send unto you from the Father, even the Spirit of truth, which proceedeth from the Father, he shall testify of me:

²⁷And ye also shall bear witness, because ye have been with me from the beginning.

ACTS 1:8 But ye shall receive power, after that the Holy Ghost is come upon you: and ye shall be witnesses unto me both in Jerusalem, and in all Judaea, and in Samaria, and unto the uttermost part of the earth.

The Holy Spirit's principal function in this age is to witness for Christ (15:26) and glorify Him (16:14 in Sec. C), both in the lives of believers and before unbelievers. He testifies who Christ is, why He came, what He offers, and how to receive Him. In part, the Holy Spirit does this witnessing to both of these groups through other believers (15:27).

E. He is the Reprover of those who need salvation.

JN 16:8 And when he [the Holy Spirit] is come, he will reprove [convict] the world of sin, and of righteousness, and of judgment:

⁹Of sin, because they believe not on me;

¹⁰Of righteousness, because I go to my Father, and ye see me no more;

¹¹Of judgment, because the prince of this world [Satan] is judged.

The Holy Spirit reproves and convicts unbelievers of their sin (16:9) by exposing their guilt under God's righteous requirements and by proving they deserve eternal condemnation. Some, He also convicts in the sense of *convince* and leads to repentance and salvation. He convinces these of Christ's perfect righteousness (v. 10) and encourages them to receive that righteousness through faith in Him. He shows them that Satan (and all his subjects) have already been judged and found guilty (v. 11). He invites these to receive Christ and escape their deserved judgment because Christ has already borne it for them.

Works of the Holy Spirit

The Holy Spirit's distinctive work in the New Testament did not wait for Pentecost. Although Christ promised to send His disciples "another Comforter" soon after His departure, the Holy Spirit already was active before and throughout Christ's life on earth. His principal work then was similar to His principal work now: namely, preparing people and circumstances to bring honor and glory to Jesus Christ. He was always in the background, seldom noticed by those present, but constantly working to effect God's plan. Most of

His activity in the Gospels was filling and guiding God's people, including (as shown below) Jesus Christ Himself.

I. The Spirit's role in Christ's birth.

A. He came upon and overshadowed Mary.

> LK 1:30 And the angel said unto her, Fear not, Mary: for thou hast found favor with God.
>
> [31]And, behold, thou shalt conceive in thy womb, and bring forth a son, and shalt call his name JESUS. . . .
>
> [34]Then said Mary unto the angel, How shall this be, seeing I know not a man?
>
> [35]And the angel answered and said unto her, The Holy Ghost shall come upon thee, and the power of the Highest shall overshadow thee: therefore also that holy thing which shall be born of thee shall be called the Son of God.

B. He brought about Christ's conception.

> MT 1:18 Now the birth of Jesus Christ was on this wise: When as his mother Mary was espoused to Joseph, before they came together, she was found with child of the Holy Ghost. . . .
>
> [20]But while he [Joseph] thought on these things, behold, the angel of the Lord appeared unto him in a dream, saying, Joseph, thou son of David, fear not to take unto thee Mary thy wife: for that which is conceived in her is of the Holy Ghost.

In a creative miracle never duplicated before or since, the Holy Spirit caused Christ's conception in the virgin Mary. He "came upon" and "overshadowed" her to produce "that holy thing . . . called the Son of God" within her. His overshadowing of Mary, although physically incomprehensible, may be somewhat similar to His activity in Genesis 1:2, where He "moved upon [hovered over] the face of the waters," with the same creative power.

II. The Spirit's announcements of the coming Messiah.

A. Through Elisabeth.

> LK 1:41 And it came to pass, that, when Elisabeth heard the salutation of Mary, the babe [John the Baptist] leaped in her womb; and Elisabeth was filled with the Holy Ghost:
>
> [42]And she spake out with a loud voice, and said, Blessed art thou among women, and blessed is the fruit of thy womb.
>
> [43]And whence is this to me, that the mother of my Lord should come to me?
>
> [44]For, lo, as soon as the voice of thy salutation sounded in mine ears, the babe leaped in my womb for joy.

⁴⁵And blessed is she that believed: for there shall be a perform- ance of those things which were told her from the Lord.

Inspired by the Holy Spirit, John the Baptist's parents each prophesied (at different times) regarding the Messiah in the months before Christ's birth. The Spirit declared through Elisabeth that Mary's son would be her Lord (v. 43), thereby proclaiming His deity and divine authority. He also confirmed through Elisabeth that the promises the angel made to Mary regarding her Son would all be fulfilled (v. 45).

B. Through Zacharias.

LK 1:67 And his [John's] father Zacharias was filled with the Holy Ghost, and prophesied, saying,

⁶⁸Blessed be the Lord God of Israel; for he hath visited and redeemed his people,

⁶⁹And hath raised up an horn of salvation for us in the house of his servant David; . . .

⁷⁶And thou, child [John], shalt be called the prophet of the Highest: for thou shalt go before the face of the Lord to prepare his ways;

⁷⁷To give knowledge of salvation unto his people by the remission of their sins,

Through Zacharias, the Holy Spirit emphasized the redemption and salvation the Messiah would bring God's people. He also foretold the nature of the ministry John would have in preparing the people by heralding the Messiah's coming. (See also Sec. I.C on p. 31, and Sec. I.A on p. 98.)

C. Through Mary.

LK 1:46 And Mary said, My soul doth magnify the Lord,

⁴⁷And my spirit hath rejoiced in God my Saviour.

⁴⁸For he hath regarded the low estate of his handmaiden: for, behold, from henceforth all generations shall call me blessed.

⁴⁹For he that is mighty hath done to me great things; and holy is his name. . . .

⁵⁴He hath helped his servant Israel, in remembrance of his mercy;

⁵⁵As he spake to our fathers, to Abraham, and to his seed for ever.

Mary's "Magnificat" (from the Latin for "magnify" in v. 46) clearly was inspired by the Holy Spirit, as were Elisabeth's declarations that preceded it. Through Mary, the Spirit revealed that, just as God had helped Israel in the past, He now was further fulfilling His promise of mercy to Abraham and his descendants. Through the coming Messiah, God would extend them His mercy forever (v. 55).

C. Through Simeon.

LK 2:25 And, behold, there was a man in Jerusalem, whose name was Simeon; and the same man was just and devout, waiting for the consolation of Israel: and the Holy Ghost was upon him.

²⁶And it was revealed unto him by the Holy Ghost, that he should not see death, before he had seen the Lord's Christ.

²⁷And he came by the Spirit into the temple: and when the parents brought in the child Jesus, to do for him after the custom of the law,

²⁸Then took he him up in his arms, and blessed God, and said,

²⁹Lord, now lettest thou thy servant depart in peace, according to thy word:

³⁰For mine eyes have seen thy salvation,

³¹Which thou hast prepared before the face of all people;

³²A light to lighten the Gentiles, and the glory of thy people Israel.

The Holy Spirit (1) promised Simeon that he would live to see the Messiah; (2) led him to the temple to meet Jesus; and (3) prophesied through him regarding Christ's salvation of both Jews and Gentiles. (See Sec. III on p. 14 for the full passage.)

III. The Spirit's involvement in Christ's ministry.

A. He anointed Christ at His baptism.

LK 3:21 Now when all the people were baptized, it came to pass, that Jesus also being baptized, and praying, the heaven was opened,

²²And the Holy Ghost descended in a bodily shape like a dove upon him, and a voice came from heaven, which said, Thou art my beloved Son; in thee I am well pleased.

Christ was baptized just prior to beginning His public ministry. At that time, the Holy Spirit "descended upon Him" and anointed Him as the Messiah. This anointing included (1) appointing Him to the task of the Messiah's ministry; (2) enabling Him to perform that ministry; and (3) presenting Him as the Messiah to those who were present.

B. He strengthened Christ for Satan's temptations.

LK 4:1 And Jesus being full of the Holy Ghost returned from Jordan, and was led by the Spirit into the wilderness,

²Being forty days tempted of the devil. And in those days he did eat nothing: and when they were ended, he afterward hungered.

Immediately after Christ's baptism (at which He was filled with the Holy Spirit, v. 1), the Spirit led Him into the wilderness. Mark 1:12 reports that the Spirit drove Him (impelled Him to go) into the wilderness, as by divine appointment. Thus prepared and led by the Spirit, Jesus endured the physical privation and, more importantly, overcame the spiritual temptations with which Satan enticed Him. (See Sec. II under on p. 360 for the full passage.)

C. He empowered Christ for His ministry.

LK 4:14 And Jesus returned in the power of the Spirit into Galilee: and there went out a fame of him through all the region round about. ¹⁵And he taught in their synagogues, being glorified of all. . . .

¹⁷And there was delivered unto him the book of the prophet Esaias. And when he had opened the book, he found the place where it was written,

¹⁸The Spirit of the Lord is upon me, because he hath anointed me to preach the gospel to the poor; he hath sent me to heal the brokenhearted, to preach deliverance to the captives, and recovering of sight to the blind, to set at liberty them that are bruised,

¹⁹To preach the acceptable year of the Lord.

JN 3:34 For he whom God hath sent [Christ] speaketh the words of God: for God giveth not the Spirit by [limited] measure unto him.

Verse 34b may be read: "For God gives the Spirit to Him [Christ] without limit." With the unlimited power of God's Holy Spirit, Christ widely proclaimed the gospel, performed miracles, and freed captives of sin (LK 4:18). Isaiah prophesied 700 years before the Messiah came that He would be filled with God's Spirit to accomplish these great works (Isa. 61:1-2).

D. He prepared Christ as the Savior for all mankind.

MT 12:16 And [Jesus] charged them that they should not make him known:

¹⁷That it might be fulfilled which was spoken by Esaias the prophet, saying,

¹⁸Behold my servant, whom I have chosen; my beloved, in whom my soul is well pleased: I will put my Spirit upon him, and he shall show judgment [proclaim justice] to the Gentiles. . . .

²¹And in his name shall the Gentiles trust.

The Jewish leaders resolutely rejected Christ as their Messiah (see the preceding verses in MT 11:20-12:15). In this context, Matthew cited Isaiah's prophecy (Isa. 42:1-4) that Christ, filled and led by the Holy Spirit, would become the Savior of the Gentiles, and not only of believing Jews. The Holy Spirit was preparing the way, in, through, and around Christ, for Christ to be the Savior for all mankind.

E. He equipped the disciples through Christ's teaching.

ACTS 1:1 The former treatise [Luke's Gospel] have I made, O Theophilus, of all that Jesus began both to do and teach,

²Until the day in which he was taken up, after that he through the Holy Ghost had given commandments unto the apostles whom he had chosen:

³To whom also he showed himself alive after his passion by many infallible proofs, being seen of them forty days, and speaking of the things pertaining to the kingdom of God:

Christ's final preparation of His disciples during the 40 days prior to His ascension was accomplished "through the Holy Spirit" (v. 2). The Spirit's principal work — before, during, and since Christ's life on earth — has been to glorify Christ for the glory of God. With Christ's departure at hand, the Holy Spirit soon would work directly in and through Christ's disciples to glorify Christ in their lives and spread the gospel throughout the earth.

17

Pictures of the Powers of Darkness

At the dawn of time, God created a host of angelic beings to serve and honor Him. One of the chief and most glorious angels was named Lucifer, which means "day star," or literally "light bearer." God said to him: "Thou sealest up the sum, full of wisdom, and perfect in beauty . . . Thou wast perfect in thy ways from the day that thou wast created, till iniquity was found in thee . . . Thine heart was lifted up because of thy beauty, thou hast corrupted thy wisdom by reason of thy brightness: I will cast thee to the ground" (Ezek. 28:12-17).

Lucifer's sin of pride and self-exaltation is detailed further in Isaiah 14: "How art thou fallen from heaven, O Lucifer, son of the morning! how art thou cut down to the ground, which didst weaken the nations! For thou hast said in thine heart, I will ascend into heaven, I will exalt my throne above the stars of God: I will sit also upon the mount of the congregation, in the sides of the north: I will ascend above the heights of the clouds; I will be like the most High. Yet thou shalt be brought down to hell, to the sides of the pit" (vv. 12-15). Note Lucifer's five "I will"s. He sought no less than to replace God and be sovereign over all creation. That remains his goal to this day.

Lucifer is identified and pictured by many other names in the Bible. The most common of these are "Satan" and "the devil." Others include: the great dragon, the serpent, the ruler of this world, the evil one, the tempter, the destroyer, and the god of this age. Christ defeated Satan at every turn during His first advent, and He will complete Satan's condemnation after His second advent. In the interim, He overcomes Satan and his allies in and through the lives of believers. This chapter illustrates how He (and we) can defeat the god of this age and the powers of darkness.

Tactics of the Adversary

God's great opponent is Satan, whose very name means "adversary." Forms of the word mean "to oppose" and "to lie in ambush." Satan opposes God and God's people with all of the substantial means at his disposal. He is a supernatural being but is not equal with God. He can overcome any and all people who face him in their own strength, but he is not omnipotent, omniscient, or omnipresent. Satan's powers and abilities are limited by God, who decreed his ultimate doom when he first rebelled against his Creator. Meanwhile, Satan works intelligently, insidiously, and incessantly to disrupt and destroy God's work and God's people on earth.

I. Satan opposes God and the truth.

A. He is the father of all who reject Christ.

JN 8:42 Jesus said unto them [hardened unbelievers], If God were your Father, ye would love me: for I proceeded forth and came from God; neither came I of myself, but he sent me.

⁴³Why do ye not understand my speech? even because ye cannot [are unable to] hear my word.

⁴⁴ᵃYe are of your father the devil,

B. He is the father of sin and death.

⁴⁴ᵇand the lusts of your father ye will [desire to] do. He was a murderer from the beginning,

C. He is the father of lies and deceit.

⁴⁴ᶜand [he] abode not in the truth, because there is no truth in him. When he speaketh a lie, he speaketh of his own [invention]: for he is a liar, and the father of it.

Christ bluntly told the religious Jews that their "father" was Satan, not God. Satan had a murderous nature "from the beginning" and resolutely determined to destroy mankind, which was created in God's image. He also has a deceitful nature and acts only in deceptive ways "because there is *no truth* in him." Satan used lies with Eve to "slay" mankind spiritually and to mold it into his image. He, therefore, is the father of all who believe and promote his destructive lies and who oppose God and His faithful representatives.

II. Satan opposed Christ's purposes and plans.

A. He tempted Christ with physical desires (the lust of the flesh).

MT 4:1 Then was Jesus led up of the spirit into the wilderness to be tempted of the devil.

²And when he had fasted forty days and forty nights, he was afterward an hungred [famished].
³And when the tempter came to him, he said, If thou be the Son of God, command that these stones be made bread.
⁴But he answered and said, It is written, Man shall not live by bread alone, but by every word that proceedeth out of the mouth of God.

Attacking at the moment and point of Christ's apparent weakness, Satan tempted Christ to satisfy His need the easy way. He sought to undermine the Son's trust in His Father's care and provision, and to persuade Christ to act in His own power and in His own interest. Christ rejected Satan's appeal by quoting from God's Word (Deut. 8:3). We have the same resource and should be prepared to use it as effectively.

Satan tempted Christ in the same three basic areas he tempted Eve and has tempted people ever since. I John 1:16 identifies these as "the lust of the flesh, and the lust of the eyes, and the pride of life." When Satan tempted Eve, "the woman saw that the tree was good for food [the lust of the flesh], and that it was pleasant to the eyes [the lust of the eyes], and a tree to be desired to make one wise [the pride of life], she took of the fruit thereof, and did eat" (Gen. 3:6).

B. He tempted Christ to flaunt His power (the pride of life).
⁵Then the devil taketh him up into the holy city, and setteth him on a pinnacle of the temple,
⁶And saith unto him, If thou be the Son of God, cast thyself down: for it is written, He shall give his angels charge concerning thee: and in their hands they shall bear thee up, lest at any time thou dash thy foot against a stone.
⁷Jesus said unto him, It is written again, Thou shalt not tempt [test] the Lord thy God.

This time, Satan quoted scripture himself (Psalm 91:11-12), though improperly applying it. In an appeal to Christ's pride, He challenged Him to prove His deity by doing a daring deed without being hurt. He tempted Christ to presume upon God's protection and "force" God to bail Him out of a self-produced predicament. In essence, he wanted Christ to seek His own glory, not God's. Christ rebutted his temptation with Deuteronomy 6:16.

C. He tempted Christ with glittering possessions (the lust of the eyes).
⁸[LK 4:5-13] Again, the devil taketh him up into an exceeding high mountain, and showeth him all the kingdoms of the world, and the glory of them {in a moment of time};

⁹**And saith unto him, All these things will I give thee, {for that is delivered unto me, and to whomsoever I will give it}, if thou wilt fall down and worship me.**

¹⁰**Then saith Jesus unto him, Get thee hence, Satan: for it is written, Thou shalt worship the Lord thy God, and him only shalt thou serve.**

¹¹**Then the devil leaveth him {for a season}, and, behold, angels came and ministered unto him.**

This temptation revealed Satan's ultimate goal: namely, to become the supreme object of worship in all creation. Through unexplained supernatural means, he gave Christ a vision of all the earthly realms he claimed as his own (although he held them only temporarily, with God's restricted permission). Satan offered these to Christ in exchange for His worship. He knew that God had already promised these realms (and more) to His Son; his temptation was for Christ to receive them without having to go through the suffering of crucifixion. When Christ declared (from Deut. 10:20) that only God should be worshipped, Satan left Him "for a season." As with us, however, Satan would return often and with many variations of these same basic temptations.

    D. He opposed Christ's work of redemption.

        MT 16:21 From that time forth began Jesus to show unto his disciples, how that he must go unto Jerusalem, and suffer many things of the elders and chief priests and scribes, and be killed, and be raised again the third day.

        ²²**Then Peter took him, and began to rebuke him, saying, Be it far from thee, Lord: this shall not be unto thee.**

        ²³**But he turned, and said unto Peter, Get thee behind me, Satan: thou art an offense unto me: for thou savourest not the things that be of God, but those that be of men.**

Satan failed in the wilderness to persuade Christ to bypass the cross (Sec. II.C above); here he attempted the same diversion through Peter. Although Peter seemed to be well-meaning, he unwittingly was being used by Satan. Christ quickly and decisively dealt with Satan's opposition, and effectively said, "Get behind me and under my authority, Satan; the issue is settled; be gone and out of my sight." Peter (and we) must desire those things that please God, rather than those that appeal to human nature.

    III. Satan opposed Christ through Judas.

        A. Judas served Satan, not Christ.

        JN 6:70 Jesus answered them [His disciples], Have not I chosen you twelve, and one of you is a devil?

        ⁷¹**He spake of Judas Iscariot the son of Simon: for he it was that should betray him, being one of the twelve.**

"Devil" means slanderer, or false accuser. Judas would fulfill the role of a devil (v. 70) when he betrayed Christ. Well before then, however, he was under the influence of the devil, who took full advantage of Judas' sinful nature. (JN 12:6 reveals that Judas was a thief and embezzler.)

> B. Satan led Judas to plan Christ's betrayal.
> **LK 22:1 Now the feast of unleavened bread drew nigh, which is called the Passover.**
> **²And the chief priests and scribes sought how they might kill him; for they feared the people.**
> **³Then entered Satan into Judas surnamed Iscariot, being of the number of the twelve.**
> **⁴And he went his way, and communed with the chief priests and captains, how he might betray him unto them.**
> **⁵And they were glad, and covenanted to give him money {thirty pieces of silver [MT 26:15]}.**
> **⁶And he promised, and sought opportunity to betray him unto them in the absence of the multitude.**

Satan "entered into Judas" (v. 3) a day or two before Passover and led him to conspire with the chief priests to betray Jesus. Because of the crowds that surrounded Jesus, the religious leaders were afraid to arrest Him during the feast. With Judas' support, however, now they could do so "in the absence of the multitude."

> C. Christ exposed Judas' plan.
> **MT 26:20 Now when the even was come, he sat down with the twelve.**
> **²¹And as they did eat, he said, Verily I say unto you, that one of you shall betray me.**
> **²²And they were exceeding sorrowful, and began every one of them to say unto him, Lord, is it I?**
> **²³And he answered and said, He that dippeth his hand with me in the dish, the same shall betray me.**
> **²⁴The Son of man goeth as it is written of him: but woe unto that man by whom the Son of man is betrayed! it had been good for that man if he had not been born.**
> **²⁵Then Judas, which betrayed him, answered and said, Master, is it I? He said unto him, Thou hast said.**
>
> **JN 13:26b And when he had dipped the sop, he gave it to Judas Iscariot, the son of Simon.**
> **²⁷And after the sop Satan entered into him. Then said Jesus unto him, That thou doest, do quickly. . . .**

³⁰He then having received the sop went immediately out: and it was night.

When Christ revealed that a traitor was in their midst, Judas feigned ignorance. He had already received the thirty pieces of silver; yet he asked, "Master, is it I?" Christ's answer means, "You have said it yourself." He further identified His betrayer by giving Judas the sop. Traditionally, a sop was unleavened bread dipped in a bowl of vinegar, salt, and bitter herbs. Giving someone a sop was a gesture of friendship. Satan then re-entered Judas for the consummation of their treachery (v. 27), and Christ permitted them to have their way.

D. Scripture foretold Judas' betrayal.

JN 17:12 [Later, Christ prayed,] While I was with them [the twelve] in the world, I kept them in thy name: those that thou gavest me I have kept, and none of them is lost, but the son of perdition; that the scripture might be fulfilled.

"Son of perdition" means "one appointed to condemnation or destruction." Judas was so appointed by God because of his willful rejection of the Messiah. His betrayal fulfilled Psalm 41:9: "Yea, mine own familiar friend, in whom I trusted, which did eat of my bread, hath lifted up his heel against me."

E. Judas betrayed Christ with feigned affection.

JN 18:2 And Judas also, which betrayed him, knew the place [Gethsemane]: for Jesus ofttimes resorted thither with his disciples.
³Judas then, having received a band of men and officers from the chief priests and Pharisees, cometh thither with lanterns and torches and weapons.

MK 14:44 And he that betrayed him had given them a token, saying, Whomsoever I shall kiss, that same is he; take him, and lead him away safely [i.e., securely; under guard].
⁴⁵And as soon as he was come, he goeth straightway to him, and saith, Master, master; and kissed him.

MT 26:50a And Jesus said unto him, Friend, wherefore art thou come?

LK 22:48b betrayest thou the Son of man with a kiss?

Jesus' "own familiar friend" betrayed Him unto death with feigned affection in gross hypocrisy. Satan, "the father of lies" and "a murderer from the beginning" (JN 8:44), pursued his evil designs through Judas' treacherous scheme and deceitful behavior.

F. God permitted Satan's "hour" of darkness.

LK 22:52 Then Jesus said unto the chief priests, and captains of the temple, and the elders, which were come to him, Be ye come out, as against a thief, with swords and staves?
⁵³When I was daily with you in the temple, ye stretched forth no hands against me: but this is your hour, and the power of darkness.

In attacking, abusing, and humiliating the incarnate Son of God through Judas and the religious establishment, Satan was making the most of his "hour" and his "power of darkness" — but only within the bounds that God had established.

G. Satan deserted Judas in the end.

MT 27:3 Then [the next day] Judas, which had betrayed him, when he saw that he [Jesus] was condemned, repented himself, and brought again the thirty pieces of silver to the chief priests and elders,
⁴Saying, I have sinned in that I have betrayed the innocent blood. And they said, What is that to us? see thou to that.
⁵And he cast down the pieces of silver in the temple, and departed, and went and hanged himself.

Judas' tragic end typifies that of many of Satan's pawns when they are no longer useful to him. Satan abandoned Judas to reap his own reward and moved on to use others (the chief priests and Sanhedrin in this case) in the next phase of his warfare against God. His allies' end often includes (1) consternation and remorse over plans and efforts that have gone horribly awry (v. 3); (2) callous rejection by former fellow travelers when they no longer need one's services (v. 4); and (3) a lonely, sorrowful, ignominious death that ends a wasted life (v. 5).

H. Religious leaders clothed Satan's work with a good deed.

⁶And the chief priests took the silver pieces, and said, It is not lawful for to put them into the treasury, because it is the price of blood.
⁷And they took counsel, and bought with them the potter's field, to bury strangers in.

With sanctimonious devotion, the chief priests scrupulously followed a technicality of their religious rules, and piously performed a charitable deed, while ignoring their own murder of the Son of God. Zechariah had prophesied over 500 years before: "And the Lord said unto me, Cast it unto the potter: a goodly price that I was prised [valued] at of them. And I took the thirty pieces of silver, and cast them to the potter in the house of the Lord" (Zech. 11:13).

IV. Satan opposes God's work in people.

    A. He snatches away the seed of God's Word.

        MT 13:19 [MK 4:15] When any one heareth the word of the kingdom, and understandeth it not, then cometh the wicked one {Satan cometh immediately}, and catcheth away that which was sown in his heart. This is he which received seed by the way side.

    B. He plants his weeds among God's wheat.

        MT 13:24 Another parable put he forth unto them, saying, The kingdom of heaven is likened unto a man which sowed good seed in his field:

        [25]But while men slept, his enemy came and sowed tares among the wheat, and went his way. . . .

        [38b]the tares are the children of the wicked one;

        [39a]The enemy that sowed them is the devil;

    C. He seeks to sift believers as grain in a sieve.

        LK 22:31 And the Lord said, Simon, Simon, behold, Satan hath desired to have you, that he may sift you as wheat:

        [32]But I have prayed for thee, that thy faith fail not: and when thou art converted, strengthen thy brethren.

These passages picture three ways in which Satan opposes God's work in people. In Part A, he comes quickly to those who have heard God's Word (both believers and unbelievers) and snatches it away before it can take root and bear fruit (see Secs. I-IV on p. 406 ff for the full parable). In Part B, he plants his false wheat among God's true wheat in an effort to choke the wheat and make it unproductive, and to claim the field (the world) as his own (see Sec. V on p. 409 for the full parable). Some believers he assaults with full frontal attacks, as he did against Job and as he sought to in Part C against Peter (see Sec. VIII on p. 181 for the full passage).

The Strong Man vs. the Stronger One

Satan exhibited his supernatural power in antiquity through Job's calamities and Pharaoh's magicians. In Christ's time, he worked primarily through demon-possessed people and demon-inspired governmental and religious authorities. In the parable below, Christ appropriately called Satan "a strong man." Satan has only the power, however, that God gave him, and God limits his exercise of that power within the bounds of His sovereign will. Christ, as Satan's creator and as God incarnate, is "stronger than he." He overcame the strong man through His ministry on earth, His death on the cross, and His work in the lives of believers.

I. Satan is "a strong man," but Christ is stronger.

    A. The Pharisees ascribed Christ's power to Satan.

       MT 12:22 [MK 3:22] Then was brought unto him one possessed with a devil [demon], blind, and dumb: and he healed him, insomuch that the blind and dumb both spake and saw.

       ²³And all the people were amazed, and said, Is not this the son of David [the Messiah]?

       ²⁴But when the Pharisees heard it, they said, {He hath Beelzebub,} This fellow doth not cast out devils, but by Beelzebub the prince of the devils.

"Beelzebub" likely means "lord of dung" or "lord of the flies" — in any case, a highly derogatory term. "The prince of the devils" refers to Satan himself. The Pharisees clearly meant that Christ was demon-possessed and received His miraculous power from Satan, not from God.

    B. But a divided house cannot stand.

       ²⁵And Jesus knew their thoughts, and said unto them {in parables, How can Satan cast out Satan?} Every kingdom divided against itself is brought to desolation; and every city or house divided against itself shall not stand:

       ²⁶And if Satan cast out Satan, he is divided against himself; how shall then his kingdom stand?

With simple and indisputable logic, Christ refuted His critics' blasphemous allegations regarding the source of His miraculous power. His further statements in Matthew regarding the Holy Spirit, the true source of His power, are presented in Section III on p. 349. The following verses from Luke and Mark report the remainder of the above parable.

    C. Christ disarmed the strong man and took his spoils.

       LK 11:21 When a strong man armed keepeth his palace, his goods are in peace:

       ²²But when a stronger than he shall come upon him, and overcome him, he taketh from him all his armor wherein he trusted, and divideth his spoils [distributes his goods among others].

Verse 21 may be read: "When a strong man who is well armed guards his palace, his possessions are secure." Satan seemed invincible in the "palace" of his earthly realm, and his "possessions" (all unbelievers) were firmly under his control. When Christ, however, who is "stronger than he," came upon and overpowered Satan, He took away both "his armor" and his possessions. Satan's armor includes his host of demons, which Christ cast out of numerous people (who had been Satan's possessions). These people now belong to

Christ, and He "distributes them" (with their testimony of His deliverance) among His followers, for their mutual blessing and edification.

> D. Christ "bound" the strong man, and "spoiled his house."
> **MK 3:27 No man can enter into a strong man's house, and spoil [take away] his goods, except he will first bind the strong man; and then he will spoil [plunder] his house.**

Mark places more emphasis on Satan's "house" (his earthly realm) than on his armor, and more on Satan's being "bound" than on his being disarmed. Christ bound Satan, not only during His earthly ministry, but even more so through His death and resurrection. Through the latter, He eternally freed those who trust in Him from their captivity by Satan. Christ will keep these "spoils" of spiritual conquest and take them to His own house in heaven.

> II. Satan fell as lightning from heaven.

> A. Christ gave certain disciples power over demons.
> **LK 10:1 After these things the Lord appointed other seventy also, and sent them two and two before his face into every city and place, wither he himself would come. . . .**
> **¹⁷[Later] And the seventy returned again with joy, saying, Lord, even the devils [demons] are subject unto us through thy name.**
> **¹⁸And he said unto them, I beheld Satan as lightning fall from heaven.**

While Christ's emissaries heralded His kingdom, they had power over demons through His name (i.e., with His authority and on His behalf). They apparently, however, had become too enamored with that power, and their misplaced focus drew a mild rebuke from Christ. In comparison with their success over demons on earth, He saw "Satan as lightning fall from heaven." This pictures either Satan's initial ejection from God's presence when he first sinned or his eventual final ejection from heaven in Revelation 12:7-10. Either way, it is Christ's complete victory over Satan that should gladden His followers the most, and His success makes possible all other spiritual victories.

> B. They would "tread on serpents and scorpions."
> **¹⁹Behold, I give unto you power to tread on serpents and scorpions, and over all the power of the enemy: and nothing shall by any means hurt you.**
> **²⁰Notwithstanding in this rejoice not, that the spirits are subject unto you; but rather rejoice, because your names are written in heaven.**

"Serpents and scorpions" probably represent predatory creatures used by demons to attack God's servants. They also picture the demons themselves, which are the spiritual offspring of "that old serpent" and "the great dragon" called Satan (Rev. 12:9). Although demons wield "the power of the enemy" (v. 19), Christ made them "subject" to those disciples (v. 20). His disciples' power over evil spirits continued notably in the early years of the church, to validate their message while the New Testament scriptures were being completed.

Believers today still "wrestle against the rulers of the darkness of this world, against spiritual wickedness in high places" (Eph. 6:12). God promised, however, that He will soon "bruise Satan under your feet" (Rom. 16:20). Christ cautioned His disciples not to rejoice in their (temporary) power over demons but rather in the joyous aspects of having their names eternally written in heaven (v. 20).

III. Christ defeated "the prince of this world."

    A. The prince was coming to war against Christ.
        JN 14:30 Hereafter I will not talk much with you: for the prince of this world cometh [is coming], and hath nothing in me.
        ³¹But that the world may know that I love the Father; and as the Father gave me commandment, even so I do. Arise, let us go hence.

Christ spoke these words to His disciples after Judas went to bring the temple guards to arrest Him. At that very moment, Satan, the prince of the world, "was coming" in the persons of Judas and the guards. He would further come against Christ through the priests and the Sanhedrin, then through Pilate and the Roman soldiers. God, however, was fully in control. When Satan's "hour" was finished and Christ had risen from the dead, everyone would know that He had fulfilled the Father's plan (v. 31).

    B. The prince was "cast out" when Christ was "lifted up."
        JN 12:31 Now is the judgment of this world: now shall the prince of this world be cast out.
        ³²And I, if I be lifted up from the earth, will draw all men unto me.
        ³³This he said, signifying what death he should die.

Verse 31, addressed earlier to the Jews, was spoken proleptically, i.e., as though the future event were already occurring. Christ was bearing "the judgment of this world" for all of its sin as He faced being "lifted up" on the cross. Also, through His death "shall the prince of this world be cast out." Christ was breaking Satan's spiritual strangle-hold on all mankind and was "casting him out" (proleptically) from his earthly domain. Satan still is vigorously pursuing his agenda but as a lame-duck prince whose time is short. Another result of Christ's being lifted up is His "drawing all men" to Himself (v. 32). Satan thus is being "cast out" of individual lives, one by one, as people trust in Christ for their salvation.

C. The prince has been judged and is now under judgment.

> **JN 16:7 Nevertheless I tell you the truth; It is expedient for you that I go away: for if I go not away, the Comforter will not come unto you; but if I depart, I will send him unto you.**
> **⁸And when he is come, he will reprove [convict] the world of sin, and of righteousness, and of judgment:**
> **⁹Of sin, because they believe not on me;**
> **¹⁰Of righteousness, because I go to my Father, and ye see me no more;**
> **¹¹Of judgment, because the prince of this world is judged.**

The phrase, "is judged" (v. 11) literally means "has been judged (and is now under condemnation)." Satan has been arraigned before God, tried, convicted, and sentenced to hell forever. Only his incarceration remains. This message is one of the three principal "convicting truths" the Holy Spirit presents to "the world" of people in need of salvation (v. 8). Unless they acknowledge and repent of their sin (v. 9) and receive Christ's righteousness by faith (v. 10), they will experience the same eternal judgment as their rebellious prince. (See also Sec. IV.E on p. 353.)

IV. Prayer protects believers from "the evil one."

A. Christ prayed that we be kept from the evil one.

> **JN 17:1 These words spake Jesus, and lifted up his eyes to heaven, and said, Father, . . .**
> **¹⁴I have given them thy word; and the world hath hated them, because they are not of the world, even as I am not of the world.**
> **¹⁵I pray not that thou shouldest take them out of the world, but that thou shouldest keep them from the evil [the evil one]. . . .**
> **²⁰Neither pray I for these alone, but for them also which shall believe on me through their word;**

B. We too should pray for deliverance from the evil one.

> **MT 6:9 After this manner therefore pray ye: Our Father which art in heaven, . . .**
> **¹³And lead us not into temptation, but deliver us from evil [the evil one]: For thine is the kingdom, and the power, and the glory, for ever. Amen.**

No human being can withstand Satan's onslaughts in his own strength. But "greater is He that is in you than he that is in the world" (I JN 4:4). Effectual prayer in Jesus' name brings God's greater power to bear on our behalf. In JN 17 above, Christ prayed for all believers of all time, including for our protection from the evil one. Since His ascension, He continues to pray for us as our "advocate with the Father" (I JN 2:1), who "ever liveth to make intercession" for us (Heb. 7:25). Christ also instructed His followers to include in their prayers a petition for their deliverance from Satan's influence and control (MT 6:13). In response to the prayers of His Son and those of His children, God readily and effectively keeps and delivers His own from the evil one.

Christ's Defeat of Satan's Host

Satan is not omnipresent, but with his army of demons he may seem so to many believers. The demons share Satan's evil nature, his hatred of God, and his superhuman powers. They will also share his condemnation in hell forever. The demons recognized Christ's deity because He was their Creator and God in their original sinless state before their fall with Satan. Christ also was and is their greatest enemy while they are "free" on earth. He will also be their future judge, as they are well aware. Throughout His ministry, Christ often demonstrated the absolute authority He eternally retains over Satan and his evil spirits.

I. Christ cast demons from numerous people.

A. He freed and healed those who were possessed.

MT 4:24 And his fame went throughout all Syria: and they brought unto him all sick people that were taken with divers [various] diseases and torments, and those which were possessed with devils [demons], . . . and he healed them.

LK 7:21 And in that same hour he cured many of their infirmities and plagues, and of evil spirits; and unto many that were blind he gave sight.

MT 8:16 When the even was come, they brought unto him many that were possessed with devils: and he cast out the spirits with his word, and healed all that were sick:

Demon possession of people, and demon activity generally, were common (and perhaps at a peak) during Christ's earthly ministry. One of the principal ways Christ demonstrated His divine authority and power was through freeing people from demonic control. The Gospels record at least seven instances in which Christ cast demons from particular people, and they cite several additional occasions (including those above) when He freed many people at a time from demons' domination.

B. He reversed the harm demons had done.

MT 9:32 As they went out, behold, they brought to him a dumb man possessed with a devil.
[33]And when the devil was cast out, the dumb spake: and the multitudes marvelled, saying, It was never so seen in Israel.

MT 12:22 Then was brought unto him one possessed with a devil, blind, and dumb: and he healed him, insomuch that the blind and dumb both spake and saw.

²³And all the people were amazed, and said, Is not this the son of David?

Many of the sicknesses and infirmities Christ cured were related to demonic influence and oppression. In each case where a physical malady accompanied demon possession, the malady was removed and its effects were reversed when the demon was expelled.

C. He broke the demons' hold on people's lives.

LK 8:1 And it came to pass afterward, that he went throughout every city and village, preaching and showing the glad tidings of the kingdom of God: and the twelve were with him,

²And certain women, which had been healed of evil spirits and infirmities, Mary called Magdalene, out of whom went seven devils,

³And Joanna the wife of Chuza Herod's steward, and Susanna, and many others, which ministered unto him of their substance.

Some of those that Christ freed from demons became His faithful followers. Mary Magdalene and other women He so freed accompanied Christ and His disciples and supplied their meals and other material needs. Others, such as the former demoniac from Gadara (in Sec. III below), became His witnesses in their communities.

II. Christ kept demons from revealing His deity.

A. The demons knew He was God.

MK 3:10 For he had healed many; insomuch that they pressed upon him for to touch him, as many as had plagues.

¹¹And unclean spirits, when they saw him, fell down before him, and cried, saying, Thou art the Son of God.

¹²And he straitly [strictly] charged them that they should not make him known.

B. The demons knew He was the Messiah.

LK 4:40 Now when the sun was setting, all they that had any sick with divers [various] diseases brought them unto him; and he laid his hands on every one of them, and healed them.

⁴¹And devils also came out of many, crying out, and saying, Thou art Christ the Son of God. And he rebuking them suffered them not to speak: for they knew that he was Christ [the Messiah].

C. The demons knew He could destroy them.

LK 4:33 And in the synagogue there was a man, which had a spirit of an unclean devil, and cried out with a loud voice,

³⁴Saying, Let us alone; what have we to do with thee, thou Jesus of Nazareth? art thou come to destroy us? I know thee who thou art; the Holy One of God.

³⁵And Jesus rebuked him, saying, Hold thy peace, and come out of him. And when the devil had thrown him in the midst, he came out of him, and hurt him not.

³⁶And they were all amazed, and spake among themselves, saying, What a word is this! for with authority and power he commandeth the unclean spirits, and they come out.

When Christ encountered demons, they often cried out His true identity, not in reverence and worship, but in hatred and fear. They knew He was more powerful than they and that He planned ultimately to destroy them. Christ, however, would not permit the demons to proclaim His deity, because their intent was not to honor His name but to disgrace it. He would reveal His own identity and mission to the people in His own way and at His own time.

III. Christ expelled a "legion" in Gadara.

A. The demons' effect on the man.

1. Violent and bizarre behavior.

MK 5:1 [MT 8; LK 8] And they came over unto the other side of the sea [of Galilee], into the country of the Gadarenes.

²And when he was come out of the ship, immediately there met him out of the tombs a man with an unclean spirit, {which had devils [a] long time,} {exceeding fierce, so that no man might pass by that way},

³ᵃWho had his dwelling among the tombs {and wore no clothes, neither abode in any house};

2. Superhuman strength.

³ᵇand no man could bind him, no, not with chains:

⁴Because that he had been often bound with fetters and chains, and the chains had been plucked asunder by him, and the fetters broken in pieces: neither could any man tame him.

3. Horrible suffering and anguish.

⁵And always, night and day, he was in the mountains, and in the tombs, crying, and cutting himself with stones {and was driven of the devil [demon] into the wilderness}.

This is the most extreme and most detailed case of demon possession in the Gospels. Evil spirits totally dominated every aspect of this man's existence — his crazed thoughts, his pitiful crying, and his fierce behavior. (Matthew reports that the man had a similarly-afflicted companion.) The "country of the Gadarenes" was southeast of the sea of Galilee and had largely a Gentile population. This is Christ's only recorded visit to that region.

    B. The demons' response to Christ.
        1. They acknowledged His deity and authority.
        ⁶But when he saw Jesus afar off, he ran and worshipped him {fell down before him},
        ⁷And cried with a loud voice, and said, What have I to do with thee, Jesus, thou Son of the most high God? I adjure thee by God, that thou torment me not. {Art thou come hither to torment us before the time?}
        ⁸For he said unto him, Come out of the man, thou unclean spirit.

"Worshipped" in verse 6 means "fell prostrate before Him" (as in LK 8:28), but not with spiritual adoration from the heart. The demons recognized Jesus' deity but responded with anger at His interference and with fear of His punishment. They knew that He planned their final judgment at a later time, rather than during His earthly ministry which was "before the time" (v. 7).

        2. They pleaded for His leniency.
        ⁹And he asked him, What is thy name? And he answered, saying, My name is Legion: for we are many {because many devils were entered into him}.
        ¹⁰And he [a demon] besought him much that he would not send them away out of the country {into the deep [the abyss]}.
        ¹¹Now there was there nigh unto the mountains a great herd of swine feeding.
        ¹²And all the devils besought him, saying, {If thou cast us out,} Send us into the swine, that we may enter into them.

        3. They obeyed His commands.
        ¹³And forthwith Jesus gave them leave {and he said unto them, Go}. And the unclean spirits went out, and entered into the swine: and the herd ran violently down a steep place into the sea, (they were about two thousand;) and were choked in the sea {and perished in the waters}.

A Roman army legion had about 6,000 men. However many demons possessed these men, it was a great number and was sufficient to enter and destroy two thousand pigs. "The deep" the demons feared (see v. 10) is the abyss or bottomless pit where some demons already are "chained in darkness" (Jude 6) and where Satan will be bound during the Millennium. It is not stated why they wanted to enter the pigs, but they soon lost that "home" also when the pigs all drowned in the sea.

C. The people's response to Christ.

1. They feared His power.

¹⁴**And they that fed the swine fled, and told it in the city, and in the country. And they went out to see what it was that was done.**

¹⁵**And they come to Jesus, and see him that was possessed with the devil, and had the legion, sitting {at the feet of Jesus}, and clothed, and in his right mind: and they were afraid.**

2. They begged Him to leave.

¹⁶**And they that saw it told them how it befell to him that was possessed with the devil {by what means he was healed}, and also concerning the swine.**

¹⁷**And they {the whole multitude of the country} began to pray him to depart out of their coasts {for they were taken with great fear}.**

The people (presumably Gentiles) had no comprehension of who was in their midst, made no rejoicing for the demoniacs' deliverance, and showed no interest in having Christ heal their other sick and infirm citizens. They seemed to care only about the loss of their pigs and to fear that this powerful Man might harm them as well. With one voice, they begged Him to leave their area.

D. The man's response to Christ.

1. He pleaded to go with Him.

¹⁸**And when he [Jesus] was come into the ship, he that had been possessed with the devil prayed him that he might be with him.**

2. He publicized what Christ did for him.

¹⁹**Howbeit Jesus suffered him not, but saith unto him, Go home to thy friends, and tell them how great things the Lord {God} hath done for thee, and hath had compassion on thee.**

²⁰**And he departed, and began to publish in Decapolis how great things Jesus had done for him: and all men did marvel.**

In Israel, Christ often commanded a healed person not to publicize his healing — to avoid further arousing a populace already focused more on His physical and material beneficence than on His spiritual message. Here, however, in a Gentile region apparently devoid of a gospel witness, Christ commissioned the healed man to proclaim the news of God's compassion, mercy, and miraculous deliverance. The man was faithful to his charge and Christ apparently received more honor among the people through his bold testimony than through his initial healing.

IV. Christ empowered His disciples to cast out demons.

A. To herald His kingdom and to free oppressed people.

LK 9:1 [MT 10:1] Then he called his twelve disciples together, and

gave them power and authority over all devils, {against unclean spirits to cast them out} and to cure diseases.

²And he sent them to preach the kingdom of God, and to heal the sick.

B. To confirm their message and to turn people from sin.

MK 6:12 And they [the twelve] went out, and preached that men should repent.

¹³And they cast out many devils, and anointed with oil many that were sick, and healed them.

C. To restrict Satan's work and to encourage His messengers.

LK 10:17 And the seventy returned again with joy, saying, Lord, even the devils are subject unto us through thy name.

At least twice, Christ sent out His disciples (the twelve first, then seventy) to proclaim that His kingdom was at hand. To certify the divine origin of their message and their authority to proclaim it, He gave them the power to cast out demons and to heal diseases. Mark records the twelve's results (6:13) and Luke reports the seventy's success (see Sec. II.A on p. 368 for the passage in LK 10).

D. To begin His church and to support its mission.

MK 16:15 And he said unto them, Go ye into all the world, and preach the gospel to every creature. . . .

¹⁷And these signs [attesting miracles] shall follow them that believe; In my name shall they cast out devils; they shall speak with new tongues [other languages];

¹⁸They shall take up serpents; and if they drink any deadly thing, it shall not hurt them; they shall lay hands on the sick, and they shall recover. . . .

²⁰·And they went forth, and preached every where, the Lord working with them, and confirming the word with signs following. Amen.

Mark's Gospel closes with Christ's commission to His eleven disciples to "preach the gospel to every creature." He also promised them miraculous power, including casting out demons. The book of Acts records many fulfillments of this promise. Others in the early church (notably Steven, Philip, Paul, and Barnabas) received similar broad powers, and many more spoke in other languages and healed the sick. As indicated in I Corinthians 13:8-10, these attesting signs of the validity of their message would cease, apparently upon the completion and dissemination of the New Testament scriptures. In our times, the Holy Spirit continues to restrain and thwart satanic activity as purposefully and effectively as He did through the apostles. He does so in accordance with the omniscient and sovereign will of God and the submissive, earnest prayers of God's people.

18

Transparencies of False Religion

Jesus said, "I am *the* way, *the* truth, and *the* life: no man cometh unto the Father, but by me" (JN 14:6). Accordingly, any other purported "way" to God and heaven, any other proclaimed "truth" about achieving salvation, any other proffered "life" beyond this present physical existence, is a false and counterfeit religion.

From the beginning, people have attempted to escape their sin and guilt and achieve salvation through their own devices rather than as God prescribes. When Adam and Eve sinned, they futilely covered their nakedness with fig leaves and tried to hide from God. In His first picture of the coming Savior's sacrifice for mankind's sin, God slew innocent animals and made coats of skins to clothe Adam and Eve, in place of the inadequate sin-covering they had fashioned for themselves (Gen. 3:21).

Similarly, Adam's son Cain disregarded God's instruction regarding sin offerings and tried to satisfy God with his own approach. He vainly offered "the fruit of the ground" rather than the animal/blood sacrifice God required (Gen. 4:17). To this day, man continues to create his own religion, rather than accept God's clearly revealed and only way of forgiveness and salvation.

Christ frequently pictured the fallacies and perils of false religion in warning the people of its evil nature. He also exposed and indicted the religious leaders — the principal practitioners and purveyors of false religion — and minced no words in condemning their ways. To the misled masses, however, He showed tender compassion, mercy, and grace. Instead of berating them for their sin, He offered them the true way of salvation and eternal life.

X-rays of False Belief

The principal feature of the widespread false religion of Christ's day was "self" — as in self-righteous, self-reliant, and self-exalting. Knowing the hearts and minds of all men, Christ saw through the selfish motives and faulty thinking behind their wrong beliefs. He presented these X-rays of their false religion to show its dead internal structure and its inability to provide salvation and spiritual life.

In counterfeit Christianity and other false religions today, the focus is still on self — such as self-esteem, self-improvement, and self-satisfaction. Entirely missing, however, are God's requirements regarding self, including self-examination in the light of His Word, self-denial in submitting to His will, and self-sacrifice in doing His work. The following pictures of false religion highlight its age-old features and facets.

I. It is based on self-esteem and pride.

A. It trusts in its own alleged goodness.
LK 18:9 And he spake this parable unto certain which trusted in themselves that they were righteous, and despised others:

B. It practices formal worship and prayer.
[10]Two men went up into the temple to pray; the one a Pharisee, and the other a publican [tax collector].

C. It claims moral superiority.
[11]The Pharisee stood and prayed thus with himself, God, I thank thee, that I am not as other men are, extortioners, unjust, adulterers, or even as this publican.

D. It promotes religious rites and deeds.
[12]I fast twice in the week, I give tithes of all that I possess.

E. It ignores man's sinful nature.
[13]And the publican, standing afar off, would not lift up so much as his eyes unto heaven, but smote upon his breast, saying, God be merciful to me a sinner.

F. It misses salvation and leads to judgment.
[14]I tell you, this man [the penitent publican] went down to his house justified rather than the other: for every one that exalteth himself shall be abased; and he that humbleth himself shall be exalted.

Christ addressed those who "trusted in *themselves* that they were righteous" (v. 9). That initial and fatal error spawned the other failings pictured here and in following passages. Although false religions typically incorporate or promote

certain deeds that appear to be good and commendable (such as those practiced by the Pharisee), the self-centeredness of these practices completely
negates their spiritual value. (See also Sec. IV on p. 186).

II. It relies on self-reformation, rather than regeneration.

**MT 12:43 When the unclean spirit is gone out of a man, he [the evil
spirit] walketh through dry places, seeking rest, and findeth none.**

**⁴⁴Then he saith, I will return into my house from whence I came out;
and when he is come, he findeth it empty, swept, and garnished.**

**⁴⁵Then goeth he, and taketh with himself seven other spirits more
wicked than himself, and they enter in and dwell there: and the last
state of that man is worse than the first. Even so shall it be also unto this
wicked generation.**

Christ pictured the Pharisees' "wicked generation" as a man who, having been
at least somewhat convicted of his sin, undertakes to "clean house" and sweep
out his moral dirt. He does so, however, through his own effort and for his
own purposes, not by repenting and turning to God for true cleansing and salvation. Such self-reformation only creates a spiritual vacuum. If that void is
not filled by receiving God's gift of salvation, the reformer makes himself an
attractive abode for more (and worse) evil spirits than plagued him initially.
Hence, he becomes more immune to the gospel than before in his "cleaned-
up" but false religion.

III. It fosters self-righteousness and hypocrisy.

**MT 16:6 Then Jesus said unto them [His disciples], Take heed and
beware of the leaven of the Pharisees and of the Sadducees.**

**⁷And they reasoned among themselves, saying, It is because we have
taken no bread. . . .**

**¹¹[Jesus said,] How is it that ye do not understand that I spake it not to
you concerning bread, that ye should beware of the leaven of the Pharisees and of the Sadducees?**

**¹²Then understood they how that he bade them not beware of the leaven
of bread, but of the doctrine of the Pharisees and of the Sadducees.**

**LK 12:1 In the mean time, when there were gathered together an innu-
merable multitude of people, insomuch that they trode one upon
another, he began to say unto his disciples first of all, Beware ye of the
leaven of the Pharisees, which is hypocrisy.**

Leaven (yeast) in scripture often typifies that which insidiously permeates and cor-
rupts, such as unconfessed sin or perverse doctrine. The Pharisees' "doctrine" of
their own self-righteousness, and the related hypocrisy of pretending to be that
which they were not, is the leaven Christ warned His followers to avoid.

In rebuking the Corinthians for not dealing with the sin in their midst, Paul wrote: "Know ye not that a little leaven leaveneth the whole lump? Purge out therefore the old leaven, that ye may be a new lump . . . not with old leaven, neither with the leaven of malice and wickedness; but with the unleavened bread of sincerity and truth" (1 Cor. 5:6-8).

IV. It produces self-delusion and false security.
> **JN 5:39 [To unbelieving Jews] Search the scriptures; for in them ye think ye have eternal life: and they are they which testify of me.**
> **⁴⁰And ye will not come to me, that ye might have life. . . .**
> **⁴⁵Do not think that I will accuse you to the Father: there is one that accuseth you, even Moses in whom ye trust.**
> **⁴⁶For had ye believed Moses, ye would have believed me: for he wrote of me.**
> **⁴⁷But if ye believe not his writings, how shall ye believe my words?**

The Pharisees used scripture, not to determine God's will, but to justify their own will. They derived a false hope of eternal life (v. 39) by selectively embracing certain passages from the Old Testament while ignoring its principal message, namely, that God would save His people from their sins through the Messiah's sacrificial death on their behalf.

Moses, who authored the first five books of the Bible, wrote of the coming Christ in Genesis (e.g., 3:15) through Deuteronomy (e.g., 18:15). He did so through pictures, prototypes, patterns, and prophecies. The Pharisees claimed to believe Moses and his writings, yet they did not believe what he wrote about Christ. Moses, therefore, (and other Old Testament prophets) is their "accuser," not their deliverer. The same is true with those today who twist the scripture to support their false beliefs.

V. It promotes liturgy, not true worship.
> **JN 4:19 The woman [at the well in Samaria] saith unto him, Sir, I perceive that thou art a prophet.**
> **²⁰Our fathers worshipped in this mountain; and ye say, that in Jerusalem is the place where men ought to worship.**
> **²¹Jesus saith unto her, Woman, believe me, the hour cometh, when ye shall neither in this mountain, nor yet at Jerusalem, worship the Father.**
> **²²Ye worship ye know not what: we know what we worship: for salvation is of the Jews.**
> **²³But the hour cometh, and now is, when the true worshippers shall worship the Father in spirit and in truth: for the Father seeketh such to worship him.**
> **²⁴God is a Spirit: and they that worship him must worship him in spirit and in truth.**

When the woman perceived that Christ was "a prophet" who fully knew her immoral life, she immediately became defensive and argumentative. She tried to sidestep her guilt by contrasting her Samaritan religion with Jewish religion. She focused on the place and system of (supposed) worship, rather than on the sole deserving object of worship and His revelation of how to worship Him. In penetrating her smokescreen, Christ observed, "Ye worship ye know not what." Then He declared, "True worshippers shall worship the Father in spirit and in truth: for the Father seeketh such to worship Him" (v. 23).

Because "God is a Spirit" (v. 24), He can only be worshiped in a person's spirit that is in harmony with His Spirit. Worshipping "in truth" includes not only with sincerity (not hypocritically), but more basically, in accordance with the principles and requirements in God's Word. ("Thy Word is truth," JN 17:17.) Thus, those who believe they can only worship at a particular place or at a set time or with a certain liturgy, "know not what they worship." They may have "the form of godliness, but deny the power thereof" (2 Tim. 3:5). (See Sec. II on p. 159.)

VI. It trusts in its religious heritage.

JN 8:33 They [unbelieving Jews] answered him, We be Abraham's seed, and were never in bondage to any man: how sayest thou, Ye shall be made free?

³⁴Jesus answered them, Verily, verily, I say unto you, Whosoever committeth sin is the servant [bond-slave] of sin. . . .

³⁸I speak that which I have seen with my Father: and ye do that which ye have seen with your father [Satan].

³⁹They answered and said unto him, Abraham is our father. Jesus saith unto them, If ye were Abraham's children, ye would do the works of Abraham.

These Jews, as physical descendants of Abraham, presumed that they were automatically the heirs to all the great and eternal promises God made to the patriarch. Christ refuted that thinking with "If ye were Abraham's children, ye would do the works of Abraham" (v. 39). Abraham's principal "work" was his faith in God and His promises: "And he believed in the Lord; and He counted it to him for righteousness" (Gen. 15:6). By rejecting God's Son and His salvation, these Jews refused to do Abraham's work of faith.

Paul identified the true children of Abraham as "all them that *believe* . . . who also walk in the steps of that faith of our father Abraham . . . [not] through the law, but through the righteousness of faith" (Rom. 4:11-13). To those who depend on their ancestors' religion, Christ replies: "Do the works of Abraham — and believe in me."

VII. It exalts tradition above God's Word.

A. It substitutes ceremonial washing for spiritual cleansing.

MK 7:2 And when they [some Pharisees] saw some of his disciples eat bread with defiled, that is to say, with unwashen, hands, they found fault.

³For the Pharisees, and all the Jews, except they wash their hands oft, eat not, holding the tradition of the elders.

⁴And when they come from the market, except they wash, they eat not. And many other things there be, which they have received to hold, as the washing of cups, and pots, brasen vessels, and of tables.

B. It places man's rules above God's commands.

⁵Then the Pharisees and scribes asked him, Why walk not thy disciples according to the tradition of the elders, but eat bread with unwashen hands?

⁶He answered and said unto them, Well hath Esaias prophesied of you hypocrites, as it is written, This people honoreth me with their lips, but their heart is far from me.

⁷Howbeit in vain do they worship me, teaching for doctrines the commandments of men.

⁸For laying aside the commandment of God, ye hold the tradition of men, as the washing of pots and cups: and many other such like things ye do.

⁹And he said unto them, Full well ye reject the commandment of God, that ye may keep your own tradition.

Over the centuries, the Jews developed a complex system of traditions based on various interpretations and extrapolations of God's Word. In time, many of their observances became accepted as law, even when these clearly contradicted God's written precepts and principles. Here, the Pharisees criticized Christ's disciples for eating without first performing their traditional ritual of ceremonial washing. He replied that their tradition was "in vain" and had replaced "the commandment of God" (vv. 7-8). His response applies equally today to traditions and practices that contravene the teaching of God's Word.

C. It creates loopholes in God's immutable law.

¹⁰For Moses said, Honor thy father and thy mother; and, Whoso curseth father or mother, let him die the death:

¹¹But ye say, If a man shall say to his father or mother, It is Corban, that is to say, a gift [dedicated to God], by whatsoever thou mightest be profited by me; he shall be free.

¹²And ye suffer him no more to do ought for his father or his mother;

¹³Making the word of God of none effect through your tradition, which ye have delivered: and many such like things do ye.

D. It cannot cleanse defilement within.

> ¹⁴**And when he had called all the people unto him, he said unto them, Hearken unto me every one of you, and understand:**
>
> ¹⁵**There is nothing from without a man, that entering into him can defile him: but the things which come out of him, those are they that defile the man. . . .**
>
> ²¹**For from within, out of the heart of men, proceed evil thoughts, adulteries, fornications, murders,**
>
> ²²**Thefts, covetousness, wickedness, deceit, lasciviousness, an evil eye, blasphemy, pride, foolishness:**
>
> ²³**All these evil things come from within, and defile the man.**

The Pharisees' tradition permitted people (mainly themselves) to evade their scriptural responsibility to care for needy parents by declaring that their funds had been dedicated to God. Their blatant disobedience of God's commands could not be purged by any amount of ceremonial washing. All sin comes "from *within*, out of the heart of men" (v. 21), and only "the washing of regeneration" (Titus 3:5) can remove such defilement.

Exposures of False Prophets

Satan's opposition to God is as sharp and intense in the realm of religion as in any other. He has always used false religion and its pliant prophets to oppose God and seduce mankind to serve him instead. To undiscerning observers, teachers of false religion often appear to be moral, spiritual, caring, and constructive. "And no marvel; for Satan himself is transformed into an angel of light. Therefore it is no great thing if his ministers also be transformed as the ministers of righteousness" (II Cor. 11:14-15). In exposing the false prophets of His day, Christ profiled their common characteristics and showed us how to identify their counterparts in our day.

I. Their deadly deceit and worthless works.

A. They are wolves masquerading as sheep.

MT 7:15 Beware of false prophets, which come to you in sheep's clothing, but inwardly they are ravening [ravenous] wolves.

Clerical garb does not make one a sheep, nor does any other accoutrement of religion. (Such garb may even be more characteristic of wolves than of sheep, as it was in Christ's day.) Clothing, however, is not the issue; what matters most is the prophet's message. The most dangerous wolves often dress their false teaching with Christian jargon and quotes from scripture to make it more plausible to gullible hearers. They deceive their sheep with misleading appearances and beguiling speech.

B. They are barren thorns and thistles.

> [16]**Ye shall know them by their fruits. Do men gather grapes of thorns, or figs of thistles?**

C. They are corrupt trees with rotten fruit.

> [17]**Even so every good tree bringeth forth good fruit; but a corrupt tree bringeth forth evil fruit.**
> [18]**A good tree cannot bring forth evil fruit, neither can a corrupt tree bring forth good fruit.**
> [19]**Every tree that bringeth not forth good fruit is hewn down, and cast into the fire.**
> [20]**Wherefore by their fruits ye shall know them.**

Regardless how high-sounding their message may seem, or how impressive their religious activities may appear, if their teaching does not accord with scripture and produce genuine spiritual fruit in their lives and ministry, they are "thorns and thistles" and "corrupt trees" to be cut down and burned. If instead of the fruit of the Spirit (Gal. 5:22-23) and the fruit of evangelism (JN 4:36), they produce the evil fruit of corrupt doctrine and sinful behavior, be aware that they are false prophets and enemies of the true gospel.

D. They are pious "workers of iniquity."

> [21]**Not every one that saith unto me, Lord, Lord, shall enter into the kingdom of heaven; but he that doeth the will of my Father which is in heaven.**
> [22]**Many will say to me in that day, Lord, Lord, have we not prophesied in thy name? and in thy name have cast out devils? and in thy name done many wonderful works?**
> [23]**And then will I profess unto them, I never knew you: depart from me, ye that work iniquity.**

Whether hypocritically or sincerely, these wolves will cry, "Lord, Lord" at the final judgment. They not only participated in religious activity; they often led the way. They had preached, cast out demons, and performed miracles — even in Christ's name! But He will call them workers of iniquity, and say, "I never knew you." As a result, they will be banished from His presence forever.

II. Their misused authority and harmful teaching.

A. They are alien plants to be uprooted.

> **MT 15:12 Then came his disciples, and said unto him, Knowest thou that the Pharisees were offended, after they heard this saying?**
> [13]**But he answered and said, Every plant, which my heavenly Father hath not planted, shall be rooted up.**

God and Satan are each actively planting their crops throughout the world. As taught in the parable of the wheat and the tares (see Sec. V on p. 409), God does not weed out every tare when it first appears. In His time, however, and certainly at the judgment if not before, He will uproot and cast out every plant that is not His own.

B. They are blind leaders of blind people.

¹⁴Let them alone: they be blind leaders of the blind. And if the blind lead the blind, both shall fall into the ditch.

The Pharisees were unable to lead anyone spiritually because of their own blindness. Both they and their misguided followers inevitably would fall into the ditch of false belief and sinful behavior. (See Sec. II on p. 105.)

C. They are unmarked graves that defile the unwary.

LK 11:44 Woe unto you, scribes and Pharisees, hypocrites! for ye are as graves which appear not, and the men that walk over them are not aware of them.

Mosaic law stated that whoever touched a dead body or a grave would be "unclean seven days" (Num. 19:16). The Pharisees' false teaching "defiled" their unsuspecting followers as though they had walked over an unmarked grave. Although the Law prescribed specific steps for cleansing and restoring those defiled by a grave, only Christ could cleanse those defiled by the Pharisees' false teaching.

D. They take away the "key of knowledge" from those seeking God.

LK 11:52 Woe unto you, lawyers! for ye have taken away the key of knowledge: ye entered not in yourselves, and them that were entering in ye hindered.

"Lawyers" were scribes, usually of the Pharisees' sect, who were expert in Old Testament law. By obscuring and perverting the true message of God's Word through their erroneous interpretations and wrong applications of scripture, they took away the keys of knowledge and prevented those who sought to know God's truth from learning it.

III. Their pompous vanity and presumed superiority.

A. They parade their deeds and clerical garb.

MT 23:5 But all their works they do for to be seen of men: they make broad their phylacteries, and enlarge the borders of their garments,

Phylacteries were small leather boxes or cases that contained verses from the Pentateuch. A devout Jew strapped them to his forehead and left arm to remind him of God's deliverance from Egypt and of God's holy law (Ex. 13:9,16). Similarly, the "borders [fringes or tassels] of their garments" were made as prescribed in Numbers 15:38-41, also to remind them of God's law. The Pharisees had abandoned the original purpose of these reminders and now used them primarily for show. To put on a bigger show, they put on bigger boxes and bigger borders.

> B. They seek prominent positions and public acclaim.
>> **⁶And love the uppermost rooms [most prominent places] at feasts, and the chief seats in the synagogues,**
>> **⁷And greetings in the markets, and to be called of men, Rabbi, Rabbi.**

> C. They usurp God's titles and honor.
>> **⁸But be not ye called Rabbi: for one is your Master [lit. Teacher], even Christ; and all ye are brethren.**
>> **⁹And call no man your father upon the earth: for one is your Father, which is in heaven.**
>> **¹⁰Neither be ye called masters [teachers, or guides]: for one is your Master, even Christ.**

Rabbi means "my lord" and was used primarily as a respectful title for recognized teachers of God's law. The Pharisees coveted the honor and acclaim that accompanied this and other elevated titles, such as *Father* and *Master*. Christ warned the people (and His disciples) that such reverential titles and honor belong to God alone. They were not to desire honor from men or exalt themselves to receive it.

> IV. Their Satanic influence and evil agenda.
>> **JN 8:38 I speak that which I have seen with my Father: and ye do that which ye have seen with your father. . . .**
>> **⁴⁴Ye are of your father the devil, and the lusts of your father ye will do. He was a murderer from the beginning, and abode not in the truth, because there is no truth in him. When he speaketh a lie, he speaketh of his own: for he is a liar, and the father of it.**

False prophets share and implement the evil agenda of their father, Satan. His principal means of opposing God's truth is denying its validity and replacing it with lies. Counterfeit religions are among his biggest lies, and their promoters are actively furthering their father's deception.

> V. Their worthless lives and final judgment.

> A. They are poisonous snakes among the people.
>> **MT 3:7 But when he [John the Baptist] saw many of the Pharisees and Sadducees come to his baptism, he said unto them, O generation of vipers, who hath warned you to flee from the wrath to come?**

> B. They have no fruit that shows salvation.
>> **⁸Bring forth therefore fruits meet for [in keeping with] repentance:**

C. They are as hard and dead as stones.

⁹**And think not to say within yourselves, We have Abraham to our father: for I say unto you, that God is able of these stones to raise up children unto Abraham.**

The religious leaders came to John, not to repent of their sins and be baptized in preparation for the coming Messiah, but to examine this strange preacher and discredit his ministry. Instead, John exposed their fallacies, and pictured them as poisonous vipers. Even they, however, could be cleansed spiritually if they would repent and demonstrate their repentance with a changed life (v. 8). As proud "children of Abraham," they saw no need to repent of anything, let alone to lower themselves to John's demeaning baptism.

D. They are barren trees to be felled and burned.

¹⁰**And now also the axe is laid unto the root of the trees: therefore every tree which bringeth not forth good fruit is hewn down, and cast into the fire.**

E. They are chaff to be purged from the wheat and burned.

¹¹**I [John] indeed baptize you [his converts] with water unto repentance: but he that cometh after me is mightier than I, whose shoes I am not worthy to bear: he shall baptize you with the Holy Ghost, and with fire:**

¹²**Whose fan is in his hand, and he will thoroughly purge his floor, and gather his wheat into the garner; but he will burn up the chaff with unquenchable fire.**

John's audiences included many who received God's message and repented of their sins. He promised these that the coming Messiah would baptize them "with the Holy Spirit" and with purifying "fire" that would cleanse their hearts and lives from their sin. (See Sec. II.B on p. 348.) In contrast, John likened the religious leaders to fruitless trees and worthless chaff, both to be discarded and burned. Verse 12 may be read: "Christ's winnowing fork [for separating wheat from chaff] is in His hand. He will completely clear His threshing floor and gather His wheat into His granary; but He will burn the chaff with unending fire." This latter fire pictures their final judgment and eternal condemnation in hell.

Negatives of Spiritual Adversaries

Photographic negatives make black seem white and white seem black. Such is the case with the positions taken by enemies of the gospel. They typically espouse, for example, man's inherent goodness, and they deny his total depravity. They presume the endless tolerance of God, and they ignore His holiness and justice. They allege the fallibility and foolishness of God's Word, and they reject all evidence of its divine inspiration. Often, their denials of truth are even more vigorous than their promulgations of error. Their greatest distortions and fiercest attacks frequently are against the person and work of Jesus Christ.

Religious opposition to Christ during His earthly ministry centered on the same key issues on which His adversaries oppose Him today. The following brief excerpts from many passages illustrate the nature, breadth, and depth of that opposition.

I. Their vicious attacks against His person.

A. They deny His deity.

LK 5:20 And when he saw their faith [that of a paralytic and his friends], he said unto him, Man, thy sins are forgiven thee.

²¹And the scribes and the Pharisees began to reason, saying, Who is this which speaketh blasphemies? Who can forgive sins, but God alone?

JN 10:30 [Jesus said,] I and my Father are one.

³¹Then the Jews took up stones again to stone him.

³²Jesus answered them, Many good works have I showed you from my Father; for which of those works do ye stone me?

³³The Jews answered him, saying, For a good work we stone thee not; but for blasphemy; and because that thou, being a man, makest thyself God.

LK 22:70 [MK 14:64] Then said they all [at His trial], Art thou then the Son of God? And he said unto them, Ye say that I am.

⁷¹And they said, What need we any further witness? for we ourselves have heard {the blasphemy} of his own mouth.

JN 19:7 The Jews answered him [Pilate], We have a law, and by our law he ought to die, because he made himself the Son of God.

B. They dispute His origin.

JN 8:41b Then said they to him, We be not born of fornication; we have one Father, even God.

⁴²Jesus said unto them, If God were your Father, ye would love me: for I proceeded forth and came from God; neither came I of myself, but he sent me. . . .

⁴⁸Then answered the Jews, and said unto him, Say we not well that thou art a Samaritan, and hast a devil?

C. They defame His nature.

JN 8:52 Then said the Jews unto him, Now we know that thou hast a devil. Abraham is dead, and the prophets; and thou sayest, If a man keep my saying, he shall never taste of death.

⁵³Art thou greater than our father Abraham, which is dead? and the prophets are dead: whom makest thou thyself ?

JN 10:20 And many of them said, He hath a devil, and is mad; why hear ye him?

All false religions deny the full deity and lordship of Jesus Christ and His equality with God the Father. Their denial may be explicit and forceful, as above, or implicit and refined, as in much of nominal Christendom today. The Jewish leaders not only denied Christ's heavenly origin and sinless nature; they also alleged that He was conceived illegitimately as a demon-possessed half-breed Samaritan (Part B above). More genteel assessments of Jesus' nature that deny His full deity, such as "a good man and a prophet," "a great teacher and example," and "a son of God," are as blasphemous as the allegations made by the scribes and Pharisees.

II. Their virulent antagonism toward His preaching.

A. They dismiss His claims.

LK 7:29 And all the people that heard him [Christ], and the publicans, justified God, being baptized with the baptism of John.

³⁰But the Pharisees and lawyers rejected the counsel of God against themselves, being not baptized of him.

JN 8:13 The Pharisees therefore said unto him, Thou bearest record of thyself; thy record is not true.

B. They detest His doctrine.

LK 11:53 And as he said these things unto them, the scribes and the Pharisees began to urge [oppose] him vehemently, and to provoke him to speak of many things [i.e., to interrogate Him intensely]:

⁵⁴Laying wait for him, and seeking to catch something out of his mouth, that they might accuse him.

C. They deride His message.

LK 16:14 And the Pharisees also, who were covetous, heard all these things: and they derided him.

D. They distort His teaching.

LK 23:2 And they began to accuse him [before Pilate], saying, We found this fellow perverting the nation, and forbidding to give tribute to Caesar, saying that he himself is Christ a King.

His adversaries could not successfully debate Christ on any issue but were always silenced by the logic and strength of His arguments. They could only ridicule and reject what they could not refute. They also intentionally distorted Christ's teaching to discredit both it and Him. His present enemies use the same tactics. Though they mislead most people (as the religious leaders eventually did in opposing Christ), their arguments are just as hollow and their "victories" just as illusory as those of their forebears.

III. Their venomous accusations against His practices.

A. They disparage His associations.

LK 15:1 Then drew near unto him all the publicans and sinners for to hear him.

²And the Pharisees and scribes murmured, saying, This man receiveth sinners, and eateth with them.

LK 7:33 For John the Baptist came neither eating bread nor drinking wine; and ye [Pharisees] say, He hath a devil.

³⁴The Son of man is come eating and drinking; and ye say, Behold a gluttonous man, and a winebibber, a friend of publicans and sinners!

B. They denounce His behavior.

LK 6:7 And the scribes and Pharisees watched him, whether he would heal on the sabbath day; that they might find an accusation against him.

JN 9:16a Therefore said some of the Pharisees, This man is not of God, because he keepeth not the sabbath day.

C. They denigrate His miracles.

MT 9:33 And when the devil [demon] was cast out, the dumb spake: and the multitudes marvelled, saying, It was never so seen in Israel.

³⁴But the Pharisees said, He casteth out devils through the prince of the devils.

MK 3:22 [on another occasion] And the scribes which came down from Jerusalem said, He hath Beelzebub, and by the prince of the devils casteth he out devils.

D. They degrade His character.

JN 9:24 Then again called they the man that [formerly] was blind, and said unto him, Give God the praise: we know that this man [Jesus] is a sinner. . . .

²⁹We know that God spake unto Moses: as for this fellow, we know not from whence he is.

JN 18:29 Pilate then went out unto them, and said, What accusation bring ye against this man?
³⁰They answered and said unto him, If he were not a malefactor, we would not have delivered him up unto thee.

MT 27:62b the chief priests and Pharisees came together unto Pilate, ⁶³Saying, Sir, we remember that that deceiver said, while he was yet alive, After three days I will rise again.

Christ's enemies attack not only His person and precepts but also His purposes and practices. There is no end to the distortions and lies they create regarding His life and ministry. They impugn His motives, fault His behavior, dismiss His miracles, and deny His power. With intellectual pride and moral superiority, they make themselves His accusers, judge, and jury, and find Him guilty of all charges.

IV. Their violent animosity toward His people.

A. They despise His followers.

MT 10:25 It is enough for the disciple that he be as his master, and the servant as his lord. If they have called the master of the house Beelzebub, how much more shall they call them of his household?

MK 13:9 But take heed to yourselves: for they shall deliver you up to councils [religious tribunals]; and in the synagogues ye shall be beaten: and ye shall be brought before rulers and kings for my sake, for a testimony against them.

B. They devastate His flock.

JN 10:8 All that ever came before me are thieves and robbers: but the sheep [true believers] did not hear them. . . .
¹⁰The thief cometh not, but for to steal, and to kill, and to destroy: I am come that they might have life, and that they might have it more abundantly.

JN 16:2b yea, the time cometh, that whosoever killeth you will think that he doeth God service.
³And these things will they do unto you, because they have not known the Father, nor me.

The principal representatives and embodiments of Christ that His enemies attack today are His message (God's Word) and His messengers (true believers). They seek to denounce, discredit, and destroy both. Christ warned His disciples that they would face such opposition and persecution — especially in the name of religion. If His enemies so attacked Christ while He was here, "how much more shall they [do so to] them of His household" (MT 10:25). He concluded His warnings, however, with "In the world ye shall have tribulation: but be of good cheer; I have overcome the world" (JN 16:33).

Proofs of Religious Wolves
(From Matthew 23)

Christ gave His final public address "to the multitude and to His disciples" (MT 23:1), a mixed assembly of curious observers, skeptical critics, and true believers. He directed most of His comments, however, at the nation's religious leaders. These contain the strongest and most comprehensive denunciation of anyone or anything He ever addressed. With a broad array of pictures and illustrations, vivid in imagery and unmistakable in intent, Christ portrayed the religious leaders' motives and methods and their results and rewards.

I. They deceive and oppress helpless people.

    A. They do not practice what they preach.

        MT 23:1 Then spake Jesus to the multitude, and to his disciples,
        ²Saying, The scribes and the Pharisees sit in Moses' seat:
        ³All therefore whatsoever they bid you observe, that observe and do; but do not ye after their works: for they say, and do not.

"Moses' seat" may refer to the chair in a synagogue from which the presiding scribe taught the Law each sabbath. The term pictures the scribes' responsibility and authority to teach the people God's Word, as Moses did. Christ told the people to "observe and do" the Law, but not to follow the perversions and circumventions of it that the scribes and Pharisees had artfully developed and regularly practiced.

    B. They load people with unbearable burdens.

        ⁴For they bind heavy burdens and grievous to be borne, and lay them on men's shoulders; but they themselves will not move them with one of their fingers.

    C. They shut heaven's door to those who would enter.

        ¹³But woe unto you, scribes and Pharisees, hypocrites! for ye shut up the kingdom of heaven against men: for ye neither go in yourselves, neither suffer ye them that are entering to go in.

The Pharisees burdened the people with numerous detailed extrapolations of the Law, to govern details of behavior not originally covered (regarding, for example, sabbath activities, oaths, ceremonial washing etc.). They piled these burdens so high (v. 4) that those who wanted to obey the Law could scarcely move under their load. Their regulations "shut heaven's door" by making entry effectively impossible. (At the same time, they created loopholes in the Law so that they themselves could evade its true requirements.) As a result, neither they nor their followers could enter God's kingdom. (See Sec. III on p. 385 for vv. 5-10, and Sec. II.D on p. 224 for vv. 11-12).

  D. They defraud the defenseless, behind pretentious prayer.
   ¹⁴Woe unto you, scribes and Pharisees, hypocrites! for ye devour widows' houses, and for a pretence make long prayer: therefore ye shall receive the greater damnation.

In unspecified ways, the Pharisees diverted for their own benefit funds and property belonging to (or given for) widows. They probably did so by exacting excessive offerings from widows or intercepting funds earmarked for their relief. Then they piously offered "long prayers" to disguise their wicked schemes.

  II. They distort and pervert God's truth.

   A. They make "children of hell" of their converts.
    ¹⁵Woe unto you, scribes and Pharisees, hypocrites! for ye compass sea and land to make one proselyte, and when he is made, ye make him twofold more the child of hell than yourselves.

Proselytes were Gentile converts to Judaism (or, here, to Pharisaism). Believing they now were earning their salvation by imitating the Pharisees' legalistic behavior, these enthusiastic new converts became twice the "children of hell" than the Pharisees themselves.

   B. They are blind guides of ignorant followers.
    ¹⁶Woe unto you, ye blind guides, which say, Whosoever shall swear by the temple, it is nothing; but whosoever shall swear by the gold of the temple, he is a debtor!
    ¹⁷Ye fools and blind: for whether is greater, the gold, or the temple that sanctifieth the gold?
    ¹⁸And, Whosoever shall swear by the altar, it is nothing; but whosoever sweareth by the gift that is upon it, he is guilty.
    ¹⁹Ye fools and blind: for whether is greater, the gift, or the altar that sanctifieth the gift?

   C. They profane God's house, His throne, and His name.
    ²⁰Whoso therefore shall swear by the altar, sweareth by it, and by all things thereon.
    ²¹And whoso shall swear by the temple, sweareth by it, and by him that dwelleth therein.
    ²²And he that shall swear by heaven, sweareth by the throne of God, and by him that sitteth thereon.

The Pharisees were blind to the essence of God's law. They perverted His commands regarding vows by creating loopholes through which a person could escape responsibility, even though he had sworn "by the temple" or "by the altar." They could not "see" the sanctity of the sacrifices to God on the altar, nor of the temple as God's meeting place with man (vv. 20-21). Nor did they honor heaven as God's throne, or God Himself as King of all creation.

D. They "strain at a gnat but swallow a camel."

²³Woe unto you, scribes and Pharisees, hypocrites! for ye pay tithe of mint and anise and cummin, and have omitted the weightier matters of the law, judgment [justice], mercy, and faith [fidelity]: these ought ye to have done, and not to leave the other undone.

²⁴Ye blind guides, which strain at a gnat, and swallow a camel.

The Pharisees tithed so rigorously that they even gave ten percent of the herbs grown in their gardens. While expanding the law to the "enth degree," they "left undone" God's greater commands regarding justice, mercy, and faithfulness. They could "strain a tiny gnat" out of their drink (i.e., observe selected rules in minute detail), but were blind to the "huge camels" of gross neglect that they swallowed without batting an eye.

II. They relish their religious rectitude.

A. They clean only the outside of their "dirty dishes."

²⁵Woe unto you, scribes and Pharisees, hypocrites! for ye make clean the outside of the cup and of the platter, but within they are full of extortion and excess [intemperance].

²⁶Thou blind Pharisee, cleanse first that which is within the cup and platter, that the outside of them may be clean also.

B. They are "whitewashed tombs full of dead men's bones."

²⁷Woe unto you, scribes and Pharisees, hypocrites! for ye are like unto whited sepulchres, which indeed appear beautiful outward, but are within full of dead men's bones, and of all uncleanness.

²⁸Even so ye also outwardly appear righteous unto men, but within ye are full of hypocrisy and iniquity [lawlessness].

The Pharisees polished and shined their public image (v. 25) but left their souls full of pollution. Again, Christ called them blind for not seeing their flagrant inconsistency and great spiritual need. Like whitewashed mausoleums, they appeared beautiful outwardly but were full of dead remains and "all uncleanness" (v. 27). They could not, however, whitewash their hearts, which brimmed with hypocrisy and lawlessness.

C. They decorate the graves of their fathers' victims.

²⁹Woe unto you, scribes and Pharisees, hypocrites! because ye build the tombs of the prophets, and garnish the sepulchres of the righteous,

³⁰And say, If we had been in the days of our fathers, we would not have been partakers with them in the blood of the prophets.

³¹Wherefore ye be witnesses unto yourselves, that ye are the children of them which killed the prophets.

³²Fill ye up then the measure of your fathers.

The Pharisees sanctimoniously honored the prophets and godly men their own ancestors had murdered, saying "We wouldn't have done that if we had been there!" (v. 30). They, however, were not only the *physical* descendants of those who killed God's prophets; they were their *spiritual* descendants as well (v. 31). As such, they would fill the measuring cup of their fathers' guilt by killing God's messengers to their generation (including Christ and His apostles). They sentenced Christ to death a few days later.

IV. They persecute God's servants.

A. They are poisonous snakes that attack God's spokesmen.

³³Ye serpents, ye generation [offspring] of vipers, how can ye escape the damnation of hell?

³⁴Wherefore, behold, I send unto you prophets, and wise men, and scribes: and some of them ye shall kill and crucify; and some of them shall ye scourge in your synagogues, and persecute them from city to city:

³⁵That upon you may come all the righteous blood shed upon the earth, from the blood of righteous Abel unto the blood of Zacharias son of Barachias, whom ye slew between the temple and the altar.

³⁶Verily I say unto you, All these things shall come upon this generation.

"Vipers" (or adders) were poisonous snakes common in the eastern hemisphere. Christ foretold that the viperous Pharisees (whom He also called serpents, picturing their smooth and crafty ways) would be great foes and tormentors of the apostles and early Christians (v. 34). The latter are the "prophets, and wise men, and scribes" that He would send to preach His gospel. As fulfilled in the book of Acts, the Pharisees and their collaborators "persecuted them from city to city."

Thus, the Pharisees continued the work of their fathers (v. 31) and share responsibility for "all the righteous blood shed upon the earth" from Abel to Zechariah, i.e., from the beginning to the end of the Old Testament (v. 35). Abel's murder is recorded in the first book (Genesis 4:8), and Zechariah's in the last book (II Chronicles 24:21), of the Jew's arrangement of the scriptures. "All these things" (v. 36) includes their punishment for persecuting God's people through the ages and the "damnation of hell" (v. 33) that is surely theirs.

B. They abuse and kill God's representatives.

³⁷**O Jerusalem, Jerusalem, thou that killest the prophets, and stonest them which are sent unto thee, how often would I have gathered thy children together, even as a hen gathereth her chickens under her wings, and ye would not!**

C. Their "house is left desolate," and God has departed.

³⁸**Behold, your house is left unto you desolate.**

³⁹**For I say unto you, Ye shall not see me henceforth, till ye shall say, Blessed is he that cometh in the name of the Lord.**

This concludes Christ's final address to the Jewish people. He used His few remaining days to prepare His disciples for His crucifixion and subsequent return to Heaven. Verses 37-39 also serve as a transition and introduction to the Olivet Discourse that He gave His disciples regarding His second coming. That discourse is presented in Chapter 20, beginning with "Signs for Christ's Return" on p. 423.

19

Blueprints for the
Kingdom and the Church

God's announced purpose in sending His Son to earth was to "save His people from their sins" (MT 1:21) and to establish "the kingdom of heaven" (MT 3:2). These are also the principal foundations on which the Messianic prophecies in the Old Testament are based. Christ linked the two in His first public statement in Mark, saying, "The time is fulfilled, and the kingdom of God is at hand: repent ye, and believe the gospel" (1:15).

Throughout the Gospels, the Jews placed a higher priority on receiving an earthly kingdom than on receiving spiritual salvation. They ultimately crucified Christ when they concluded that His priorities were in the reverse order of theirs. When it was clear that the religious leaders would not accept His spiritually-based kingdom, Christ revealed privately to His disciples God's previously-hidden plan to build such a kingdom in the form of His church. (He would establish His Messianic kingdom when He comes again and the Jews as a nation receive Him as king.) This chapter includes Christ's principal revelation regarding God's kingdom and His promised church.

The Multi-Faceted Kingdom of God

God ordained and raised up earthly kingdoms and governments, in part to picture His own sovereign authority and power. Similarly, the respect and the obedience that are due monarchs and magistrates portray the greater reverent submission and obedient service that are due Almighty God as the ultimate King of all creation.

Christ spoke often of "the kingdom of God" and "the kingdom of heaven." What are these kingdoms, and are they the same or do they differ? "The kingdom of heaven" appears only in Matthew, and about 30 times. All four Gospels cite "the kingdom of God," and Mark and Luke use the term for the same instances that Matthew uses "kingdom of heaven." It appears, therefore, that the terms are synonymous and are used interchangeably. Christ did discuss two distinct divine kingdoms but they are not differentiated by the words "of God" and "of heaven."

One of the two kingdoms is Christ's Messianic kingdom. This is the kingdom promised throughout the Old Testament and offered by Christ to Israel. Although Israel rejected it, this kingdom will be established on earth for a thousand years when Christ returns. The other kingdom is the eternal rule of God over all creation. This kingdom includes God's dominion over nature and the nations and also over the spirit realm. It especially involves God's personal relationship with His people in every age and place, and His beneficent rule in their hearts and lives.

The kingdom of God, therefore, includes Christ's Messianic kingdom but extends well beyond it. This section focuses on God's rule in the lives of believers and on passages that refer to that aspect of His kingdom.

    I. God's kingdom is primarily a spiritual kingdom.

        A. He seeks to reign in lives more than in lands.
> **JN 18:36 Jesus answered [Pilate], My kingdom is not of this world: if my kingdom were of this world, then would my servants fight, that I should not be delivered to the Jews: but now is my kingdom not from hence [not from this world].**
> **³⁷Pilate therefore said unto him, Art thou a king then? Jesus answered, Thou sayest that I am a king. To this end was I born, and for this cause came I into the world, that I should bear witness unto the truth. Every one that is of the truth heareth my voice.**

The word for kingdom can also mean "kingship," as in verse 36. God's kingdom and kingship generally refer more to His active rule over the affairs of His subjects than to the physical nature of His realm. Thus, Christ's kingship is "not of this world," but operates within "every one that is of the truth" (v. 37). Christ affirmed to Pilate that He was indeed a king, and was born to be such, but not (at that time) the kind of king Pilate understood. (His earthly kingdom would come later, after His second coming.)

B. His kingdom is perceived (and received) more inwardly than outwardly.
LK 17:20 And when he was demanded of the Pharisees, when the kingdom of God should come, he answered them and said, The kingdom of God cometh not with observation:
²¹Neither shall they say, Lo here! or, lo there! for, behold, the kingdom of God is within [or "among"] you.

The Pharisees demanded that Christ tell them when the kingdom of God (they meant the Messianic kingdom) would be established. He replied obliquely that the kingdom of God (in the sense of His kingship) does not come with an outward display of its approach (v. 20). In other words, the establishment of God's kingship in a person's life is not preceded by any particular visible indications of its coming.

Christ added, "the kingdom of God is within you," or, "*within* a person." (It obviously was *not* "within" those Pharisees at that time.) It is experienced inwardly by those who willingly acknowledge the King and submit to His kingship. The word for "within" can also mean "among" or "in the midst of." God's kingdom already was "among" the Pharisees in the person of the King and through His declaration of the spiritual principles on which His kingdom would be established.

II. Sinful people cannot enter God's kingdom.

Passages in Sections II through V relate God's kingdom to topics covered more fully elsewhere, as referenced in these sections.

A. Materialistic and self-sufficient people.
MT 19:23 Then said Jesus unto his disciples, Verily I say unto you, That a rich man shall hardly enter into the kingdom of heaven.
²⁴And again I say unto you, It is easier for a camel to go through the eye of a needle, than for a rich man to enter into the kingdom of God.

There is nothing wrong with having wealth, and riches may be the blessing of God on those who are faithful with what they have. The problem is with a *selfish desire* to have riches. (Poor people can be just as materialistic as the wealthy.) A longing to achieve material things prevents many from entering God's kingdom. (Note that Christ used "kingdom of heaven" and "kingdom of God" interchangeably in the same passage.) (See the full passage in Sec. II on p. 244.)

B. Self-centered and lustful people.

MK 9:43a And if thy hand offend thee [causes you to sin], cut it off: . . .
⁴⁵ᵃAnd if thy foot offend thee, cut it off: . . .
⁴⁷And if thine eye offend thee, pluck it out: it is better for thee to enter into the kingdom of God with one eye, than having two eyes to be cast into hell fire:
⁴⁸Where their worm dieth not, and the fire is not quenched.

If your hand (what you do), your foot (where you go), or your eye (what you gaze upon and desire) becomes a stumbling block to your full acceptance of God's kingship, "cut out" that offending thing for the sake of your eternal soul. (See Sec. II on p. 449.)

C. Self-righteous and hypocritical people.

MT 23:12 And whosoever shall exalt himself shall be abased; and he that shall humble himself shall be exalted.
¹³But woe unto you, scribes and Pharisees, hypocrites! for ye shut up the kingdom of heaven against men: for ye neither go in yourselves, neither suffer ye them that are entering to go in.

MT 21:31b. Jesus saith unto them [the chief priests and elders], Verily I say unto you, That the publicans and the harlots go into the kingdom of God before you.

The religious leaders exalted themselves and their system of salvation through good works, but neither they nor those who followed their teaching would enter God's kingdom. (See Sec. I.C on p. 392.) Admitted sinners who repented of their disobedience were far ahead of the self-righteous religionists in approaching God's kingdom.

III. God's kingdom is entered only through salvation.

A. Entrance requires willing acceptance of God's truth.

MK 12:32 And the scribe said unto him, Well, Master, thou hast said the truth: for there is one God; and there is none other but he:
³³And to love him with all the heart and with all the understanding, and with all the soul, and with all the strength, and to love his neighbor as himself, is more than all whole burnt offerings and sacrifices.
³⁴ᵃAnd when Jesus saw that he answered discreetly [intelligently], he said unto him, Thou art not far from the kingdom of God.

This scribe had greater spiritual perception than his colleagues had. He properly understood Deuteronomy 6:4-5 (cited in vv. 32-33), and recognized that satisfying God required full and willing submission of his heart, mind, soul, and strength to Him, not mere performance of religious rituals. Thus, he was "not far from the kingdom." He still needed, however, to take the next step and believe in Jesus as the Christ.

> B. Entrance requires coming to Christ in simple faith.
> > **LK 18:16 But Jesus called them unto him, and said, Suffer little children to come unto me, and forbid them not: for of such is the kingdom of God.**
> > **¹⁷Verily I say unto you, Whosoever shall not receive the kingdom of God as a little child shall in no wise enter therein.**

Small children picture the way each person must come to Christ in simple child-like faith, by simply taking Him at His word and trusting Him fully to meet every spiritual need (see Sec. IV on p. 83).

> C. Entrance requires a new birth through God's Spirit.
> > **JN 3:3 Jesus answered and said unto him, Verily, verily, I say unto thee, Except a man be born again, he cannot see the kingdom of God.**
> > **⁴Nicodemus saith unto him, How can a man be born when he is old? can he enter the second time into his mother's womb, and be born?**
> > **⁵Jesus answered, Verily, verily, I say unto thee, Except a man be born of water and of the Spirit, he cannot enter into the kingdom of God.**

Only those born again can "see" (v. 3) and enter (v. 5) God's kingdom. Nicodemus did not understand that God's Spirit produces this new birth within a person and that salvation does not result from physical lineage or from obeying moral and religious rules (see Sec. I on p. 81). It appears, however, that later he understood these truths and became a believer in Christ (see Sec. IV on p. 66).

> IV. God's kingdom offers privileges and carries responsibilities.

> > A. Receiving God's kingdom requires bearing its fruits.
> > > **MT 21:43 Therefore say I unto you [the Jewish leaders], The kingdom of God shall be taken from you, and given to a nation bringing forth the fruits thereof.**

Israel rejected Christ's offer of God's kingdom by failing to acknowledge Him as its King. God's kingdom, therefore, would be given to "a nation" (the body of all believers in Christ; His church) which would bear spiritual fruit in and through its citizens. Bearing fruit is not a condition of receiving God's kingdom but a natural outgrowth of it. God expects such fruit of His people. (See Sec. VII on p. 128.)

> > B. Receiving God's kingdom permits the use of its keys.
> > > **MT 16:19 And I will give unto thee [Peter, as a leader in the church] the keys of the kingdom of heaven: and whatsoever thou shalt bind**

on earth shall be bound in heaven: and whatsoever thou shalt loose on earth shall be loosed in heaven.

Christ promised to give "the keys of the kingdom" to His church and its leadership. Peter here represents all the apostles and other leaders called by God to oversee the proper use of these keys in and by the church. The keys "bind" or "loose" certain things on earth and in heaven (see also MT 18:17-18). The passage is reviewed in Section IV on p. 404.

V. Sacrifice for God's kingdom brings great reward.

A. Through God's provision of daily needs.

MT 6:33 But seek ye first the kingdom of God, and his righteousness; and all these things [the necessities of life] shall be added unto you.

B. Through abundant temporal and eternal blessings.

LK 18:29 And he said unto them, Verily I say unto you, There is no man that hath left house, or parents, or brethren, or wife, or children, for the kingdom of God's sake,
30Who shall not receive manifold more in this present time, and in the world to come life everlasting.

God promises to meet all the basic needs of the faithful citizens of His kingdom (v. 33). He will also repay *in this life* many times more than they sacrifice for His kingdom's sake (v. 30). Thereafter, they will enjoy the untold blessings of "life everlasting in the world to come." (See Sec. III on p. 253 on MT 6, and Sec. I.C on p. 279 for parallel passages to LK 18.)

The Foundation of Christ's Church

The "kingdom of God" in this present age is manifested primarily in Christ's church — the universal body of all true believers in Him. His church is not equivalent to His Messianic kingdom but is a separate and unique entity of which He is the Head. It is founded on Christ's sacrificial death and resurrection and is entered solely by receiving God's grace through faith in Christ for salvation.

Christ's disciples did not understand, at the time, much of what He said regarding His future church. He promised them, however, that when the Holy Spirit would come, "He shall teach you all things, and bring all things to your remembrance, whatsoever I have said unto you" (JN 14:26). "These things" included His declarations in the following passage on how His church would be built, what message it would proclaim, and what was required of its members. Christ laid its foundation both with His teaching and with the sacrifice of His life. It would be His church in every respect; He would create it, direct it, and reward it, through His wisdom and power.

I. The fundamental testimony of His church.

MT 16:13 When Jesus came into the coasts of Caesarea Philippi, he asked his disciples, saying, Whom do men say that I the Son of man am?

¹⁴And they said, Some say that thou art John the Baptist: some, Elias [Elijah]; and others, Jeremias [Jeremiah], or one of the prophets.

¹⁵He saith unto them, But [you!,] whom say ye that I am?

¹⁶And Simon Peter answered and said, Thou art the Christ, the Son of the living God.

The opinions held by the general populace regarding Jesus' identity fell short of "the Messiah, the Son of God." Peter, as spokesman for the twelve, however, gave clear, unequivocal testimony to Jesus' deity and incarnation as the promised Christ. Belief in and confession of this essential understanding of Jesus' identity is the basis of every believer's salvation (Rom. 10:9), and it is the common bond that unites them in His body, the church.

II. The divine Designer of His church.

¹⁷And Jesus answered and said unto him, Blessed art thou, Simon Bar-jona [son of Jonah]: for flesh and blood hath not revealed it unto thee, but my Father which is in heaven.

Paramount in Christ's statement is the basic truth that spiritual perception and a proper response to it are not the result of human intellect or effort but of God's sovereign working in the heart and life of each person He draws to Christ. In commending Peter's response, Christ also reminded him of the fundamental differences in their respective origins and natures. He addressed Peter as "son of Jonah," in contrast to His own divine Sonship through "my Father . . . in heaven."

III. The foundational "Rock" of His church.

¹⁸And I say also unto thee, That thou art Peter [Petros], and upon this rock [petra] I will build my church; and the gates of hell shall not prevail against it [not overpower it].

Although in our English translation, it may appear that Christ will build His church on Peter, the Greek indicates He will build it on *Himself*. Petros means "a detached rock or stone," while petra means "a massive rock or rocky peak." Christ will build His church on "the massive rock" of His own deity and redemptive work.

That Christ is "the rock" is shown in other scripture, including Peter's application of Old Testament prophecies to Christ: e.g., "I lay in Zion a chief cornerstone" and "a living stone disallowed indeed of men but chosen of God and precious" (I Peter 2:4-8). Paul added: "For other foundation can no man lay than that is laid, which is Jesus Christ" (I Cor. 3:11) and "ye are . . . the household of God; and are built upon the foundation of the apostles and prophets, Jesus Christ himself being the chief corner stone" (Eph. 2:19-20).

Some take "this petra" to mean the divine revelation of Christ's true identity and a believer's confession of it, through which each believer becomes a member of His church. The two views appear to be two sides of the same coin; the former focuses on Christ's role as the church's foundation; the latter, on each believer's faith in and confession of Christ as that foundation. Both are required for building His church.

IV. The authoritative "keys" in His church.
¹⁹And I will give unto thee the keys of the kingdom of heaven: and whatsoever thou shalt bind on earth shall be bound in heaven: and whatsoever thou shalt loose on earth shall be loosed in heaven.

In building His church, Christ would give Peter a set of keys for *binding* or *loosing* certain things on earth and in heaven. Through preaching the gospel, Peter did open the church to the Jews on Pentecost, and he unlocked its doors to the Gentiles beginning with Cornelius. The "whatsoever" in verse 19, however, refers to things rather than to people. Also, binding and loosing were terms used by rabbis to mean forbidding and permitting. Therefore, whatever Peter (and the apostles and godly leaders after them) either forbad or permitted in exercising spiritual leadership in the church carried the weight of divine authority. This granting of authority over the church's doctrine and deportment to Spirit-filled men was particularly needful before the New Testament was completed. The principle still applies today with respect to biblical church discipline of erring members (see Sec. VII on p. 219).

V. The required sacrifice for His church.
²⁰Then [strongly] charged he his disciples that they should tell no man that he was Jesus the Christ.
²¹From that time forth began Jesus to show unto his disciples, how that he must go unto Jerusalem, and suffer many things of the elders and chief priests and scribes, and be killed, and be raised again the third day.

Christ gave the command in verse 20 in His last year of ministry. The Jewish leaders had already rejected His claims and message, and they attributed His power to Satan (MT 12). He would continue to speak publicly (but less extensively) while spending more time preparing His disciples for His departure. He foretold His violent death at the hands of the religious authorities, but He promised to rise again. Although these predictions shocked and dismayed His disciples (see v. 22), these crucial events were essential for Christ's building His church.

VI. The principal enemy of His church.

²²Then Peter took him, and began to rebuke him, saying, Be it far from thee, Lord: this shall not be unto thee.

²³But he turned, and said unto Peter, Get thee behind me, Satan: thou art an offense unto me: for thou savourest not [you have no mind for] the things that be of God, but those that be of men.

Satan uses all means at his disposal to prevent Christ from building His church — including deceiving unwary church leaders and members (such as Peter here) regarding how Christ's church should be built. Every believer, therefore, must set his mind to diligently seek "the things of God" in order to avoid thinking and acting like those who are following Satan's agenda (v. 23). (See Sec. II.D, on p. 362.)

VII. The sacrificial calling of His church.

²⁴Then said Jesus unto his disciples, If any man will come after me, let him deny himself, and take up his cross, and follow me.

²⁵For whosoever will save his life shall lose it: and whosoever will lose his life for my sake shall find it.

²⁶For what is a man profited, if he shall gain the whole world, and lose his own soul? or what shall a man give in exchange for his soul?

Christ's sacrificial death on the cross was first and foremost to purchase our salvation. But it was also for our example. He calls every believer to "take up his cross" and follow Him with the same degree of self-denial and self-sacrifice in living for Him that He willingly accepted and endured in dying for us. (See Sec. VI on p. 249.)

VIII. The eternal reward for His church.

²⁷For the Son of man shall come in the glory of his Father with his angels; and then he shall reward every man according to his works.

An eternal perspective motivates and encourages the members of Christ's church to remain faithful to their calling. When Christ returns, He will reward every believer's selfless works and devoted service for Him. His return to earth will be unspeakably glorious (v. 27), and so will be His rewards for His servants. Both the church Christ is building and the rewards its members will receive will abide in heaven forever. (See Sec. IX on p. 446.)

Parables on Professing Christendom

Sowers and Seeds; Soils and Sprouts

Matthew 13 presents a collage of related parables on God's kingdom. They deal primarily with how God is building His kingdom on earth, who among those seeking to enter it actually do so, and how God views and deals with true believers versus false professors. Hindsight through the epistles and two millennia of church history makes it clear that these parables relate particularly to professing Christendom in this present age. Some of these parables picture the presentation of God's Word and responses to it by individual people. Others relate to the professing church collectively and why it will eventually incur God's judgment.

Several of these parables (with others about God's kingdom) are also recorded in Mark 4 and Luke 8 and 13. The parables are presented in the order given in Matthew, with additional details from Mark and Luke inserted in braces.

I. Christ used parables to teach spiritual truth.

MT 13:1 The same day went Jesus out of the house, and sat by the sea side. ²And great multitudes were gathered together unto him, so that he went into a ship, and sat; and the whole multitude stood on the shore. ³And he spake many things unto them in parables, saying, Behold, a sower went forth to sow;

Although Christ previously had taught with parables, from here on He employed them more frequently. The change largely followed His complete rejection by the religious leaders in MT 12 when they attributed His power to Satan. Later, the crowds would begin to abandon Him as well when He claimed to be "the Bread of life" in JN 6.

II. The sower and the soils: why many fall short of salvation.

A. Unproductive soils that yield no fruit.

⁴And when he sowed, some seeds fell by the way side {and it was trodden down}, and the fowls {fowls of the air} came and devoured them up: ⁵Some fell upon stony places {upon a rock}, where they had not much earth: and forthwith {immediately} they sprung up, because they had no deepness of earth: ⁶And when the sun was up, they were scorched; and because they had no root, they withered away {because it lacked moisture}. ⁷And some fell among thorns; and the thorns sprung up {with it}, and choked them {and it yielded no fruit}.

B. Fertile soil that produces fruit.

⁸But other fell into good ground, {and sprang up,} and brought forth fruit, some an hundredfold, some sixtyfold, some thirtyfold. ⁹{And when he had said these things, he cried,} Who hath ears to hear, let him hear.

Sowers in Israel would typically broadcast seed by hand as they walked through a field. The "way side" in verse 4 refers to a hardened footpath where fallen seeds were exposed to preying birds. The "stony places" in verse 5 does not mean full of stones but shallow soil because of rock strata near the surface. The "thorns" in verse 7 had their own seeds and/or roots already in the soil and quickly outgrew and choked the good seedlings. The "good ground," however, produced bountifully.

III. Parables both reveal and conceal spiritual truth.

A. The disciples received insight that others could not receive.

¹⁰And the disciples came, and said unto him, Why speakest thou unto them in parables?

¹¹He answered and said unto them, Because it is given unto you to know the mysteries of the kingdom of heaven, but to them it is not given. {unto them that are without, all these things are done in parables}.

¹²For whosoever hath, to him shall be given, and he shall have more abundance: but whosoever hath not, from him shall be taken away even that he hath.

¹³Therefore speak I to them in parables: because they seeing see not; and hearing they hear not, neither do they understand.

To those who earnestly desire it, God gives spiritual insight into the otherwise hidden "mysteries" (v. 11) of Christ's person and work and the kind of king-dom He is offering. Verse 12 may be understood: "For whoever has a desire to know God's truth, to him shall be given such knowledge and understanding, and he shall have it abundantly. But whoever does not have such a desire, from him shall be taken even the little knowledge that he has." Christ's parables revealed truth to those who "saw and heard" with willing eyes and ears, but they concealed truth from those with no real desire to see or hear from God.

B. Most people's hearts were closed to God.

¹⁴And in them is fulfilled the prophecy of Esaias, which saith, By hearing ye shall hear, and shall not understand; and seeing ye shall see, and shall not perceive:

¹⁵For this people's heart is waxed gross [become thick and heavy], and their ears are dull of hearing, and their eyes they have closed; lest at any time they should see with their eyes, and hear with their ears, and should understand with their heart, and should be converted, {and their sins should be forgiven them} and I should heal them.

Christ cited Isaiah 6:9-10 and applied that prophecy to the people of His day. They had willfully hardened their hearts against God and closed their ears to His message and their eyes to His miracles. As a result, they forfeited their opportunity to receive spiritual healing and salvation. (See "Sight and Blindness" Sec. I.B and II.B on p. 104 ff.)

 C. The disciples witnessed what their forebears longed for.
> **¹⁶But blessed are your eyes, for they see: and your ears, for they hear. ¹⁷For verily I say unto you, That many prophets and righteous men have desired to see those things which ye see, and have not seen them; and to hear those things which ye hear, and have not heard them.**

God had promised a coming Savior ever since Adam fell in sin (Gen. 3:15). "Many prophets and righteous men" since Adam longed to see and experience the Messiah's presence and kingdom, but were not privileged to do so. Christ's disciples, however, were now seeing and hearing these things first hand. More importantly, they were seeing and hearing with a degree of perception and spiritual understanding.

 D. This parable is key for "knowing all parables."
> **¹⁸{And when he was alone, they that were about him with the twelve asked of him the parable. . . . And he said unto them, Know ye not this parable? and how then will ye know all parables? [MK 4:10-13]}. Hear ye therefore the parable of the sower.**

Christ said, in essence, "Don't you understand this parable? If you can't grasp this relatively simple and straightforward parable, how will you be able to interpret other and deeper parables?" He not only wanted them to learn the lessons in the parable of the sower, but also how to view, decipher, and apply all of His parables.

IV. The soils picture the hearts of hearers.

 A. Soil by the wayside: hardened hearts closed by Satan.
> **¹⁹{The sower soweth the word. The seed is the word of God.} When any one heareth the word of the kingdom, and understandeth it not, then cometh {immediately} the wicked one {Satan} and catcheth away that {word} which was sown in his heart. This is he which received seed by the way side.**

The critical element in the parable is the condition of the soil (i.e., the hearts of people) into which the seed of God's Word is sown. Its primary application relates to people's responses to the gospel of salvation. The principle, however, also applies to believers: the condition of one's heart directly affects his response to God's Word and his related fruitfulness. Hardened soil repels the seed and permits Satan to "snatch it away" before it takes root.

B. Rocky ground: no commitment or real faith.

²⁰But he that received the seed into stony places, the same is he that heareth the word, and anon {immediately} with joy receiveth it; ²¹Yet hath he not root in himself, but [en]dureth for a while: for when tribulation or persecution ariseth because of the word, by and by {immediately} he is offended {and in time of temptation fall[s] away}.

The parable makes it clear that each person is responsible for the condition of his own heart and for his response to God's Word (both for salvation and for Christian living thereafter). A superficial fair-weather commitment will not withstand the inevitable trials of adversity and opposition that will arise "because of the Word." Conversely, true decisions will be lasting decisions and will be reinforced and strengthened (by God's Spirit and His Word) in times of trial.

C. Thorn-covered ground: choked by the cares of this world.

²²He also that received seed among the thorns is he that heareth the word; and the care of this world, and the deceitfulness of riches, {and pleasures of this life, and the lusts of other things entering in} choke the word, and he becometh unfruitful {and bring[s] no fruit to perfection}.

The "thorns" identified here are present in seed form, if not in active growth, in every hearer's life. They can block and prevent salvation initially or thwart spiritual growth in the lives of believers. These thorns can even choke previously fruitful plants if they are not rooted out at their first appearance.

D. Fertile ground: willing hearts that respond and bear fruit.

²³But he that received seed into the good ground is he that heareth the word, and understandeth it, which also beareth fruit, and bringeth forth, some an hundredfold, some sixty, some thirty. {the good ground are they, which in an honest and good heart, having heard the word, keep it, and bring forth fruit with patience.}

All "good ground" will bear at least some fruit that testifies of salvation. There are substantial differences, however, among believers in their relative fruitfulness. Luke's account indicates that our degree of fruitfulness is related to our honesty (humble transparency), purity of heart and life, attention and obedience to God's Word, and patient faithfulness in God's service.

V. The tares and the wheat: why unbelievers exist in the church.

A. The enemy sowed weeds among the wheat.

²⁴Another parable put he forth unto them, saying, The kingdom of heaven is likened unto a man which sowed good seed in his field:

> ²⁵But while men slept, his enemy came and sowed tares among the wheat, and went his way.
> ²⁶But when the blade was sprung up, and brought forth fruit, then appeared the tares also.

The tares are probably darnel, a grass-like weed that looks like wheat in its early stages of growth. Tares not only compete with the wheat for nourishment, their seeds can host a fungus that is poisonous to people and animals. Here, the enemy sowed tares among the wheat for maximum disruptive and damaging effect. When the wheat "brought forth fruit," the fruitless tares became clearly distinguishable.

B. Both will grow together until the harvest.

> ²⁷So the servants of the householder came and said unto him, Sir, didst not thou sow good seed in thy field? from whence then hath it tares?
> ²⁸He said unto them, An enemy hath done this. The servants said unto him, Wilt thou then that we go and gather them up?
> ²⁹But he said, Nay; lest while ye gather up the tares, ye root up also the wheat with them.
> ³⁰Let both grow together until the harvest: and in the time of harvest I will say to the reapers, Gather ye together first the tares, and bind them in bundles to burn them: but gather the wheat into my barn.

The roots of the tares became so intertwined with those of the wheat that the tares could not easily be uprooted without harming the wheat. When wheat matures, however, it bows under the weight of its kernels, and the taller tares can be harvested first, and burned. After telling additional parables in verses 31-35 (see Sec. II on p. 413), Christ gave the following explanation of the parable of the tares.

C. The tares are "the children of the wicked one."

> ³⁶Then Jesus sent the multitude away, and went into the house: and his disciples came unto him, saying, Declare unto us the parable of the tares of the field.
> ³⁷He answered and said unto them, He that soweth the good seed is the Son of man;
> ³⁸The field is the world; the good seed are the children of the kingdom; but the tares are the children of the wicked one;
> ³⁹ᵃThe enemy that sowed them is the devil;

The tares are not merely obstacles and hindrances (of which Satan creates many) to the spread of the gospel and the growth of believers; they are large numbers of *people* who are "children of the wicked one." Satan plants them among "the children of the kingdom" who were planted by Christ with the "good seed" of God's Word. The parable pictures the world-wide professing church in which true believers and false professors "grow together" (v. 30) side by side in this present age.

D. The tares will be "burned in the fire."

³⁹ᵇthe harvest is the end of the world; and the reapers are the angels.
⁴⁰As therefore the tares are gathered and burned in the fire; so shall it be in the end of this world.
⁴¹The Son of man shall send forth his angels, and they shall gather out of his kingdom all things that offend, and them which do iniquity;
⁴²And shall cast them into a furnace of fire: there shall be wailing and gnashing of teeth.

The tares enjoyed a comfortable existence while living in God's field among the wheat. They shared in His sunshine and rain and initially were admired as healthy plants. Although appearing to be wheat, they possessed from the beginning Satan's diabolical nature and designs. They can only "do iniquity" and "offend" God, and they will be forcibly removed from His kingdom (v. 41).

The present church age will culminate at "the harvest" (v. 39) when Christ returns. The tares will be burned "in a furnace of fire" (v. 42), but they will not be burned up. They will be eternally conscious of their deserved punishment and will wail forever in constant torment.

E. The wheat will "shine as the sun" forever.

⁴³Then shall the righteous shine forth as the sun in the kingdom of their Father. Who hath ears to hear, let him hear.

The wheat will be "gathered into [God's] barn" (v. 30). In that heavenly kingdom, believers will shine as the sun with their Father forever. Verse 43b may be understood: "Whoever will listen and learn from this lesson, let him heed it by acting on it."

Parables on Professing Christendom

Light or Leaven? Fish or Fowl?

The preceding parables on the soils and the tares, along with their explanation by Christ, laid the foundation for understanding God's kingdom as it relates to this present age. Christ followed these parables with others that picture additional aspects of professing Christendom during this interval between His ascension and His second coming. Although He "expounded all things" in these parables to His disciples, these explanations were not recorded for our benefit. Our task, therefore, is to apply biblical principles of interpretation to these parables to understand their instruction regarding professing Christendom and our own relationship to Christ.

I. The spreading and working of God's Word.

The following three parables in Mark and Luke may have been told after the one about the soils in MT 13. Christ gave these to His earnest followers (the twelve plus others) to assure them that in spite of opposition and hardship, God's purposes eventually will prevail — in the world, in the church, and in their individual lives.

A. The shining lamp: presenting truth to those in darkness.
MK 4:21 [LK 8:16] And he said unto them, Is a candle [lamp] brought to be put under a bushel, or under a bed? and not to be set on a candlestick [lampstand]? {No man, when he hath lighted a candle, covereth it with a vessel, or putteth it under a bed; but setteth it on a candlestick, that they which enter in may see the light.} ²²For there is nothing hid, which shall not be manifested; neither was any thing kept secret, but that it should {be known and} come abroad. ²³If any man have ears to hear, let him hear.

The parable teaches that the gospel is to be proclaimed fully and openly — and not withheld or obscured from those who need its light. Christ previously declared that God's kingdom has come among men through His person and work, and that this kingdom is entered by hearing and heeding His Word. This illuminating message about Christ is the lamp that is to be held high for all to see.

The principal "secret" (in v. 22) to be published abroad is God's previously-undisclosed plan of salvation through the sacrifice of His Son for mankind's sin. That plan, presented in veiled form to Israel in the Old Testament, would be manifested to all mankind following Christ's death and resurrection.

B. The increasing measure: the more we heed, the more we receive.
²⁴And he said unto them, Take heed what {how} ye hear: with what measure ye mete [you measure with], it shall be measured to you: and unto you that hear shall more be given. ²⁵For he that hath, to him shall be given: and he that hath not, from him shall be taken even that which he hath {seemeth to have}.

The picture here is not of a measuring *device* (such as a cup or a scale), but of the measuring *process* and the particular thing being measured. Verse 24b may be understood: "With the same measure or degree that you heed my Word, its beneficial results will be 'measured back' to you. And when you heed what you have received, you will be given more truth and understanding." Verse 25 adds that those who do not heed what they have already heard will lose the limited spiritual understanding they initially seemed to have.

    C. The growing plant: God's and man's roles in His kingdom.
        ²⁶And he said, So is the kingdom of God, as if a man should cast seed into the ground;
        ²⁷And should sleep, and rise night and day, and the seed should spring and grow up, he knoweth not how.
        ²⁸For the earth bringeth forth fruit of herself; first the blade, then the ear, after that the full corn in the ear.
        ²⁹But when the fruit is brought forth, immediately he putteth in the sickle, because the harvest is come.

Different interpretations of this parable have been offered. One, however, is precluded — namely, that the sower is Christ. He could not be said, as in verse 27, to "know not how" the seed germinates and grows. In the context of the parables in MT 13, this one also seems to picture the progressive growth of God's kingdom among men. If so, the seed (as in the other parables) is God's Word, sown by His servants throughout the world and throughout the ages. The "blade, ear, and full corn" may represent the growth and development of Christ's church of true believers until "the harvest" when He returns.

Another interpretation views the seed as the gospel which is sown by a believer in the life of an unbeliever and which works within the latter through God's unseen power until it produces the harvest of salvation. Yet another is that each faithful believer sows God's Word into his own life, where the Holy Spirit uses it quietly and inwardly to bring about his progressive sanctification. The harvest, then, is the full-grown result of those spiritual seeds.

    II. Perversion in church membership and doctrine.

      A. The mustard tree: fowls roosting in the church.
        MT 13:31 [MK 4; LK 13] Another parable put he forth unto them, saying, {Whereunto shall we liken the kingdom of God? or with what comparison shall we compare it?} The kingdom of heaven is like to a grain of mustard seed, which a man took, and sowed in his field {and it grew, and waxed [became] a great tree}:
        ³²Which indeed is the least of all seeds: but when it is grown, it is the greatest among herbs, and becometh a tree, so that the birds {fowls} of the air come and lodge in the branches thereof.

This parable and the related one that follows it have been interpreted in diametrically opposite ways. The exceptional growth pictured for the kingdom is seen as good by some and as bad by others. Because of the negative connotations of the vastly overgrown herb and "the fowls of the air" (and, in the next parable, of leaven), it appears that Christ is preparing His followers for the adverse, not the favorable, aspects of the professing church's future growth.

Mustard seeds are tiny but they can produce large shrubs 10-20 feet tall. Such shrubs, however, have multiple, spindly stems that are relatively weak and insubstantial. The shrub in the parable "became a great tree," suggesting abnormal expansion of the professing church, as well as its departure from its original nature.

Luke calls the birds "the fowls of the air" — perhaps the same creatures that "came and devoured" the good seed by the wayside in the parable of the soils. Such fowls would include Satanically-used unbelievers who infiltrate the church, oppose its purpose, and pervert its activity. This view is consistent with the mixed membership seen in the professing church today and with other prophecies that apostate leaders and members increasingly will inhabit the church in the end times.

B. The leaven: false doctrine spreading in the church.

³³Another parable spake he unto them; The kingdom of heaven is like unto leaven, which a woman took, and hid in three measures of meal, till the whole was leavened.

Christ warned His disciples in MT 16:6-12: "Beware of the leaven of the Pharisees and of the Sadducees . . . not the leaven of bread, but of their *doctrine*." When related to moral matters, leaven in scripture uniformly pictures evil. Use of leaven, for example, was forbidden during the feasts of Passover and Unleavened Bread and in sacrifices and offerings to God made with fire. Paul, in confronting sin in the church at Corinth, warned that "a little leaven leaveneth the whole lump," as Christ pictured here. The meal here represents true doctrine that is being corrupted with falsehood. The woman pictures apostate ecclesiastical organizations and leaders that mix truth with error until their whole message (and the church in general) is permeated with heresy.

III. Parables the people should have understood.

³⁴All these things spake Jesus unto the multitude in parables {And with many such parables spake he the word unto them, as they were able to hear it}; and without a parable spake he not unto them: {and when they were alone, he expounded all things to his disciples}.
³⁵That it might be fulfilled which was spoken by the prophet, saying, I will open my mouth in parables; I will utter things which have been kept secret from the foundation of the world.

Christ taught His followers through parables "as they were able to hear." He graciously suited each picture to their capacity at that juncture for grasping spiritual truth. He presented enough that was apparent so that an earnest hearer could deduce its application. The Jewish people had waited 1,000 years for the fulfillment of Psalm 78:2 (cited in v. 35), but very few recognized it when it came. Afterward, Christ "expounded all things to His disciples," including things "kept secret from the foundation of the world." (After v. 35, Christ explained the parable of the tares in vv. 36-43; see Sec. V.C-E on p. 410.)

IV. Treasure purchased with all a man had.

A. The treasure hidden in a field.

⁴⁴Again, the kingdom of heaven is like unto treasure hid in a field; the which when a man hath found, he hideth, and for joy thereof goeth and selleth all that he hath, and buyeth that field.

B. The one pearl of great price.

⁴⁵Again, the kingdom of heaven is like unto a merchant man, seeking goodly pearls:

⁴⁶Who, when he had found one pearl of great price, went and sold all that he had, and bought it.

These similar parables relate to God's greatest treasure on earth. The "treasure hid in a field" pictures all the people throughout the world who ever have trusted or will yet trust in His revealed way for their salvation. Christ gave all that He had to buy that treasure (and also to obtain the right to rule over the world in which He found it). More particularly, the "one pearl of great price" depicts the unique body of all true believers in Christ (His universal church) during this present age. For a further discussion of these parables, see Section III on p. 52.

V. Summaries of Christ's parables on Christendom.

A. The net full of fish: separating true from false believers.

⁴⁷Again, the kingdom of heaven is like unto a net [a dragnet], that was cast into the sea, and gathered of every kind:

⁴⁸Which, when it was full, they drew to shore, and sat down, and gathered the good into vessels, but cast the bad away.

⁴⁹So shall it be at the end of the world: the angels shall come forth, and sever the wicked from among the just,

⁵⁰And shall cast them into the furnace of fire: there shall be wailing and gnashing of teeth.

This parable summarizes those before it that deal with the fundamental difference between true believers and false professors. It also emphasizes the horrible judgment that awaits "the bad" and "the wicked." (It has the same concluding verse as the parable on the tares.) Like the others, this parable highlights a major aspect of professing Christendom — namely, that all manner of people will be drawn from the sea of mankind into its physical network. When the professing church is "full" at the end of the age, the "good" will be gathered and taken to their new home. A wide variety of "bad" critters also will be in the church; these must be "severed" from the good and cast into "the furnace of fire."

> B. The householder and his treasure: old truth for new applications.
> **⁵¹Jesus saith unto them [His disciples], Have ye understood all these things? They say unto him, Yea, Lord.**
> **⁵²Then said he unto them, Therefore every scribe which is instructed unto the kingdom of heaven is like unto a man that is an householder, which bringeth forth out of his treasure things new and old.**

This brief, concluding parable is representative of those that deal with each believer's understanding and application of God's truth for his own spiritual growth and presentation to others. Verse 52 may be understood: "Every student of God's Word who is well taught regarding God's kingdom is like the head of a household who brings out of his treasure chest [God's Word] things new and things old."

The *old things* are God's timeless truths that undergird our faith and our relationship with Him. The *new things* are new insights and fresh applications that we draw daily from our treasure chest as we seek and find its precious jewels. Uncovering these ageless truths and applying them newly in our current circumstances brings some of the greatest joy we can experience as God's children. What an encouragement that, in spite of the failures in the professing church and in our individual lives, these old treasures "fail not; they are new every morning" (Lam. 3:22-23).

20

Previews of Christ's Second Coming

Before Christ fulfilled His purpose in coming to earth (i.e., to purchase our salvation on the cross), He began preparing His disciples for His departure and return. They had not yet grasped the reason for His first coming, and now He was talking about a second coming. Further, much of His instruction was in pictures and parables they did not understand. Christ told them, however, "These things have I spoken unto you in proverbs [veiled sayings]: but the time cometh, when I shall no more speak unto you in proverbs, but I shall show you plainly of the Father" (JN 16:25).

Christ began to unveil these sayings for His disciples after His resurrection, and the Holy Spirit continued that work for all believers beginning on Pentecost. Now, viewed with hindsight through the remainder of the New Testament, the puzzles and parables can be resolved and the pictures be seen with understanding. Their subjects vary, but they all include the underlying thought: "Watch ye, therefore, and pray always, that ye may be accounted worthy to escape all these things that shall come to pass, and to stand before the Son of man" (LK 21:36).

Puzzles of Going and Coming

Most of Christ's prophecies regarding His leaving earth and coming again were intentionally vague. Especially to disbelieving Jews, who had already rejected Him as their Messiah, Christ made only brief and veiled allusions to His plans. Revealing the details to them would have been fruitless. Invariably, they were either baffled or angered by His puzzling pronouncements.

Even the prophecies Christ gave His disciples were often veiled in mystery and seeming ambiguity. Luke reports, "They understood none of these things: and this saying was hid from them" (18:34). It was not yet time for them to understand God's plan for the future. Christ promised, however, that "when he, the Spirit of truth, is come, he will guide you into all truth . . . and he will show you things to come" (JN 16:13).

I. Christ would go away in "a little while."

A. The Jews were perplexed by His puzzles.

JN 7:33 Then said Jesus unto them [the Jews], Yet a little while am I with you, and then I go unto him that sent me.

³⁴Ye shall seek me, and shall not find me: and where I am, thither ye cannot come.

³⁵Then said the Jews among themselves, Whither will he go, that we shall not find him? will he go unto the dispersed among the Gentiles, and teach the Gentiles?

³⁶What manner of saying is this that he said, Ye shall seek me, and shall not find me: and where I am, thither ye cannot come?

JN 8:21 Then said Jesus again unto them, I go my way, and ye shall seek me, and shall die in your sins: whither I go, ye cannot come.

²²Then said the Jews, Will he kill himself ? because he saith, Whither I go, ye cannot come.

²³And he said unto them, Ye are from beneath; I am from above: ye are of this world; I am not of this world.

These exchanges occurred about six months before Christ's death. The Jews could not comprehend where He was going nor why they could not follow Him there. Bewildered, they asked one another, "Will he go and teach the Jews dispersed throughout the world [the Diaspora]? Will He teach the Gentiles too?" (v. 35). They even conjectured: "Will he kill himself?" (v. 22).

Disbelieving Jews could not go where Christ was going (to heaven) because they were "from beneath" (v. 23) and were under Satan's control. Also, they were "of this world" and were preoccupied with selfish and temporal concerns. As a result, they would die in their sins (v. 21). In a way they never expected, Christ would indeed voluntarily die, and (through His emissaries) go to the Diaspora and also "teach the Gentiles." These others would hear the gospel that the Jews in Israel had rejected.

B. Peter was troubled by His sayings.

> JN 13:33 [To His disciples:] Little children, yet a little while I am with you. Ye shall seek me: and as I said unto the Jews, Whither I go, ye cannot come; so now I say to you. . . .
>
> ³⁶Simon Peter said unto him, Lord, whither goest thou? Jesus answered him, Whither I go, thou canst not follow me now; but thou shalt follow me afterwards.
>
> ³⁷Peter said unto him, Lord, why cannot I follow thee now? I will lay down my life for thy sake.
>
> ³⁸Jesus answered him, Wilt thou lay down thy life for my sake? Verily, verily, I say unto thee, The cock shall not crow, till thou hast denied me thrice.

The night Christ was betrayed, the disciples still did not grasp what He was saying. Peter asked, in effect: "What country or city are you going to? and why can't I go along?" Christ's answer, "You will follow me afterward," can be taken two ways: (1) Peter would follow Him eventually to heaven, or (2) Peter would follow Him in death by crucifixion (see Sec. IV.C on p. 266).

C. The disciples were confused by His proverbs.

> JN 14:19 Yet a little while, and the world seeth me no more; but ye see me: because I live, ye shall live also.
>
> ²⁰At that day ye shall know that I am in my Father, and ye in me, and I in you. . . .
>
> ²²Judas saith unto him, not Iscariot, Lord, how is it that thou wilt manifest thyself unto us, and not unto the world?
>
> ²³Jesus answered and said unto him, If a man love me, he will keep my words: and my Father will love him, and we will come unto him, and make our abode with him.

The disciples could not understand how the world would not be able to see Christ while they could see Him (v. 19). Thaddaeus (called Judas here and in LK 6:16) asked how He could reveal Himself to them as the Messiah without everyone else also seeing Him as king. Christ answered that He and His Father would come and indwell each believer personally (v. 23). Jointly, they would reveal Christ as Lord and King to those who love and obey Him. This promise, however, was beyond their comprehension for the time being.

II. The disciples would see Christ again "in a little while."

    A. They wanted to know what He meant.

> JN 16:16 A little while, and ye shall not see me: and again, a little while, and ye shall see me, because I go to the Father.
>
> [17]Then said some of his disciples among themselves, What is this that he saith unto us, A little while, and ye shall not see me: and again, a little while, and ye shall see me: and, Because I go to the Father?
>
> [18]They said therefore, What is this that he saith, A little while? we cannot tell what he saith.
>
> [19]Now Jesus knew that they were desirous to ask him, and said unto them, Do ye enquire among yourselves of that I said, A little while, and ye shall not see me: and again, a little while, and ye shall see me?

This "a little while and ye *shall* not see me" (v. 16) is followed by "a little while and ye shall see me." It appears to refer simultaneously to two separate pairs of coming events. The first is Christ's death and burial ("you will not see me") and His resurrection ("you will see me"). The second is His ascension ("not see me") and His return to them at Pentecost in the person of His Holy Spirit ("will see me"). Both pairs of events would occur in "a little while." The first began the next day; the second, less than two months later.

    B. They would weep for a while, but then rejoice.

> [20]Verily, verily, I say unto you, That ye shall weep and lament, but the world shall rejoice: and ye shall be sorrowful, but your sorrow shall be turned into joy.
>
> [21]A woman when she is in travail hath sorrow, because her hour is come: but as soon as she is delivered of the child, she remembereth no more the anguish, for joy that a man is born into the world.
>
> [22]And ye now therefore have sorrow: but I will see you again, and your heart shall rejoice, and your joy no man taketh from you.

These verses also have two possible applications. The first refers to Christ's death, over which "the world" would rejoice while they sorrow, and to His resurrection, which would turn their sorrow to joy. The second looks ahead to the persecution and suffering they and believers after them would experience before Christ's second coming, while the world revels in its defiance of God. That sorrow would turn to joy when they rejoin Christ through death or when He comes again for them from heaven.

    C. They finally began to perceive His proverbs.

> JN 16:25 These things have I spoken unto you in proverbs [veiled sayings]: but the time cometh, when I shall no more speak unto you in proverbs, but I shall shew you plainly of the Father. . . .

²⁸I came forth from the Father, and am come into the world: again, I leave the world, and go to the Father.

²⁹His disciples said unto him, Lo, now speakest thou plainly, and speakest no proverb

³⁰Now are we sure that thou knowest all things, and needest not that any man should ask thee: by this we believe that thou camest forth from God.

D. But full understanding was still to come.

³¹Jesus answered them, Do ye now believe?

³²Behold, the hour cometh, yea, is now come, that ye shall be scattered, every man to his own, and shall leave me alone: and yet I am not alone, because the Father is with me.

³³These things I have spoken unto you, that in me ye might have peace. In the world ye shall have tribulation: but be of good cheer; I have overcome the world.

JN 16 is part of Christ's final message to His disciples before the cross. To the end, He used pictures and proverbs they struggled to perceive. The light, however, finally began to dawn in verses 29-30: "Now you are speaking plainly, and not with hidden meaning." Christ acknowledged the dawning of their understanding by asking, "Are you just now beginning to believe?" (v. 31). He warned that great trials of their faith were still ahead — beginning momentarily when they would flee and forsake Him. Though facing the cross, Christ ended His message with triumph and encouragement: "Be of good cheer; I have overcome the world."

III. Believers long for His coming, but must wait.

A. His coming, though delayed, will occur in a flash.

LK 17:22 And he said unto the disciples, The days will come, when ye shall desire to see one of the days of the Son of man, and ye shall not see it.

²³And they shall say to you, See [it is] here; or, see [it is] there: go not after them, nor follow them.

²⁴For as the lightning, that lighteneth out of the one part under heaven, shineth unto the other part under heaven; so shall also the Son of man be in his day.

Christ revealed here that His second coming would follow a waiting period of some length (v. 22). Then it will come as suddenly as lightning (v. 24). (This passage refers to His return to earth to establish His kingdom, but His return "in the air" to rapture His church will occur just as suddenly.) Christ's Olivet Discourse in subsequent sections contains a detailed exposition of this prophecy.

B. His coming in glory must follow His rejection on earth.

²⁵**But first must he suffer many things, and be rejected of this generation.**

Here is why Christ typically veiled the future in puzzles and proverbs. He was still offering Himself as Israel's Messiah and the nation's rejection of Him was not yet complete. His first task was to suffer and die at the hands of "this generation." Until that was accomplished, neither unbelieving Jews nor His own disciples could comprehend God's plan for future. His disciples began to understand these things after His resurrection, but Israel as a nation will not recognize Him as its Messiah until shortly before His glorious return.

IV. Christ's promised coming encourages His own.

A. It dispels their fears and comforts their hearts.

JN 14:1 Let not your heart be troubled: ye believe in God, believe also in me.

²**In my Father's house are many mansions [dwelling places]: if it were not so, I would have told you. I go to prepare a place for you.**

³**And if I go and prepare a place for you, I will come again, and receive you unto myself; that where I am, there ye may be also.**

The disciples were greatly troubled by Christ's "where I go ye cannot come" and His revelation that Peter (and they all) would forsake Him. Christ gave them, therefore, these reassuring promises to confirm that He would return to take them to dwell with Him in heaven. Ever since, His promised return has given comfort and encouragement to troubled believers.

B. It gives them peace, assurance, and joy.

JN 14:27 Peace I leave with you, my peace I give unto you: not as the world giveth, give I unto you. Let not your heart be troubled, neither let it be afraid.

²⁸**Ye have heard how I said unto you, I go away, and come again unto you. If ye loved me, ye would rejoice, because I said, I go unto the Father: for my Father is greater than I.**

²⁹**And now I have told you before it come to pass, that, when it is come to pass, ye might believe.**

Christ declared that the fulfillment of His prophesied death, resurrection, and ascension would confirm and strengthen His followers' faith in Him (v. 29). That fulfillment would also give them great peace and assurance that He is fully in control of all things and will surely come again as He promised (v. 28). Until then, He gives all receptive believers His own perfect peace and joy to encourage their hearts and strengthen their spirits as they live in anticipation of His return.

Signs for Christ's Return
From the Olivet Discourse
(MT 24; MK 13; LK 21)

As the time for His crucifixion drew near, Christ grieved that God's chosen people had rejected their Messiah. Sadly but solemnly, He declared that their "house is left desolate" and that His earthly kingdom would be delayed indefinitely. His disciples asked: "When shall these things be? and what shall be the sign of thy coming, and of the end of the age?" In response, Christ cited the "signs" presented in the following pages.

Signs are events or conditions that signal the approach or arrival of a predicted occurrence. These signs for Christ's return are from His Olivet Discourse (named for the Mount of Olives, where He gave it to His disciples). Matthew's account is the most complete and is presented here in order. Related material from Mark and Luke is inserted where appropriate.

    I. Summary: Three eras of Israel's history.

        A. Israel's rejection of the prophets from Moses through Christ.

        MT 23:37 O Jerusalem, Jerusalem, thou that killest the prophets, and stonest them which are sent unto thee, how often would I have gathered thy children together, even as a hen gathereth her chickens under her wings, and ye would not!

From the time God delivered Israel from Egypt (about 1450 B.C.), through the time of Christ, the nation repeatedly rejected God's leadership and rule by rejecting God's emissaries. Jesus is speaking here not only as the Christ they have rejected for three and one-half years, but as the God they have rejected for over 1,000 years.

        B. Israel's desolation between Christ's comings.

        [38]Behold, your house is left unto you desolate.

The Jews' "house" certainly included the temple, in which Christ made these statements. More broadly, it included the entire system of temple worship. God Himself soon would end that system by severing the veil in the holy of holies to signify His replacement of the Old Covenant with the New. The Jews' house also encompassed the city of Jerusalem and the nation-state of Israel. These, along with the temple, were destroyed by the Romans in A.D. 70 (see below). Although the city and nation have been partially restored physically and politically, they remain desolate in spiritual terms (Romans 9-11). The temple remains desolate in every sense of the word to this day.

C. Israel's blessing when Christ returns as its King.

³⁹For I say unto you, Ye shall not see me henceforth, till ye shall say, Blessed is he that cometh in the name of the Lord.

For devout Jews awaiting God's kingdom, this was the worst news of all. Their rejected King was leaving and taking their hope for the kingdom with Him. He would not be seen again by the Jewish nation until He returns as its majestic Lord. Believing Jews will then bless and worship Him as their Messiah. He in turn will bless them by fulfilling all the prophecies concerning His (and their) millennial kingdom.

II. Initial signs before Christ's coming.

A. The temple will be "thrown down."

MT 24:1 [MK 13:1; LK 21:5] And Jesus went out, and departed from the temple: and his disciples came to him for to show him the buildings of the temple. {One of his disciples saith unto him, Master, see what manner of [beautiful] stones and what [magnificent] buildings are here!}

²And Jesus said unto them, See ye not all these things? verily I say unto you, There shall not be left here one stone upon another, that shall not be thrown down.

This conversation immediately followed Christ's solemn predictions at the end of chapter 23 above. His disciples must have been shocked that God's holy temple would be left desolate. They showed Him the temple area, as if to say, "Surely you don't mean this magnificent and beautiful place!" But Christ underscored His prophecy by adding that no stone of all the buildings in the temple area would be left in place.

B. He will not return until "the end of the age."

³And as he sat upon the mount of Olives, the disciples {Peter and James and John and Andrew} came unto him privately, saying, Tell us, when shall these things be? and what shall be the sign of thy coming, and of the end of the world [age] {when all these things shall be fulfilled}?

Christ's four closest disciples asked what sign would signal His coming and the temple's destruction. Although they had not understood many of His previous prophecies, they apparently connected some knowledge of Old Testament eschatology with Christ's prior teaching to conclude (correctly) that He would return at "the end of the age." The remainder of the chapter contains Christ's answer.

C. Many false Christs will deceive many people.

⁴And Jesus answered and said unto them, Take heed that no man deceive you.

⁵For many shall come in my name, saying, I am Christ; and shall deceive many. {Go ye not, therefore, after them.}

D. War and fighting will be widespread.

⁶And ye shall hear of wars and rumors of wars: see that ye be not troubled: for all these things must {first} come to pass, but the end is not yet.
⁷ᵃFor nation shall rise against nation, and kingdom against kingdom:

E. "Natural" calamities will abound.

⁷ᵇand there shall be famines, and pestilences, and earthquakes, in divers places {and fearful sights and great signs shall there be from heaven}.

F. Much more is yet to come.

⁸All these are [only] the beginning of sorrows [birth pains].

Although the signs in verses 5-7 have been present in the world in varying degrees since His ascension, Christ indicated they will increase in frequency, scope, and intensity as His coming approaches. That these do not signal the end of the age is clearly stated in verse 6 ("the end is not yet") and verse 8 ("these are the *beginning* of sorrows"). These "birth pains" will reach their greatest severity during the seven-year Tribulation described in Revelation chapters 6-18. For the present, these recurring tragedies are a reminder that the world in general will not materially improve spiritually, socially, or physically (all human effort notwithstanding) until Christ returns and reorders all creation.

III. Initial signs related to Israel.

A. Jerusalem will be destroyed by Gentile armies.

LK 21:20 And when ye shall see Jerusalem compassed with armies, then know that the desolation thereof is nigh.
²¹Then let them which are in Judaea flee to the mountains; and let them which are in the midst of it depart out; and let not them that are in the countries enter thereinto.
²²For these be the days of vengeance [days when justice is meted out], that all things which are written may be fulfilled.
²³But woe unto them that are with child [pregnant], and to them that give suck [nurse infants], in those days! for there shall be great distress in the land, and wrath upon this people.

B. The Jews will be dispersed "into all nations."

²⁴ᵃAnd they shall fall by the edge of the sword, and shall be led away captive into all nations:

C. Jerusalem will be dominated by Gentiles until Christ returns.

²⁴ᵇand Jerusalem shall be trodden down of the Gentiles, until the times of the Gentiles be fulfilled.

Luke's account explains how the Jews' house would be left desolate and every stone thrown down. It parallels MT 24:15-22, which also foretells a climactic desolation of Jerusalem and Judea. With a dual perspective, Christ foretold two separate events in one broad prediction. Such prophetic melding is used in both Testaments, especially when the first event is a type or picture of the second, as is the case here.

Christ predicted here the destruction of Jerusalem, which occurred in A.D. 70 at the hands of the Roman army. Its desolation (v. 20) would be followed by world-wide dispersion of the Jewish people and a lengthy period of Gentile domination of the city (v. 24). Luke's account is inserted at this point because of its early historical fulfillment. Matthew pictures a similar but still-future onslaught against the Jews by the Antichrist (see Sec. VII).

IV. Signs regarding believers' problems.

A. Severe persecution by governments and religious organizations.

MT 24:9 [MK 13:9] Then shall they deliver you up {to councils} to be afflicted, and shall kill you {and in the synagogues ye shall be beaten}: and ye shall be hated of all nations for my name's sake.

¹⁰And then shall many be offended, and shall betray one another, and shall hate one another.

B. Frequent betrayal by family and friends.

LK 21:16 [MK 13:12] And ye shall be betrayed both by parents, and brethren, and kinsfolks, and friends; and some of you shall they cause to be put to death. {Now the brother shall betray the brother to death, and the father the son; and children shall rise up against their parents, and shall cause them to be put to death.}

¹⁷And ye shall be hated of all men for my name's sake.

C. Widespread apostasy, sin, and apathy among professing believers.

MT 24:11 And many false prophets shall rise, and shall deceive many.

¹²And because iniquity [lawlessness] shall abound, the love of many shall wax [grow] cold.

¹³But he that shall endure unto the end, the same shall be saved [delivered from death].

These problems (A, B, C), tragically, have afflicted the body of believers in varying degrees since Pentecost. In some lands, severe persecution of believers is commonplace today. Also, the sins identified in Part C have always been a major problem in professing Christendom, and they seem to be on the increase. Other passages (e.g., II Tim. 3:1-9) state that these conditions will increase and abound during these "last days." As with the signs in verses 5-7, these too will reach their peak during the Tribulation. Christ asked earlier, "When the Son of man cometh, shall he find faith on the earth?" (LK 18:8).

V. Signs regarding preaching the gospel.

    A. Power for believers to speak for Christ.

        LK 21:12 [MK 13:11] But before all these, they shall lay their hands on you, and persecute you, delivering you up to the synagogues, and into prisons, being brought before kings and rulers for my name's sake.

        ¹³And it shall turn to you [to your advantage] for a testimony.

        ¹⁴Settle it therefore in your hearts, not to meditate before what ye shall answer:

        ¹⁵For I will give you a mouth and wisdom, which all your adversaries shall not be able to gainsay [contradict] nor resist [refute] {but whatsoever shall be given you in that hour, that speak ye: for it is not ye that speak, but the Holy Ghost}.

    B. Physical protection for God's messengers.

        LK 21:18 But there shall not an hair of your head perish.

        ¹⁹In your patience possess ye your souls.

During the Tribulation, a remnant of 144,000 Jews will acknowledge Christ as Messiah and be "sealed [as] the servants of God" (Rev. 7:1-8). Also, an additional large number of Jews will "keep the commandments of God, and have the testimony of Jesus Christ" (Rev. 12:17). God will give these Jews unusual power to present and defend the gospel (Part A above), and will protect them physically throughout their ministry (Part B above). Verse 19 may be understood: "Through steadfast endurance, your lives will be saved."

    C. World-wide evangelism.

        MT 24:14 And this gospel of the kingdom shall be preached in all the world for a witness unto all nations; and then shall the end come.

The "end" will not come until the gospel is preached "in all the world . . . unto all nations." Although missionary efforts the last 2,000 years have sought to spread the gospel throughout the world, large areas today still appear to have no gospel witness. During the Tribulation, an innumerable multitude of Gentiles will be saved (Rev. 7:9), apparently in large part through the zealous witness of Jewish believers.

VI. Signs regarding the "Great Tribulation."

    A. Antichrist standing as God in the temple.

        MT 24:15 When ye therefore shall see the abomination of desolation, spoken of by Daniel the prophet, stand in the holy place {where it ought not}, (whoso readeth, let him understand:)

One of Daniel's prophecies regarding the Antichrist states: "the daily sacrifice [in the temple] shall be taken away, and the abomination that maketh desolate set up" (12:11). That prophecy (made about 540 B.C.) is another example of melding two separate but similar future events. Its first fulfillment occurred in 167 B.C. when Antiochus IV (Epiphanes), a Syrian Seleucid king, banned the Jewish religion, converted the temple to worship of Zeus, and offered swine's flesh on the altar. That "abomination" prefigured the future Antichrist's action at the mid-point of the Tribulation cited in verse 15 above. Then shall "that man of sin be revealed, the son of perdition, who opposeth and exalteth himself above all that is called God, or that is worshipped; so that he as God sitteth in the temple of God, showing himself that he is God" (II Thes. 2:3-4).

    B. Unprecedented persecution, especially for Jews.

        [16]Then let them which be in Judaea flee into the mountains:

        [17]Let him which is on the housetop not come down to take any thing out of his house:

        [18]Neither let him which is in the field return back to take his clothes.

        [19]And woe unto them that are with child [pregnant], and to them that give suck [nurse infants] in those days!

        [20]But pray ye that your flight be not in the winter, neither on the sabbath day:

    C. World-wide tribulation for all mankind.

        [21]For then shall be great tribulation {affliction}, such as was not since the beginning of the world to this time, no, nor ever shall be.

        [22]And except those days should be shortened, there should no flesh be saved: but for the elect's sake {whom he hath chosen} those days shall be shortened.

The second half of the Tribulation will be "great tribulation," especially for God's "elect," i.e., His chosen ones. God calls Israel His elect in Isaiah, and He uses the same term for Christians throughout the epistles. Here, "the elect" probably refers to believing Jews, but the message applies to all who have trusted Christ and are alive near the end of the Tribulation. To spare those believers from certain physical annihilation, God will bring those horrible days to a quick conclusion.

D. False Christs with miracle-working power.

> [23]Then if any man shall say unto you, Lo, here is Christ, or there; believe it not.
>
> [24]For there shall arise false Christs, and false prophets, and shall show great signs and wonders; insomuch that, if it were possible, they shall deceive the very elect.
>
> [25]Behold, I have told you before. {But take ye heed ... I have foretold you all things.}
>
> [26]Wherefore if they shall say unto you, Behold, he is in the desert; go not forth: behold, he is in the secret chambers; believe it not.

God will permit Satan to empower the Antichrist and his false prophet (and possibly others) to perform miracles during the Tribulation to persuade the peoples of the earth to worship the Antichrist (Rev. 13:11-15). Christ warned believers not to be deceived by these "false Christs," or by reports that He has already returned to earth and can be found in some "secret place" (v. 26).

VII. The ultimate sign of Christ's return.

A. His coming as a flash of lightning.

> [27]For as the lightning cometh out of the east, and shineth even unto the west; so shall also the coming of the Son of man be.

B. His slaying the enemies of God.

> [28]For wheresoever the carcass is, there will the eagles be gathered together.

Verse 28 appears to refer to Christ's slaughter of Antichrist's armies at Armageddon at the moment of His return (Rev. 19:11-21). His statement uses the imagery of Job 39:27-30, which pictures eagles that feast on the blood of the slain. At Armageddon, an angel will summon "the fowls that fly in the midst of heaven" to eat the flesh of those slain in the battle (Rev. 19:17-18).

C. His shaking the heavens and earth.

> [29]Immediately after the tribulation of those days shall the sun be darkened, and the moon shall not give her light, and the stars shall fall from heaven, and the powers of the heavens shall be shaken:
>
> {And there shall be signs in the sun, and in the moon, and in the stars; and upon the earth distress of nations, with perplexity; the sea and the waves roaring; men's hearts failing them for fear, and for looking after those things which are coming on the earth: for the powers of heaven shall be shaken [LK 21:25-26].}

D. His appearing with "great glory" to all people.

> [30]**And then shall appear the sign of the Son of man in heaven: and then shall all the tribes of the earth mourn, and they shall see the Son of man coming in the clouds of heaven with power and great glory.**

E. His gathering together of all believers.

> [31]**And he shall send his angels with a great sound of a trumpet, and they shall gather together his elect from the four winds, from one end of heaven to the other {from the uttermost part of the earth to the uttermost part of heaven.}**

"*The sign* of the Son of man" (v. 30) will appear as a flash of lightning (v.27). Against a sky previously darkened (v. 29), Christ will suddenly appear in a brilliant blaze of glory. In one majestic sweep, the King of kings and Lord of lords will shake the heavens and the earth (v. 29), appear visibly and simultaneously to all people worldwide (v. 30), slay the wicked hosts assembled against Him by the Antichrist (v. 28) and gather to Himself all believers from all parts of God's creation (v. 31).

This is the climax toward which all human history has pointed, and for which believers in all ages have waited. The last prayer in the Bible pleads: "Even so, come, Lord Jesus" (Rev. 22:20).

Parallels for the End Times

At this point in His Olivet Discourse, Christ revisited the period that will precede His return and inserted further prophecies of events and conditions that will characterize that time. He framed these in the following parables and parallels, using objects and topics well known to His disciples. These illustrations present additional indicators of His coming as well as admonitions to watch and be ready for His return.

I. Israel's position as "the fig tree."

A. Its "budding branches" will signal the end.

> **MT 24:32 [LK 21:29] Now learn a parable of the fig tree {and all the trees}; When his branch is yet tender, and putteth forth leaves, ye know that summer is nigh:**
> [33]**So likewise ye, when ye shall see all these things, know that it {the kingdom of God} is near, even at the doors.**

God told Israel: "I saw your fathers as the first-ripe [fruit] in the fig tree" (Hosea 9:10). As the nation, however, progressively rejected its Messiah, Christ pictured Israel first as a fruitless fig tree (see Sec. IV on p. 4) and later as a cursed fig tree (Sec. VIII on p. 301). These pictures focused on Israel's *spiri-*

tual condition, not its political status. Its budding in verse 32, therefore, likely refers to its spiritual rebirth when it recognizes Christ as its Messiah during the Tribulation period. "All the trees" in LK 21 likely refers to the Gentile nations. When the events Christ prophesied for Israel and the nations of the world begin to unfold as new leaves on trees, "the kingdom of God is near" (v. 33).

B. Its "generation" will see the end.

³⁴**Verily I say unto you, This generation shall not pass {away}, till all these things be fulfilled.**

³⁵**Heaven and earth shall pass away, but my words shall not pass away.**

Verse 34 puzzles many believers. Some take it to mean that the generation living (or commencing) at the time of Israel's "budding" as an independent nation (in 1948) will live to see "all these things fulfilled." Alternatively, the word translated "generation" can mean "a race of people." If Christ intended the latter, then, in spite of the Jews' dispersion throughout the world and the determined efforts of their enemies throughout the ages to destroy them, the Jews' *race* "shall not pass away." Not even Satan's Antichrist with his mighty armies (vv. 15-21) will be able to destroy God's chosen people.

II. Moral degeneration as an indicator.

A. Preoccupation with pleasure, as in Noah's day.

³⁶**But of that day and hour knoweth no man, no, not the angels of heaven, but my Father only.**

³⁷**But as the days of Noe [Noah] were, so shall also the coming of the Son of man be.**

³⁸**For as in the days that were before the flood they were eating and drinking, marrying and giving in marriage, until the day that Noe entered into the ark,**

³⁹**And knew not until the flood came, and took them all away; so shall also the coming of the Son of man be.**

In Noah's time, "God saw that the wickedness of man was great in the earth, and that every imagination of the thoughts of his heart was only evil continually" (Gen 6:5). So shall it be at Christ's coming (v. 37). The activities in verse 38 are not wrong in themselves, but are sinful when pursued with selfish motives and in ungodly ways. God's prior judgment through the flood illustrates the breadth and severity of the judgment that will accompany Christ's return.

B. Decadence and materialism, as in Lot's day.

LK 17:28 Likewise also as it was in the days of Lot; they did eat, they drank, they bought, they sold, they planted, they builded;

²⁹**But the same day that Lot went out of Sodom it rained fire and brimstone from heaven, and destroyed them all.**
³⁰**Even thus shall it be in the day when the Son of man is revealed.**

Sodom's sin was "very grievous" (Gen. 18:20), and God destroyed the city with fire from heaven. The moral decadence and unbridled materialism that typified Lot's day will also typify "the day when the Son of man is revealed" (v. 30). God's judgment of unbelievers at Christ's return will be as sudden and severe as Sodom's judgment. (Luke adds this comparison with Lot to Matthew's comparison with Noah.)

C. The hold of worldliness, as on Lot's wife.
³¹**In that day [when Antichrist stands in the temple], he which shall be upon the housetop, and his stuff in the house, let him not come down to take it away: and he that is in the field, let him likewise not return back {to take his clothes}.**
³²**Remember Lot's wife.**
³³**Whosoever shall seek to save his life shall lose it; and whosoever shall lose his life shall preserve it.**

Verse 31 refers to the Jews, who should flee immediately for their lives upon seeing the Antichrist stand as God in the temple (see Sec. VI.A and B on p. 428). The passage also contains a warning not to become attached to worldly things and ways, as Lot's wife apparently was. She disobeyed God's command, "Look not behind thee" (Gen. 19:17), and "became a pillar of salt" (19:26). Her reason for disobeying is not given in Genesis, but this passage suggests it was her attachment to the worldly belongings and life-style she enjoyed in Sodom. Christ warned, therefore, "Whosoever shall seek to save [hold on to and keep] his life shall lose it" (v. 33).

Noah and Lot (with their small families) each lived among wicked people who willfully, openly, and continually disobeyed God's moral code. Both Noah and Lot had godly backgrounds and received instruction regarding God's will for their lives. Noah prepared well for the day of judgment; Lot and his wife, scarcely at all. The application for believers is clear.

III. The dividing of people for judgment.
³⁴**[MT 24:40] I tell you, in that night there shall be two men [two people] in one bed; the one shall be taken, and the other shall be left.**
³⁵**Two women shall be grinding together {at the mill}; the one shall be taken, and the other left.**
³⁶**Two men shall be in the field; the one shall be taken, and the other left.**

³⁷**And they [His disciples] answered and said unto him, Where, Lord? And he said unto them, Wheresoever the body [the corpse] is, thither will the eagles be gathered together. {Watch therefore: for ye know not what hour your Lord doth come.}**

These verses refer to Christ's visible return to earth, not to the rapture of believers that occurs at least seven years earlier. They mean that one shall be taken in death and to judgment, and the other left alive to enter Christ's kingdom. They depict the cataclysmic judgment of all unbelievers who are alive when Christ returns at the end of the Tribulation. Christ previously compared their judgment with (1) the flood which "took them all away," with Noah left alive, and (2) the fire from heaven which "destroyed them all," with Lot left alive. The disciples' question may mean "Where will this happen?" or "Where will those who are taken be taken to?" Christ's answer implies that their judgment and death will be sudden and violent, as at Armageddon (see Sec. VII.B on p. 429.)

IV. The *beginning* of these signs means the end is near.
> **LK 21:28 And when these things begin to come to pass, then look up, and lift up your heads; for your redemption draweth nigh.**

The moral degeneration prophesied for the end time (Sec. II above) and the spiritual, physical, and political troubles predicted in MT 24:5-12, are already present throughout the earth to a major degree. They will reach their peak, however, just before Christ's return. For believers in this age awaiting the rapture, and for those in the Tribulation awaiting His revelation, Christ promises: "Surely, I come quickly" (Rev. 22:20). "When these things *begin to come to pass*, . . . your redemption draweth nigh."

Particular People at Christ's Return

The preceding sections deal with Christ's return primarily from a global standpoint. They emphasize epochal events, the interplay of nations and societies, and world-wide problems and upheavals — all in the context of the pervasive spiritual battle waged by Satan and his hosts against God and His children. Within that macrocosm, however, are a multitude of microcosms, one for each person on earth. Christ's coming is all-important on both scales. How each person prepares for that day is also all-important; it determines his eternal destiny.

This section, from the concluding portion of the Olivet Discourse, presents parables that picture the attitudes and responses of various people to Christ's coming return. The issues and choices they faced are the same issues and choices we face. Similarly, the consequences of their choices foretell the results that our own choices will bring.

I. Christ's coming is imminent.

A. Watch, for no one knows the time.

MK 13:32 But of that day and that hour knoweth no man, no, not the angels which are in heaven, neither the Son, but the Father.
[33]Take ye heed, watch and pray: for ye know not when the time is.

B. Wake and work, "lest He find you sleeping."

[34]For the Son of man is as a man taking a far journey, who left his house, and gave authority to his servants, and to every man his work, and commanded the porter [doorkeeper] to watch.
[35]Watch ye therefore: for ye know not when the master of the house cometh, at even, or at midnight, or at the cockcrowing, or in the morning:
[36]Lest coming suddenly he find you sleeping.
[37]And what I say unto you I say unto all, Watch.

The Son of man has taken a "far journey" back to heaven and left His "house" (His earthly ministry) in the care of His servants until He returns. They do not know the day or time of day that He will come back. Christ admonished His servants, therefore, to be constantly alert and continually watching for His coming. "Take ye heed" (v. 33) may be read: "Always be on guard, all of you."

C. Walk worthily and alertly to avoid the snare.

LK 21:34 And take heed to yourselves, lest at any time your hearts be overcharged with surfeiting [indulging in pleasure], and drunkenness, and cares of this life, and so that day [of His return] come upon you unawares.
[35]For as a snare shall it come on all them that dwell on the face of the whole earth.
[36]Watch ye therefore, and pray always, that ye may be accounted worthy to escape all these things that shall come to pass, and to stand before the Son of man.

Christ's coming is likened to a snare that will catch by surprise those absorbed in pleasure-seeking and the "cares of this life" (v. 34). To those saved during the Tribulation, Christ urges, "Watch and pray continually that you may escape God's judgment of this earth and stand approved before me when I come" (v. 36). Believers today should be equally diligent in preparing to stand approved at the judgment seat of Christ (II Cor. 5:10). The rapture of the church, like Christ's return to earth in verse 35, also will be as a snare that catches many unawares.

II. People must be ready when He comes.

A. Some will be caught off guard, as by a thief.

MT 24:42 Watch therefore: for ye know not what hour your Lord doth come.

⁴³But know this, that if the goodman [owner] of the house had known in what watch the thief would come, he would have watched, and would not have suffered his house to be broken up [broken into].

⁴⁴Therefore be ye also ready: for in such an hour as ye think not the Son of man cometh.

Christ portrays those who are unprepared for His coming as an unwary homeowner whose house is broken into by a thief. The unsuspecting owner represents both the unsaved person who disregards God's offer of security in Christ and the unwise believer who stores his treasure on earth. Both will lose everything they held dear when Christ suddenly returns.

B. Some are "faithful and wise servants."

⁴⁵Who then is a faithful and wise servant, whom his lord hath made ruler over his household, to give them meat [their food] in due season?

⁴⁶Blessed is that servant, whom his lord when he cometh shall find so doing.

⁴⁷Verily I say unto you, That he shall make him ruler over all his goods.

Verse 45b may be read: "to give his fellow servants their food at the proper time." The Master will return to His household (His body of believers) and determine the degree to which each of His servants has been faithful and wise in carrying out his assigned responsibilities during His absence. Christ stressed the importance of being actively engaged in His work at the time He returns (v. 46). Because that time is unknown, it behooves each servant to be about the Master's business continually. He will reward each faithful servant accordingly.

C. Some doubt that Christ is coming at all.

⁴⁸[LK 12:45] But and if that evil servant shall say in his heart, My lord delayeth his coming;

⁴⁹And shall begin to smite his fellowservants, and to eat and drink with the drunken;

⁵⁰The lord of that servant shall come in a day when he looketh not for him, and in an hour that he is not aware of,

⁵¹And shall cut him asunder, and appoint him his portion with the hypocrites {unbelievers}: there shall be weeping and gnashing of teeth.

Just because someone calls Christ "my lord" does not necessarily mean that he possesses salvation. He may only be grudgingly admitting that Christ is a superior being. Christ described this so-called servant as "evil" (v. 48) and consigned him as an unbeliever to everlasting punishment (v. 51). His fatal error was in thinking that any coming judgment was far in the future and was of no concern at the present time.

> D. Some consciously choose not to prepare.
>> **LK 12:47 And that servant, which knew his lord's will, and prepared not himself, neither did according to his will, shall be beaten with many stripes.**

> E. Others fail to prepare out of ignorance.
>> **⁴⁸But he that knew not, and did commit things worthy of stripes, shall be beaten with few stripes. For unto whomsoever much is given, of him shall be much required: and to whom men have committed much, of him they will ask the more.**

Neither of these servants is a true believer, and both will receive eternal punishment. The one who "knew his lord's will" but refused to do it (v. 47) will be punished more severely than the one who "knew [it] not" (v. 48). (Even the latter had sufficient revelation, through nature and his conscience at the least, to make him fully responsible for his sin.) These verses indicate that, just as there are degrees of reward in heaven, there are also degrees of punishment in hell. Even the least punishment, however, includes unbearable torment for all eternity. The more revelation one has been given, the more responsible he will be for his lack of preparation (v. 48b).

> III. Many invited guests will miss Christ's wedding.

> A. "Foolish" guests mingle with "the wise" who await the Groom.
>> **MT 25:1 Then shall the kingdom of heaven be likened unto ten virgins, which took their lamps, and went forth to meet the bridegroom. ²And five of them were wise, and five were foolish.**

> B. They have a "form of godliness" but no power.
>> **³They that were foolish took their lamps, and took no oil with them: ⁴But the wise took oil in their vessels with their lamps.**

The difference between the wise and foolish guests was that the latter "took no oil with them." Although all ten had been invited to the wedding, and outwardly they all appeared ready, being truly prepared depended on having oil in their lamps. Some see the oil as representing God's saving grace, "through which He hath made us accepted in the beloved [i.e., in Christ]" (Eph. 1:6). Our acceptance in Christ, the bridegroom, includes our future admission to the "marriage supper of the Lamb" (Rev. 19:9).

Others see the oil as a symbol of the Holy Spirit, whom God gives to everyone who accepts Christ as his Savior. The oil used in lamps was pressed from olives, and such oil also was used in Old Testament times in anointing kings and priests for their God-ordained service. (It also was used in preparing foods, treating wounds, and anointing honored guests.) Since Pentecost, every believer is anointed by God with the Holy Spirit at the time of his salvation (II Cor. 1:21-22). That anointing is the source of each believer's spiritual enlightenment (I John 2:20, 27) and spiritual power (Acts 1:8). The Holy Spirit also provides each believer's spiritual nourishment, spiritual healing, and spiritual enjoyment, as God's all-sufficient oil. In the parable, the foolish unbelievers had "a form of godliness" (their physical lamps and religious activity) but not "the power" of God's energizing oil (see II Tim. 3:5).

C. They will not be prepared when the Groom returns.

> ⁵While the bridegroom tarried, they all slumbered and slept.
> ⁶And at midnight there was a cry made, Behold, the bridegroom cometh; go ye out to meet him.
> ⁷Then all those virgins arose, and trimmed their lamps.
> ⁸And the foolish said unto the wise, Give us of your oil; for our lamps are gone out.
> ⁹But the wise answered, saying, Not so; lest there be not enough for us and you: but go ye rather to them that sell, and buy for yourselves.

God's "oil" is not transferable from one person to another. The wise virgins properly advised the others to go and buy from those who sell (v. 9). In this regard, God calls: "Come ye, buy [from me], and eat; yea, come, buy wine and milk without money and without price" (Isa. 55:1). Salvation is costly, but God paid the price in full with the death of His Son. We must come to Him and receive His salvation "without money or price," that is, without our own effort or good works. God's unspeakable gift includes an inexhaustible supply of His life-giving oil.

D. They will not take part in the marriage.

> ¹⁰And while they went to buy, the bridegroom came; and they that were ready went in with him to the marriage: and the door was shut.
> ¹¹Afterward came also the other virgins, saying, Lord, Lord, open to us.
> ¹²But he answered and said, Verily I say unto you, I know you not.
> ¹³Watch therefore, for ye know neither the day nor the hour wherein the Son of man cometh.

Wise believers, who prepared in advance, will go in with the Groom "to the marriage" (v. 10). Foolish and unprepared unbelievers, however, will find the door shut. Although they will claim that Christ is their Lord and will plead for admittance, He will reply, "I know you not." In applying the parable, Christ again urged His followers: "Watch!" and always be ready for His imminent return.

Immediately after Christ's return, He will judge and "reward every man according to his works" (MT 16:27). Christ concluded His Olivet Discourse with two vivid pictures of that judgment. His parable of the servants and talents deals primarily with the rewards that He will give to faithful believers (see Sec. II on p. 255). Then, in an analogy to the dividing of sheep from goats, He pictured the judgment and eternal reward of both believers and unbelievers (see Sec. VIII on p. 444). The Discourse ends with His solemn declaration: "And these [unbelievers] shall go away into everlasting punishment: but the righteous into life eternal." These judgments and rewards are the principal focus of the next chapter.

21

Previews of Eternal Destinies

Christ's second coming will launch a series of momentous events and experiences that will affect every person who ever lived. For believers in this present age, these will be glorious beyond description. Whether we are alive when He returns or we die first, our bodies will be changed instantly "like unto His glorious body" (Phil. 3:21). We will never again experience grief, pain, temptation, or sin — only God's blessing, perfection, and glory. "And so shall we ever be with the Lord" (I Thes. 4:17).

In summary, those who believe in Christ receive eternal spiritual life at their salvation, eternal physical life at their rapture or resurrection, and eternal heavenly life at their death or translation to glory. In contrast, unbelievers face eternal death, doom, and damnation. Their death will bring only untold suffering; their resurrection, only judgment and condemnation; and their eternity, only torment and burning in hell forever.

Christ often addressed these coming events to persuade His hearers to prepare for them while they still have the opportunity. He graphically described the unbelievers' fate and contrasted it to the wonders that await those who trust in Him. He poured out His heart, and then His life, to spare us from torment and take us to glory.

Mankind's Resurrection and Judgment

Christ solemnly declared: "The hour is coming in which all that are in the graves . . . shall come forth . . . unto the resurrection of life . . . [or] unto the resurrection of damnation" (JN 5:28-29). The grave is not the end of the line; it is the door to all eternity. Death temporarily separates one's spirit from his body, but the two will be rejoined at the body's resurrection and will remain united forever. Where and how resurrected people spend eternity is determined here and now by their response to Christ and His word.

I. "The God of the living" will resurrect everyone.

A. The Sadducees' sad doctrine and sad story.

MT 22:23 [MK 12:18; LK 20:27] The same day came to him the Sadducees, which say that there is no resurrection, and asked him,

²⁴Saying, Master, Moses said, If a man die, having no children, his brother shall marry his wife, and raise up seed unto his brother.

²⁵Now there were with us seven brethren: and the first, when he had married a wife, deceased, and, having no issue, left his wife unto his brother:

²⁶Likewise the second also, and the third, unto the seventh.

²⁷And last of all the woman died also.

²⁸Therefore in the resurrection whose wife shall she be of the seven? for they all had her.

The Sadducees were a sect of religious liberals, largely from the priestly and upper classes. They did not believe in resurrection or in the soul's life after death. They also did not believe in angels, did not accept rabbinic traditions, and generally placed political and economic objectives above spiritual concerns. The Mosaic regulation they cited (from Deut. 25:5-6) originally was intended to prevent a deceased brother's line from dying out and losing its inheritance in the land. The Sadducees fabricated this sad tale in an effort to discredit both Christ and His teaching on resurrection.

B. Christ's rebuke of their erroneous belief.

²⁹Jesus answered and said unto them, Ye do err, not knowing the scriptures, nor the power of God.

³⁰For in the resurrection they neither marry, nor are given in marriage, but are as the angels of God in heaven. {Neither can they die any more: for they are equal unto the angels; and are the children of God, being the children of the resurrection (LK 20:36).}

The Sadducees erred in (1) "not knowing the scriptures," such as Daniel 12:2: "And many of them that sleep in the dust of the earth shall awake, some to everlasting life, and some to shame and everlasting contempt," and (2) underestimating "the power of God" to accomplish what He promised. Christ corrected them on both the resurrection and the existence of angels by stating that, with respect to marriage, resurrected people will be as the angels, which do not marry.

    C. Scriptural evidence that all will be raised.

        [31]But as touching the resurrection of the dead {that they rise}, have ye not read {in the book of Moses} that which was spoken unto you by God {how, in the bush, God spoke unto him}, saying,

        [32]I am the God of Abraham, and the God of Isaac, and the God of Jacob? God is not the God of the dead, but {the God} of the living; {for all live unto him}. {Ye, therefore, do greatly err.}

        [33]And when the multitude heard this, they were astonished at his doctrine.

Regarding the dead, Christ confirmed "that they rise" (MK 12:26). He also quoted from Exodus 3:6 to show that the patriarchs' souls were still alive and with God (v. 32). God is thus "the God of the living." Christ added: "for *all* live [are alive] unto God" (LK 20:38). This indicates that the souls of all who have died are still alive, and that they will be reunited with their bodies at a future resurrection.

    II. All will be raised "at the last day."

        A. Believers will be raised for eternal reward.

        JN 6:39 And this is the Father's will which hath sent me, that of all which he hath given me I should lose nothing, but should raise it up again at the last day.

        [40]And this is the will of him that sent me, that every one which seeth the Son, and believeth on him, may have everlasting life: and I will raise him up at the last day. . . .

        [44]No man can come to me, except the Father which hath sent me draw him: and I will raise him up at the last day. . . .

        [54]Whoso eateth my flesh, and drinketh my blood, hath eternal life; and I will raise him up at the last day.

        B. Unbelievers will be raised for condemnation.

        JN 12:48 He that rejecteth me, and receiveth not my words, hath one that judgeth him: the word that I have spoken, the same shall judge him in the last day.

        MT 10:14 And whosoever shall not receive you, nor hear your words, when ye depart out of that house or city, shake off the dust of your feet.

> ¹⁵**Verily I say unto you, It shall be more tolerable for the land of Sodom and Gomorrah in the day of judgment, than for that city.**

"The last day" will include mankind's resurrection in the end time for final judgment. As indicated below, that "day" covers a period of over 1,000 years. The Jews also connected the term with the Messiah's coming and His bestowal of eternal blessing on resurrected believers. Job declared, "I know that my redeemer liveth, and that he shall stand at the latter day upon the earth: And though after my skin worms destroy this body, yet in my flesh shall I see God" (19:25-26). Whether saved or unsaved, everyone's resurrection and judgment will occur at "the last day," when he receives either heavenly rewards or eternal condemnation.

III. The saved and the unsaved will be resurrected separately.

> **JN 5:28 Marvel not at this: for the hour is coming, in the which all that are in the graves shall hear his [Christ's] voice,**
> ²⁹**And shall come forth; they that have done good, unto the resurrection of life; and they that have done evil, unto the resurrection of damnation.**

Everyone who dies will be raised in one of two resurrections. Believers' bodies will be raised and joined with their living souls at "the resurrection of life" (v. 29). Other passages indicate that this resurrection will occur in two phases: the first, at the rapture of believers who have died during this present Church age; and the second, after the tribulation, for believers from other ages. Both phases will precede the millennium, so that all believers from all ages may participate in it. Unbelievers also will be raised, but "unto the resurrection of damnation" 1,000 years later. Their bodies and souls will be reunited after the millennium, for judgment and condemnation at God's great white throne (Rev. 20:11-15).

Everyone will enter eternity with a physical body. At their resurrection, believers will receive perfect, glorified bodies similar to Christ's resurrected body (see I JN 3:2). Unbelievers, however, apparently will suffer eternally in bodies similar to their present bodies, but with no physical death ever to relieve them (Rev. 20:13-15).

IV. Christ Himself is "the resurrection and the life."

A. Old Testament believers anticipated their resurrection.

> **JN 11:21 Then said Martha unto Jesus, Lord, if thou hadst been here, my brother [Lazarus] had not died.**
> ²²**But I know, that even now, whatsoever thou wilt ask of God, God will give it thee.**
> ²³**Jesus saith unto her, Thy brother shall rise again.**

²⁴Martha saith unto him, I know that he shall rise again in the resurrection at the last day.

Based on Old Testament teaching, Martha assumed that Christ was referring to Lazarus' resurrection "at the last day," and she stated her faith that he would be raised at that time. She probably had in mind passages such as Daniel 12:2 and Job 19:26 cited in Sections I.B and II.B above.

B. Christ is the means of all believers' resurrection.

²⁵Jesus said unto her, I am the resurrection, and the life: he that believeth in me, though he were dead, yet shall he live:

²⁶And whosoever liveth and believeth in me shall never die. Believest thou this?

²⁷She saith unto him, Yea, Lord: I believe that thou art the Christ, the Son of God, which should come into the world.

As "the resurrection and the life," Christ is the source, the basis, and the means of every believer's promised resurrection and eternal life. Further, His own resurrection and eternal life guarantee ours. Verses 25b-26 may be understood: "He that believes in me, though he dies [physically], yet shall he [be resurrected and] live. And whoever lives and believes in me shall never die [i.e., never die spiritually after salvation, or die physically after resurrection]." Martha's answer demonstrated her faith that Christ as the Son of God is the guarantor of her own future resurrection and eternal life.

V. Salvation itself is a spiritual resurrection.

JN 5:21 For as the Father raiseth up the dead, and quickeneth them [gives them life]; even so the Son quickeneth whom he will. . . .

²⁴Verily, verily, I say unto you, He that heareth my word, and believeth on him that sent me, hath everlasting life, and shall not come into condemnation; but is passed from death unto life.

²⁵Verily, verily, I say unto you, The hour is coming, and now is, when the dead shall hear the voice of the Son of God: and they that hear shall live.

The Father and the Son, equal in the Godhead, each have the power to "raise up" the physically dead and also the spiritually dead. The latter are "raised up" through salvation. By hearing and believing the gospel, they pass "from death unto life" (v. 24). That verse 25 refers to salvation is evident in the phrase: "The hour . . . *now* is when the dead shall hear . . . and live." Now is the time for the spiritually dead to be raised to spiritual life. Their spiritual resurrection assures that they will also take part in the physical "resurrection of life" when Christ returns (JN 5:29).

VI. The Father made Christ the judge of all men.

JN 5:22 For the Father judgeth no man, but hath committed all judgment unto the Son:

²³That all men should honor the Son, even as they honor the Father. He that honoreth not the Son honoreth not the Father which hath sent him. . . .

²⁶For as the Father hath life in himself; so hath he given to the Son to have life in himself;

²⁷And hath given him authority to execute judgment also, because he is the Son of man.

The Father does not work independently of the Son (nor vice versa), but works *through* the Son, including here in the matter of mankind's judgment. The Father, therefore, has given the Son the authority (in His capacity as the Son of man; i.e., as the Messiah and God incarnate) to "execute all judgment" (vv. 22 and 27) for every human being. Their joint purpose in this is that the Father and the Son be honored equally (v. 23).

VII. Everyone will be judged by the words from his heart.

MT 12:34 O generation of vipers, how can ye, being evil, speak good things? for out of the abundance of the heart the mouth speaketh.

³⁵A good man out of the good treasure of the heart bringeth forth good things: and an evil man out of the evil treasure bringeth forth evil things.

³⁶But I say unto you, That every idle word that men shall speak, they shall give account thereof in the day of judgment.

³⁷For by thy words thou shalt be justified, and by thy words thou shalt be condemned.

In scripture, the heart pictures a person's essence — what he is spiritually by nature. Each heart is like a treasure chest filled with good things or evil things (v. 35). Before its new birth, the heart is inherently evil (Rom. 3:10-18), and the words and deeds that issue from it are inherently evil. At salvation, each believer receives a "new heart" (a new nature) that produces "good things," i.e., godly words and deeds. (A believer's old nature, however, will not be fully eradicated until his death.) At the judgment, Christ will cite a person's words as evidence of the true nature of his heart. Either rewards or condemnation will follow as a result.

VIII. Christ will judge the living at His return.

A. He will divide "His sheep from the goats."

MT 25:31 When the Son of man shall come in his glory, and all the holy angels with him, then shall he sit upon the throne of his glory:

³²And before him shall be gathered all nations: and he shall separate them one from another, as a shepherd divideth his sheep from the goats:

³³And he shall set the sheep on his right hand, but the goats on the left.

Earlier sections focus primarily on the resurrection and judgment of those who die before Christ's glorious return. Many will be alive, however, when He comes to earth as King. At that time, all Gentiles who survived the tribulation will be brought before His throne for judgment. Christ Himself will divide "His sheep from the goats" (i.e., believers from unbelievers), and will judge each group accordingly. (Jews apparently will be judged separately, as indicated in Ezekiel 20:36-38.)

B. His sheep will enter His kingdom.

³⁴Then shall the King say unto them on his right hand, Come, ye blessed of my Father, inherit the kingdom prepared for you from the foundation of the world:

³⁵For I was an hungered, and ye gave me meat: I was thirsty, and ye gave me drink: I was a stranger, and ye took me in:

³⁶Naked, and ye clothed me: I was sick, and ye visited me: I was in prison, and ye came unto me.

C. They had graciously served Christ's brethren.

³⁷Then shall the righteous answer him, saying, Lord, when saw we thee an hungered, and fed thee? or thirsty, and gave thee drink?

³⁸When saw we thee a stranger, and took thee in? or naked, and clothed thee?

³⁹Or when saw we thee sick, or in prison, and came unto thee?

⁴⁰And the King shall answer and say unto them, Verily I say unto you, Inasmuch as ye have done it unto one of the least of these my brethren, ye have done it unto me.

Conditions on earth during the tribulation will be unimaginably horrible. All believers, and Jewish believers especially, will be persecuted severely for their relationship to God. Unbelievers will so hate God (for pouring out His judgment on them) and will so hate His people, that only true believers will extend a helping hand to any of Christ's suffering "brethren" (Jewish believers). The believers' refusal to accept the mark of the Antichrist (Rev. 13:16) will identify them clearly both to their enemies and to each other. Their smallest acts of charity to one another will be clear and valid indicators of their salvation and will be appropriate grounds for their eternal rewards.

D. The goats will be cast into everlasting fire.

⁴¹Then shall he say also unto them on the left hand, Depart from me, ye cursed, into everlasting fire, prepared for the devil and his angels:

⁴²For I was an hungered, and ye gave me no meat: I was thirsty, and ye gave me no drink:

⁴³I was a stranger, and ye took me not in: naked, and ye clothed me not: sick, and in prison, and ye visited me not.

E. They had ignored the Shepherd and His needy sheep.

⁴⁴Then shall they also answer him, saying, Lord, when saw we thee an hungered, or athirst, or a stranger, or naked, or sick, or in prison, and did not minister unto thee?

⁴⁵Then shall he answer them, saying, Verily I say unto you, Inasmuch as ye did it not to one of the least of these, ye did it not to me.

Good deeds are not the ground of salvation, but they will invariably grow from that ground. James declared, "Show me thy faith without thy works [a logical and practical impossibility], and I will show thee my faith by my works" (2:18). As with all unbelievers, the goats' fatal failure was their rejection of God's gift of salvation. Because of their rebellion against God, none of these unbelievers would so much as give a drink of water to any of Christ's sheep. If they had had any relationship with Christ, they would have shown some concern for the fate of those identified with Him. Their failure to do so provided clear evidence of their just condemnation.

F. The sheep will enter "life eternal"; the goats, condemnation.

⁴⁶And these shall go away into everlasting punishment: but the righteous into life eternal.

Although this particular judgment is for specific groups of people, it indicates how the judgment of other believers and unbelievers may be conducted. At the conclusion of each judgment, unbelievers will go "into everlasting punishment" and "the righteous into life eternal."

IX. Believers will be judged and rewarded for their service to God.

A. Their rewards will be personal and equitable.

MT 16:27 For the Son of man shall come in the glory of his Father with his angels; and then he shall reward every man according to his works.

B. Their rewards will be appropriate and commensurate.

LK 14:13 But when thou makest a feast, call the poor, the maimed, the lame, the blind:

¹⁴And thou shalt be blessed; for they cannot recompense thee: for thou shalt be recompensed at the resurrection of the just.

C. Their rewards will be bountiful and eternal.

MK 9:41 For whosoever shall give you a cup of water to drink in my name, because ye belong to Christ, verily I say unto you, he shall not lose his reward.

God will reward every believer's service for Him, and particularly deeds of love and kindness rendered in His name. (As illustrated above, we serve God primarily through helping and serving other people.) Although little is said in scripture about the exact nature of these rewards, we know that they will immeasurably exceed any related sacrifice on our part, and will do so in quantity, quality, and duration. Obtaining rewards, however, should not be our principal objective. Our primary goal should be to honor and please God with our lives through faithful love, worship, obedience, and service to Him. That is the least (and the most) we can do in response to who He is and all that He has done for us.

The Horrors of Hell

Christ spoke more often, and in greater detail, about hell (as an abode after death) than He did about heaven. God initially prepared hell for the devil and his demons (MT 25:41) but, tragically, most people will end there too (MT 7:13). Christ repeatedly warned all who would listen of the certain and imminent judgment that unbelievers face in hell.

The principal word Christ used for hell is *gehenna*, meaning "place of fire." The word itself is a graphic picture of terrible torment. Historical Gehenna is the valley of Hinnom outside of Jerusalem, where idolatrous Jews burned their children alive as sacrifices to Molech and Baal (II Chron. 28:3; Jer. 19:5). Gehenna later was used as a rubbish dump where trash burned continuously, with nauseous stench, acrid smoke, and filthy pollution. Because of the unspeakable evil committed there, God declared that it would be called "the valley of slaughter" and would overflow with unburied corpses (Jer. 7:30-33). The eternal gehenna is infinitely worse than its earthly namesake. Called "the lake of fire" in Revelation, gehenna will be the everlasting abode of all unbelievers.

The other word translated "hell" in the Gospels is *hades*. Hades is the present and future abode of the spirits of all dead unbelievers while they await their final consignment to gehenna at God's Great White Throne of final judgment (Rev. 20:11-15). As shown below, hades has many of the horrible characteristics of gehenna. When the bodies of dead unbelievers are resurrected for final judgment, these will be reunited with their spirits from hades, and both will be cast into gehenna forever.

I. Hell is for those with no time for God.

A. Everyone dies, rich and poor alike.
LK 16:19 There was a certain rich man, which was clothed in purple and fine linen, and fared sumptuously every day:

²⁰And there was a certain beggar named Lazarus, which was laid at his gate, full of sores,

²¹And desiring to be fed with the crumbs which fell from the rich man's table: moreover the dogs came and licked his sores.

²²And it came to pass, that the beggar died, and was carried by the angels into Abraham's bosom: the rich man also died, and was buried;

Unstated but understood was Lazarus' salvation before his death and the rich man's lack of saving faith. The rich man evidently had made his money the god of his life. His wealth, however, could not buy him immortality or, failing that, an entrance into heaven. In contrast, Lazarus' spirit was carried "into Abraham's bosom," a place of unending comfort and bliss (as discussed in Sec. III.B on p. 456).

B. Unbelievers end in "torments" and "flame."

²³And in hell [hades] he lift up his eyes, being in torments, and seeth Abraham afar off, and Lazarus in his bosom.

²⁴And he cried and said, Father Abraham, have mercy on me, and send Lazarus, that he may dip the tip of his finger in water, and cool my tongue; for I am tormented in this flame.

Several horrific aspects of hell are identified here: (1) the full consciousness of its captives; (2) their recollection of associations and experiences on earth that could have helped them avoid being there; (3) the unmitigated torment and unsatisfied desires they experience; and (4) the unrelenting flame that envelops them continuously.

C. Priorities before death determine positions after death.

²⁵But Abraham said, Son, remember that thou in thy lifetime receivedst thy good things, and likewise Lazarus evil [adverse] things: but now he is comforted, and thou art tormented.

The rich man in life received "good things," and lavishly reveled in his wealth. He never acknowledged that everything he had came directly or indirectly from God, but treated everything he received as his own. Lazarus on the other hand experienced only "adverse things" on earth. Now the tables were turned and their results magnified.

D. Hell's separation from God is "fixed" and impassable.

²⁶And beside all this, between us and you there is a great gulf fixed: so that they which would pass from hence to you cannot; neither can they pass to us, that would come from thence.

Additional terrible aspects of hell are (1) complete separation from God and from every good thing that God provides; (2) no hope or means whatever of escaping its confinement; and (3) no possible source of relief from any of its consequences. To its captives, hell is all-encompassing and all-pervading.

E. God's Word offers the only alternative to hell.

²⁷Then he said, I pray thee therefore, father, that thou wouldest send him to my father's house:

²⁸For I have five brethren; that he may testify unto them, lest they also come into this place of torment.

²⁹Abraham saith unto him, They have Moses and the prophets; let them hear them.

³⁰And he said, Nay, father Abraham: but if one went unto them from the dead, they will repent.

³¹And he said unto him, If they hear not Moses and the prophets, neither will they be persuaded, though one rose from the dead.

The rich man's living brothers evidently shared his temporal, materialistic values. He pleaded, therefore, that Lazarus be sent to warn them to repent before they too ended in hell. In reply, Abraham cited the ready availability of God's Word and its sufficiency. If they reject the message already given, no other message or messenger would persuade them. Abraham's further response in verse 31 is amply confirmed by unbelievers' continued rejection of Christ's message of salvation — even though He returned from the dead and (through His representatives) urges them to repent rather than proceed on their way to hell.

II. Hell is for those who serve sinful pleasures.

A. Their sinful deeds will convict them.

MK 9:43 And if thy hand offend thee [causes you to stumble and sin], cut it off: it is better for thee to enter into life maimed, than having two hands to go into hell [gehenna], into the fire that never shall be quenched:

⁴⁴Where their worm dieth not, and the fire is not quenched.

B. Their wayward path will destroy them.

⁴⁵And if thy foot offend thee, cut it off: it is better for thee to enter halt into life, than having two feet to be cast into hell, into the fire that never shall be quenched:

⁴⁶Where their worm dieth not, and the fire is not quenched.

C. Their lustful desires will condemn them.

⁴⁷And if thine eye offend thee, pluck it out: it is better for thee to enter into the kingdom of God with one eye, than having two eyes to be cast into hell fire:

⁴⁸Where their worm dieth not, and the fire is not quenched.

This passage links the central issue of who or what controls one's life to where he will spend eternity. Those who live to satisfy selfish desires will be "cast into hell." In contrast, those who renounce these for Christ's sake will enter "life" and the "kingdom of God." These sinful appetites are pictured by the hand, foot, and eye. The problem is not with the physical organs, but with the selfish and lustful activities they pursue under the direction of a sinful heart and mind. Together, they lead the whole body to hell. Sinful pleasures last only a while, but hell's fire will never be quenched and its gnawing worms will never die.

D. Their deserved end will torment them.

⁴⁹For every one shall be salted with fire, and every sacrifice shall be salted with salt.

In the context of the preceding verses, verse 49a appears to be a reaffirmation of the certainty that everyone who lives for sinful pleasures will bear the consequences in hell's eternal fire. In contrast, verse 49b seems to apply to believers, who alone can make any sacrifice acceptable to God. Mosaic law required: "thy meat [meal, or grain] offering shalt thou season with salt . . . with all thine offerings thou shalt offer salt" (Lev. 2:13). Believers are to be "living sacrifices" pleasing to God and "the salt of the earth" on His behalf.

III. Hell is for those who reject God's authority.

A. The devil, his demons, and his disciples.

MT 25:41 Then shall he [Christ the King] say also unto them on the left hand, Depart from me, ye cursed, into everlasting fire, prepared for the devil and his angels: . . .

⁴⁶And these [unbelievers] shall go away into everlasting punishment: but the righteous into life eternal.

God prepared the "everlasting fire" of hell for the devil and his demons (v. 41). Hell is their ordained punishment for rebelling against God's dominion and authority. By the same token (and for the same reason), all those who cast their lot with Satan by rejecting God's dominion and authority over their lives will join Satan and his demons in hell forever. (See Sec. VIII on p. 444 for the full passage.)

B. Apostate teachers of false doctrine.

MT 23:15 Woe unto you, scribes and Pharisees, hypocrites! for ye compass sea and land to make one proselyte, and when he is made, ye make him twofold more the child of hell than yourselves. . . .

³³Ye serpents, ye generation of vipers, how can ye escape the damnation of hell?

The scribes and Pharisees had turned away from God's truth in the Old Testament and perverted it into a man-made, self-serving religion. Thus, Christ called them children of gehenna, that is, belonging to, deserving of, and destined for the lake of fire. Their proselytes (unbelievers converted to Pharisaism) became children of hell "twice over" through their fervent devotion to the Pharisees' false religion. (See p. 392 ff for the full passage).

C. False servants and religious hypocrites

MT 24:48 [LK 12:45] But and if that evil servant shall say in his heart, My lord delayeth his coming;

⁴⁹And shall begin to smite his fellowservants, and to eat and drink with the drunken;

⁵⁰The lord of that servant shall come in a day when he looketh not for him, and in an hour that he is not aware of,

⁵¹And shall cut him asunder, and appoint him his portion with the hypocrites {unbelievers}: there shall be weeping and gnashing of teeth.

The "evil servant" in the parable did not believe his master would return any time soon to hold him accountable. His unbelief spawned the sinful and debauched way of life in which the returning lord found him. He was justly consigned to hell "with the hypocrites," those who pose as believers but have no true faith. (See Sec. II.C on p. 435.)

IV. Hell is for those with no good fruit.

A. They are corrupt trees, to be felled and burned.

MT 7:18 A good tree cannot bring forth evil fruit, neither can a corrupt tree bring forth good fruit.

¹⁹Every tree that bringeth not forth good fruit is hewn down, and cast into the fire. [See Sec. VI on p. 127 for the full passage.]

B. They are dead branches, to be gathered and burned.

JN 15:6 If a man abide not in me, he is cast forth as a branch, and is withered; and men gather them, and cast them into the fire, and they are burned. [See Sec. II.B on p. 122 for the full passage.]

C. They are worthless chaff, to be winnowed and burned.

MT 3:12 [Speaking of Christ] Whose fan [winnowing shovel] is in his hand, and he will throughly purge his [threshing] floor, and gather his wheat into the garner [granary]; but he will burn up the chaff with unquenchable fire. [See Sec. V on p. 387 for the full passage.]

D. They are troublesome tares, to be culled and burned.

MT 13:40 As therefore the tares are gathered and burned in the fire; so shall it be in the end of this world.

⁴¹The Son of man shall send forth his angels, and they shall gather out of his kingdom all things that offend, and them which do iniquity; ⁴²And shall cast them into a furnace of fire: there shall be wailing and gnashing of teeth. [See Sec. V on p. 409 for the full passage.]

These horticultural analogies all convey the same message that unbelievers cannot produce anything in or with their lives that has any value whatsoever before God. In each case, the worthless growth is cut off and burned in the fire. A winnowing shovel (LK 3) is used to toss threshed wheat and its chaff into the air. The wind blows away the chaff, while the heavier grain falls to the threshing floor. The tares (in MT 13) are weeds that look like wheat but produce no grain and interfere with the growth of the wheat.

V. Hell is for those who practice sin.

MT 5:21 Ye have heard that it was said by them of old time, Thou shalt not kill . . .

²²But I say unto you, That whosoever is angry with his brother without a cause shall be in danger of the judgment: and . . . whosoever shall say, Thou fool, shall be in danger of hell fire.

²⁷Ye have heard that it was said by them of old time, Thou shalt not commit adultery:

²⁸But I say unto you, That whosoever looketh on a woman to lust after her hath committed adultery with her already in his heart.

²⁹And if thy right eye offend thee, pluck it out, and cast it from thee: for it is profitable for thee that one of thy members should perish, and not that thy whole body should be cast into hell.

MT 10:28 And fear not them which kill the body, but are not able to kill the soul: but rather fear him [God alone] which is able to destroy both soul and body in hell.

Every human being deserves to be in hell. Even if someone claims never to have committed any of the sins cited in prior sections (certainly a far-fetched claim), Christ declared that even a *desire* for anything that is wrong is a sin that justly condemns one to hell. No one is innocent of such sin. Further, with our inborn sinful nature, each of us has committed a multitude of additional sins. More to be feared than anything is to stand before God with unforgiven sin (10:28). He will justly consign us to hell — or will forgive us our sin if we have trusted in Christ as our personal Savior.

VI. Hell is for those who neglect salvation.

A. They fail to receive God's spiritual clothing.

MT 22:2 The kingdom of heaven is like unto a certain king, which made a marriage for his son, . . .

> ¹¹And when the king came in to see the guests, he saw there a man which had not on a wedding garment:
> ¹²And he saith unto him, Friend, how camest thou in hither not having a wedding garment? And he was speechless.
> ¹³Then said the king to the servants, Bind him hand and foot, and take him away, and cast him into outer darkness; there shall be weeping and gnashing of teeth.

The unfit guest failed to accept the king's prior provision of the required wedding garment (which assuredly he was offered when he was brought to the wedding). He pictures unbelievers who neglect God's offer to clothe them in His righteousness. (See Sec. III on p. 130 for the full parable.) The man's condemnation included his banishment to "distant darkness," far from the king's wedding feast. There he remains, bound and in pain, wailing in anguish forever.

B. They miss the "narrow gate" and the "narrow way."

> MT 7:13 Enter ye in at the strait [narrow] gate: for wide is the gate, and broad is the way, that leadeth to destruction, and many there be which go in thereat:
> ¹⁴Because strait is the gate, and narrow [hard] is the way, which leadeth unto life, and few there be that find it.

The broad way that leads to hell is a crowded highway. It is full of people flowing with the crowd and oblivious to where it leads and ends. That road may be paved with good intentions but it leads to eternal destruction. In contrast, relatively few will enter the "narrow gate" of salvation in Christ and take the way "that leads to life." (See Sec. VI on p. 84.)

C. They disregard the works and words of God.

> MT 11:20 Then began he to upbraid the cities wherein most of his mighty works were done, because they repented not: . . .
> ²³And thou, Capernaum, which art exalted unto heaven, shalt be brought down to hell [hades]: for if the mighty works, which have been done in thee, had been done in Sodom, it would have remained until this day.
> ²⁴But I say unto you, That it shall be more tolerable for the land of Sodom, in the day of judgment, than for thee.

The people of Sodom were unimaginably wicked, and God destroyed them with fire from heaven (Gen. 19:24). In comparison, Capernaum was Christ's home base in Galilee and its people witnessed many of His miracles and messages. He said that with equivalent revelation, Sodom would have repented and been spared its conflagration. Capernaum, therefore, (and people today who reject the greater revelation of God's completed Word) "will be brought down to hell" with greater condemnation than Sodom's in the day of final judgment. (See Sec. III.A on p. 292.)

Christ's detailed knowledge of hell compelled His effort to keep us from going there. He used every available opportunity and every available means to warn us of hell's torment and restrain us from entering its door. Ultimately, He provided our only way of escape from hell's reach, by bearing our hell in our place on His cross. Anyone, however, who fails to accept Christ's sacrificial payment for his sin will have to bear his own hell — without limit, without relief, without end.

The Glories of Heaven

Heaven is both the celestial abode of God and the blissful abode of departed believers. It is glorious beyond imagination, with "fullness of joy" at God's right hand and "pleasures for evermore" (Psalm 16:11). The most wonderful and remarkable aspect of being there will be to experience personally the infinitely glorious presence of God. All of the other unspeakable glories of heaven will pale in comparison with beholding and worshipping the God of our salvation.

The Gospels provide relatively few details about heaven, leaving most of that information for the epistles and the book of Revelation. Christ revealed enough about heaven, however, to motivate us in God's service, to encourage us in our distresses, and to fill us with anticipation of dwelling there forever.

I. Heaven is God's celestial home.

    A. God the Father dwells there.

        MT 6:9 After this manner therefore pray ye: Our Father which art in heaven, Hallowed be thy name.
        [10]Thy kingdom come. Thy will be done in earth, as it is in heaven.

        MT 5:34 But I say unto you, Swear not at all; neither by heaven; for it is God's throne:
        [35]Nor by the earth; for it is his footstool: neither by Jerusalem; for it is the city of the great King.

    B. God the Son dwells there.

        JN 3:13 And no man hath ascended up to heaven, but he that came down from heaven, even the Son of man which is in heaven. . . .
        [31]He that cometh from above is above all: he that is of the earth is earthly, and speaketh of the earth: he that cometh from heaven is above all.

C. God the Holy Spirit dwells there.

JN 1:32 And John bare record, saying, I saw the Spirit descending from heaven like a dove, and it abode upon him.
³³And I knew him not: but he that sent me to baptize with water, the same said unto me, Upon whom thou shalt see the Spirit descending, and remaining on him, the same is he which baptizeth with the Holy Ghost.

D. God's angels dwell there.

MT 18:10 Take heed that ye despise not one of these little ones; for I say unto you, That in heaven their angels do always behold the face of my Father which is in heaven.

JN 1:51 And he saith unto him [one of His disciples], Verily, verily, I say unto you, Hereafter ye shall see heaven open, and the angels of God ascending and descending upon the Son of man.

The Gospels refer often to heaven as the particular abode of the Trinity. Christ referred to the "Father in heaven" more than a dozen times. He declared that He Himself had "come from heaven," and that He would return to His former home. God sent His Spirit visibly from heaven at Christ's baptism in ordaining His Son for His ministry. One day soon, believers will join the angels who "always behold the face of the Father [and the Son and the Spirit] in heaven."

II. Christ will take all believers to heaven.

A. He is preparing mansions for us there.

JN 14:2 In my Father's house are many mansions [dwelling places]: if it were not so, I would have told you. I go to prepare a place for you.
³And if I go and prepare a place for you, I will come again, and receive you unto myself; that where I am, there ye may be also.

Christ described heaven as His "Father's house," an expansive mansion so spacious that it contains "many mansions" within it. He is presently preparing these dwelling places as a glorious home for all believers. When He returns to take us there, He will receive us to Himself, so that He and we may enjoy one another forever. Personal face-to-face communion with Christ will be the heart of our heavenly bliss.

B. He longs that we be with Him there.

JN 17:24 Father, I will [I greatly desire] that they also, whom thou hast given me, be with me where I am; that they may [continually] behold my glory, which thou hast given me: for thou lovedst me before the foundation of the world.

In this prayer on the eve of His crucifixion, Christ revealed the great longing of His heart that all those whom the Father had given Him (as His eternal inheritance) would soon be with Him in heaven. When we join Him there, we will behold, enjoy, and share His infinite glory, with unceasing worship and praise.

    C. He will welcome us to "life eternal."
        MT 25:31 When the Son of man shall come in his glory, and all the holy angels with him, then shall he sit upon the throne of his glory: . . .
        ³⁴Then shall the King say unto them on his right hand [believers], Come, ye blessed of my Father, inherit the kingdom prepared for you from the foundation of the world: . . .
        ⁴⁶And these [unbelievers] shall go away into everlasting punishment: but the righteous into life eternal.

At His return, Christ will warmly welcome living believers into His kingdom and "into life eternal." All believers from all ages also will enter that kingdom. It begins with but transcends Christ's millennial (1,000-year) reign; it also includes the subsequent eternal state called "the kingdom of their Father" (see MT 13:43 in Sec. VI.B below). Christ's earthly kingdom will have a number of heaven-like qualities, including His glorious presence with resurrected believers, and will serve as a prelude to even greater blessings in God's eternal heaven.

    III. Heaven is a paradise of comfort and enjoyment.

    A. Christ received the repentant thief in paradise.
        LK 23:42 And he said unto Jesus, Lord, remember me when thou comest into thy kingdom.
        ⁴³And Jesus said unto him, Verily I say unto thee, Today shalt thou be with me in paradise.

Christ promised the dying thief that he would be with Him in paradise that same day. The pain and shame of his horrible crucifixion would be replaced instantly with joyous celebration in God's presence. (See Sec. VI.C on p. 17 for the full passage.) Scripture equates paradise with "the third heaven" (God's celestial abode) where God gave Paul unspeakably glorious experiences (II Cor. 12:2-4). Also, heaven is called "the paradise of God", where its residents eat freely of "the tree of life" (Rev. 2:7).

    B. Angels carried Lazarus to "Abraham's bosom."
        LK 16:22 And it came to pass, that the beggar [Lazarus] died, and was carried by the angels into Abraham's bosom: the rich man also died, and was buried;
        ²³And in hell [hades] he lift up his eyes, being in torments, and seeth Abraham afar off, and Lazarus in his bosom. . . .

²⁵But Abraham said, Son, remember that thou in thy lifetime receivedst thy good things, and likewise Lazarus evil [adverse] things: but now he is comforted, and thou art tormented.

Christ gave this account of the comfort, rest, and satisfaction that Lazarus received when he was transported to "Abraham's bosom" at his death. (See Sec. I on p. 447 for the full passage.) Abraham is called "the father of all them that believe" (Rom. 4:11), and his "bosom" pictures the full relief and freedom from earthly problems and sorrows that believers will experience in the celestial home where Abraham already dwells. It also portrays the warm reception they will receive and the intimate fellowship they will enjoy with other believers when they enter that blissful abode.

In this present age, the spirits of all believers go immediately at death to be with the Lord in heaven (II Cor. 5:8). Most believe that this has always been the case. Some hold, however, that before Christ died, hades (v. 23 above) had separate compartments for the saved, called Abraham's bosom, and for the lost, called the place of torment. They conclude (from passages such as Eph. 4:8-10) that Christ took those in Abraham's bosom with Him to heaven following His death. (In either view, the spirits of unbelievers will remain in torment until their resurrection for judgment after the millennium.)

IV. Believers should be storing up "treasures in heaven."

A. They are the only treasures that last forever.

MT 6:19 Lay not up for yourselves treasures upon earth, where moth and rust doth corrupt, and where thieves break through and steal:
²⁰But lay up for yourselves treasures in heaven, where neither moth nor rust doth corrupt, and where thieves do not break through nor steal:

JN 12:25 He that loveth his life shall lose it; and he that hateth his life in this world shall keep it unto life eternal.

B. They result from faithful service for God.

JN 4:35b Behold, I say unto you, Lift up your eyes, and look on the fields; for they are white already to harvest.
³⁶And he that reapeth receiveth wages, and gathereth fruit unto life eternal: that both he that soweth and he that reapeth may rejoice together.

C. They result from willing sacrifice for God.

MK 10:21 Then Jesus beholding him loved him, and said unto him, One thing thou lackest: go thy way, sell whatsoever thou hast, and give to the poor, and thou shalt have treasure in heaven: and come, take up the cross, and follow me.

LK 12:33 Sell that ye have, and give alms; provide yourselves bags which wax not old, a treasure in the heavens that faileth not, where no thief approacheth, neither moth corrupteth.
³⁴For where your treasure is, there will your heart be also.

D. They result from bearing persecution for Christ's sake.

MT 5:11 Blessed are ye, when men shall revile you, and persecute you, and shall say all manner of evil against you falsely, for my sake.
¹²Rejoice, and be exceeding glad: for great is your reward in heaven: for so persecuted they the prophets which were before you.

A martyred missionary is quoted, "He is no fool who gives up what he cannot keep to gain what he cannot lose." The ephemeral nature of earthly possessions and the eternal duration of "treasures in heaven" should make this choice clear and easy. Yet many an unbeliever rejects salvation to clutch what he cannot keep. And many a believer forgoes what he could not lose to pursue illusory temporal gains. Christ does not specifically identify these "treasures in heaven" other than to indicate that they stem from dedicated effort (JN 4:36), surrendered resources (MK 10:21), and steadfast testimony in the face of opposition (MT 5:11) that believers faithfully give in God's service.

V. Heaven will be changed, but only for the better.

A. God will make a new heaven and a new earth.

MK 13:31 Heaven and earth shall pass away: but my words shall not pass away.

MT 5:18 For verily I say unto you, Till heaven and earth pass, one jot or one tittle shall in no wise pass from the law, till all be fulfilled.

God will recreate the universe following the millennium and the judgment of all unbelievers. At that time, "the heavens shall pass away with a great noise, and the elements shall melt with fervent heat, the earth also and the works that are therein shall be burned up" (2 Peter 3:10). God will replace these with "a new heaven and a new earth: for the first heaven and the first earth were passed away" (Rev. 21:1). This new creation will remain forever, with all the glories that scripture associates with heaven.

B. Believers will live in the new heaven forever.

MT 13:41 The Son of man shall send forth his angels, and they shall gather out of his kingdom all things that offend, and them which do iniquity;
⁴²And shall cast them into a furnace of fire: there shall be wailing and gnashing of teeth.
⁴³Then shall the righteous shine forth as the sun in the kingdom of their Father. Who hath ears to hear, let him hear.

Although these verses from the parable of the tares deal primarily with the end of the present church age, they also apply to the end of Christ's millennial kingdom and the beginning of the new eternal state. "The kingdom of their Father" (v. 43) includes the new heaven and new earth referred to in Part A above. Paul wrote: "Then cometh the end, when he [Christ] shall have *delivered up the kingdom to God, even the Father*; when he shall have put down all rule and all authority and power. For he must reign, till he hath put all enemies under his feet. The last enemy that shall be destroyed is death" (I Cor. 15:24-26). Death will finally be destroyed at the end of the millennium, in preparation for the perfection of the new eternal state.

Believers from all ages will dwell eternally with God in that new heaven and new earth. Christ in His ineffable glory then will outshine the sun, and believers also will "shine forth as the sun in the kingdom of their Father." Referring to that time, John wrote: "And I heard a great voice out of heaven saying, Behold, the tabernacle of God is with men, and he will dwell with them, and they shall be his people, and God himself shall be with them, and be their God" (Rev. 21:3). Until then, Christ told His followers, "Rejoice because your names are written in heaven."

Subject Index

Selected references to the following subjects are on the pages shown, with principal references in bold print. Several basic subjects with frequent references throughout the book (e.g., "believe" and "salvation") are not listed.